THE SHIFTING TERRAIN

# The Shifting Terrain

## Non-profit Policy Advocacy in Canada

Edited by
NICK J. MULÉ AND GLORIA C. DESANTIS

McGill-Queen's University Press
Montreal & Kingston • London • Chicago

© McGill-Queen's University Press 2017

ISBN 978-0-7735-4864-0 (cloth)
ISBN 978-0-7735-4865-7 (paper)
ISBN 978-0-7735-4866-4 (ePDF)
ISBN 978-0-7735-4867-1 (ePUB)

Legal deposit second quarter 2017
Bibliothèque nationale du Québec

Printed in Canada on acid-free paper that is 100% ancient forest free (100% post-consumer recycled), processed chlorine free

McGill-Queen's University Press acknowledges the generous contributions of the University of Regina President's Publication Fund, York University Subvention Fund, The Muttart Foundation, and the Max Bell Foundation.

McGill-Queen's University Press acknowledges the support of the Canada Council for the Arts for our publishing program. We also acknowledge the financial support of the Government of Canada through the Canada Book Fund for our publishing activities.

---

Library and Archives Canada Cataloguing in Publication

The shifting terrain : non-profit policy advocacy in Canada / edited by Nick J. Mulé and Gloria C. DeSantis.

Includes bibliographical references and index.
Issued in print and electronic formats.

ISBN 978-0-7735-4864-0 (cloth). – ISBN 978-0-7735-4865-7 (paper).
ISBN 978-0-7735-4866-4 (ePDF). – ISBN 978-0-7735-4867-1 (ePUB)

1. Nonprofit organizations – Political activity – Canada.  2. Social advocacy – Canada.  I. DeSantis, Gloria author, editor  II. Mulé, Nick J., 1963–, author, editor

HD2769.2.C3S55 2017         361.7632         C2017-900237-6
                                              C2017-900238-4

---

This book was typeset by Apex CoVantage, LLC in 10.5/13 Sabon.

*To all those who participate in public policy advocacy in Canada.*

NJM

*To my children, Ali, Stefan, and Aidan ... the next generation of advocates in Canada.*

GCD

# Contents

Tables and Figures  ix

Acknowledgments  xi

Foreword: The Insiders  xiii
PETER R. ELSON

1 Advocacy: A Contested yet Enduring Concept in the Canadian Landscape  3
GLORIA C. DESANTIS AND NICK J. MULÉ

2 Shifting Legal Terrain: Legal and Regulatory Restrictions on Political Advocacy by Charities  33
ADAM PARACHIN

3 Advocates Anonymous: A Study of Advocacy Coalitions in Ontario  63
ANNA BURROWES AND RACHEL LAFOREST

4 The Changing Face of the Non-profit Sector: Social Enterprise Legislation in British Columbia  82
CAROL LIAO

5 Saskatchewan Disability Income Support Coalition: Advocacy for a New Disability Benefit Program  110
KATHLEEN THOMPSON AND BONNIE MORTON

6 Who Is Minding the First Nations during the Flood? Failing Advocacy at Every Policy Turn during a Human/Environmental Crisis  140
MYRLE BALLARD

7 Poverty Free Ontario: Cross-Community Advocacy for Social Justice   172
CHRISTA FREILER AND PETER CLUTTERBUCK

8 The Québec Act to Combat Poverty and Social Exclusion: A Case of Democratic Co-construction of Public Policy   200
YVES VAILLANCOURT AND FRANÇOIS AUBRY

9 Reinventing Democracy through Public Advocacy: The Case of the Anti-shale Gas Movement in New Brunswick   230
SUZANNE DUDZIAK AND MARK D'ARCY

10 Canada's Northern Communications Policies: The Role of Aboriginal Organizations   259
ROB MCMAHON, HEATHER E. HUDSON, AND LYLE FABIAN

11 A "Political Activity": The Inherent Politicization of Advocacy   293
NICK J. MULÉ AND GLORIA C. DESANTIS

Contributors   321

Index   325

# Tables and Figures

**TABLES**

4.1 Features of the BC Community Contribution Company  97

5.1 The underlying process goals, intervention, and outcomes of collaborative advocacy  115

5.2 Activities included in collaborative advocacy interventions  116

5.3 List of DISC partner organizations  123

6.1 List of select legislation under which first Nations are forced to live  146

6.2 Summary of DFAA eligibility on First Nations reserves  153

9.1 Advocacy activities of the New Brunswick Anti-shale Gas Movement (2011–14)  234

9.2 Timeline of the dismantling of environmental regulations and policies (2005–14)  243

10.1 ICT4D in the Canadian North: Key stakeholders  263

10.2 Summary of Indigenous ICT4D initiatives in the Canadian North  280

## FIGURES

1.1 Collective advocacy lies at the intersection of numerous theories  8

4.1 Anglo-American hybrid legal structures  90

5.1 SAID event timeline – 1995–2015  122

6.1 Lake St Martin is located in the Interlake region of Manitoba between Lake Manitoba and Lake Winnipeg.  142

6.2 LSMFN members claimed Site #9 between Grahamdale and Moosehorn for their new community.  151

6.3 LSMFN members took part in many peaceful protests but their voices were not heard.  164

6.4 LSMFN members' protests for a new community and wanting to go home were ignored.  164

6.5 LSMFN members were asked what they wanted to see in their new community during a planning meeting.  165

7.1 Timeline of anti-poverty advocacy in Ontario 2007–13  186

10.1 Indigenous non-profit networks discussed in this chapter  269

# Acknowledgements

We would like to express great thanks to all the contributors from across Canada who are featured in this book. They spent an enormous amount of their time writing their chapters in addition to their advocacy work, teaching, research, policy work, etc. This thanks includes Peter Elson, who provided us with an insightful foreword for the collection.

We would like to extend special thanks to our editor, Jacqueline Mason, at McGill-Queen's University Press for her warm engagement on this project and steady hand in seeing it through. Of course, we would also like to extend thanks to McGill-Queen's University Press itself for seeing the importance of a collection of original works that depicts the various ways public policy advocacy is taken up in the non-profit sector across Canada, and ensuring those stories are told.

To the funders, a big thank you for assisting in bringing this book to fruition. It is wonderful to have the financial support of each of the editors' institutions, the University of Regina and York University. Given the nature of our book, it is a thrill to have the financial support of community organizations: the Max Bell Foundation and The Muttart Foundation.

We would also like to extend our thanks to advocates everywhere in Canada who inspired us in the creation of the title of our first chapter, "Advocacy: A Contested yet Enduring Concept in Our Canadian Landscape." Your contribution to the growth and betterment of this country is invaluable.

Finally, we sincerely thank one another as co-editors for the mutual respect, support, and work that went into creating, developing, and producing this book. It has been an incredible journey of learning!

Nick J. Mulé and Gloria C. DeSantis

# Foreword: The Insiders

PETER R. ELSON

"The Insiders," a popular CBC television national political panel, is an apt analogy for this book (CBC News 2016). On this CBC panel people with an inside knowledge of the machinery of the three main political parties in Canada share their insights behind headline-making news. While the authors in this anthology have very different experiences and perspectives that they have chosen to share, they all have this insider characteristic in common.

So what does a political insider bring to the table? First, an insider brings a sense of history. They have usually worked with a political party since high school or university days, leading or participating in a youth caucus and progressing to work on campaigns, leadership races, and riding constituency matters. If the politician in question gets elected, these young people are often eager recruits to either the legislative or constituency office. Throughout this period, they build an institutional memory of what worked, what didn't, and why. Their knowledge of internal party systems, protocols, and personalities is important information in advocacy strategy development. This cultural history provides an insight into how policies are developed, the importance of policy timing, and the potential appeal of a particular policy proposal, both inside and outside the party. It's no coincidence that long-serving policy insiders are often recruited by external government relations firms. A sense of history takes on added importance in common law, as precedents provide the foundation on which cases are adjudicated. Adam Parachin (chapter 2) shines a welcome light on this legal "black box"; particularly when seemingly arbitrary court decisions distort the role of political activities by charities and are subsequently applied by other judges.

Second, these insiders bring a partisan perspective on issues and events, firmly grounded in the paradigm and perspectives of the party they support. This partisanship reflects a keen sense of loyalty to party values and policies (e.g., The Green Party and the environment). The understanding of each of these divergent world views are critical for any advocate. Party insiders certainly make it their business to track developments in other political parties. Sometimes it's not easy or comfortable to take the time to understand all core political values, particularly when they can be so different from your own. But that's the point. It is essential to being able to clearly stake out a policy position and analyse its potential for adoption. There are an abundant number of examples of this strategy in this anthology: See Carol Liao (chapter 4), Kathleen Thompson and Bonnie Morton (chapter 5), Christa Freiler and Peter Clutterbuck (chapter 7), and Yves Vaillancourt and François Aubry (chapter 8).

Coalitions, as discussed by Anna Burrows and Rachel Laforest in chapter 3, are one way to reduce political exposure and at the same time build political capital and create a policy tent that takes into account different political perspectives. Within coalitions, the focus is on the core policy issue rather than, in most cases, political ideology. When taking political ideologies into account, omit any partisan bias in the development or execution of one's own research work. I have seen instances where a sound policy proposal was rejected because it was tainted with a perception of political bias. An excellent counter case-in-point is the success of the Saskatchewan Disability Income Support Coalition (DISC) as profiled by Kathleen Thompson and Bonnie Morton in chapter 5.

Third, an insider brings important insights into working "within" the political system. Almost by definition, advocacy is dominated by outsiders, trying to find the right combination to unlock the opportunity for a desired policy change. Insiders don't fight the existing political system, they work to influence it from within. These long-time insiders have also learned the art of political compromise. They realize that they can't win every policy debate, but that having that debate can result in incremental successes in some cases and important changes in others. If Canada is cautiously entering an era of "collaborative politics," building meaningful relationships with political insiders would appear to be a worthwhile and strategic policy investment (Denzil Nash 2006). Yves Vaillancourt and François

Aubry (chapter 8) provide a sound example of collaborative policy development and, in this case, blend in the two other characteristics of policy insiders, the importance of history and a partisan social justice lens.

ADVOCACY INSIDERS

To turn the table on the political insiders and turn our attention to advocacy insiders, what do they bring to the table? The short answer is: the same, but different.

First, their sense of history. Examples in this anthology abound. The profile of "Poverty Free Ontario: Cross-Community Advocacy for Social Justice" by Christa Freiler and Peter Clutterbuck in chapter 7 is one example. The internal tensions inherent in coalition building combined with attempts to frame and re-frame child poverty is truly instructive. Their chapter highlights the old adage that all politics is local; but at the same time, the causes of these local issues can also be global in scale, systemic local poverty a byproduct of New Public Management, neoliberalism, and globalization. Other excellent examples of a shared history are Myrle Ballard's analysis of the evacuation of the Lake St Martin First Nation from their traditional territory during the 2011 flood in Manitoba (chapter 6); and Rob McMahon, Heather Hudson, and Lyle Fabian's analysis in "Canada's Northern Communications Policies: The Role of Aboriginal Organizations" (chapter 10). While Ballard's chapter is an all-too-familiar story of modern-day colonialism and provincial abdication of constitutional rights, McMahon, Hudson, and Fabian profile the renaissance of Aboriginal self-determination. This self-determination and dogged perseverance over time both uses and advocates for a wide range of information and communication technologies across Canada's North, including broadband internet connection, radio, television, and telecommunications.

Second, a partisan perspective on issues and events. In this context, social activism is firmly grounded in a social justice paradigm and people in need. This is highlighted in chapter 9 by Suzanne Dudziak and Mark D'Arcy. In their chapter, "The Case of the Anti-Shale Gas Movement in New Brunswick," they profile how, in the absence of any legitimate public forum, a public space for debate and democratic engagement was created to both profile the social and environmental consequences of shale gas development and to build a community-based agenda for a clean economy and local sustainability. Another example is the chapter by Carol Liao (chapter 4), where determined and experienced social enterprise policy insiders worked to align their desire to foster social enterprises with a market-oriented provincial government. Paramount to "creative exploitation" in the overall evolution of social enterprises, this C3 legislation is one way to blend the interest in creating social value returns on private investment (Elson & Hall 2012).

Third, an advocacy insider brings important insights into working "within" the advocacy system. Several authors address this dynamic from a number of perspectives. Anna Burrowes and Rachel Laforest capture the internal dynamics and self-censorship of coalitions within the context of an "advocacy chill" in chapter 3. The result is education and evidence as advocacy, a wolf in sheep's clothing. Christa Frieler and Peter Clutterbuck (chapter 7), bring home the tensions inherent in addressing an issue as large and complex as poverty. This chapter is an echo of a social justice–political pragmatism debate that occurred in Québec following the Women's March against Poverty, better known as the Bread and Roses March against Poverty, in 1995 (Panet-Raymond 1999). The Québec Act to Combat Poverty and Social Exclusion, profiled in detail by Yves Vaillancourt and François Aubry in chapter 8 discusses the positive consequence of creating space to express the collective need for social justice. Chapter 5, "Saskatchewan Disability Income Support Coalition: Advocacy for a New Disability Benefit Program Legislation," by Kathleen Thompson and Bonnie Morton, is another example. These authors provide an in-depth analysis of social justice and at its core – the mobilization of self-advocates – people with disabilities and family members of people living with disabilities.

## A WORD ON ADVOCACY FAILURE

So how convincing do you have to be to change policy? The contributions in this anthology analyze both policy change successes and failures in candid detail. This alone is a worthy contribution to coalitions and advocates everywhere. What may underlie some advocacy failures is a sustained reinforcement of misconceptions to which the addition of evidence not only makes no difference, but can actually reinforce the bias held by the recipient. This could be particularly true when adhering to "evidence-based decision making" at the expense of policy framing strategies. Brendan Nyhan and his colleague Jason Reifler (2010) describe the failure of clear evidence to convince an adherent of an opposing belief system as the "backfire effect." Their research revealed that not only did the response to mock newspaper stories vary by ideology and the credibility of the source documents rebuked when the stories provided corrections (factual evidence) that countered the initial perception, it actually strengthened misperceptions in some groups (Nyhan & Reifler 2010).

This is a sobering finding for those who believe that evidence-based decision making is a prevailing policy-making tool. In many cases it is. But in policy arenas where the political stakes are both high and contentious, more evidence may not create a tipping point. Myrle Ballard's excellent analysis of the Lake St Martin First Nation evacuation from their traditional territory during the 2011 flood in Manitoba (chapter 6) is a case in point. Before you read this chapter, I encourage you to take time to read *The Truth and Reconciliation Commission Report: Calls to Action* (Truth and Reconciliation Commission of Canada 2015).

Institutional inertia at all levels of government is regularly defended and protected in the face of evidence that challenges the status quo. This defence is grounded in politics, policy, and performance. As the authors in this book, including editors Gloria DeSantis and Nick Mulé (chapters 1 and 11), have ably demonstrated, collective civic action is one tool that appears to have the capacity to create a crack in institutional armour.

REFERENCES

CBC News. (2016). The Insiders. Accessed 20 June 2016. http://www.cbc.ca/player/news/TV%20Shows/The%20National/The%20Insiders.

Elson, P.R., and P.V. Hall. 2012. "Canadian Social Enterprises: Taking Stock." *Social Enterprise Journal* 8 (3): 216–36. http://dx.doi.org/10.1108/17508611211280764.

Nash, Denzil. 2006. "Contradictions of Collaborative Politics." *Social Alternatives* 25 (2): 43–7.

Nyhan, B., and J. Reifler. 2010. "When Corrections Fail: The Persistence of Political Misperceptions." Political Behavior 32 (2): 303–30. http://dx.doi.org/10.1007/s11109-010-9112-2.

Panet-Raymond, J. 1999. "A Postscript: Community Development in Quebec: Between Hope and Doubt." *Community Development Journal: An International Forum* 34 (4): 340–5. http://dx.doi.org/10.1093/cdj/34.4.340.

Truth and Reconciliation Commision of Canada. (2015). *Truth and Reconciliation Commission: Calls to Action*. Winnipeg. http://www.trc.ca/websites/trcinstitution/File/2015/Findings/Calls_to_Action_English2.pdf.

# THE SHIFTING TERRAIN

# 1

# Advocacy: A Contested yet Enduring Concept in the Canadian Landscape

GLORIA C. DESANTIS AND NICK J. MULÉ

Has advocacy become a dirty word in Canada? We believe it has and it is for this reason that we were inspired to write a book about it. For the past twenty-five years, we have been advocates involved in many public policy issues through the non-profit sector[1] as well as academics engaged in research and teaching advocacy at the undergraduate and graduate levels. During this time, we have seen advocacy evolve and take many hits, yet endure on an unsympathetic landscape–one dominated by a rise in government surveillance, ongoing cyclical government funding cuts, and a corresponding increase in the non-profit sector sense of confusion and fear. Advocacy has always been a core function of the non-profit sector (Elson 2011; DeSantis et al. 2014) and interestingly, funded by governments during certain periods of time (e.g., during the 1970s and 1980s, advocacy was funded by the federal Department of the Secretary of State) (Laforest 2013). Yet advocacy is still one of the most contentious aspects of relations between the non-profit sector and governments.

The origins of this shift can be traced back to the mid-1990s (see chapter 3 in this collection). However, in 2006, the federal government began to systematically eliminate or radically reduce the funding for organizations that have advocated for progressive public policies (e.g., National Council of Welfare, First Nations Statistical Council, Canadian Council for Refugees, Court Challenges Program, Status of Women Canada, Federation of Saskatchewan Indian Nations, North-South Institute, Nova Scotia-based Mersey Biodiversity Centre, Canadian Environmental Network). In fact, this is exactly what happened in 2013 to the lead charity facilitating the disability coalition in Saskatchewan (see chapter 5). However, non-profits that do not engage in advocacy work have also experienced funding cuts. Further, in addition to funding cuts, in June 2012 the federal government announced that some organizations had been selected for Canada Revenue Agency audits. These focused on compliance rules about "political activities" and the legal definition of charitable activities (Kirkby 2014). This government surveillance created anxiety for non-profits and cautious behaviour surrounding advocacy work that is still ongoing (see chapter 3 especially).

Provincial governments have also been cutting funding to non-profit organizations that have been engaged in advocacy work (between 2013 and 2015, examples include the Welfare Rights Centre in Regina, Deafness Advocacy Association Nova Scotia, HIV Edmonton). The difficulty we encountered as we explored this target-and-silence phenomenon – better known as "advocacy chill" – as both provincial and federal governments cut funds to non-profits, is that there appear to be no Canadian studies that systematically analyze patterns of provincial government funding cuts to the entire range of organizations in the sector. Were organizations' funds cut because their services were no longer deemed necessary by the government or because they advocated against certain government policies? Further, while provincial governments have reduced funding to some non-profits, they have increased funding to others. We thus need to better understand what types of organizations were targeted, which organizational functions were targeted (e.g., service delivery versus advocacy or both), whether they were registered charities or registered non-profits, and what were both implicit and explicit reasons stated by the government for this targeting. Regardless, "advocacy chill" has been part of the Canadian literature for the past few decades and this chill has influenced organizations' perceptions and participation in public policy-making processes (DeSantis 2008; Kirkby 2014). Paradoxically, we also know that non-profit-driven advocacy persists in many forms in Canada. Thus, advocacy endures, but in general, it is being undertaken with varying degrees of unease.

In this book, we set out to expose, and encourage reflection on, the shifting terrain of collective public policy advocacy as practised by non-profits across Canada. We want readers to see *what* these shifts are and ponder what these shifts represent philosophically, ideologically, theoretically, politically, and practically. We invite readers to contemplate *why* these shifts are occurring and their possible implications for democracy and citizen participation. Finally, we urge readers to think about what advocacy is and how it is regulated in Canada.

This book is a cross-Canada journey that offers a glimpse of the public policy advocacy being undertaken in different regions across Canada, focusing primarily on provincial governments. The collection of chapters is intended to show Canada's regional and geographic diversity and expose the various facets of advocacy that, when taken together, bring us to a precipice of cutting-edge observations and questions about advocacy, participation, and democracy in Canada. The chapters are multidisciplinary and will be of interest to those studying environmentalism, health studies, human rights and equity studies, law, policy studies, political science, social work, sociology, and telecommunications.

The contributors to this book offer historical and contemporary examinations of advocacy from different regions in Canada via many perspectives. They are non-profit or charitable organization staff, lawyers, academics, and activists – all of whom engage in various types of public advocacy work. Thus, the chapters are full of insider knowledge, including what worked and what failed in advocacy processes, shedding light on the complexity of advocacy, including shifts in discourse, contested concepts, restrictions, challenges, and opportunities. Throughout the book, we discuss the implications for shaping public policies and programs as well as the effects on democracy. Although the chapters provide valuable insights based on analyses, a major aim of this anthology is to stimulate further dialogue on the issue of collective public policy advocacy.

## THEORIZING AND SITUATING ADVOCACY

Boyce et al. (2001), differentiate between *policy advocacy* that is initiated and occurs outside government walls and *policy participation* that occurs from inside governments. Phillips and Orsini (2002, 3) explain that in policy-making processes, uninvited involvement by non-profits and citizens "is usually referred to as advocacy." Stienstra (2003) is more pointed: governments consult, non-profits advocate. Taken together, the chapters in this book offer the defining features of collective public policy advocacy as practised and theorized in Canada. Two key statements draw boundaries around the type of advocacy that is our focus. First, advocacy is "the act of speaking or of disseminating information intended to influence individual behaviour or opinion, corporate conduct, or public policy and law" (Government of Canada 1999, 50). Second, and more specifically, advocacy consists of the intentional efforts of non-profits and charities to change existing or proposed government policies and programs along with other organizations and/or with marginalized people (adapted from Ezell 2001; DeSantis 2013, 459). This book concentrates on collective public advocacy that results in more equitable outcomes – essentially advocacy is about seeking out collective goods that are in the public's interest (Boris and Mosher-Williams 1998).

Throughout this book, we use the term public policy in its broadest sense. Public policies are about choices made by governments (Graham, Swift, and Delaney 2003; Vaillancourt 2009) and are usually expressed in formal government instruments such as acts, regulations, and bylaws. They are then translated into programs and may be implemented by governments, the non-profit sector, and/or the private sector. Some of the contributors to this anthology focus on specific legislation (e.g., anti-poverty legislation) while others speak more broadly about public policies that they are advocating against (e.g., environmental policies).

## Advocacy Is Process-Oriented

Advocacy is a form of citizen engagement and civic participation in which non-profits play a vital part (Phillips and Orsini 2002; Salamon and Lessans Geller 2008). Recent Canadian literature shows a shift toward viewing volunteerism as civic engagement (Volunteer Canada 2012 edition, 5). Scholars involved in conceptualizing a non-profit sector civic footprint explain that these organizations encourage civic engagement by engaging volunteers and donors, involve organizations within and beyond the community, and promote community awareness (Shier et al. 2014, 57). As such, advocacy involves a wide range of people whose participation ebbs and flows over time depending on the nature of the advocacy work and volunteers' abilities and time availability (DeSantis 2010).

## Advocacy Is about Myriad Different Strategies and Fluid Processes

Advocacy processes are fluid processes; different strategies are adopted in different phases. DeSantis (2013) provides an overview of strategies that are used in advocacy processes: raise public awareness; make direct contact with governments; conduct research; cross-fertilize issues and network across groups; monitor governments and make strategic decisions; and pursue policy enforcement routes (e.g., force the application of city bylaws). Often advocacy work must persist beyond formal approval of new legislation for actual implementation; this is what occurred in both Saskatchewan (see chapter 5) and Québec (see chapter 8). Further, major shifts have occurred as advocacy work has moved to online platforms and social media (Hick and McNutt 2002; Guo and Saxton 2014).

## *Advocacy in Theory Can Be Explained from Different Perspectives*

Given the diverse nature of the non-profit sector and the public policies that it seeks to alter, a collection of theoretical approaches is needed to help explain advocacy in Canada. Advocacy can be characterized as a fluid process that comprises several phases that are influenced by different degrees of intent on the part of activists: it is inspired by an unjust situation that has been identified by a group, and it is shaped by the interaction of certain conditions and the sociopolitical context. The result can be unpredictable (Boris and Mosher-Williams 1998; Schmid et al. 2008; Nicholson-Crotty 2009; Guo and Saxton 2010; Mosley 2010, 2011; DeSantis 2013). A schema that places various fields or bodies of theory together that help explain advocacy can help to highlight the features of this characterization – what this means is that non-profit–facilitated collective advocacy lies at the intersection of many fields. Figure 1.1 provides a sample of some of these fields, including social movement theories and advocacy coalition frameworks, non-profit organizational theories, rational choice theories, public-policy-making theories, and governance theories. It is noteworthy that although these fields are compartmentalized in the figure, in reality the lines between them are blurred. For example, the advocacy coalition framework is a theory that embraces non-profit beliefs, government institutions, policy subsystems, and external system events (Sabatier 1998). Further, scholars have tested a blending of theories, such as punctuated equilibrium theory (public policy changes only incrementally but is punctuated by sudden major transformative changes, such as a change in government) and the advocacy coalition framework in an attempt to explain changes in public policies (Beard 2013).

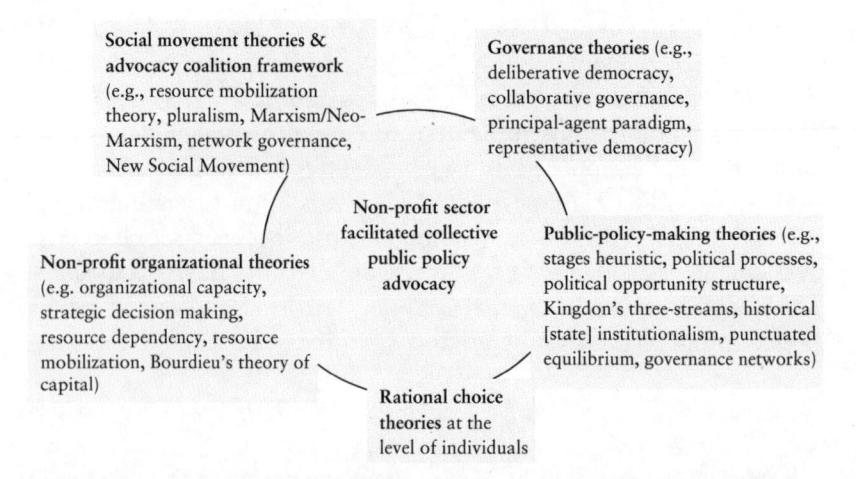

```
Social movement theories &           Governance theories (e.g.,
advocacy coalition framework         deliberative democracy,
(e.g., resource mobilization         collaborative governance,
theory, pluralism, Marxism/Neo-      principal-agent paradigm,
Marxism, network governance,         representative democracy)
New Social Movement)
                    \      Non-profit sector
                     \     facilitated collective
                           public policy            Public-policy-making theories (e.g.,
Non-profit organizational theories   advocacy      stages heuristic, political processes,
(e.g. organizational capacity,                     political opportunity structure,
strategic decision making,                         Kingdon's three-streams, historical
resource dependency, resource                      [state] institutionalism, punctuated
mobilization, Bourdieu's theory of                 equilibrium, governance networks)
capital)                  Rational choice
                          theories at the
                          level of individuals
```

Figure 1.1 Collective advocacy lies at the intersection of numerous theories. Please see the following works as some examples of various theories: Mosley (2010), Sabatier (1998), Beard (2013), Evans and Shields (2000), Laforest (2013), Elson (2011), Bryce (2005), Neigh (2012), and Smith (2008).

It is worth drawing attention to the collective or coalitional nature of advocacy in this book. Coalitions form when "organizations agree to act in concert on particular issues of common interest," often giving up the "right to act independently on this particular issue" (Lee 1999, viii) but maintaining their individual organizational identity. The classic advocacy coalition framework developed by Jenkins-Smith and Sabatier (1994) and Sabatier (1998) helps to explain collective advocacy efforts and public policy change. Many of the salient elements of the model are also reflected in the case studies in this book (Sabatier 1998, 99–102) (e.g., policy subsystems containing a variety of actors, coalition beliefs, and resources influence strategy choices; relatively stable parameters such as socio-cultural values and social structure; and external system events such as changes in public opinion and governments in power, etc.).

## Advocacy and Participatory Governance

"Governance is most fundamentally about the overarching co-ordination of public policy" (Evans and Shields 2000, 14). This includes the involvement of and interaction among a variety of state and non-state actors from the local to the international levels. More specifically, this book discusses the concept of multilevel governance, which includes four levels of government (i.e., federal, provincial, municipal, and Aboriginal) that interact with each other as well as with myriad private-sector and non-profit-sector actors that are also influenced by state policies and their discourses (Laforest 2013).

The public policy world and policy-making processes are constantly evolving (Orsini and Smith 2007). Some aspects of this evolution involve rethinking governance and participation (Hajer 2003) while others focus on conceptualizing citizen diversity and the need to incorporate new knowledges and discourses into public policies (Orsini and Smith 2007). Critical perspectives on policy making reveal a shift in importance toward greater democratic governance, especially enhanced deliberate, participatory approaches and the use of local knowledge (Fischer 2003; Hajer and Wagenaar 2003). For example, engaging multiple actors in deliberations on a science-based policy process enriched the policy itself, as well as democracy (Burgess 2014). Nonetheless, some would argue that the shift is of a particular nature, a "shift toward market driven policy governance" (or neoliberalism) that currently dominates western liberal democracies (Phillips 2006, 59) and ends up excluding the non-profit sector. Also, government engagement strategies are known to "arrange and contain" non-profit participation, resulting in a form of regulated advocacy (Murray 2012; DeSantis 2013) (see also chapters 3 and 7). Further, some scholars are of the opinion that democratic space has shrunk in Canada (see chapter 9) (see also Abelson et al. 2003).

Ballard presents a compelling antithesis to participatory engagement and democracy in Manitoba in chapter 6. She presents the tragic story of her Lake St Martin First Nation Anishinaabe community which was left to struggle alone through a public policy quagmire created by the federal and provincial governments that resulted in the flooding and complete destruction of her community. Both historic (e.g., Indian Act of 1876) and current federal and provincial government policies united to control and silence the Lake St Martin First Nation; the province controls land and water policies while the federal government controls First Nations policies. These governments and their policies affected the degree to which the community was entitled to participate in decisions that directly affected them, despite the paradox that they had a constitutional right to participate in the decisions made before the flood, during the evacuation, and in resettlement plans after the flood. This is a case of multilevel governance and democracy heavily influenced by colonization.

Any curtailment of non-profit participation in policy governance limits democracy. Laforest (2013) explains that the scope for non-profit participation at the federal government level has narrowed since the 1970s and 1980s, despite the Voluntary Sector Initiative hosted over five years by the federal government which began in 2000. The Initiative failed to lead to a more formal relationship between the non-profit sector and the federal government. Interestingly, non-profit leadership in various federal policy areas was strong during that earlier era because "the federal government supported and encouraged political representation in a way that the provinces never have" (Laforest 2013, 243). Evans and Shields (2000, 13) believe the shift is quite intentional: "A new architecture of governance is being erected ... The third sector is being positioned to contribute to the silencing of voices by serving as the mediating agent of conflict and producer of social goods. In essence, it becomes a buffer sector for the state."

This hypothesis is supported beyond Canada. The book *The Revolution Will Not Be Funded* (INCITE! Women of Color against Violence 2009) exposes how the "non-profit industrial complex" controls and shapes advocacy and consequently impedes needed change – indeed a serious critique of sector advocacy. By contrast, Liao points out in chapter 4 that new hybrid non-profit and for-profit organizations may be able to open up new forms of advocacy given the emergent blurring of boundaries between the private market and non-profits.

## THE NON-PROFIT SECTOR IN CANADA – A BRIEF OVERVIEW

There are a multitude of labels for this sector: third sector, voluntary sector, non-profit sector, community-based organizations, charities, social economy organizations, and civil society organizations. These various labels have been adopted by the contributors to this book and reflect the regional labels that are unique to those geographic areas. Some of these terms have specific legal meanings. For example, "registered charity" is a legal term used by the Canada Revenue Agency and refers to organizations that fit certain criteria, have tax-exempt status, and have limitations on their advocacy work (see the next section on non-profit-sector advocacy). In contrast, "registered non-profits" refer to those that are registered through a province/territory or through Innovation, Science, and Economic Development Canada and do not have any limits imposed on their advocacy work. Some organizations register as both charities and non-profits.

The sector provides both targeted and public benefit services and undertakes advocacy. By definition, this sector is independent from the private market and governments, has its own self-governing structure and processes, exists to serve a public benefit, does not distribute profits to its directors or members, and depends to varying degrees on volunteers (Government of Canada 2002; Hall et al. 2004).[2] The International Classification of Nonprofit Organizations states that there are fourteen categories: arts/culture, sports/recreation, education/research, universities and colleges, health, hospitals, social services, environment, development/housing, law/advocacy/politics, grant-making/fundraising/voluntarism, international development, religion, and business and professional associations (Hall et al. 2004). In Canada, based on data collected more than a decade ago, which is also the most recent and comprehensive data, the non-profit sector has $112 billion in revenue, approximately 161,000 registered charities and non-profit organizations, employs more than two million people, and has millions of volunteers (Hall et al. 2004).

The statistics just cited reveal the size and scope of the non-profit sector, but how much advocacy facilitated by the non-profit sector actually goes on in Canada? The chapters in this book reveal that advocacy is undertaken by registered charities, registered non-profits, unregistered entities, and coalitions that are hosted by registered charities – indeed, advocacy is driven by a multitude of combinations. Yet, how many sector staff engage in advocacy, how many volunteer advocates are there, and how many hours do they engage in advocacy each year in Canada? There are few data to answer these questions clearly (Carter 2011; Northcott 2014). In one study, a sample of 1,625 non-profit leaders were interviewed and 39 per cent said they "engaged in permitted political activities over the previous year" (Imagine Canada 2010). In another study, organizations were asked what type of public policy activities they undertake (Carter, Plewes, and Echenberg 2005, 6):

- 89 per cent reported "identifying issues, raising awareness and getting issues on the public policy agenda";

- 66 per cent reported "developing policy solutions through research and analysis"; and
- 58 per cent reported actually developing policy solutions and promoting them.

The advocacy function of the non-profit sector is its foundation. Some have posited that "the history of advocacy parallels the development of democratic societies" (Rektor 2002, 3). We would add that advocacy precedes the formation of new non-profit organizations. For example, in Saskatchewan, the Anti-Tuberculosis League became an incorporated non-profit in 1911 after community volunteers rallied together to advocate for public policies, programs, and sanatoria to treat people with the deadly disease. This non-profit organization then ran these hospitals and advocated for healthy public policy for decades (DeSantis et al. 2014) (see Elson 2011 for additional historical details). Nonetheless, "advocacy and funding are two of the most controversial areas of government and voluntary sector relations" (Brock and Banting 2001, 10). There was hope that the federal government's Voluntary Sector Initiative would pave the way for more open discussion about advocacy – especially with the release of *A Code of Good Practice on Policy Dialogue* (Government of Canada 2002). Based on the chapters in this book, the outcome is not encouraging.

## NON-PROFIT-SECTOR ADVOCACY: SHIFTING TERRAIN

The shifting terrain refers to changes in the use of the term advocacy as well as advocacy discourses and processes. It also refers to the many contexts, environments, and spaces within which advocacy as a concept has evolved. Both within and across these many contexts, advocacy and its discourses are contested by practitioners and scholars – it is a term with many meanings and interpretations. The terrain explored in this book includes shifting advocacy discourse as well as shifts in the regulatory, political, ideological, public policy, and geographical contexts.

Shifting advocacy discourse was one of our primary areas of interest in writing this book. Discourse may be defined as "a system of meaning that provides a way of interpreting or understanding a set of objects in the world ... Discourses are organized, maintained and resisted by talk and action" (Carroll 2004, 273) and, as such, are forms of social practice and interactions that require an understanding of context (Phillips and Hardy 2002; Titscher et al. 2007). Today, many terms are being used to refer to the advocacy work of non-profits. The following list offers some examples:

- "policy dialogue" was made prominent through the Voluntary Sector Initiative when there seemed to be serious federal government interest to work on its relationship with the sector (Government of Canada 2002);
- "engage in public policy" refers to non-profit organizations' participation in public policy and can be divided into three main activity areas (i.e., awareness raising and public education, policy research for solutions, and promoting/mobilizing the adoption of a policy solution) (Carter, Plewes, and Echenberg 2005);
- "collaboration on policy" is the dominant language adopted in a practical manual that encourages the community and government to work together to design public policies (Caledon Institute of Social Policy 2009);
- "policy co-construction" refers to a theoretical construct that reflects shifting discourse in Québec which sees advocacy for public policy change as something done in partnership with the provincial government – some of which is funded by the provincial government (see chapter 8);
- "our intention is to educate" is language that has been adopted by many non-profits because they believe they do not have a mandate to advocate and many are afraid of the potential consequences of engaging in advocacy activities (from chapter 3).

This shifting discourse also begs questions about shifts in advocacy approaches. While the intention here is not to offer an in-depth historical comparison of advocacy approaches, there are some notable points. In chapter 7, Freiler and Clutterbuck hypothesize about a trend toward greater insider advocacy in Canada – also known as institutional advocacy – and believe the evolution of anti-poverty advocacy is such a case study. Their hypothesis appears to be supported by other scholars writing from international perspectives (Lang 2014). Freiler and Clutterbuck explain that non-profits working inside and more closely with governments is not a bad thing in itself, especially if more relevant public policies and programs that tackle community problems, as defined by communities, are developed as a result. However, they and others (Chandler 2004; Lang 2014) express concerns that insider approaches have serious risks, including political accommodation, exclusion of groups, non-profit mission drift, and non-profit co-optation – all of which are threats to democracy.

It is also important to examine the variety of advocacy environments. First, the regulatory environment and attempts to define it and shape it publicly have shifted over the past few decades. The Voluntary Sector Initiative acknowledged that advocacy and policy participation were "inherent to debate and change in a democratic society" (Voluntary Sector Initiative 2001, 8; 2002) but the dialogue on advocacy that took place during that Initiative was limited because the government was reluctant to discuss it (Mulé 2011). Further, the Canada Revenue Agency (CRA) has not yet made substantive changes to the Income Tax Act, or its regulations, to which "registered charities" are bound. This act is based on a 400-year-old Elizabethan English model of charity (Bridge 2002) which accepts the status quo and in which there is no place for advocating change. Parachin argues in chapter 2 that the attendant CRA regulations are too restrictive (see also Broder 2014) and can have a chilling effect on advocacy.

Over the past ten years, CRA has scaled up its web presence and regularly circulates information to non-profits through its elist. Since 2003, when it released circular CPS-022, CRA has created webpages, produced interpretations of the Income Tax Act, released a video series titled "Charities and their Participation in Political Activities" and held webinars, intending to help registered charities better understand the advocacy rules. Research shows that many non-profits are still confused and anxious about what is permitted (DeSantis 2013). Imagine Canada, a national non-profit, responded by developing resources for non-profits to use, freely accessible on its website. Imagine Canada also partnered with Carters Professional Association to offer webinars such as "Political Activities by Charities: If you do it, do it smart!" Locally based non-profits also began offering resources and workshops. For example, in the spring of 2014, the Calgary Chamber of Voluntary Organizations offered a half-day workshop, "Strategic Advocacy: How to Develop a Government Relations Plan to Strategically Address Policy Issues."

A second area where shifting terrain is evident is the political environment, particularly at the federal government level. If we simply take a look at the past twenty-five years, the back and forward movement is clear. Chapter 3 describes how the federal government funded non-profit-facilitated advocacy in the 1990s (see also Laforest 2011). Then, in 2000, the Voluntary Sector Initiative led to much excitement about a more collaborative relationship between the federal government and the non-profit sector. However, as we have already stated, since 2006, when the Conservative Party of Canada took office, there have been many cuts to advocacy-focused non-profits as well as the advocacy work of other non-profits (Phillips 2009; Elson 2011; Laforest 2011).[3] Many of these cuts led to public outcries, petitions, editorials, and stories in newspapers, and calls to action across social media. To make matters worse for charities, in 2012 the Conservative government dedicated an additional $13 million to the CRA to support an increase in the number of auditors required to check into the "political activities" of organizations (see chapter 11 for more details). The terrain shifted suddenly in 2015, when the Liberal Party of Canada was elected to office and the new prime minister, Justin Trudeau, issued public mandate letters to all cabinet ministers, including a letter to the Minister of National Revenue, which contained instructions to reduce the "political harassment" of charities and modernize the rules (Government of Canada 2015). It is too early to tell whether this instruction and shift in tone will result in a fundamental shift in practice about how the federal government deals with charities and their advocacy function.

Third, the ideological landscape has shifted too. Advocacy is defined and operationalized by the beliefs of those who work or volunteer in the non-profit sector. In chapter 8, Vaillancourt and Aubry highlight the work of scholars who explain that advocates are driven to do their work based on different ideologies, which in turn influence their choice of strategies and targets. For example, Lamarche and Greason (2009, 146–7) describe how some human rights activists and organizations adopt *legal approaches* based on "human rights frameworks" developed by the United Nations, while others, such as anti-poverty activists and organizations, are bound to *ethical approaches* based on values of dignity and social justice. We would add that much terrain is still unexplored, for example the *constitutional rights approaches* of First Nations people on the "duty to consult" that is required by all governments and the attendant implications for self-determination. In chapter 6, Ballard describes the absence of this latter approach regarding her Anishinaabe First Nation community in Manitoba. What does advocacy look like in this latter case and should this even be conceived as advocacy?

Fourth, the public policy environment and accompanying discourses on everything from poverty to northern telecommunications are constantly shifting. Freiler and Clutterbuck explain in chapter 7 how the public discourse on poverty, for example, shifted in 1989 when poverty was reframed as "child poverty" and all political parties in the House of Commons voted unanimously to eliminate it by the year 2000. The advocacy work of anti-poverty activists changed over that ten-year period, as there seemed to be a greater government–non-profit-sector sense of "we are all working together to eliminate child poverty." In chapter 10, McMahon, Hudson, and Fabian offer a poignant example of how shifts in discourse in information and communication technologies in Canada's far north influenced advocacy and people's participation; their advocacy work is currently reshaping public policy discourse to focus on the "First Mile" instead of the last mile. Other scholars have written about the ongoing ebb and flow of what is trendy and what is not (e.g., immigrants, childcare) (Kobayashi 2000; Thériault 2009).

Finally, an exploration of shifting terrain in Canada simply cannot ignore geographic and spatial variables. "Voluntary action commonly develops in response to localized needs and interests that change over time and space" (Milligan and Conradson 2006, 7). Place, location, distance, and scale are known to influence disability policy activism (Kitchin and Wilton 2003) as well as how non-profit organizations react to government-driven restructuring (Skinner 2008), which can result in human, funding, and resource reductions. Evidence from a small-scale Canadian study shows that advocacy behaviour is different in remote and/or northern communities, towns located in isolated rural landscapes, and towns located close to regional centres and cities (DeSantis 2013). Several chapters in this book, such as chapter 9, which discusses fracking in New Brunswick, further illustrate this diversity.

## THE SOILING OF "ADVOCACY"

At least five main mechanisms have driven the soiling of advocacy in Canada. These mechanisms are: government rules, non-profits' perception and understanding of those government rules, muzzle clauses in some non-profit contracts with governments, personal muzzling attempts on individuals, and funding cuts made by governments to non-profits. We now briefly turn to each of these.

The federal government's CRA regulations and rules based on the Income Tax Act define permissible activities. In summary,

> Registered charities are limited by Canada Revenue Agency (CRA) in the types of public awareness and policy activities they can engage in. Allowable public awareness and policy activities fall into two general categories: *charitable activities* and *permitted political activities*. Activities that fall outside the boundaries of these categories (e.g., politically partisan activities, activities not related to the charity's purpose, etc.) are generally not permitted. (Imagine Canada 2010, 1)

As we explained in preceding sections, CRA regulations under the Income Tax Act are not clear and there have been many calls to change them. In chapter 2, Parachin explains many of these issues, especially "the 10% rule," and that if charities break these rules, their charitable status may be revoked by the CRA. Further, CRA heightens its presence during elections. One study showed how CRA sent e-newsletters out to registered charities during the 2007 federal election reminding them about CRA rules, which resulted in organizations' role in public election conversations and activities being reduced (DeSantis 2008).

Lobbyist registries at various levels of government have also evolved since 1989. Serious questions arose when lobbyist registries and policies were drafted and rolled out by federal, provincial/territorial, and municipal governments, including public debates about whether non-profits should be exempt from these registries. To date, most registries exempt non-profits. However, all of these discussions laid a collective blanket of caution on non-profits who were already feeling the heaviness of CRA rules.

Second, non-profit staff and volunteers' perceptions and level of understanding of advocacy, both formally and informally, are problematic. Evidence from one study showed that 59 per cent of the non-profit respondents indicated that their concern about potentially violating the rules is a fairly potent barrier to doing advocacy (Imagine Canada 2010).

Third, some government funding relationships with non-profits have muzzle clauses. There is evidence that some government funding contracts have clauses that require the non-profit not to speak out against them (DeSantis 2008). In other cases, the muzzling is more informal. For example, we experienced this muzzling effect first-hand in our own advocacy work, when a women's emergency shelter executive director responded to a newspaper reporter's questions about a new provincially-funded initiative. After the story ran in the local newspaper, a provincial government staff person phoned the non-profit and denounced her media coverage as too negative about the government. The non-profit staffer later stated she would not respond to any more media queries. Thus, the community will no longer hear this non-profit's perspective on emergency shelter issues.

Fourth, personal muzzling of individuals who are actively advocating for certain policies also occurs. This is a kind of informal muzzling that goes on in communities when volunteers and staff from non-profits attempt to speak out and are threatened with personal consequences (DeSantis 2008). Interview data revealed two examples in particular. In one instance, a single mother on social assistance was told by her provincial social worker that he would find a way to cut her social assistance cheque if she continued to speak out against the provincial government's housing policy. In a second example, an advocate who was part of a coalition speaking out against a property tax policy at municipal council was told by the oil company he worked for that he would lose his job if he kept speaking out (ibid.). These conversations then spread throughout communities and increased advocacy chill.

Fifth, we have already explained that government funding cuts destabilize non-profits, which then influences how they make their advocacy decisions. Some non-profits choose to focus their fewer resources on their service delivery role only (Brooks 2001). This sets up a domino effect wherein non-profits, competing with each other for fewer dollars, are then reluctant to cooperate on advocacy campaigns (Luther and Prempeh 2003).

In sum, for many non-profits, advocacy is a dirty word – it makes them nervous and they choose to curtail their advocacy activities because of the possible negative consequences, the most severe of which is having their charitable status revoked. There is a cruel irony to all of this. Public opinion polls undertaken by The Muttart Foundation and Imagine Canada have shown that non-profits are the most trusted of a variety of groups in Canada and are expected to speak out about problems in communities. The following offers evidence of this (Lasby and Barr 2013):

- 79 per cent of Canadians "say they have some or a lot of trust in charities" and this remains virtually unchanged since the 2000 survey (p. 29); and
- 62 per cent of "Canadians generally believe that the opinions charities express on issues of public concern have value because they represent a public interest perspective" (as opposed to only representing a particular interest) (p. 84).

## SOCIAL JUSTICE VERSUS NEOLIBERAL IDEOLOGY

Justice generally and social justice specifically define the scope of this anthology. Our understanding of justice is that it focuses our attention on the search for equitable outcomes for the greatest public good in parallel with reducing the marginalization of certain societal issues. In this book, marginalized societal issues include: disability support systems, poverty, the forced displacement of Aboriginal communities, fracking in rural areas, and telecommunications connections for remote communities in northern Canada.

It is this participatory dimension that is of essence in our and our contributors' examination of advocacy. Social justice espouses the involvement of various groups of people based on their knowledge of the existence of a societal problem, who are directly affected by a new or modified public policy (Mullaly 1997; DeSantis 2010). Collective advocacy processes usually see an ebb and flow of people depending on the length of these processes; for example, middle-class advocates are usually able to participate for longer periods because they do not have the same material and survival issues that tend to reduce marginalized groups' engagement, thus compromising justice. Sen (2009) draws a link between the pursuit of social justice and democracy as "government by discussion." The ongoing project of public advocacy work in creating, developing, and upholding ideas of social justice within a democratic governance framework, where governance refers to the sum of all the ways we run our communities, is underscored by the works of numerous scholars (Smith 1759; Wollstonecraft 1790, 1792; Rawls 1971, 1993, 2001; Sen 2009). Indeed, participation is a defining criterion of democratic nations like Canada, but some have argued there is a "democratic deficit" (Canadian Policy

Research Networks and Ascentum Inc. 2005, 6), making a book about the participatory nature of public policy advocacy especially timely. Therein lies a critical tension that we hope to expose: the recent adoption of terms like "policy participation" and "policy dialogue" should serve social justice and democracy purposes, but do they in reality? Based on our own advocacy work, we would answer that in many cases they do not.

Marginalized societal issues, such as those examined in this book, lie outside current mainstream neoliberal ideology, thus it is important for us to frame and examine public policy advocacy within this ideological context. Neoliberalism is currently seen as supporting the market economy via economically liberalized policies that include reduced state intervention, deregulation, privatization, free trade, cuts in government spending, and austerity measures, serving to enhance the role of the private sector in an already powerful capitalist economy (Jones, Parker, and Ten Bos 2005; Boas and Gans-Morse 2009; Arac 2013). Such a perspective supports globalization in strengthening the economy instead of attending to marginalized societal issues. This allows governments and corporations to place responsibility for societal problems such as pollution and poverty on individuals, eschewing any interest in or responsibility for the structural and systemic causes (Chomsky 2011), thus discouraging collective action such as public policy advocacy on these issues.

In the non-profit sector, the neoliberal agenda problematizes organizations that take on broader structural and systemic issues, and ignores policies that redistribute resources equitably (Evans, Richmond, and Shields 2005) and goals of fair and equitable outcomes. In turn, this work becomes questioned and labelled as "political." As a result, charities drift from their missions (Kivel 2007; Mulé 2011; Mulé 2015). This neoliberal governance structure has been imposed upon non-profits and charities specifically. It includes professionalized bureaucratic procedures that negatively affect already under-resourced non-profits, further limiting their capacity while compromising their autonomy and ability to advocate (Evans, Richmond, and Shields 2005). An example of this would be the increase in paper work to respond to heightened accountability measures imposed by governments.

## ADVOCACY AND TRADITIONAL NEWS MEDIA

Traditional mass news media are public communication technologies (e.g., television, radio, and newspapers). For advocates, the media is simultaneously: a part of the larger neoliberal ideological context that they must monitor and understand to carefully frame their messages and strategize their delivery, and a tool for spreading mass messages to educate the public and governments. Traditional media can positively affect advocacy work because it puts the spotlight on issues and it speaks to large numbers of people and encourages involvement, thus serving democracy, but it can also have negative effects because advocacy messages and groups can be misrepresented (Dobson 2003). Today, traditional news media have been augmented by newer technologies, including organization websites, blogs, email protests, Facebook, Twitter, and the like, where advocacy messages can be written and promoted without organizations having to use traditional media.

Traditional news media are known to have a powerful influence on mediating culture and a sense of community (Hick and Reich 2002) as well as on affecting advocacy messages and tactics (Hoefer 2006). "Given that journalists play a substantial role in gatekeeping based on their news values, norms, and practices, the relationship between advocacy groups' publicity efforts and news organizations' representation of a group's efforts" (Min and Kim 2012, 226) is a salient factor in advocacy work. The news media influences what and how we think about societal problems as well as viable alternatives (Dorfman and Krasnow 2014, 296). Non-profits and their many marginalized societal messages "operate at a symbolic and material disadvantage" in which their public policy *issues* are downplayed, ignored (Greenberg, May and Elliott 2005, 132), or portrayed negatively (Hackett and Carroll 2004). However, mass media is also not monolithic and some organizations have been able to achieve their social change objectives through these media (Greenberg, May, and Elliott 2005) (see also chapter 5). Finally, even though advocacy through traditional media is believed to foster democratic processes because it engages larger communities in public decision making (Dorfman and Krasnow 2014), we know from our own advocacy work that some *advocacy tactics* are denounced and framed negatively by some journalists (e.g., a First Nations blockade of railway tracks, a sit-in organized by environmentalists trying to protect a wetland).

## CROSS-CANADA ADVOCACY EXPERIENCES

This book is a cross-Canada advocacy journey. Each chapter explores, in different ways, various facets of the participatory aspect of public policy advocacy that is a form of civic engagement; the ebbs and flows of advocacy processes, including who is engaged and who is not over time; and the search for positive social justice change on marginalized societal issues within an increasingly threatening landscape coloured by neoliberalism.

The first three chapters in this book help to set the context and encourage us to think about the future of advocacy in Canada. In chapter 2, Adam Parachin explains the rules governing the work of registered charities and argues that since the charitable sector concentrates on community interests and civic engagement – as contrasted with the economic self-interest of the marketplace – the sector is rightly positioned to drive democratic renewal and reform. In chapter 3, despite their respondents' fear about participating in advocacy research, Anna Burrowes and Rachel Laforest explain how coalitions create an important space for advocacy and political participation as well as examine the discourses of coalitions while exposing how practices and meaning systems in advocacy are shifting. In chapter 4, Carol Liao describes new hybrid corporation legislation – the first was enacted in British Columbia – and encourages us to think about the advantages and disadvantages of these hybrids and how they affect potential new advocacy processes and impacts.

The ensuing six chapters are case studies that take us deep inside advocacy processes:

- In chapter 5, Kathleen Thompson and Bonnie Morton describe the history of advocacy for/with people who have disabilities in Saskatchewan, including shifting relations with the provincial government, while using a collaborative advocacy model;
- In chapter 6, Myrle Ballard presents a compelling antithesis to participatory engagement and democracy in Manitoba, as she describes how a First Nation community was left to advocate within a federal-provincial government policy quagmire that systematically silenced them, revealing that multilevel governance is still influenced by colonization;
- Chapter 7 by Christa Freiler and Peter Clutterbuck reveals that we cannot disconnect public policy advocacy from either the present policy context or the policy legacy of decades ago and that political accommodations and different public policy goals (e.g., poverty reduction versus poverty elimination) can lead to

fragmented networks, tensioned processes, and watered-down policy outcomes;
- In chapter 8, Yves Vaillancourt and François Aubry analyze a case study in Québec that unfolded over a ten-year period that began with civil society organizations in a bottom-up phase but evolved to become a highly participatory co-construction process that saw both civil society organizations as well as government actors being engaged;
- Chapter 9 is based in New Brunswick where Suzanne Dudziak and Mark D'Arcy analyze a current marginalized public policy issue – shale gas exploration and hydraulic fracturing (i.e., fracking) – including their observations about the creation of new democratic space through new urban–rural and Aboriginal–non-Aboriginal alliances;
- In chapter 10, Rob McMahon, Heather Hudson, and Lyle Fabian provide a longitudinal analysis of advocacy for information and communication technologies for development (ICT4D) in Canada's Far North and demonstrate how a greater diversity of Aboriginal non-profits and coalitions joined with experienced consumer organizations, expert witnesses, and academics to shape public policies as well as secure new products in remote and rural communities.

Advocacy is a contested yet enduring concept in the Canadian landscape. As the contributors to this book demonstrate, collective public policy advocacy is flourishing in many forms in Canada, despite the increase in government surveillance; constant and cyclical government funding cuts to non-profits; and the concomitant struggles, challenges, and anxiety for non-profits. All five case study chapters – except for Manitoba's – conclude optimistically about the power of advocacy to make progressive change, despite the fear, anxiety, and accompanying political accommodations that were made (e.g., see chapter 7 especially, on insider–outsider strategies). Indeed, there is both advocacy chill and advocacy warmth depending on the policy issue, the points in advocacy life cycles that one analyzes, the political context, and the actors. Readers will come away from this book with a much greater understanding of advocacy theory, practice, trends, strategies, politics, and impacts. The findings will speak to those with an interest in justice and democracy in this country, as the book addresses the extent to which the act of public policy advocacy, a form of civic engagement, is and can be undertaken in Canada.

NOTES

1 The term "non-profit sector" is a general term used throughout this chapter that is intended to be inclusive of a variety of organizations including registered non-profits and registered charities. Further in the chapter though, the legal difference between registered charities and registered non-profits is made, especially with regards to how registered non-profits do not have limits imposed on their advocacy work but registered charities do.
2 This definition excludes co-operatives and credit unions, for example.
3 It is known that funding cuts destabilize non-profits and depending on the severity of the cut, results in the closure of organizations (Scott 2003; Hall et al. 2005). In her chapter, Liao explains that social enterprises and new hybrid organizations that are able to diversify and solidify their financial bases may not face the same degree of instability in the future. This territory remains to be explored.

REFERENCES

Abelson, J., P.-G. Forest, J. Eyles, P. Smith, E. Martin, and F.-P. Gauvin. 2003. "Deliberations About Deliberative Methods: Issues in the Design and Evaluation of Public Participation Processes." *Social Science & Medicine* 57 (2): 239–51. http://dx.doi.org/10.1016/S0277-9536(02)00343-X.

Arac, J. 2013. "Prologue." In *Social Resilience in the Neoliberal Era*, edited by P. Hall and M. Lamont, xv–xviii. Cambridge, UK: Cambridge University Press, xvi–xvii. http://dx.doi.org/10.1017/CBO9781139542425.002.

Beard, V. 2013. "A Theoretical Understanding of Housing and Homelessness: Federal Homelessness and Housing Policy through the Lenses of Punctuated Equilibrium Theory and Advocacy Coalition Frameworks." *Poverty & Public Policy* 5 (1): 67–87. http://dx.doi.org/10.1002/pop4.16.

Boas, T., and J. Gans-Morse. 2009. "Neoliberalism: From New Liberal Philosophy to Anti-Liberal Slogan." *Studies in Comparative International Development* 44 (2): 137–61. http://dx.doi.org/10.1007/s12116-009-9040-5.

Boris, E., and R. Mosher-Williams. 1998. "Nonprofit Advocacy Organizations: Assessing the Definitions, Classifications and Data." *Nonprofit and Voluntary Sector Quarterly* 27 (4): 488–506. http://dx.doi.org/10.1177/0899764098274006.

Boyce, W., M. Tremblay, M.A. Mccoll, J. Bickenbach, A. Crichton, S. Andrews, N. Gerein, and A. D'aubin. 2001. *A Seat at the Table: Persons with Disabilities and Policy Making*. Kingston, ON: McGill-Queen's University Press.

Bridge, R. 2002. "The Law Governing Advocacy by Charitable Organizations: The Case for Change." *Philanthropist* 17 (2): 3–33.

Brock, K., and K. Banting. 2001. "Introduction." In *The Nonprofit Sector and Government in a New Century*, edited by K. Brock and K. Banting, 1–20. Kingston, ON: McGill-Queen's University Press.

Broder, P. 2014. "Pemsel Case Foundation Launched to Foster Canadian Charity Law." *Philanthropist* 25 (4): 207–14.

Brooks, N. 2001. "The Role of the Voluntary Sector in a Modern Welfare State." In *Between State and Market: Essays on Charities Law and Policy in Canada*, edited by Jim Phillips, B. Chapman, and D. Stevens, 166–216. Kingston, ON: McGill-Queen's University Press.

Bryce, H. 2005. *Players in the Public Policy Process: Nonprofits as Social Capital and Agents*. New York, NY: Palgrave MacMillan.

Burgess, M. 2014. "From 'Trust Us' to Participatory Governance: Deliberative Publics and Science Policy." *Public Understanding of Science (Bristol, England)* 23 (1): 48–52. http://dx.doi.org/10.1177/0963662512472160.

Caledon Institute of Social Policy. 2009. *Collaboration on Policy: A Manual Developed by the Community-Government Collaboration on Policy*. Ottawa, ON: Caledon Institute of Social Policy. Accessed 21 January 2015. http://www.caledoninst.org/Publications/PDF/772ENG.pdf.

Canadian Policy Research Networks, and Ascentum Inc. 2005. *Trends in Public Consultation in Canada*. Ottawa, ON: Canadian Policy Research Networks.

Carroll, W., ed. 2004. *Critical Strategies for Social Research*. Toronto, ON: Canadian Scholars' Press.

Carter, S. 2011. "Public Policy and the Nonprofit Sector." *Philanthropist* 23 (4): 427–35.

Carter, S., B. Plewes, and H. Echenberg. 2005. *Civil Society and Public Policy: A Directory of Nonprofit Organizations Engaged in Public Policy*. Edmonton, AB: Muttart Foundation, McConnell Family Foundation, Maytree Foundation, Walter and Duncan Gordon Foundation.

Chandler, D. 2004. "Building Civil Society 'from Below'?" *Millennium* 33 (2): 313–39. http://dx.doi.org/10.1177/03058298040330020301.

Chomsky, N. 2011. *How the World Works*. Berkeley, CA: Soft Skull Press.

DeSantis, G.C. 2008. A Critical Exploration of Voluntary Sector Social Policy Advocacy with Marginalized Communities Using a Population Health Lens and Social Justice. PhD dissertation, Canadian Plains Studies, University of Regina, Regina, SK.

– 2010. "Voices from the Margins: Policy Advocacy and Marginalized Communities." *Canadian Journal of Nonprofit and Social Economy Research* 1 (1): 23–45. Accessed 17 November 2014. http://www.anserj.ca/index.php/cjnser/article/viewFile/24/8.

– 2013. "Policy Advocacy Experiences of Saskatchewan Nonprofit Organizations: Caught between Rocks and Hard Places with Multiple Constituents?" *Canadian Geographer* 57 (4): 457–73. http://dx.doi.org/10.1111/j.1541-0064.2013.12043.x.

DeSantis, G.C., T. Todd, P. Hackett, J. Daschuk, T. McIntosh, N. Sari, and J. Bascu. 2014. *Saskatchewan Voluntary Sector Early Work on the Determinants of Health 1905–1950: Some Unsettling Questions Inspired by History*. Regina, SK: University of Regina, Saskatchewan Population Health and Evalution Research Unit.

Dobson, C. 2003. *The Troublemaker's Teaparty: A Manual for Effective Citizen Action*. Gabriola Island, BC: New Society Publishers.

Dorfman, L., and I.D. Krasnow. 2014. "Public Health and Media Advocacy." *Annual Review of Public Health* 35 (1): 293–306. http://dx.doi.org/10.1146/annurev-publhealth-032013-182503.

Elson, P. 2011. *High Ideals and Noble Intentions: Voluntary Sector-Government Relations in Canada*. Toronto, ON: University of Toronto Press.

Evans, B.M., T. Richmond, and J. Shields. 2005. "Structuring Neoliberal Governance: The Nonprofit Sector, Emerging New Modes of Control and the Marketisation of Service Delivery." *Policy and Society* 24 (1): 73–97. http://dx.doi.org/10.1016/S1449-4035(05)70050-3.

Evans, B.M., and J. Shields. 2000. *Neoliberal Restructuring and the Third Sector: Reshaping Governance, Civil Society and Local Relations (Working Paper Series)*. Toronto, ON: Ryerson University, Faculty of Business, Centre for Voluntary Sector Studies.

Ezell, M. 2001. *Advocacy in the Human Services*. Belmont, CA: Wadsworth/Thomson Learning.

Fischer, F. 2003. *Reframing Public Policy: Discursive Politics and Deliberative Practices*. New York, NY: Oxford University Press. http://dx.doi.org/10.1093/019924264X.001.0001.

Government of Canada, Office of the Prime Minister. 2015. *Minister of National Revenue Mandate Letter.* Accessed 27 November 2015. http://pm.gc.ca/eng/minister-national-revenue-mandate-letter.

Government of Canada, Voluntary Sector Initiative. 2002. *A Code of Good Practice on Policy Dialogue: Building on an Accord between the Government of Canada and the Voluntary Sector.* Ottawa, ON: Privy Council of Canada.

Government of Canada, Voluntary Sector Initiative, Privy Council Office. 1999. *Working Together: A Government of Canada/Voluntary Sector Joint Initiative - Report of the Joint Tables.* Ottawa, ON: Privy Council Office, Government of Canada.

Graham, J., K. Swift, and R. Delaney. 2003. *Canadian Social Policy: An Introduction.* Toronto, ON: Prentice Hall.

Greenberg, J., T. May, and C. Elliott. 2005. "Homelessness and Media Activism in the Voluntary Sector: A Case Study." *Philanthropist* 20 (2): 131–52.

Guo, C., and G.D. Saxton. 2010. "Voice-in, Voice-Out: Constituent Participation and Nonprofit Advocacy." *Nonprofit Policy Forum* 1 (1): 1–25. http://dx.doi.org/10.2202/2154-3348.1000.

– 2014. "Tweeting Social Change: How Social Media Are Changing Nonprofit Advocacy." *Nonprofit and Voluntary Sector Quarterly* 43 (1): 57–79. http://dx.doi.org/10.1177/0899764012471585.

Hackett, R., and W. Carroll. 2004. *Critical Social Movements and Media Reform.* Vancouver: Simon Fraser University, electronic resource. Accessed 4 December 2014. http://www.sfu.ca/~hackett/CriticalSocialMovements.htm.

Hajer, M. 2003. "Policy without Polity? Policy Analysis and the Institutional Void." *Policy Sciences* 36 (2): 175–95. http://dx.doi.org/10.1023/A:1024834510939.

Hajer, M., and H. Wagenaar, eds. 2003. *Deliberative Policy Analysis: Understanding Governance in the Network Society.* Cambridge, UK: Cambridge University Press. http://dx.doi.org/10.1017/CBO9780511490934.

Hall, M., A. Andrukow, C. Barr, K. Brock, M. De Wit, D. Embuldeniya, L. Jolin, D. Lasby, B. Levesque, E. Malinsky, et al. 2005. *The Capacity to Serve: A Qualitative Study of the Challenges Facing Canada's Nonprofit and Voluntary Organizations.* Toronto, ON: Canadian Centre for Philanthropy.

Hall, M., M. De Wit, D. Lasby, D. Mciver, T. Evers, C. Johnston, J. Mcauley, K. Scott, G. Cucumel, L. Jolin, et al. 2004. *Cornerstones of Community: Highlights of the National Survey of Nonprofit and*

*Voluntary Organizations*. Ottawa, ON: Ministry of Industry, Statistics Canada, catalogue no. 61–533-XIE. Accessed 21 September 2016. http://sectorsource.ca/resource/file/cornerstones-community-highlights-national-survey-nonprofit-and-voluntary-o

Hick, S., and J. McNutt, eds. 2002. *Advocacy, Activism and the Internet: Community Organization and Social Policy*. Chicago, IL: Lyceum Books Inc.

Hick, S., and E. Reich. 2002. "Can You Have Community on the Net?" In *Advocacy, Activism and the Internet: Community Organization and Social Policy*, edited by S. Hick and J. McNutt, 34–42. Chicago: Lyceum Books Inc.

Hoefer, R. 2006. *Advocacy Practice for Social Justice*. Chicago, IL: Lyceum Books Inc.

Imagine Canada. 2010. "Factsheet 2: Public Awareness and Policy Activity, Top-Line Summary." *Imagine Canada's Sector Monitor* 1 (3): 1–2.

INCITE! Women of Color against Violence, ed. 2009. *The Revolution Will Not Be Funded: Beyond the Non-Profit Industrial Complex*. Cambridge, MA: South End Press.

Jenkins-Smith, H.C., and P. Sabatier. 1994. "Evaluating the Advocacy Coalition Framework." *Journal of Public Policy* 14 (2): 175–203. http://dx.doi.org/10.1017/S0143814X00007431.

Jones, C., M. Parker, and R. Ten Bos. 2005. *For Business Ethics*. New York, NY: Routledge. http://dx.doi.org/10.4324/9780203458457.

Kirkby, G. 2014. *An Uncharitable Chill: A Critical Exploration of How Changes in Federal Policy and Political Climate Are Affecting Advocacy-Oriented Charities, Communication and Culture*, Master's thesis, Royal Roads University, Victoria, BC.

Kitchin, R., and T. Wilton. 2003. "Disability Activism and the Politics of Scale." *Canadian Geographer* 47 (2): 97–115. http://dx.doi.org/10.1111/1541-0064.00005.

Kivel, P. 2007. "Social Service or Social Change." In *The Revolution Will Not Be Funded: Beyond the Non-Profit Industrial Complex*, ed. INCITE! Women of Color Against Violence, 1–39. Cambridge, MA: South End Press.

Kobayashi, A. 2000. "Advocacy from the Margins: The Role of Minority Ethnocultural Associations in Affecting Public Policy in Canada." In *The Nonprofit Sector in Canada: Roles and Relationships*, ed. K. Banting, 229–61. Montreal and Kingston: McGill-Queen's University Press.

Laforest, R. 2011. *Voluntary Sector Organizations and the State*. Vancouver, BC: UBC Press.

– 2013. "Shifting Scales of Governance and Civil Society Participation in Canada and the European Union." *Canadian Public Administration* 56 (2): 235–51. http://dx.doi.org/10.1111/capa.12016.

Lamarche, L., and V. Greason. 2009. *Poverty Impact Analysis (PIA) and Government Action: "Made in Québec" Again?* Montreal, QC: Accessed 14 October 2014. file:///C:/Users/Terra4/Desktop/Poverty%20 Impact%20Analysis%20(PIA)%20and%20Governmental%20 Action%20lamarche%20greason%202009.pdf.

Lang, S. 2014. NGOs, *Civil Society and the Public Sphere*. New York, NY: Cambridge University Press.

Lasby, D., and C. Barr. 2013. *Talking About Charities 2013: Canadians' Opinions on Charities and Issues Affecting Charities*. Toronto, ON: Muttart Foundation and Imagine Canada.

Lee, B. 1999. *Pragmatics of Community Organization*. Mississauga, ON: CommonAct Press.

Luther, R., and E. Prempeh. 2003. *Advocacy Matters: Reviving and Sustaining Community Advocacy Networks to Support Multiculturalism and Anti-Racism in the Ottawa Region*. Ottawa, ON: Community Advocacy Action Committee on Access and Equity.

Milligan, C., and D. Conradson. 2006. "Contemporary Landscapes of Welfare: The Voluntary Turn?" In *Landscapes of Voluntarism*, edited by C. Milligan and D. Conradson, 1–14. Bristol, UK: The Policy Press. http://dx.doi.org/10.1332/policypress/9781861346322.003.0001.

Min, S.-J., and Y.M. Kim. 2012. "Choosing the Right Media for Mobilization: Issue Advocacy Groups' Media Niches in the Competitive Media Environment." *Mass Communication & Society* 15 (2): 225–44. http://dx.doi.org/10.1080/15205436.2011.568316.

Mosley, J.E. 2010. "Organizational Resources and Environmental Incentives: Understanding the Policy Advocacy Involvement of Human Service Nonprofits." *Social Service Review* 84 (1): 57–76. http://dx.doi.org/10.1086/652681.

– 2011. "Institutionalization, Privatization and Political Opportunity: What Tactical Choices Reveal About the Policy Advocacy of Human Service Nonprofits." *Nonprofit and Voluntary Sector Quarterly* 40 (3): 435–57. http://dx.doi.org/10.1177/0899764009346335.

Mulé, N.J. 2011. "Advocacy Limitations on Gender and Sexually Diverse Activist Organizations in Canada's Voluntary Sector." *Canadian Journal of Nonprofit and Social Economy Research* 2 (1): 5–23.

– 2015. "The Politicized Queer, the Informed Social Worker: Dis/Re-Ordering the Social Order." In *LGBTQ People and Social Work:*

*Intersectional Perspectives*, edited by B.J. O'Neill, T.A. Swan, and N.J. Mulé, 17–35. Toronto, ON: Canadian Scholars' Press.

Mullaly, B. 1997. *Structural Social Work: Ideology, Theory and Practice*. Don Mills, ON: Oxford University Press.

Murray, K. 2012. "Regulating Activism: An Institutional Ethnography of Public Participation." *Community Development Journal: An International Forum* 47 (2): 199–215. http://dx.doi.org/10.1093/cdj/bsr022.

Neigh, S. 2012. *Resisting the State: Canadian History through the Stories of Activists*. Winnipeg, MB: Fernwood.

Nicholson-Crotty, J. 2009. "The Stages and Strategies of Advocacy among Nonprofit Reproductive Health Providers." *Nonprofit and Voluntary Sector Quarterly* 38 (6): 1044–53. http://dx.doi.org/10.1177/0899764009332467.

Northcott, A. 2014. "Creating Better Public Policies: The Roles of Canadian Charities." *Philanthropist* 25 (4): 201–7.

Orsini, M., and M. Smith, eds. 2007. *Critical Policy Studies*. Vancouver, BC: UBC Press.

Phillips, N., and C. Hardy. 2002. *Discourse Analysis: Investigating Processes of Social Construction*. Thousand Oaks, CA: Sage Publications Inc. http://dx.doi.org/10.4135/9781412983921.

Phillips, R. 2006. "The Role of Nonprofit Advocacy Organizations in Australian Democracy and Policy Governance." *Voluntas* 17 (1): 57–73. http://dx.doi.org/10.1007/s11266-005-9004-y.

Phillips, S. 2009. "The Harper Government and the Voluntary Sector: Whither a Policy Agenda?" In *The New Federal Policy Agenda and the Voluntary Sector*, edited by R. Laforest, 7–34. Kingston, ON: McGill-Queen's University Press.

Phillips, S., and M. Orsini. 2002. *Mapping the Links: Citizen Involvement in Policy Processes*. Ottawa, ON: Canadian Policy Research Networks.

Rawls, J. 1971. *A Theory of Justice*. Cambridge, MA: Harvard University Press.

– 1993. *Political Liberalism*. New York, NY: Columbia University Press.

– 2001. *Justice as Fairness: A Restatement*. Cambridge, MA: Harvard University press.

Rektor, L. 2002. *Advocacy – the Sound of Citizens' Voices. A Position Paper from the Advocacy Working Group*. Ottawa, ON: Government of Canada, Voluntary Sector Initiative Secretariat.

Sabatier, P. 1998. "The Advocacy Coalition Framework: Revisions and Relevance for Europe." *Journal of European Public Policy* 5 (1): 98–130. http://dx.doi.org/10.1080/13501768880000051.

Salamon, L., and S. Lessans Geller. 2008. *Nonprofit America: A Force for Democracy (Communique No. 9)*. Baltimore, MD: Centre for Civil Society Studies, Institute for Public Policy, John Hopkins University; Accessed 21 September 2016. http://ccss.jhu.edu/wp-content/uploads/downloads/2011/09/LP_Communique9_2008.pdf,.

Schmid, H., M. Bar, and R. Nirel. 2008. "Advocacy Activities in Nonprofit Human Service Organizations: Implications for Policy." *Nonprofit and Voluntary Sector Quarterly* 37 (4): 581–602. http://dx.doi.org/10.1177/0899764007312666.

Scott, K. 2003. *Funding Matters: The Impact of Canada's New Funding Regime on Nonprofit and Voluntary Organizations*. [Electronic Resource] Ottawa, ON: Canadian Council on Social Development and Coalition of National Voluntary Organizations. Accessed 21 September 2016. http://vsi-isbc.org/eng/funding/fundingmatters/introduction.pdf.

Sen, A. 2009. *The Idea of Justice*. Cambridge, MA: Harvard University Press.

Shier, M., F. Handy, and L. Mcdougle. 2014. "Nonprofits and the Promotion of Civic Engagement: A Conceptual Framework for Understanding the "Civic Footprint" of Nonprofits within Local Communities." *Canadian Journal of Nonprofit and Social Economy Research* 5 (1): 57–75.

Skinner, M. 2008. "Voluntarism and Long-Term Care in the Countryside: The Paradox of a Threadbare Sector." *Canadian Geographer* 52 (2): 188–203. http://dx.doi.org/10.1111/j.1541-0064.2008.00208.x.

Smith, A. 1759. *The Theory of Moral Sentiments*. London: General Books. http://dx.doi.org/10.1093/oseo/instance.00042831.

Smith, M. 2008. *Group Politics and Social Movements in Canada*. Peterborough, ON: Broadview Press.

Stienstra, D. 2003. "Listen, Really Listen, to Us: Consultation, Disabled People and Governments in Canada." In *Making Equality: History of Advocacy and Persons with Disabilities in Canada*, edited by D. Stienstra and A. Wight-Felske, 33–47. Concord, ON: Captus Press Inc.

Thériault, L. 2009. "Moving Back into the Shadows: Social Economy, Social Policy, and the Harper Government." In *The New Federal Policy Agenda and the Voluntary Sector*, edited by R. Laforest, 61–80. Kingston, ON: McGill-Queen's University Press.

Titscher, S., M. Meyer, R. Wodak, and E. Vetter. 2007. *Methods of Text and Discourse Analysis: In Search of Meaning*. London, UK: Sage Publications Ltd.

Vaillancourt, Y. 2009. "Social Economy in the Co-Construction of Public Policy." *Annals of Public and Cooperative Economics* 80 (2): 275–313. http://dx.doi.org/10.1111/j.1467-8292.2009.00387.x.

Voluntary Sector Initiative. 2001. *An Accord between the Government of Canada and the Voluntary Sector*. Ottawa, ON: Privy Council Office, Government of Canada.

– 2002. *A Code of Good Practice on Policy Dialogue*. Ottawa, ON: Voluntary Sector Initiative, Government of Canada.

Volunteer Canada. 2012 edition. *The Canadian Code for Volunteer Involvement: Values, Guiding Principles, and Standards of Practice*. Ottawa, ON: Volunteer Canada. https://volunteer.ca/content/canadian-code-volunteer-involvement-2012-edition.

Wollstonecraft, M. 1790. *A Vindication of the Rights of Men in a Letter to the Right Honourable Edmund Burke, Occasioned by His Reflections on the Revolution in France*. London: J. Johnson.

– 1792. *A Vindication of the Rights of Women with Strictures on Political and Moral Subjects*. London: T. Fisher Unwin.

# 2

# Shifting Legal Terrain: Legal and Regulatory Restrictions on Political Advocacy by Charities

ADAM PARACHIN

## I: INTRODUCTION

Charities face a strange contradiction surrounding the role they are permitted to play in the law and policy-making processes of government. On the one hand, charities are, in many senses, uniquely suited to actively and constructively participate in the process of law and policy reform. Owing to their frontline experience and grassroots connections, charities frequently have valuable insights into the unique and varying needs of the constituencies served by government programming. This combination of field experience, specialized knowledge, and closeness to the community gives charities a basis for commenting meaningfully on the effectiveness of existing, or the need for new, government programming.

Charities are also ready sources of normative perspectives on law and policy. Whereas the marketplace relies upon economic self-interest to unite people who otherwise lack a basis for collective action, the organizing principle behind the charitable sector is idealism. The sector brings together people who share a concern over, and core values surrounding, matters of collective interest (see chapter 1). Since the basis for action in the charitable sector is entirely civic, one might say that charities are where principled conviction and community experience come together to form a vibrant and proficient source of democratic renewal and reform.

Owing to the above, charities will often have the ability to authentically represent and speak about marginal societal issues. While the charitable sector is diverse, providing goods and services to populations spanning the entire socioeconomic spectrum, the institution of charity is largely, if not primarily, concerned with voluntary wealth redistribution from those who have to those who lack. Significant pockets of the charitable sector have direct contact and experience with communities lacking a voice in public debate. In addition, charities can promote public awareness on issues – e.g., environmental conservation – that might not otherwise attract public attention. In this sense, charities are uniquely positioned to enrich public dialogue, raising public awareness surrounding matters of collective interest, and/or speaking on behalf (or with) community stakeholders otherwise lacking a voice. Hence, charities have the ability to facilitate participatory forms of justice.

Nevertheless, charity law, through the rule known as the doctrine of political purposes, severely restricts the ability of charities to function as agents of reform. While charities are permitted under Canadian law to engage in a limited amount of political *activity* (excluding partisan participation in election campaigns), no institution can qualify as charitable (or continue to so qualify) if it has (or adopts) a political *purpose*. Perhaps not surprisingly, this means that charitable status is not available to any institution whose purposes entail campaigning for or against candidates for public office. Less expected is that it also disqualifies institutions whose purposes expressly or by necessary implication entail seeking changes to the laws or administrative practices of any government (foreign or domestic). In addition, the charitableness of public awareness campaigns is a matter of some debate. Courts have never squarely established that promoting a point of view – absent a specific goal to achieve law or policy reform – is political and thus non-charitable. However, in its published policy statement on political activities (the "Policy Statement"), the Charities Directorate of the Canada Revenue Agency (CRA) contemplates that public awareness is political unless it conforms to specific criteria (section 7.1) (CRA 2003). These include the requirement that public awareness be based on factual information. Public awareness campaigns that appeal to conceptions of social justice are not necessarily going to meet this requirement. They are therefore at risk of being characterized by CRA auditors as political.

The implications of the doctrine of political purposes are, in some senses, radical. Under current Canadian law, charitable purposes cannot entail, either expressly or by necessary implication, political advocacy, not even in relation to areas of law and policy that dovetail with charitable purposes. So, for example, a relief-of-poverty organization must have as its purpose the direct relief of poverty rather than advocating in favour of any particular anti-poverty strategy or raising public awareness about the blight of poverty. Likewise, an educational charity must provide educational services rather than operate for the purpose of promoting any given education policy. Public awareness campaigns are permissible for charities. However, as we shall see, they have to be carefully scripted to avoid being categorized as political.

The doctrine of political purposes evidences a shifting terrain in the legal definition and regulation of charities. At one time, the law posed little to no restriction on the freedom of charities to pursue aims that under current law would be characterized as non-charitable political purposes. With the twentieth century came new regulatory restrictions that progressively muzzled charities in the area of political advocacy. The cases expanding the doctrine of political purposes have been widely criticized for being poorly reasoned and excessively restrictive on charities (Sheridan 1980; Brooks 1983; Santow 1999; Bridge 2002; Harvie 2002; Parachin 2008; Chia, Harding, and O'Connell 2011; and Dunn 2014).

Recent developments reveal a trend – at least outside of Canada – in favour of a more liberal tradition. Breaking from the established precedents, the decision of the High Court of Australia in *Aid/Watch Incorporated v. Commissioner of Taxation* concluded that an Australian watchdog organization qualified as charitable even though it was established and operated for the sole purpose of shaping public opinion on government policy on foreign aid. This landmark case established, albeit for the purposes of Australian law only, that it is charitable to encourage public debate for those aspects of government policies and practices linked with purposes considered charitable at law, e.g., relieving poverty. Likewise, the New Zealand Supreme Court in *Re Greenpeace* recently concluded that a "blanket exclusion" for political advocacy "should no longer be applied in New Zealand."[1]

Until recently, Canadian law was showing no signs of loosening the restrictions on charities in this area. The Canadian Federal Court of

Appeal lost no time in concluding in *News to You Canada v. Minister of National Revenue* that the relaxed Australian position adopted in *Aid/Watch* would not be followed in Canada. While no Canadian court has yet had the opportunity to consider *Re Greenpeace*, there is no reason to believe that it will receive a better reception than *Aid/Watch* did. Further, the 2012 federal budget affirmed the then Conservative government's support for the doctrine of political purposes. While it did not specifically narrow the scope of permissible advocacy, it did set out new rules facilitating the enforcement of the doctrine by the Charities Directorate of the Canada Revenue Agency (CRA).[2] In addition, the CRA received a multi-million dollar budget to carry out an audit of political activities by registered charities over several years (see chapters 1 and 11).

However, the election of a majority Liberal government in the October 2015 federal election has changed the prognosis for Canadian law and regulatory practices in this area. The Liberal Party platform included the following election promise:[3]

> We will allow charities to do their work on behalf of Canadians free from political harassment, and will modernize the rules governing the charitable and not-for-profit sectors.
>
> This will include clarifying the rules governing "political activity," with an understanding that charities make an important contribution to public debate and public policy. A new legislative framework to strengthen the sector will emerge from this process.

The Liberal government's promise to revisit this aspect of charity law and regulation invites a re-examination of what is wrong with the status quo. This chapter therefore critically examines how and why the doctrine of political purposes restricts the autonomy of charities to participate in public debate. Employing a case law and policy analysis, it explores the thesis that the doctrine imposes an artificial constraint on the boundaries of legal charity. Currently, law and regulatory practices prevent charities from realizing their potential (as outlined at the beginning of this chapter) to constructively contribute to public debate. Part II situates the doctrine within the cases dealing with the legal meaning of charity. Part III discusses the effect of the doctrine on the operations of charities. Part IV reveals the superficial rationales articulated by courts to support the doctrine.

Part V links the doctrine with the rise of fiscal considerations in the legal definition and regulation of charity. Part VI proposes reforms to the doctrine that are designed to preserve a principled distinction between charity and politics, while ridding the law of the excessive restraints it currently poses against political advocacy by charities.

## II: SHIFTING LEGAL TERRAIN: THE RISE OF THE DOCTRINE OF POLITICAL PURPOSES

The law of charity has witnessed a shifting legal and regulatory terrain. Advocacy activities that were a tolerated, if not embraced, feature of legal charity at one time would, under current law, render an institution ineligible for charitable status. Over time, the law has witnessed an expansion in the sorts of pursuits characterized as political in the non-charitable sense and a corresponding contraction in the legal meaning of charity. Given that the doctrine of political purposes is fundamentally concerned with what pursuits qualify as charitable at law, it is helpful to begin by locating this doctrine in the jurisprudence that deals with the legal meaning of charity.

Eligibility for charitable status under Canadian law, including income tax law, is determined on the basis of the common law meaning of charity. Common law defines charity by referring to the preamble to a 1601 English statute variously known as the Statute of Charitable Uses and the Statute of Elizabeth. This was an unlikely source for the legal meaning of charity because the preamble itself does not define charity, nor was it intended to inform attempts to define charity. It was instead enacted to regulate what were, at the time of its enactment, abuses in the administration of charitable trusts. The preamble simply gave context to the statute's regulatory aims by listing – by way of example only – the sorts of purposes for which charitable trusts were being established.[4] Nevertheless, courts began to consult the preamble as a reference point for determining whether putative charitable trusts were indeed established for exclusively charitable purposes. It eventually became the law that a purpose could qualify as charitable only if it was specifically listed in the preamble, analogous to a purpose specifically listed in the preamble, or analogous to a purpose that had previously been found by a court to be charitable.

Through the passage of time, the cases dealing with the legal meaning of charity grew to form a somewhat muddled body of judicial pronouncements. To help bring better understanding to this area of law, Lord Macnaghten in *Commissioners for Special Purposes of the Income Tax v. Pemsel* offered a fourfold classification of the purposes that had to date been characterized as charitable. In what is easily the most widely quoted statement ever made in charity law, Lord Macnaghten said: "'Charity' in its legal sense comprises four principal divisions: trusts for the relief of poverty; trusts for the advancement of education; trusts for the advancement of religion; and trusts for other purposes beneficial to the community, not falling under any of the preceding heads" (*Pemsel* 583). It remains the case today that no purpose will qualify as charitable under Canadian common law unless all of its purposes meet a "public benefit" requirement and fall within one or more of these four so-called heads of charity.

The *Pemsel* "heads" of charity do not pose any immediately obvious conflict with political engagement. There is, for example, nothing in the phrase "relief of poverty" necessitating the conclusion that pursuing poverty relief through, say, law reform, is necessarily non-charitable. Indeed, at one time, trusts with purposes whose attainment required a change to law were upheld as charitable (Luxton 2001, 225). Courts of the nineteenth century concluded that trusts to promote temperance legislation (*Farewell v. Farewell*), secure the abolition of vivisection (*In re Foveaux*), and establish a new bishopric (*Re Villers-Wilkes*) were exclusively charitable. Perhaps more telling is that at one time the political involvement of charities is said to have been largely unquestioned (Chesterman 1979, 44, 78, and 359; Gladstone 1982, 99–100; and Webb 2000, 16 and 127–9).

All of this changed in 1917 when Lord Parker of the House of Lords observed in *Bowman v. Secular Society* that "a trust for the attainment of political objects has *always* been held invalid" (442). While this statement was neither historically accurate nor necessary to resolve the case before the court, it formed the basis of the modern-day restriction against political advocacy by charities. Every single case dealing with the non-charitableness of political advocacy either cites *Bowman* directly or cites cases following *Bowman*.

Building on the foundation of *Bowman*, courts in future cases elaborated on what it means to have a "political" object. These cases reveal an ongoing expansion of what qualifies as political, such that the law has evolved from having little to no restriction against political advocacy to now having a robust restriction against advocacy. The list of purposes characterized as political has expanded to now include electioneering (*McGovern v. Attorney General*) and campaigning for changes to the laws or policies of a domestic or foreign government (*McGovern v. Attorney General*). Courts have never concretely established that advocacy unrelated to electioneering and law / policy reform, such as public awareness campaigns through which charities stimulate public debate, is political. However, there is always the risk that such campaigns could be interpreted as having an underlying goal of altering the law or the practices of government. For example, courts have concluded that it is political to promote attitude of mind (*Anglo-Swedish Society v. Commissioners of Inland Revenue*), advocate in favour of one side of a controversial social issue (*Human Life International in Canada Inc. v. M.N.R.* and *Re Positive Action Against Pornography and M.N.R.*), and create a climate of opinion (*Buxton and Others v. Public Trustee and Others*) where the ultimate purpose is to thereby achieve a shift in government policy.

In addition to the case law authorities, there are the administrative practices of the CRA. The CRA has published a policy statement (the "Policy Statement") summarizing its administrative interpretation of the relevant case law (CRA 2003). Though the policy statement lacks the force of law, it is authoritative in that it informs the audit practices of the CRA. Among other things, the policy statement elucidates an important distinction between political activities and political purposes. Though charities are prohibited from having political *purposes*, they are permitted to engage in a certain number of political *activities*, including (1) communicating to the public that some law or policy should be changed or (if reform is being contemplated) retained and (2) encouraging the public to contact public officials urging them to either oppose or support a proposed change to law or policy (CRA 2003, section 6.2).

Subsections 149.1(6.1) and (6.2) of the Income Tax Act also address the issue of political advocacy by charities. These provisions provide a "safe harbour" for charities. They legislatively establish that charities engaging in political activities will be deemed to be operating for exclusively charitable activities / purposes provided certain criteria are met. The political activity must not, directly or indirectly, include support of (or opposition to) a political party or candidate for public office. The political activity must be ancillary and incidental to charitable activities/purposes. Also, "substantially all" the charity's resources must be applied to charitable activities/purposes.

Current law does not have a bright-line test for determining when a political activity has ceased to be ancillary and incidental to charitable activities / purposes. The basic issue is one of discerning when a political activity has become an end in itself so that the institution in question can no longer be considered to be established and operated for exclusively charitable purposes. One of the relevant factors is the extent of a charity's resources devoted to political activities. As a general guideline, the CRA applies a 10 per cent rule, meaning no more than 10 per cent of a charity's resources – property, staff, volunteers, directors, etc. – can be applied to political activities. The percentage is adjusted upwards for small charities. The ceiling is 20 per cent for charities with annual incomes less than $50,000, 15 per cent for charities with annual incomes between $50,000 and $100,000, and 12 per cent for charities with annual incomes between $100,000 and $200,000 (CRA 2003, section 9). If the applicable threshold is exceeded, an otherwise permissible political activity risks being audited by the CRA from the vantage point that the activity discloses a non-charitable political purpose, the consequence of which is loss of charitable status.

The policy statement also sets out CRA's understanding of the distinction between charitable public information campaigns and non-charitable political messaging. Public awareness campaigns, the policy statement notes, only qualify as charitable if stringent criteria are met. To qualify as charitable, a public awareness campaign must, among other things, be based on a "well-reasoned" position, which the policy statement defines as follows: "A position based on factual information that is methodically, objectively, fully, and fairly analyzed. In addition, a well-reasoned position should present/address serious arguments and relevant facts to the contrary" (CRA 2003, Appendix I).

The policy statement expressly notes that providing information is not itself a charitable purpose unless it meets the formal requirements for the advancement of education. Among the requirements that educational charities must meet are the requirements that the materials presented qualify as "reasonably objective" and "well-reasoned." Education must not rely upon an "appeal to emotions" or be undertaken to "create a climate of opinion or to advocate a particular cause." (CRA 2003, section 8). Again, this is an exacting standard. The distribution of empirically demonstrable "facts" enjoys the cover of charitable status but communications drawing on ideals alone risks being relegated to the political category.

While there is obviously much more that could be said about how the cases and CRA distinguish charity from politics, the description set out here will suffice for present purposes. Clearly, charity law has shifted from a position that at one time had few restrictions on political engagement to a position that strictly regulates the scope of lawfully permissible political advocacy for charities.

### III: REGULATORY IMPACT ON CHARITIES

The implications of the doctrine of political purposes for charities are far-reaching, if not radical. Take, for example, the non-charitableness of law reform. Obviously, this precludes charities from being established for the express purpose of securing a change to law. Less obvious, however, is that it also disqualifies institutions whose purposes merely imply the need for, and perhaps even the desirability of, law or policy reform. The breadth of the principle is illustrated by the holding in *McGovern v. Attorney-General* in which the House of Lords concluded that the Nobel-Peace-Prize-winning Amnesty International Trust was non-charitable because one of its purposes – pursuing the abolition of human torture – implicitly contemplated a change to law. The court reasoned that abolishing human torture would ultimately tend toward pursuing law reform. How can one truly *abolish* human torture other than making it contrary to law?[5] The same reasoning was applied by the House of Lords in *National Anti-Vivisection Society v. I.R.C.* where it was concluded (contrary to earlier authorities) that pursuing the abolishment of vivisection was not a charitable purpose.

Likewise, the precedents contemplating that promoting a point of view or attitude of mind is political (at least where the goal is to thereby effect a change in law or government policy) have the potential to remove charities from public debate. Again, courts have not concretely established that promoting a point of view or attitude of mind is necessarily political. But there is always the potential that these sorts of pursuits could be characterized as non-charitable. This could occur if a law/policy reform agenda is alleged to exist. Alternatively, a literal application of the CRA's requirement that public awareness campaigns be fact-based rules out awareness campaigns that promote conceptions of social justice. This reflects a legal ordering in which charities risk being valued as suppliers of "facts" and tangible goods and services but not as suppliers of normative ideals capable of enriching public deliberation.

The common law authorities bear out the jeopardy faced by awareness organizations. Institutions found by courts to be non-charitable include those established and/or operated for the purpose of promoting a view on abortion (*Human Life International in Canada Inc. v. M.N.R.* and *Alliance for Life v. M.N.R.*), promoting greater understanding between societies in conflict (*Anglo-Swedish Society v. Commissioners of Inland Revenue* and *Toronto Volgograd Committee v. Canada*), promoting the view that pornography is harmful (*Re Positive Action Against Pornography and M.N.R.*), promoting the desirability of any particular political doctrine or perspective (*Re Loney, Re Hopkinson, Bonar Law Memorial Trust v. I.R.C., Re Knight,* and *Re Bushnell*),[6] and promoting the view that peace is best secured by demilitarization (*Southwood & Another v. Her Majesty's Attorney General*). The final case referenced in this list reveals the considerable extent to which courts have sought to remove charities from public deliberation. The court took no issue with a charity promoting the view that peace is preferable to war. The bar to charitableness was that the institution in question was advancing the view that disarmament was the *best* way to achieve peace. As this is a matter of considerable controversy, the promotion of this view was not considered charitable.

Perhaps one of the most significant effects of the doctrine of political purposes is one that cannot be directly observed, namely, self-censorship by charities. The cases suggest that neutrality and objectivity are hallmarks of legal charity. It has been held, for example, that charitableness will be absent where there is no attempt to "educate the public so that they [can] choose for themselves, starting with neutral information, to support or oppose" any particular position (*Re Bushnell*). So while courts have recognized that it can be charitable to educate people "from a particular political or moral perspective," they have concluded that charitableness is vitiated once the goal becomes promoting a political or moral perspective (*Challenge Team v. Canada* and *Vancouver Society of Immigrant and Visible Minority Women v. Canada*). The distinction is so fine and so difficult to draw in practice that it weighs heavily in favour of charities either altogether removing themselves from public debate or restricting public communications to temperate remarks. This kind of chilling effect may well represent the single biggest impact of the doctrine on charities.

Of particular concern is that the doctrine of political purposes creates something of an unequal playing field. Although the doctrine is facially neutral because it applies with like force to all charities, it has the effect of marginalizing certain perspectives while privileging others. For example, the non-charitableness of law and policy reform privileges supporters of the status quo over those calling orthodoxy into question. Since the latter can only achieve their mission by campaigning for change, they are the ones who disproportionately bear the brunt of the doctrine of political purposes. Supporters of the status quo typically need not engage in advocacy and therefore need not contend with the doctrine of political purposes. Likewise, the principle that charitable education must be "well-reasoned" and cannot rely upon an "appeal to emotions" (see Part II above) prejudices certain perspectives. Whether any particular content, be it an educational curriculum or information relayed through a public campaign, incites emotions will often turn on whether the underlying message affirms or opposes established norms. Institutions questioning orthodoxy will presumably be more likely to fail this requirement because their message will be more likely to attract strong emotional responses. Further, the well-reasoned requirement goes some distance in restricting charitable education and information campaigns to empirically demonstrable statements.[7] Perspectives drawing on ideals not readily amenable to empirical demonstration, e.g., "social justice," will struggle to meet this requirement and thus stand a greater chance of being characterized as political.

Certain of the factors employed to distinguish charity from politics also seem to run at cross purposes with how voluntary associations are formed. Consider the idea (discussed in Part II above) that charitable education can be distinguished from political propaganda based on whether relevant counter-arguments are identified and addressed. At some level, this is a sensible basis on which to distinguish between genuine attempts to inform and attempts to indoctrinate. However, in another sense it runs contrary to how voluntary associations form and attract audiences. One commentator rhetorically asks whether a "group against impaired driving [would] have to give the 'other side' of impaired driving" (Webb 2000, 42). For better or worse, value neutrality is not what inspires people to form, participate in, and contribute to charities. So while it is true that polemical information campaigns might properly fail to qualify as educational, overemphasizing value neutrality as a hallmark of charity runs the risk of entrenching into law a sterile understanding of charity.

In short, the doctrine of political purposes has a profound impact on charities. The doctrine prohibits the idealism forming the basis for collective action in the charitable sector from taking full expression in the activities of charities. The question addressed in the next part is why courts have interpreted charity in this manner. The reasons offered by courts are surprisingly shallow.

## IV: STATED RATIONALES FOR THE DOCTRINE OF POLITICAL PURPOSES

The jurisprudence is notable for the superficial rationales courts have articulated in support of the doctrine of political purposes. As these rationales have been thoroughly discussed and critiqued elsewhere (Parachin 2008), it will suffice for present purposes to identify the core claim recurring in the jurisprudence. Most of the cases rest on the idea that the doctrine of political purposes is a necessary concession to the institutional limits of the judiciary. The reasoning is as follows: Given that public benefit is a prerequisite for charitable status, a finding by a court that a given purpose qualifies as charitable at law is neither value neutral nor agnostic. To the contrary, at some level it is an affirmation that the purposes being pursued are desirable, that they confer a recognizable benefit on some segment of society qualifying as "a public." Much of the jurisprudence is concerned with articulating reasons why it would be inappropriate for courts to find public benefit in, and thus affirm, political purposes.

One particularly anemic line of reasoning posits that the law would stultify itself – contradict or cause itself to appear illogical – if it were to recognize public benefit in law reform (*National Anti-Vivisection Society v. I.R.C.*, 50 and 62, and *McGovern v. Attorney General*, 333–7). The essential idea is that law reform could only be of public benefit if the law were imperfect to begin with. Since the law should not recognize its own imperfection, charity law cases, so the reasoning goes, should be decided from the premise that the law is perfect as it is. In this view, law reform initiatives are necessarily non-charitable because their goal is to take the law from a state of perfection to something that could only be inferior. With respect, this shallow reasoning is hardly even worth critically dissecting as no serious student of the law is very likely to accept the premise that the law is perfect. Perfection is at most an aspiration of the law but not an achieved characteristic. Ironically, one of the leading cases dealing with the doctrine of political purposes openly commented on the imperfection of the doctrine itself (*Human Life International in Canada Inc. v. M.N.R.*, paragraph 19).

Other cases emphasize the need for courts to maintain an appearance of neutrality in matters of controversy. Justice Slade reasoned in *McGovern v. Attorney General* that finding public benefit in political purposes would be problematic because it would "usurp the functions of the legislature" (337), result in the court "prejudicing its reputation for political impartiality" (337), and "be a matter more for political than for legal judgment" (339). Other authorities have reasoned similarly, with the common theme being that judges ought to refrain from ruling on the public benefit of advocacy as a way of preserving the institutional legitimacy of courts (*Alliance for Life v. M.N.R., Bowman v. Secular Society, National Anti-Vivisection Society v. I.R.C., Human Life International in Canada Inc. v. M.N.R.,* and *Jackson v. Phillips*).[8]

If nothing else, this reasoning helps put into context decisions like *McGovern v. Attorney General* in which the court declined to find public benefit in the advocacy work of the Nobel-Peace-Prize-winning Amnesty International Trust. It is not as if the court concluded that Amnesty lacked public benefit. The court simply declined to make a determination one way or the other as a way of preserving its impartiality. Non-charitableness was not a positive finding but rather the practical effect of no conclusion being drawn as to the presence or absence of the public benefit requirement. Likewise, in *Human Life International in Canada Inc. v. M.N.R.* and *Re Positive Action Against Pornography and M.N.R.*, the court did not conclude that the pro-life and anti-pornography perspectives lacked public benefit. Instead, the court declined altogether to address the matter as a way of upholding the institutional neutrality of courts.

Two notable fallacies are evident in this approach.

The first fallacy lies in the assumption that neutrality is necessarily preserved through a failure to rule one way or the other on the public benefit of political purposes. Just as granting charitable status is not a value-neutral exercise, neither is withholding it. The neutrality that courts purport to be preserving by making no finding on the issue of public benefit is compromised by the fact that this does not bring the cases to a neutral conclusion. Cases dealing with charitable status only have two possible outcomes – charitable or non-charitable. "Maybe but maybe not" is not one of the possible outcomes.

So when a court declines to make any finding on the issue of public benefit, the default result is that the particular institution before the court will fail to qualify as charitable. Even though the court is not specifically finding that the institution is non-charitable on the basis that it lacks public benefit, the ultimate effect is the same. In both instances, the institution in question faces the stigma of having lost its legal battle for charitable status. As this is not a neutral outcome, it does not preserve the neutrality of the judiciary in the way that courts assume.

Further, a failure to rule on the issue of public benefit is tantamount to a finding that public benefit may or may not be present. That is, courts are accepting that the purposes before them are of such a nature that reasonable people might agree to disagree on the issue of benefit without either side contradicting any inviolable principle of law or justice. There are certainly contentious issues where this reasoning is apt.[9] However, what about cases like *McGovern v. Attorney General* and *Action by Christians for the Abolition of Torture v. Canada* dealing with the abolition of human torture? The court's failure to rule on public benefit implies that human torture may have a place in a democratic society committed to just law. This is not altogether value neutral.

The second fallacy lies in the assumption that a grant of charitable status necessarily entails the court condoning the *specific* law reform or the *specific* point of view being advocated. One might say that a distinction exists between the desirability inhering in the particular *purposes* being pursued and the desirability inhering in the *pursuit* of those purposes. Charitable status could be granted on the strength of the conclusion that it is of public benefit for there to be public debate over matters relating to the legally recognized categories of charity. Benefit need not necessarily be found in the particular point of view being advanced by any given institution in such debates. This, incidentally, is how the law tends to find benefit in religion without aligning itself with any particular religion. The law accepts that there is benefit in religious inquiry without necessarily endorsing all the individual beliefs of any given religion.[10] There is no reason why the same approach could not be taken with political purposes.[11]

The cases have struggled to adequately account for why the law distinguishes charity from politics in the manner that it does but the various explanations offered by courts tend to raise more questions than they answer. Whatever good reasons might exist for distinguishing charity from politics, those reasons do not find concrete expression in the precedents.

## V: ROLE OF INCOME TAX CONSIDERATIONS

How then do we account for the doctrine of political purposes? After years of having little to no restriction on the political advocacy activities of charities, why did the law assume an increasingly restrictive approach? A cynical view is that the doctrine manifests an emergent disrespect for freedom of expression, particularly by governments seeking to minimize public criticism. Consistent with this view, the income tax amendments facilitating CRA's enforcement of the doctrine of political purposes enacted as part of the 2012 federal budget have been characterized as a political response to criticism of the then federal government's environmental policy from within the charitable sector (McCarthy 2012). One could, however, legitimately question whether the doctrine of political purposes is best viewed in this light. The doctrine does not forbid any person from holding or expressing any point of view. That is, any institution denied charitable status on the grounds that it has a political purpose remains free to reorganize and operate as a non-charitable not-for-profit institution. The doctrine of political purposes is not therefore focused on the limits of free expression as much as on the limits of charitableness.

But this only redirects us back to asking what it is about charity that has inspired jurists to distinguish it from politics. Interestingly, the cases do very little to establish an intrinsic incompatibility between charity and advocacy. One might even say that the cases are incoherent to the extent that they accept the inherent charitableness of religious proselytization but nevertheless characterize as political the advancement of views on controversial social issues. Is there anything more controversial than religious dogma? However, criticizing the cases for failing to consistently distinguish charity from politics according to some substantive metric might very well miss the point. It is at least possible that the doctrine of political purposes is not a response to some perceived incompatibility between charity and politics as much as it is a response to an assumed incongruity between charitable *status* and politics. That is, courts may well have developed the doctrine of political purposes from the vantage point of an instrumental view of charity under which the principal concern is less whether any given purpose has the true character of a charitable purpose and more whether it should enjoy the benefits, primarily the income tax benefits, that follow from a grant of charitable status (Swann 2000, 161; Dunn 2000, 75; Luxton 1995, 28; Rickett 1982, 176; and Secretary of State 1989, chapter 2). In this understanding, the doctrine of political purposes can be attributed to a mostly undisclosed, perhaps even subconsciously held, view of charitable status as a policy instrument for determining eligibility for a state subsidy in the form of income tax concessions. Such an approach conflates the question "is this charitable?" with the question "should this institution be state subsidized through tax concessions?" The denial of charitable status to institutions with political purposes can perhaps then be thought of as reflecting at some level the determination that certain forms of advocacy, regardless of whether they are truly charitable, should not be state-subsidized through income tax concessions and should thus be denied charitable status.

Admittedly, this interpretation of the cases is provocative in the sense that it locates the true rationale for the doctrine of political purposes not in the text but rather in the subtext of the cases, the reasoning of which tends to avoid linking the doctrine with subsidy considerations. Some will object to this thesis on the grounds that the reasons for judgment articulated by courts ought to be taken seriously as just that – the reasons by which legal conclusions are reached – rather than dismissed as mere window dressing. Nonetheless, the thesis that tax subsidy considerations might be playing a buried role in jurisprudence does not strain credulity. The formal reasoning of charity cases generally, and the cases that distinguish charity from politics specifically, often seem artificial, suggesting that additional undisclosed considerations might also be playing a role. Notably, the doctrine of political purposes is a twentieth century phenomenon that closely paralleled the growth and development of the modern income tax regime. With the arrival of income tax came new technical and policy considerations that could perhaps be viewed as justifying new restrictions on political engagement. Charity law became infused with a fiscal dimension owing to the income tax concessions that charities have enjoyed since, effectively, the outset of income tax. It became possible to view grants of charitable status as something posing a tangible public cost. Unlike before the advent of income tax, a rule restricting political advocacy by charities now made sense as a tool for more efficiently targeting the state subsidy inherent in charitable status (Swann 2000, 166–7), protecting taxpayers from indirectly financially supporting special interest lobbying (Secretary of State 1989, para. 2.41), and preserving scarce income tax revenues.[12]

Lending credence to this thesis is the fact that judges, though they tend to studiously avoid expressly attributing their interpretations of charity to fiscal considerations, have from time to time candidly acknowledged the role of such considerations. In one of the leading Canadian cases, the Federal Court of Appeal tellingly framed the doctrine of political purposes not as achieving a denial of charitableness per se but rather a "denial of tax exemption to those wishing to advocate certain opinions" (*Human Life International in Canada Inc. v. M.N.R.*, para. 18). Even the Supreme Court of Canada, in a recent case dealing with the legal meaning of charity, expressly connected its decision to withhold charitable status to the anticipated *fiscal* cost (*Amateur Youth Soccer Association v. Canada Revenue Agency*). Though this decision did not deal specifically with the doctrine of political purposes, it bears out the thesis that fiscal cost benefit analysis plays a role in the judicial interpretation of charity.

There is at least a case then for viewing the doctrine of political purposes as representing on some level a shift in thinking, further to which charitable status has come to be viewed and understood by courts and regulators principally as an instrument for awarding a state subsidy. One concern is that this paradigm shift has brought to the case law a form of cost benefit analysis for which courts are poorly suited and under which applications for charitable status tend to be adjudicated from the vantage point of whether granting charitable status is worth what it costs. This kind of cost benefit analysis favours applicants for charitable status who supply concrete goods and services, especially in instances where the demand for those goods and services might otherwise fall upon government. The economic benefits conferred by such institutions are observable and measurable. In contrast, asking whether a grant of charitable status to an advocacy organization will be worth what it will cost the public treasury is more of an imponderable. This is why fiscal considerations will tend to work against recognizing advocacy as charitable: the case for subsidizing advocacy is simply more difficult to make out, especially where the views being advocated challenge orthodoxy. What we are witnessing then with the doctrine of political purposes is arguably an increasingly economic-driven paradigm of "charity" under which charities have come to be valued not for the normative ideals they can bring to public discourse but rather for the resources they can spare governments through the supply of goods and services.

## VI: REFORM

So far, I have suggested that the doctrine of political purposes reflects a shifting legal terrain in which restrictions on advocacy previously unknown to charity law have now become entrenched into current law. I have connected the rise of the doctrine to fiscal considerations that lack any discernable relevance to the true meaning of charity. The question I consider in this part is whether the doctrine of political purposes should be altogether abolished or salvaged in a modified form. I argue in favour of the latter. The ultimate premise of the doctrine – that there exists a principled distinction between charity and politics – is sound. It is just that the doctrine of political purposes is excessively broad in its current form. So in this part of the chapter I return to first principles with a view to refining and refocusing the doctrine more consistently with a principled way to understand the distinction between charity and politics.

A useful first step is to identify quintessential instances of non-charitable political advocacy and to reflect on why they should not qualify as charitable. If we can identify a characteristic that truly non-charitable political purposes share, then we will at least have identified a referent for refining the doctrine of political purposes. In my anecdotal experience, most people tend to agree with the suggestion that institutions established specifically for the purposes of electioneering and/or lobbying represent archetypical instances of non-charitable political institutions. The relevant feature shared by electioneering and lobbying is that they both entail a call on government to respond in some way to a social, economic, environmental, or like problem. In some instances this will entail a call for interventionist governmental measures in the form of new or revised regulations. In others it will entail efforts to secure governmental deregulation so as to make room for what are perceived to be superior non-governmental solutions. Even though these militate in opposite policy directions, they are both equally concerned at the end of the day with the proper role and function of government. Therein, arguably, lies the incongruity with charitableness. Even if the goal ultimately being pursued through electioneering or lobbying dovetails with a lawful charitable purpose, e.g., the relief of poverty, the immediate focus of the activity is not the attainment of that purpose but rather securing a governmental response perceived as conducive to the attainment of that purpose.

Why should this make any difference? One reason might be that electioneering and lobbying are too remotely connected to the attainment of anything qualifying as charitable. Even accepting that electing a particular government or enacting a particular law reform will achieve greater poverty relief, these activities only indirectly contribute to that goal. The most proximate cause is governmental action, not the actions contributing to the government action. Electioneering and lobbying do not therefore meet the requirement that the direct effect of activities must be the attainment of charitable goals.

A less technical, and perhaps more normatively appealing, answer is that government and charity, though they might at times pursue similar goals, are ultimately distinct from one another. If true, there is a basis for concluding that a purpose qualifying as charitable at law might not remain charitable when pursued through government, and by extension through actions directed at determining who forms the government through electioneering or shaping the outputs of government (e.g., laws and regulations) through lobbying. In this view, charity is not simply concerned with the attainment of ends that qualify as charitable. It is concerned with attaining those ends privately, meaning other than via government or law. The charitableness of an endeavour could therefore be said to be compromised when an end capable of qualifying as charitable, e.g., poverty relief, if pursued other than through government, is instead pursued through government or law.

The suggestion that such a stark distinction between charity and government exists might prove controversial. This was not always the case. At one time the distinctiveness of charity and government would have been taken to be obvious. Back when charities were effectively the sole suppliers of goods and services whose aim was to attain charitable ends, there was no basis for even considering whether charitable ends remained charitable when pursued through government. The issue was moot since governments were not generally pursuing the same goals as charities. This remains true today for some charitable purposes, such as the advancement of religion, where a clear distinction continues to exist between charity and the state. However, in other areas, such as poverty relief, health, and education, a blending of the ends pursued by charity and government has occurred. Further blurring the boundaries between charity and government is the propensity of government to increasingly rely upon charities to deliver government-funded programming (Warburton and Morris 1991, 419; Chesterman 2000, 249; and Dunn 2008). Given the increased entanglement of charities and governments (see chapters 3, 5, 7, and 8), it has become necessary to re-examine the distinctiveness of the two.

There are admittedly certain respects in which current thinking about legal charity accepts a close similarity of charity and government. At a high level of generalization, charity and government are both concerned with attaining the common good. It is in this very general sense that Matthew Harding observes that "government and charity – at least charity in the legal sense – are in the same business" (Harding 2009, 559–60). But, as Harding observes, charity and government continue to share some territory even when we transition from the general to the more specific. For example, certain purposes recognized as charitable at law seem to be overtly governmental in nature. It has been established that donations to government for the purpose of paying down the national debt qualify as charitable at law (*Newland v. A.G.*). Likewise, trusts to build roads and bridges qualify as charitable at law, notwithstanding that this activity can only be carried by or under the control of government (*Central Bayside (HCA)*). Further, trusts for the relief of taxes, which effectively means trusts providing revenue streams for governmental programming that would otherwise have to be raised through government revenue tools, have been recognized as charitable (*Attorney-General v. Bushby*). Indeed, one could say that the immediate purpose of such trusts is not to achieve governmental ends per se but rather to reduce the burden of tax associated with governmental ends. Nonetheless, these authorities are clearly contemplating some sort of overlap between charity and government.

The theoretical thinking behind the preferred income tax treatment of charitable donations also draws to some extent upon an assumed similarity of charity and government. One line of reasoning posits that charitable donations should not be taxed because they do not qualify as "income" in the first place (Andrews 1972). A premise of this reasoning is the idea that charitable donations achieve the essential aims of income tax, including the redistribution of wealth through the production of collective goods and services that would go underfunded without an income tax (Andrews 1972, 346). Obviously, this reasoning only holds true if it is accepted that charitable goods and services bear a resemblance of some sort to government supplied goods and services.

Another line of reasoning maintains that the preferred income tax treatment of charitable donations can be justified as an indirect state subsidy for charities. A state subsidy for charities is said to be warranted because of a failure of government to directly supply the goods and services supplied by charities and a corresponding failure of the market to supply charities with the optimal level of funding (Hall and Colombo 1991, 1423–5; Crimm 1998; and Ben-Ner and Gui 2003, 3). The state could directly subsidize charities through direct transfers but an indirect subsidy delivered through donation tax incentives is said to be preferable for a variety of reasons. One idea is that donation incentives better allocate the costs of charitable programming to taxpayers who value that programming than would a system of direct state provision (Gergen 1988, 1399–406). Another idea is that donation incentives foster a form of direct democracy whereby taxpayers are permitted to vote (through charitable donations) how public funds are allocated (Levmore 1998). Yet another idea is that donation incentives offer efficiency advantages over direct state grants because they attract more donations than they cost in foregone tax revenue (Vickrey 1962, 31; Feldstein 1975; Gergen 1988, 1404; Wiedenbeck 1985; Colombo 2001; and Duff 2004).

This reasoning quite clearly draws upon an assumed similarity of charitable and governmental purposes. The government failure thesis casts into doubt the very existence of the charitable sector as a consequence of government failing to supply the full range of public goods that would be supplied by an ideal government. In this view, there would not even be a need for the charitable sector if the government were providing the optimal level of public goods and services. Likewise, the idea that donation incentives foster a form of direct democracy implicitly analogizes between charitable goods and services and the kinds of governmental goods and services that form the basis for democratic votes. Even the idea that donation incentives are a more efficient model of program delivery than direct state provision takes for granted that charitable goods and services could be directly supplied by government.

And yet I maintain nonetheless that charity law should be developed on the footing that charity is separate and apart from government.

Those authorities that characterize purposes with an overt governmental orientation as charitable purposes are the exception rather than the rule. Alongside these authorities exist other authorities who establish that donations to governmental departments for their general purposes, as well as trusts whose purpose is to carry out governmental policy, are not charitable (Harding 2009, 561–3). In addition, while it is true that a blurring of government and charity has in some senses occurred over time, this does not compel us to deny that charity remains distinct from government. There is a simple reason why charitable trusts can remain charitable even when established and/or funded by government. It is well-established that neither the motive nor the identity of the contributor to (or settlor of) a charitable trust is in any way relevant to whether the trust qualifies as charitable at law. The focus is always on what is being achieved rather than the source of funding or the motive behind the funding. So if all else remains equal, it simply does not matter to the charitableness of a putative charitable trust whether the settlor of or contributor to the trust is or is not government. That is, charitable ends remain charitable even when subsidized by the state. This is not to say that governmental involvement is incapable of vitiating the charitableness of a trust. The UK Charity Commission observes that charitable trusts must be independent from government (Charity Commission 2001). In the view of the Commission, if the purpose of a trust is ultimately to implement the policies of government, or if the trust operates such that it merely carries out the directions of government, then it will not qualify as charitable. The best explanation for this is that charities are not government and cannot be operated or established as an arm of government.

One way to summarize the preceding is to say that governments cannot "do government" through charities. The only exception is if the goal of government in supporting charity is to "do charity." Of course, this is not really an exception to the rule since it merely reveals that governments are just like everybody else in the sense that they are able to support (though neither direct nor control) the work of charities. The doctrine of political purposes can be understood as simply applying this principle in reverse. When courts say that electioneering and lobbying for law and regulatory reform are non-charitable they might simply mean the following: Just as governments cannot "do government" through charities, charities cannot "do charity" through governments. Since government and charity are separate and distinct, government cannot be the means for charitable ends any more than charity can be the means for governmental ends. The doctrine of political purposes is therefore perhaps misnamed because it is arguably less concerned with the non-charitableness of politics than it is with the non-charitableness of government.

If I have correctly identified a theoretically defensible rationale for the doctrine of political purposes, then we have a principled basis for concluding that the doctrine of political purposes as currently applied is excessive. For the reasons noted, the distinction between charity and government grounds a case for continuing to characterize electioneering and lobbying as non-charitable political pursuits. However, this leaves open the charitableness of shaping (and contributing to) public debate through public awareness campaigns. Admittedly, the cultivation of certain values or perspectives might tend to influence the demands that people make of government. However, since this is also true of, say, education and religion, it cannot in and of itself supply a basis for concluding against the charitableness of public awareness campaigns. Even purposes whose ultimate fulfillment might, strictly speaking, entail law reform – e.g., the *abolition* of human torture or vivisection, as in *McGovern* and *National Anti-Vivisection*, respectively – they need not automatically disqualify an institution from charitable status, at least not when the institution understands and approaches its mission not as one of securing law or regulatory reform through electioneering, lobbying, or expressly inciting the public to engage in lobbying, but rather as one of participating in public debate. That is, supplying the public with reasons, be they empirical, moral, practical, or controversial in nature, to favour one side of a contentious issue should not necessarily be equated with campaigning in favour of a particular candidate for public office or directly pressing the government to legislate consistently on one side of a contentious issue. Current law and regulatory practices have not done enough to distinguish these. To the extent that this has imposed a more robust restraint on advocacy than what a principled understanding of the distinction between charity and politics might be said to support, it should be revisited (see chapter 11).

Whatever else this might entail, the idea (perpetuated in the CRA's policy statement) that charitable public awareness must be confined to factual information should be abandoned. If, as I have suggested, the doctrine of political purposes serves the purpose of policing the distinction between charity and government, then the CRA requirement for factual information is specious. A public awareness campaign is no more or no less governmental in nature whether it is based on facts versus normative conceptions of social justice. More fundamentally, though, the CRA requirement for factual information has the effect – intentionally or otherwise – of restricting the extent to which charities can draw on unprovable normative ideals in their public messaging. This is difficult to reconcile with the reality that practically all charitable programming is loaded with value-laden messaging. The idea that charities can somehow be restricted to benign and uncontroversial missions devoid of normative messaging is inconsistent with much of what charities do.

For example, the very act of relieving poverty through some specific poverty relief strategy deliberately endorses a view about poverty to the public. Identifying a given population as "poor" communicates a potentially controversial message about the basic standards of living below which no one should be left to languish. Indeed, it is impossible to engage in the act of relieving poverty without necessarily communicating a value-laden message about which wealth disparities are too extreme to leave unaddressed. Likewise, even something as seemingly uncontentious as a scholarship fund promotes potentially controversial ideas about the sorts of criteria that should be used to identify meritorious scholarship candidates (e.g., gender, religion, financial need, geographic residence, disadvantaged ancestry, military service, etc.), the sorts of athletic and academic pursuits worthy of financial support, and so on. Charities established to grapple with the issue of impaired driving are transparent in their goal to shape public attitudes on the issue of impaired driving. Human rights charities unavoidably shape public values in a wide array of contentious socio-legal issues. Environmental charities instill a sense of environmental stewardship and cognizance of environmental impact. Religious charities, especially in the context of proselytizing religions, necessarily provide non-neutral instruction on the most controversial issues imaginable. In fact, churches – because they commend to parishioners comprehensive religious belief systems – do far more to shape attitudes and opinions than the sorts of single-issue advocacy organizations that are sometimes thought of as political.

Law and regulation in this area could be improved by giving greater recognition to the reality that with the idealism inspiring charitable works comes ideals. Allowing charities to enrich public discourse by contributing these ideals to the marketplace of ideas is not a deviation from what charities ought to be doing but rather a fulfillment of it.

## CONCLUSION

Charity law has shifted from initially having little to no restriction on political advocacy to now having what might be fairly described as a vigorous rule distinguishing charity from politics. The current state of the law is vulnerable to numerous criticisms. The law characterizes as political an excessively broad range of pursuits. It squanders the capacity of charities to speak about marginalizing societal issues, compromising the exercising of justice in the process. Further, the case law authorities have never articulated a persuasive rationale for the doctrine. Arguably, the doctrine reflects an increased tendency for courts and policy-makers to approach legal charity as more of a fiscal concept than an intelligible and coherent ideal. This has resulted in charities being valued more for the goods and services they supply than for the normative ideals they espouse. None of which is meant to altogether repudiate the doctrine of political purposes. The distinctiveness of charity and government grounds a case for some form of rule against political purposes, just not the rule as constituted under current Canadian law. When the current Liberal government makes good on its promise to revisit the distinction between charity and politics, expanding the parameters of charitable public awareness campaigns would be a good place to start.

### NOTES

1. Paragraph 3 (per Elias CJ).
2. In particular, the 2012 Budget amended the Income Tax Act R.S.C. 1985, c. 1 (5th Supp.) [Income Tax Act], as amended to (1) make clear that it is a political activity for one charity to make gifts to another charity to support the latter charity's political activities (2) provide that a registered charity's gift receipting privileges could be suspended for one year if the charity engages in excessive political activity or fails to accurately report the scope of its political activities.
3. "Real Change: A New Plan for a Strong Middle Class." https://www.liberal.ca/realchange/.

4 The preamble identified the following as charitable purposes:

> [T]he relief of aged, impotent, and poor people; the maintenance of sick and maimed soldiers and mariners; schools of learning; free schools and scholars in universities; the repair of bridges, ports, havens, causeways, churches, sea banks, and highways; the education and preferment of orphans; the relief, stock, or maintenance of houses of correction; marriages of poor maids; support, aid, and help of young tradesmen, handicraftsmen and persons decayed; the relief or redemption or prisoners or captives; and the aid or ease of any poor inhabitants covering payments of fifteens, setting out of soldiers, and other taxes.

5 This reasoning has been followed in Canada in *Action by Christians for the Abolition of Torture* v. *Canada*.
6 For a general discussion of these cases and others on this point, see O. Tudor 1929, 51–4 and Brooks 1983, 149.
7 This is implicit in the requirement for a well-reasoned position based on factual information.
8 See also Ontario Law Reform Commission Report on the Law of Charities 1997, 219–20.
9 For example, the CRA discusses a hypothetical charity advocating a view in a municipal debate over whether pedestrian safety would be best achieved through a marked pedestrian crosswalk or a traffic light (CRA 2003).
10 In *Gilmour* v. *Coats*, it was expressly held by Lord Reid at 459 that a "religion can be regarded as beneficial without it being necessary to assume that all its beliefs are true."
11 The High Court of Australia adopted similar reasoning in *Aid/Watch Incorporated and Commissioner of Taxation*, 44–5.
12 As far back as *Commissioners for Special Purposes of the Income Tax v. Pemsel*, it was recognized by Lord Halsbury at 551 that "every [tax] exemption throws an additional burden on the rest of the community."

REFERENCES

*Action by Christians for the Abolition of Torture v. Canada* (2002), 225 D.L.R. (4th) 99.
*Aid/Watch Incorporated and Commissioner of Taxation* [2010] H.C.A. 42.
*Alliance for Life v. M.N.R.*, [1999] 3 F.C. 504 (F.C.A.).

*Amateur Youth Soccer Association v. Canada Revenue Agency*, [2007] S.C.J. No. 42.
Andrews, W. 1972. "Personal Deductions in an Ideal Income Tax." *Harvard Law Review* 86 (2): 309-85. http://dx.doi.org/10.2307/1339894.
*Anglo-Swedish Society v. Commissioners of Inland Revenue* (1931), 16 T.C. 34 (K.B.).
*Attorney-General v. Bushby* [1857]53 ER 373.
Ben-Ner, A., and B. Gui. 2003. "The Theory of Nonprofit Organizations Revisited." In *The Study of Nonprofit Enterprise: Theories and Approaches*, edited by H.K. Anheier and A. Ben-Ner, 3–26. New York: Plenum Publishers. http://dx.doi.org/10.1007/978-1-4615-0131-2_1.
*Bonar Law Memorial Trust v. I.R.C.* (1933) 49 T.L.R. 220.
*Bowman v. Secular Society* [1917] A.C. 406 (H.L.).
Bridge, R. 2002. "The Law of Advocacy by Charitable Organizations: The Case for Change." *Philanthropist* 17:2–33.
Brooks, N. 1983. *Charities: The Legal Framework*. Ottawa: Secretary of State.
*Buxton and Others v. Public Trustee and Others* (1962), 41 T.C. 235.
Canada Revenue Agency. 2003. Document CPS-022, *Political Activities*. http://www.cra-arc.gc.ca/chrts-gvng/chrts/plcy/cps/cps-022-eng.html#N10452.
*Central Bayside (HCA)* (2006) 228 CLR 168.
*Challenge Team v. Canada* [2000] F.C.J. No. 433 (F.C.A.).
Charity Commission for England and Wales. 2001. *RR7 – The Independence of Charities from the State*.
Chesterman, M. 1979. *Charities, Trusts and Social Welfare*. London: Weidenfeld and Nicolson.
– 2000. "Foundations of Charity Law in the New Welfare State." In *Foundations of Charity*, edited by C. Mitchell and S.R. Moody, 249. Portland: Hart Publishing.
Chia, J., M. Harding, and A. O'Connell. 2011. "Navigating the Politics of Charity: Reflections on *Aid/Watch Inc. v. Federal Commissioner of Taxation*." *Melbourne University Law Review* 35:353–93.
Colombo, J.D. 2001. "The Marketing of Philanthropy and the Charitable Contributions Deduction: Integrating Theories for the Deduction and Tax Exemption." *Wake Forest Law Review* 36 (3):657–703.
*Commissioners for Special Purposes of the Income Tax v. Pemsel* [1891] A.C. 531 (H.L.).
Crimm, N.J. 1998. "An Explanation of the Federal Income Tax Exemption for Charitable Organizations: A Theory of Risk Compensation." *Florida Law Review* 50:419–62.

Duff, D. 2004. "Tax Treatment of Charitable Contributions in Canada: Theory, Practice, and Reform." *Osgoode Hall Law Journal* 42 (1):47–97.

Dunn, A. 2000. "Charity Law as a Political Option for the Poor." In *Foundations of Charity*, edited by C. Mitchell and S.R. Moody, 57–78. Portland: Hart Publishing.

– 2008. "Demanding Service or Servicing Demand? Charities, Regulation and the Policy Process." *Modern Law Review* 71 (2):247–70. http://dx.doi.org/10.1111/j.1468-2230.2008.00690.x.

Dunn, A. 2014. *Charity, Law and Politics: Radicals, Conservatives or Subversives*. Oxford: Hart Publishing.

*Farewell v. Farewell* [1892] O.J. No. 173 (Ont. H.C.J.).

Feldstein, M. 1975. "The Income Tax and Charitable Contributions." *National Tax Journal* 28:81–100.

Gergen, M. 1988. "The Case for a Charitable Contributions Deductions." *Virginia Law Review* 74 (8): 1399. http://dx.doi.org/10.2307/1073279.

*Gilmour v. Coats* [1949] AC 426 (H.L.)

Gladstone, F. 1982. *Charity, Law and Social Justice*. London: Bedford Square Press.

Hall, M., and J. Colombo. 1991. "The Donative Theory of the Charitable Tax Exemption." *Ohio State Law Journal* 52:1379–476.

Harding, M. 2009. "Distinguishing Government from Charity in Australian Law." *Sydney Law Review* 31:559–78.

Harvie, B. 2002. *Regulation of Advocacy in the Voluntary Sector: Current Challenges and Some Responses*. http://www.vsi-isbc.org/eng/policy/pdf/regulation_of_advocacy.pdf.

*Human Life International in Canada Inc. v. M.N.R.*, [1998] F.C.J. No. 365 (F.C.C).

*In re Foveaux* [1895] 2 Ch. 501.

*Jackson v. Phillips* (1867), 96 Mass. 539.

Levmore, S. 1998. "Taxes as Ballots." *University of Chicago Law Review. University of Chicago. Law School* 65 (2): 387. http://dx.doi.org/10.2307/1600226.

Luxton, P. 1995. "Charitable Status and Political Purpose." *N.L.J. Annual Charities Rev.* 24:28.

– 2001. *The Law of Charities*. Oxford: Oxford University Press.

McCarthy, S. 2012. "Minister Defends Tory Environment Plan, Dials back Criticism of Charities," *The Globe and Mail*, 7 May. http://www.theglobeandmail.com/news/politics/ottawa-notebook/minister-defends-tory-environment-plan-dials-back-criticism-of-charities/article4105318/.

*McGovern v. Attorney-General* [1982] 1 Ch. 321.
*Newland v. A.G.* (1809), 36 E.R. 262.
*News to You Canada v. Minister of National Revenue* [2011] 5 C.T.C. 176.
Ontario Law Reform Commission. 1979. *Report on the Law of Charities.* Toronto: Ontario Law Reform Commission.
Parachin, A. 2008. "Distinguishing Charity and Politics: The Judicial Thinking Behind the Doctrine of Political Purposes." *Alberta Law Review* 45:871–99.
*Re Bushnell* [1975] 1 W.L.R. 1596.
*Re Greenpeace* [2014] NZSC 105.
*Re Hopkinson,* [1949] 1 All E.R. 346.
*Re Knight* [1937] O.R. 462 (H.C.J.).
*Re Loney* (1953), 61 Man. R. 214 (Q.B.).
*Re Positive Action Against Pornography and Minister of National Revenue* (1988), 49 D.L.R. (4th) 74 (F.C.A.).
*Re Villers-Wilkes* [1895] 72 L.T. 323.
Rickett, C.E.F. 1982. "Charity and Politics." *N.Z.U.L. Rev.* 10:176.
Santow, G.F.K. 1999. "Charity in Its Political Voice: A Tinkling Cymbal or a Sounding Brass?" *Current Legal Problems* 52 (1): 255–85. http://dx.doi.org/10.1093/clp/52.1.255.
Secretary of State for the Home Department. 1989. *Charities: A Framework for the Future.* Cmd: 694.
Sheridan, L.A. 1980. "Charitable Causes, Political Causes and Involvement." *Philanthropist* 2:5–20.
*Southwood & Another v. Her Majesty's Attorney General* 2000 WL 877698.
*Statute of Elizabeth* 1601 (43 Eliz. 1), c. 4.
Swann, S. 2000. "Justifying the Ban on Politics in Charity." In *The Voluntary Sector, the State and the Law*, edited by A. Dunn, 161–76. Portland: Hart Publishing.
*Toronto Volograd Committee v. Canada,* [1988] 3 F.C. 251.
Tudor, O. 1929. *Tudor on Charities; A Practical Treatise on the Law Relating to Gifts and Trusts for Charitable Purposes.* 5th ed. London: Sweet & Maxwell.
*Vancouver Society of Immigrant and Visible Minority Women v. Canada (M.N.R.),* [1999] 1 S.C.R. 10.
Vickrey, W. 1962. "One Economist's View of Philanthropy." In *Philanthropy and Public Policy*, edited by F.G. Dickinson, 31–56. New York: National Bureau of Economic Research.

Warburton, J. and Morris, D. 1991. "Charities and the Contract Culture." *The Conveyancer*, 419.

Webb, K. 2000. *Cinderella's Slippers? The Role of Charitable Tax Status in Financing Canadian Interest Groups*. Vancouver: SFU-UBC Centre for the Study of Government and Business.

Wiedenbeck, P. 1985. "Charitable Contributions: A Policy Perspective." *Missouri Law Review* 50:85–140.

# 3

# Advocates Anonymous: A Study of Advocacy Coalitions in Ontario

ANNA BURROWES AND RACHEL LAFOREST

Advocacy has long been one of the core functions of non-profit organizations (Berger and Neuhaus 1977; Frumkin 2002; Jenkins 2006; Smith and Pekkanen 2012). Advocacy involves supporting and enabling constituencies to voice their views and concerns to society and to the state. It is a vital process of democratic governance because it contributes to the articulation, aggregation, and organization of interests in society. This is how non-profit organizations provide a vehicle for communities to come together to share ideas and beliefs. Non-profit organizations advocate as an expression of the needs of their constituency, and their understanding of existing social relations. However, the way non-profit organizations engage in advocacy has changed significantly over the past decade, undermining the essential role they play in political representation.

Typical analyses of advocacy have tended to define advocacy as a broad set of activities ranging from writing letters, to petitioning, contacting legislators, and protesting; and quantifying these practices (Boris and Mosher-Williams 1998; Reid 2000; Salamon 1995). However, these studies associate advocacy with a series of characteristics and may misrepresent the true effect of changes that have occurred in advocacy over the past decade. Rather than treating advocacy as an objective variable, defined by a strict category of activities and examining the extent to which organizations engaged in these activities, advocacy needs to be thought of as made up of active players with their own strategies and interests. We contend that these meaning systems can be uncovered by analyzing discourses that influence thoughts and practices.

Indeed, notions of what constitutes advocacy vary over time, and are context specific. Political environments and the state play a big part in this as they encourage some kinds of group formation and collective action, but not others. One way to capture the shifting terrain of advocacy is to focus on the ideas and discourses of actors who are directly engaged in the practice of advocacy. This chapter focuses on the work of coalitions in Ontario. Coalitions are umbrella organizations and, as such, are vehicles for non-profit organizations to pool their resources to influence policy. Coalitions have become important spaces for advocacy. Non-profit organizations in Ontario have increasingly focused their practices on more mainstream approaches that involve working through coalitions because of their own organizations' financial constraints and tighter regulations. Because coalitions are generally not formed as charities, they tend not to be constrained by advocacy regulations to the same extent. We chose them as a case study because, theoretically, members can channel their advocacy activities through them without fear of reprisal. Coalitions form one basis of participation in the policy process which, unfortunately, researchers have tended to ignore. By examining the discourses of coalitions, we aim to expose how practices and meaning systems in advocacy are shifting on the ground.

Drawing on the analysis of fifteen coalitions, this chapter illustrates how the current political, social, and regulatory environment for organizations in Ontario has left coalitions struggling in three key areas: (1) to engage in advocacy with often barebones resources; (2) to engage members active and sustainable fashion; and (3) to maintain a wide scope of advocacy activities given government's preference for evidence-based strategies. This, however, is not just a story of coalitions submitting to the pressures imposed by the state. What is most troubling, we argue, is that these norms have been so internalized that many coalitions now want to be dissociated from advocacy practices. This internalization illustrates just how penetrating these changes have been and speak to the pernicious normalizing tendencies of neoliberalism. This internalization of norms about advocacy has had a negative effect on the agency capacity of non-profit organizations, and for democratic governance as a whole.

In this chapter, we first define coalitions and consider their role as vehicles for advocacy. Second, we examine the broad political environment, at both the federal and provincial levels, that shapes government and non-profit-sector relations. We then analyze the shifting norms that have defined coalition efforts in Ontario over the past decade (for examples of coalitional work in other provinces and territories, see chapter 9 [New Brunswick], chapter 10 [Yukon, Northwest Territories, and Nunavut], chapter 5 [Saskatchewan], and chapter 8 [Quebec] in this book). Finally, we discuss the broader implications of these findings for Canadian democracy.

## STUDYING COALITIONS

Building coalitions to generate awareness around a policy issue has long been an advocacy strategy used by non-profit organizations (Hojnacki 1997). Because coordinating multiple, at times disparate, actors involves framing the issue, organizing action, and raising public awareness, coalitions themselves can be seen as advocacy actors. For the purposes of this chapter, we define coalitions as "alliances of individuals or organizations that strive to influence public policy and resource allocation decisions within political, economic, and social systems and institutions" (Advocacy Institute 2004). One of the reasons we chose this definition is that it encompasses many different types of coalitions such as alliances, networks, coalitions, or associations – all of which pursue an external advocacy role. With very little existing research on coalitions in Canada, we felt it was important to cast the net wide. Hence, the coalitions we analyzed focused on a range of policy fields, including three from environment, one from immigrant settlement, three from poverty reduction, one from labour policy, three from social justice, and four from health policy. Two of the coalitions were registered charities and the remainder were registered and non-registered non-profits. We selected two registered charities as a counterfactual to assess whether charitable status had an impact on a coalition's perception of advocacy. As will become evident, the dynamics we observed in the majority of coalitions are that, regardless of an organization's charitable status, advocacy has become a stigmatized activity. That is, the advocacy chill is so pervasive that even those organizations that are not directly regulated have begun to embody the new norms and dissociate themselves from advocacy activities that are more critical and confrontational.

Coalitions have their own identity and are composed of multiple entities (usually other organizations). In our sample, the formality, type, and scope of membership between coalitions varied widely. Some only accepted organizational representatives, others were primarily composed of individuals, and the rest were made up of a combination of both individuals and organizational representatives. Formality of membership also varied, from coalitions whose members paid a membership fee, to coalitions that defined their members loosely as those who "participate in the activities of the organization and come to meetings." Finally, there was a wide variety, both between and within coalitions, around the level of involvement of their members from "receiving newsletters ... and that's about it" to being actively involved in the advocacy activities of the coalition. Moreover, funding sources for coalitions vary. Some receive external support from government agencies or labour unions, while others rely solely on membership fees. Clearly, coalitions involve a wide range of relationships. While these may be worth examining in the longer term, our focus here is on the way discourses around advocacy are constructed within coalitions.

Although coalitions are important actors in the policy realm, much of the literature to date has focused on capacity building (Wolff 2001; Zakocs and Edwards 2006). In fact, we know very little about trends in coalition organizing over time. Coalitions have long served as a way for organizations to share information and increase their power in the policy process. Anecdotally, however, the respondents we interviewed reported that coalitions have become more attractive as a vehicle for political expression because of the widespread advocacy chill and growing financial constraints imposed on individual organizations. Although the Trudeau government reinvested in advocacy activities early in its mandate by supporting women's organizations and reinstating the Court Challenges program of Canada, it will surely take some time before the advocacy chill defrosts, given how internalized the dismissal of this activity has become across the non-profit sector. What is more, coalitions are seen as effective ways of leveraging the resources of organizations that come together around a common goal or objective. Perhaps more important, coalitions reportedly offer anonymity for organizations that enable them to engage in advocacy without directly being singled out by the state. Not surprisingly then, coalitions have become safeguards for organizations fearing direct reprisal from government for engaging in advocacy (Acheson and Laforest 2013; Shapcott 2009; Shields 2013). They provide an outlet through which organizations can channel their opposition and express their concerns without putting individual organizations at risk of losing funding.

Moreover, respondents noted that the rise of coalition activity can be attributed to the fact that non-profit organizations are increasingly called upon to do more with less. The financial and administrative burdens that currently hinder non-profit organizations' ability to deliver services and advocate require non-profits to find new and innovative ways to work together (Shapcott 2009). Imagine Canada (2010), for example, found that 42 per cent of all operating charities collaborated with other organizations to reduce expenses following the 2008 fiscal crisis. While this data does not distinguish between informal collaboration and formal collaboration via coalitions, there is a general tendency toward a pooling of resources, both financial and human. Weisner (1983, 298) has also gone so far as to argue that "the degree to which non-profit organizations are successful in fighting back in a period of austerity will depend in part on their ability to use coalitions effectively to shape public opinions and influence the political process." Resources and capacity are an important factor in the ability of non-profit organizations to undertake advocacy (Berry and Arons 2003). The importance of coalitions in the policy process will most likely continue to grow in the future given the scarcity of resources for non-profit organizations and the "chilly" political and regulatory environment in which they operate – to which we turn next.

## THE SHIFTING ADVOCACY ENVIRONMENT IN CANADA

One of the unique features of non-profit organizing in Canada is that up until the mid-1990s the federal government was a strong supporter, both financially and institutionally, of non-profit organizations, and of advocacy in particular (Pal 1993; Jenson and Phillips 1996). In fact, the federal government constructed a financial regime early on to support collective-action efforts as a way of enabling citizens to attain and practise citizenship skills (Phillips, Laforest, and Graham 2010). By mobilizing disadvantaged segments of Canadian society, the federal government strongly believed that it could promote the formation and maintenance of a Canadian identity. Not only was core funding made available to support advocacy groups, access to the federal government was also institutionalized through the

Secretary of State programs and the creation of Status of Women Canada. In the mid-1990s, the government and the general public grew sceptical of non-profit organizations as a result of a number of widely publicized scandals and alleged abuses within the sector. This resulted in the legitimacy of non-profit advocacy being questioned by government, and a slew of funding cuts that were specifically targeted at advocacy organizations followed. Because funding for advocacy and collective action has generally been tied to the federal government in Canada, it is important to examine broader macro-dynamics as well, if we are to understand coalition trends in Ontario.

The dismantling of this federal funding regime in the late 1990s had important repercussions on non-profit organizations at the provincial level (Phillips, Laforest, and Graham 2010). When the funding door closed at the federal level, it meant that organizations had to turn to other sources of funding – such as provincial governments or foundations – to secure resources to support advocacy activities. However, as the advocacy "chill" spread, securing advocacy support from these new sources would also prove increasingly difficult.

The federal government is also an important player in shaping the provincial advocacy landscape because, even though these may be provincially incorporated non-profit entities, it has authority over the taxation benefits of charitable organizations through the Canada Revenue Agency. The trends are quite clear and have been widely documented (see chapter 2). The charitable rules are prohibitive and have contributed to an advocacy chill in the non-profit sector. The restrictions have created a reluctance that extends beyond just charities to all non-profit organizations – and have even affected the coalitions in our case study.

The federal government's announcement in the 2012 federal budget that it would allocate an additional $8 million dollars to police charities only further accentuated this advocacy "chill." This initiative was prompted by the media attention surrounding the Northern Gateway Pipeline and the allegation that environmental charities had used foreign money to build opposition to the project. This regulatory climate and the potentially grim repercussions of engaging in prohibited activities (including the loss of charitable status) were the source of much reluctance among charities to engage in advocacy, and they may have further decreased the already low levels of engagement in political activities within the charitable sector. In 2014, there were fifty-two specific political-activity-related audits underway affecting organizations as diverse as environmental, foreign aid, human rights, and poverty groups (Kirby 2014; see also chapter 11). The current Liberal government's commitment to allowing charities to operate without political harassment, and its move to wind down the charity audit program, has led to optimism for some within the sector. However, because norms regarding advocacy have been internalized, the effects of the chill may linger for years to come.

Further changes in the political and funding environment at the federal level have also limited the ability of non-profit organizations to engage in advocacy activities at the provincial level. Faced with a growing deficit, the federal government embarked on a modernizing effort called Program Review in 1994–97 that was strongly influenced by New Public Management (NPM). This program led to massive funding cutbacks and the reorienting of funding away from core funding toward project-based funding. Project funding and contracts are less likely to cover organizations' ongoing advocacy activities or networking costs, so their introduction struck a blow to many national and provincial advocacy groups. Katherine Scott, vice-president of research and policy at the Canadian Council on Social Development, for example, observed that many non-profit organizations ended up self-restricting their advocacy activities for fear of losing funding (Scott 2003). Project-based funding also siphons off already limited resources so organizations can meet the requirements and conditions of the contractual agreements (Phillips and Levasseur 2004). Non-profit organizations are increasingly concerned about the administrative burden resulting from the demands that funders are placing on them. The time spent on the application and reporting processes, and in following the compliance requirements, drains non-profit organizations of valuable time – time they could be dedicating toward advocacy.

Taken together, these shifts have rendered the perception of advocacy as negative and controversial rather than positive and charitable. This negative portrayal is paradoxical, as governments have come increasingly to rely on the knowledge and services of non-profit organizations. The previous Conservative federal government made it clear that it would fund projects, rather than organizations, that efficiently use public funds for ends that are compatible with federal government priorities. As Phillips stated, the previous government sent a clear message to the non-profit sector: it needs "to deliver services efficiently and be quiet" (Phillips 2009, 2). Some researchers have also pointed to high-profile funding cuts to well-established non-profit organizations that have spoken out against government policies as an explanation for the growing fear of reprisals in the non-profit sector (Laforest 2012; Shields 2013). Notable examples include the Canadian Arab Foundation, KAIROS, the Canadian Council for Social Development (CCSD), the Canadian Policy Research Networks (CPRN), and the International Centre for Human Rights and Democratic Development (R&D) Shields (2013, 18), who interviewed non-profit organizations across Canada, argued that, "a strong belief exists among non-profits that using voice can have negative consequences for state funding. In this sense 'advocacy chill' is a reality in the sector and it greatly influences actions by non-profit bodies in Canada." Many observers have already noted the advocacy "chill" that has befallen the non-profit sector in Canada (Kirby 2014; Laforest 2011, 2012; Phillips 2009; Richmond 2004). New norms for advocacy have been embodied in drastic funding cuts to organizations deemed too political and a progressive tightening of rules around charities' political activities (Levasseur 2012). While the tide appears to be changing with the election of a Liberal federal government, it will nonetheless take time for internal practices to adapt to the new openness to advocacy.

## THE SHIFTING ADVOCACY ENVIRONMENT IN ONTARIO

Provincial trends for advocacy have reflected these broad macro trends. Just as in the federal government, the Ontario government had to deal with a skyrocketing deficit and rising unemployment in the mid-1990s. The newly elected Progressive Conservative government in 1995, under Mike Harris, also proceeded to cut funding to non-profit organizations, adopting NPM contracting practices. So when the federal funding doors closed, so did the provincial ones. The Harris regime was particularly regressive, making it difficult for non-profits to gain access at a provincial level, as it offloaded many social programs to local governments (Marquardt 2007/2008). While this shift had a major effect on organizations, it also affected coalitions in important ways.

According to Berry and Arons (2003), access to government is an important determinant of whether or not an organization will engage in advocacy. In our sample, all but one of the coalitions strove to influence policy by attempting to gain access and develop relationships with the provincial government over this period. In fact, the majority of our sample – eleven of the fifteen coalitions – reported a shift in the way they accessed funding and resources over this period. The federal and provincial governments had previously provided funding for advocacy activities. However, core funding, which provided stable funding for advocacy, subsided as governments moved toward funding service delivery projects such as running crisis lines or after-school programs. Not surprisingly, given these funding trends, securing resources has become a constant preoccupation for coalitions. One respondent noted that its coalition was so vulnerable that it changed its entire funding strategy so as "never to depend on only one source." Others also stated they were now "always struggling to get funding together," "constantly looking for funding," or "always dealing with the funding issue." Finally, some noted that they had to increasingly dedicate energy to the pursuit of new funds and new funders, whether it was another level of government, the private sector, or foundations. This had important organizational effects. One consequence of limited financial resources was the amount of time spent searching for new sources of funding, thereby taking away valuable time that could otherwise be spent on programming work or advocacy. For example, one coalition mentioned that when "times were tight," they had to spend up to 50 per cent of their time on fundraising activities, which left little time for advocacy or other activities. Another coalition even came to question the amount of time it dedicated to securing resources, lamenting, "What am I fundraising for if I don't have time to advocate?"

This new funding environment can significantly influence advocacy trends. Research has repeatedly shown that the constant pursuit of funds can lead to "mission drift" or "diluted advocacy" when non-profit organizations mould their mandate to meet the requirements of the contract or dilute their advocacy message to mitigate potential opposition (Smith and Lipsky 1993; Brown and Troutt 2004; Katz 2001; Salamon 1995; Scott 2003). Our analysis of coalitions in Ontario echoed these findings. The constant preoccupation with the pursuit of new funds also fostered internal tensions within coalitions. In particular, coalitions' greatest concern was their ability to achieve their mission. For example, one coalition noted that it had to ease the tension "between limited resources and being able to mobilize." Other coalitions struggled with "balancing ability to deliver with capacity" and "doing what you can and working within the budget." Coalitions were cognizant of the potential gravity of this tension as funders want to fund effective coalitions and failing to meet expectations can result in losing existing funding. As one coalition discovered, "we were not effective so funders left."

Resources – or the lack thereof – and the constant search for new resources were also found to significantly influence how coalitions framed their issues and the strategies they used to influence government. In a funding context where project-based funding is so prevalent, it is not surprising to see a form of mission drift in our sample. One coalition that was interviewed noted that they had contemplated "switching the direction of the coalition to find an area that could be funded." Another coalition admitted to "doing a scan of what is going on in the external environment through newspapers and media to align ourselves with these topical issues." A third noted they had "lost funding and as a result had diversified their initiative to seek out alternative sources of funding." While this may be an effective way to "get heard" by government, it may have a mainstreaming effect that we should be attentive to in policy studies.

Nevertheless, even those coalitions that had successfully diversified their funding sources found themselves vulnerable in this new funding context. Losing one source of funding would start a domino effect. For example, one coalition found that once funding was cut by one funder, it aroused concern, causing others to pull funding. Another summarized that "those who still get money fear to speak in support of those who have been cut off." Clearly, the level of vulnerability and instability faced by coalitions is palpable.

We also know from the breadth of non-profit research that the funding environment affects advocacy strategies adopted by non-profit organizations (See for example, Chaves, Stephens, and Galaskiewicz 2004; Kimberlin 2010; Mosley 2011; Smith and Pekkanen 2012). It is therefore not surprising to observe non-profit organizations turning to coalitions as a way to collaborate, to share valuable resources, and to create support for particular issues. There is safety in numbers. Membership trends in our sample illustrate just how attractive coalitions became for organizations in Ontario over this time. Although resources were declining, we observed that membership across coalitions had been on the rise since the late 1990s.

As one respondent explicitly stated, "the key to advocacy is indeed coalition building." Ten coalitions we examined saw their membership base increase over the course of their existence – although the rate of increase varied. As a case in point, one organization noted that its membership had increased significantly, from 400 to 26,000, in five years, whereas another experienced more modest growth of only nineteen members after ten years.

While the quantity of members may have increased, the level of engagement of members within coalitions also changed over this period of time. Eight of the ten coalitions whose membership increased described this as an increase in peripheral, not core, membership. For example, the increase to 26,000 members is largely due to an increase in more "passive" or "peripheral" members, that is, members who are on an email list, but do not engage meaningfully with the coalition. Some coalitions spoke to the importance of keeping a presence in the community and making sure their name and work is known. These coalitions believed in "remaining on people's radar" or maintaining a large peripheral network (see also chapters, 5, 8, and 9). Indeed, respondents noted that some of their members were not able to bring as much as they once could to the table given the constrained financial context that they also faced as organizations. A greater number of organizations satisfied themselves with the gesture of putting their name on the list of coalition members, without really investing time or energy in the cause, in the hopes of multiplying their allies. Since organizations may not have sufficient resources to invest directly in coalition activities, coalitions may be obtaining more breadth of involvement at the expense of depth (see chapter 7). However, it can also be argued that as space for advocacy is being constrained, more organizations have recognized that coalitions and the ties they create within the sector are an important source of solidarity among civil society actors and a valuable space where issues can be debated and strategies deployed.

For the remaining coalitions in our sample, membership was a challenge because of the constrained funding environment. A couple of coalitions saw their core memberships recede whereas the rest had maintained their membership base. One coalition noted a decrease in its membership as "people got scared off as a result of the loss of funding."

Having examined how the context of advocacy has evolved in Canada and in Ontario, it is now important to turn to how these signals were interpreted and internalized by coalitions to truly understand how the shifting norms of advocacy have affected their behaviour.

## SHIFTING ADVOCACY NORMS: MAINSTREAMING TOWARD "EDUCATION" AND "EVIDENCE"

The terms of access to the policy process are dynamic and contingent because they are socially constructed and inform practice. With this understanding, we can start to identify and analyze how norms regarding advocacy are changing. One of the biggest insights we gained from this research, and also one of the challenges we faced, was the realization that many coalitions were extremely fearful of participating in our research project and thereby being labelled as advocates. Almost two decades ago, non-profit organizations in Canada defined advocacy as "the act of speaking or of disseminating information intended to influence individual behavior or opinion, corporate conduct, or public policy and law" (Government of Canada/Voluntary Sector Joint Initiative 1999). Since then, the biggest change has been that the attitudes, values, and opinions of governments toward advocacy have been internalized into organizations' sense of self to the extent that many coalitions now want to be dissociated from advocacy practices. Advocacy is no longer viewed as good and moral; there is now a great deal of shame and social stigma attached to it.

Indeed, as we have discussed earlier, coalitions that engage in advocacy have become aware that they are being treated differently by governments and that they may not receive funding as a result. In fact, one respondent in our sample eloquently noted, "the message is: Be careful what you say, the price you pay will be high." What is perhaps more telling is that even though our respondents engaged in advocacy activities, as stated in the 1999 definition, in the course of the interviews they felt more comfortable labelling their work as "educational" even when these educational programs were directed at policy-makers and the desired effect was to change policy. For example, one respondent strongly stated, "Our organization is mandated NOT to advocate. We work very closely with municipalities and certainly have influenced political agendas, but that has not been our intention. Rather our intention is to educate, write or re-write policy, change behavior and ultimately change attitudes." In fact, only one of the coalitions in our sample admitted to engaging in direct advocacy activities. This coalition, which happened to receive funds from external sources, also reported having lost funding due to its use of more controversial or direct advocacy tactics. The respondent noted that the coalition had to constantly deal with "large fluctuations in funding levels that were dependent on the actions they were taking at any given period of time." Clearly, these quotes illustrate that over the past decade, it has become risky for non-profit organizations to engage in advocacy given the political climate because of the stigma that has been affixed to advocacy activities. Moreover, it is important to note that this sentiment toward advocacy was shared by the majority of coalitions regardless of their charitable status. Even those coalitions that could technically engage in unlimited advocacy because they were not charities felt the pressure to not engage in these activities.

Another telling change in behaviour we observed was that many coalitions consciously chose to refocus their advocacy activities on evidence-based practices because these were deemed more acceptable by governments (Laforest and Orsini 2005). In fact, in our sample, the coalitions with resources for research were the same coalitions that reported having a positive influence on government decisions. For example, one coalition specifically attributed its policy success to the decision to hire an independent research group to conduct research on their key issue. The respondent stated, "The results of the research supported our mandate and this independent verification was a key factor in getting the government to start really listening to us." Another coalition described its primary advocacy strategy as involving "researching the latest facts, and writing a report card that includes policy recommendations." This coalition also accredited its success in gaining access to government to the provision of "information based on solid research." Finally, a third coalition mentioned the importance of "providing evidence that a policy maker would want to see." Coalitions reported wanting to support their advocacy work with hard facts and quantifiable measures. Interestingly, those coalitions that advocated for social justice issues attributed their lack of access to the public sphere to their inability to produce quantifiable measures.

The growing preference for evidence-based policy making by government privileges certain advocacy coalitions while excluding those that lack the skills and resources for research or those that advocate on issues that cannot easily be supported by research. Moreover, rigorous research requires significant resources. Coalitions struggling to get funding or access to government are being asked to prove themselves before they are heard or receive funding, when, paradoxically, without this initial funding, they cannot create the research needed to get in the door. We observed that younger coalitions were more successful than more established coalitions at navigating an evidence-based relationship with the Ontario government. Budding coalitions used a discourse that strategically centred on building allies in government by "acting as a resource for government" or "providing information and advice, rather than being confrontational or critical" (see chapter 7). For example, one respondent noted that its coalition had attracted government attention by "helping government with the ground work and making it easy for them to say yes." Young coalitions firmly believed that their research-centred focus was what had helped them secure legitimacy. Interestingly, Child and Gronbjerg (2007), studying advocacy in the US, also found that older, well-established organizations had more confrontational advocacy strategies than newer organizations did. Despite the distinction between older and newer coalitions, in Ontario most respondents described evidence-based practices as a safe channel through which coalitions could advocate.

In sum, building coalitions and focusing on providing education and evidence, rather than more traditional forms of advocating, are two ways that organizations are shying away from "advocacy" as a practice. Both trends also emerged as ways to gain legitimacy in the eyes of government. Coalitions that were able to provide evidence to support their issue saw increased government involvement as they were likely deemed more legitimate policy contributors. Likewise, coalitions that were able to maintain their membership base saw that as an important signal that they were focusing on issues that mattered. A large breadth of support was helpful in their efforts to influence government. This trend would suggest, conversely, that organizations working in isolation on issues that are difficult to quantify will struggle to gain access to government and have their voices heard.

## CONCLUSION

Concerns about the state of advocacy – whether through coalitions or organizations – are intimately connected to the question of democratic governance. Thus it is important to unpack the consequences of neoliberalism on agency and democratic governance. Perhaps the most important lesson to reflect on from this research is recognizing the profound fear coalitions have of being identified as advocates. There is a profound stigma surrounding advocacy. This stigma has been internalized by organizations that now consciously avoid confrontational tactics and gravitate toward evidence-based practices. This fear of reprisal has only been accentuated by the waves of federal and provincial funding cuts that have occurred over the past decade and has led to a profound shift in advocacy norms, decentring the role of advocacy in policy making with perhaps important implications for democracy in the long term.

Taken together, the narrowing of the scope for action, plus the move away from advocacy, does not bode well for the ability of non-profit organizations and coalitions to contribute to the development of policy. As evidence becomes an increasingly valued input, the non-profit sector's involvement in decision making may be depoliticized, challenging the sector's unique role in enlarging opportunities for citizen engagement in public decision making (Basok and Ilcan 2004). Early research has shown that a move toward evidence-based policy making shifts the "repertoires of action" for advocacy, as organizations tend to revert to research-based approaches to shape policy decisions, rather than using multiple routes to influence policy (Laforest and Orsini 2005). As evidence becomes the currency of policy making, it also means that policy debates are becoming increasingly technical, insular, and far removed from the average citizen. Agency, the capacity to effect change, to empower members of the community, is therefore constrained by these new power dynamics that do not allow for confrontational and disruptive strategies.

We should also be wary of the superficial nature of the existing ties between organizations working together within coalitions. Non-profit organizations are central institutions for the transmission of unmet community needs and emerging trends into public policy. They help citizens articulate their interests, claims, and demands for the political system. Putnam (2000) and Skocpol (2003) have both raised the issue of eroding ties between non-profit organizations and citizens. If coalitions come to serve as the main vehicles for advocacy claims within civil society, then how sustainable can they be over time if they rely on weak ties to connect the voices of citizens with advocacy channels? Moreover, the greater recourse to coalitions and the effect of the mainstreaming of organizational practice may be problematic, specifically for marginalized groups. As coalition size increases and membership diversifies, it may be harder for smaller communities and more marginalized groups to have a say in policy – even via coalitions (DeSantis 2010; Frisken and Wallace 2003; Stasiulis, Hughes, and Amery 2011). Rather than multiplying spaces for agency and empowerment, these spaces can, in effect, be limiting.

Reversing the current chilly advocacy climate will be one of the most central issues facing non-profit organizations in the future. Some progress has already been made under the newly elected Liberal federal government. However, it will take time before non-profit organizations adapt their internal practices. The non-profit sector will have to face these issues in a context where governments, provincial and federal, as well as the general public remain sceptical of the role of "special interest groups" in policy making. Moreover, provincial governments and the federal government may be reluctant to open up political space to their critics in a context where they themselves are subject to intense scrutiny and greater demands for accountability. Nevertheless, the non-profit sector needs to find a way to communicate with government, and with its members, how important and valuable advocacy is to the policy process and to analysis. If governments continue to discredit advocacy, the implications for our democratic systems, as we have seen, will be significant.

REFERENCES

Acheson, N., and R. Laforest. 2013. "The Expendables: Community Organizations and Governance Dynamics in the Canadian Settlement Sector." *Canadian Journal of Political Science* 46 (3): 597–616. http://dx.doi.org/10.1017/S0008423913000450.

Advocacy Institute. 2004. *What Is 'Advocacy'?* Washington, DC. Retrieved 03/2004, from www.advocacy.org.

Basok, T., and S. Ilcan. 2004. "The Voluntary Sector and the Depoliticization of Civil Society: Implications for Social Justice." *International Journal of Canadian Studies* 28:113–31.

Berger, P., and R. Neuhaus. 1977. *To Empower People*. Washington, DC: American Enterprise Institute.

Berry, J.M., and A.F. Arons. 2003. *A Voice for Nonprofits*. Washington, DC: Brookings Institution Press.

Boris, E., and R. Mosher-Williams. 1998. "Nonprofit Advocacy Organizations: Assessing the Definitions, Classifications, and Data."

*Nonprofit and Voluntary Sector Quarterly* 27 (4): 488–506. http://dx.doi.org/10.1177/0899764098274006.

Brown, L., and E. Troutt. 2004. "Funding Relations Between Nonprofits and Government: A Positive Example." *Nonprofit and Voluntary Sector Quarterly* 33 (1): 5–27. http://dx.doi.org/10.1177/0899764003260601.

Chaves, M., L. Stephens, and J. Galaskiewicz. 2004. "Does Government Funding Suppress Nonprofits' Political Activity?" *American Sociological Review* 69 (2): 292–316. http://dx.doi.org/10.1177/000312240406900207.

Child, C.D., and K.A. Gronbjerg. 2007. "Nonprofit Advocacy Organizations: Their Characteristics and Activities." *Social Science Quarterly* 88 (1): 259–81. http://dx.doi.org/10.1111/j.1540-6237.2007.00457.x.

DeSantis, G. 2010. "Voices from the Margins: Policy Advocacy and Marginalized Communities." *Canadian Journal of Nonprofit and Social Economy Research* 1 (1): 23–45.

Frisken, F., and M. Wallace. 2003. "Governing the Multicultural City-Region." *Canadian Public Administration* 46 (2): 153–77. http://dx.doi.org/10.1111/j.1754-7121.2003.tb00910.x.

Frumkin, P. 2002. *On Being Nonprofit: A Conceptual and Policy Primer*. Cambridge, MA: Harvard University Press. http://dx.doi.org/10.4159/9780674037403.

Government of Canada/Voluntary Sector Joint Initiative. 1999. *Working Together: Report of the Joint Tables*. Ottawa: PCO.

Hojnacki, M. 1997. "Interest Groups' Decisions to Join Alliances or Work Alone." *American Journal of Political Science* 41 (1): 61–87. http://dx.doi.org/10.2307/2111709.

Imagine Canada. 2010. *Sector Monitor* 1(1). http://www.imaginecanada.ca/files/www/en/sectormonitor/sectormonitor_vol1_no1_2010.pdf.

Jenkins, C. 2006. "Nonprofit Organizations and Political Advocacy." In *The Nonprofit Sector: A Research Handbook*, 2nd ed., edited by W.W. Powell, 307–32. New Haven, CT: Yale University Press.

Jenson, J., and S.D. Phillips. 1996. "Regime Shift: New Citizenship Practices in Canada." *International Journal of Canadian Studies* 14:11–36.

Katz, M. 2001. *The Price of Citizenship: Redefining the American Welfare State*. New York: Metropolitan Books, Henry Holt & Co.

Kimberlin, S.E. 2010. "Advocacy by Nonprofits: Roles and Practices of Core Advocacy Organizations and Direct Service Agencies." *Journal of Policy Practice* 9 (3–4): 164–82. http://dx.doi.org/10.1080/15588742.2010.487249.

Kirby, G. 2014. *Is It Getting Chilly?: How are Changes in Federal Governing Charities, and the Changing Political Climate, Impacting Advocacy-oriented Canadian Charities?* Master's thesis, Royal Roads University, Canada.

Laforest, R. 2011. *Voluntary Sector Organizations and the State.* Vancouver: UBC Press.

Laforest, R. 2012. "Rerouting Political Representation: Canada's Social Infrastructure Crisis." *British Journal of Canadian Studies* 25 (2): 181–97. http://dx.doi.org/10.3828/bjcs.2012.10.

Laforest, R., and M. Orsini. 2005. "Evidence Based Engagement in the Voluntary Sector: Lessons from Canada." *Social Policy and Administration* 39 (5): 481–97. http://dx.doi.org/10.1111/j.1467-9515.2005.00451.x.

Levasseur, K. 2012. "In the Name of Charity: Institutional Support and Resistance for Redefining the Meaning of Charity in Canada." *Canadian Public Administration* 55 (2): 181–202. http://dx.doi.org/10.1111/j.1754-7121.2012.00214.x.

Marquardt, R. 2007/2008. "The Progressive Potential of Local Social Policy Activism." *Canadian Review of Social Policy* 60/61:21–38.

Mosley, J. 2011. "From Skid Row to the Statehouse: How Nonprofit Homeless Service Providers Overcome Barriers to Policy Advocacy Involvement." Paper presented at the conference Nonprofits and Advocacy, Georgetown University, March.

Pal, L.A. 1993. *Interests of State: The Politics of Language, Multiculturalism and Feminism in Canada.* Montreal: McGill-Queen's University Press.

Phillips, S.D. 2009. "Canada's 'New Government' and the Voluntary Sector: Whither a Policy Agenda." In *The New Federal Policy Agenda and the Voluntary Sector*, edited by R. Laforest, 7–34. Montreal, Kingston: McGill-Queen's University Press.

Phillips, S.D., R. Laforest, and A. Graham. 2010. "From Shopping to Social Innovation: Getting Public Financing Right in Canada." *Policy and Society* 29 (3): 189–99. http://dx.doi.org/10.1016/j.polsoc.2010.06.001.

Phillips, S.D., and K. Levasseur. 2004. "The Snakes and Ladders of Accountability: Contradictions between Contracting and Collaboration for Canada's Voluntary Sector." *Canadian Public Administration* 47 (4): 451–74. http://dx.doi.org/10.1111/j.1754-7121.2004.tb01188.x.

Putnam, R. 2000. *Bowling Alone: The Collapse and Revival of American Community.* New York: Simon and Schuster. http://dx.doi.org/10.1145/358916.361990.

Reid, E. 2000. "Understanding the Word 'Advocacy': Context and Use." In *Structuring the Inquiry into Advocacy. Nonprofit Advocacy and the Policy Process: A Seminar Series*, vol. 1, edited by E. Reid.

Richmond, T. 2004. *Promoting Newcomer Civic Engagement: The Role of Umbrella Organizations in Social Citizenship*. Available at: http://laidlawfdn.org. (Accessed September 23, 2013).

Salamon, L. 1995. *Partners in Public Service: Government-Nonprofit Relations in the Modern Welfare State*. Baltimore: Johns Hopkins University Press.

Scott, K. 2003. *Funding Matters: The Impact of Canada's New Funding Regime on Nonprofit and Voluntary Sector Organizations*. Ottawa: Canadian Council on Social Development in partnership with the Coalition of National Voluntary Sector Organizations.

Shapcott, M. 2009. "Housing." In *Social Determinants of Health: Canadian Perspectives*, edited by D. Raphael, 222–34. Toronto: Canadian Scholars Press.

Shields, J. 2013. *Nonprofit Engagement with Provincial Policy Officials: The Case of Canadian Immigrant Settlement Services*. Paper presented to the 1st international conference on public policy, Grenoble.

Skocpol, T. 2003. *Diminished Democracy: From Membership to Management in American Civil Life*. Norman, OK: University of Oklahoma Press.

Smith, S.R., and M. Lipsky. 1993. *Nonprofits for Hire: the Welfare State in the Age of Contracting*. Cambridge, MA: Harvard University Press.

Smith, S.R., and R. Pekkanen. 2012. "Revisiting Advocacy by Non-profit Organisations." *Voluntary Sector Review* 3 (1): 35–49. http://dx.doi.org/10.1332/204080512X632719.

Stasiulis, D., C. Hughes, and Z. Amery. 2011. "From Government to Multi-level Governance of Immigrant Settlement in Ontario's Cities." In *Immigrant Settlement Policy in Canadian Municipalities*, edited by E. Tolley, 73–147. McGill-Queen's University Press.

Weisner, S. 1983. "Fighting Back: A Critical Analysis of Coalition Building in the Human Services." *Social Service Review* 57 (2): 291–306. http://dx.doi.org/10.1086/644518.

Wolff, T. 2001. "A Practitioner's Guide to Successful Coalitions." *American Journal of Community Psychology* 29 (2): 173–91. http://dx.doi.org/10.1023/A:1010366310857.

Zakocs, R.C., and E.M. Edwards. 2006. "What Explains Community Coalition Effectiveness?: A Review of the Literature." *American Journal of Preventive Medicine* 30 (4): 351–61. http://dx.doi.org/10.1016/j.amepre.2005.12.004.

# 4

# The Changing Face of the Non-profit Sector: Social Enterprise Legislation in British Columbia

CAROL LIAO

### INTRODUCTION

The non-profit sector in Canada has had a long and storied tradition of participating in public policy advocacy that has been directed at marginalized societal issues, including efforts to enhance community development and improve the common good. Non-profit organizations (NPOs) and charities gain special knowledge in their engagement with the communities that they seek to serve, becoming experts in specific societal issues, thereby adding a critical voice in the policy-making process. The relationship between the non-profit sector and policy-makers can be mutually beneficial and go a long way in promoting social justice and the public good, but this relationship rests on tenuous ground given the number of challenges these organizations face every day. NPOs and charities are under enormous pressure to maintain their funding and influence. The sector gets the bulk of its money through governmental, corporate, and other types of donations, and has difficulty growing once funding sources are tapped. The considerable strain put upon these organizations has led many within the sector to rethink their business plans to survive and maintain their influence as advocates for social change.

Unlike the other chapters in this collection, which offer case studies on advocacy efforts, this chapter provides the opportunity to think about how to influence the advocacy work of the sector in the future. Current legislative shifts in corporate and non-profit law are paving the way for the creation of "hybrid" organizations – those that embrace both for-profit and non-profit characteristics.

The last decade has seen a growing awareness of the "social enterprise" – a term with no legal force in Canada that commonly refers to either a for-profit company trying to do social good or an enterprising NPO/charity. Many organizations are incorporating for-profit subsidiaries, and finding other creative and at times legally questionable ways to get around laws that hamper their abilities to use the engine of the market to enhance the greater public good. Because social enterprises are not falling within the set boundaries of the for-profit and non-profit sectors, legislators are being persuaded to create alternative corporate entities to meet growing demands from entrepreneurs and activists seeking legal infrastructure to house their social businesses. Legislation for new hybrid organizations represents yet another dimension of the shifting advocacy terrain in Canada.

As more Canadian NPOs, charities, and for-profit companies express the desire to pursue both social justice and economic value in their mandates, policy-makers and legislators have struggled to keep up with the pace of innovation. This chapter explores the changing face of the non-profit landscape in Canada, specifically how legal changes in British Columbia mark the possible beginning of Canada's participation in the international trend of emerging new hybrid legal structures that embody both social justice and business components. This chapter is divided into four sections. The first section will discuss the non-profit dilemma that is forcing many NPOs and charities to explore new funding sources so they can deliver public benefit services while maintaining a strong advocacy voice. The second section examines the growth of social enterprises and the global emergence of "hybrid" corporations – legal entities that are intended to enable businesses to pursue both economic and public benefit mandates. The third section examines the 2013 lead-up to and final implementation of social enterprise legislation in BC, including an assessment of the United Kingdom legislation on which the BC community contribution company is almost wholly-based. The fourth section considers the ripple effects of the emergence of hybrids – what do these changes mean for the sector and public policy advocacy going forward? Critics may argue that hybrids only further the neoliberal agenda underpinning a market economy. The final section surmises whether new hybrid innovations signal an evolution in the for-profit and non-profit dichotomy, and pinpoints areas in need of greater research, as well as significant risks that policy-makers, legislators, and public benefit advocates should be aware of in the next critical stages of hybrid development.

## THE NON-PROFIT DILEMMA

Despite the significant role NPOs and charities play in our communities and in the Canadian economy, the sector is subject to a number of challenges that affect its future vitality. It stands to reason that an NPO or charity cannot be effective in its advocacy if it is struggling to find funding to keep its doors open (see chapter 11). Registered charities have inherent limitations since, unlike NPOs, they are prohibited from engaging in "political activities" under ss. 149.1(6.1) and 149.1(6.2) of the Income Tax Act (Canada) (ITA). The interpretation of "political activities" has historically been a considerable source of tension. In 2003 it led to the issuance of Policy Statement CPS-022 from the Canada Revenue Agency (CRA) detailing the differences between political and charitable activities, with further updates in 2012. NPOs, on the other hand, are subject to s. 149(1)(l) of the ITA, which requires them to be exclusively for "social welfare, civic improvement, pleasure, recreation, or any other purpose except profit." NPOs are not, however, prohibited from engaging in "incidental" or "ancillary" business activities, which means that a non-profit can only make a profit if it is by accident. In 2012, the CRA issued two technical interpretations, CRA doc. no. 2012-0454251E5 and 2012-0468581E5, which were in line with a more restrictive position on revenue generation. They stated that any NPO or charity carrying on a business activity with the intent of making a profit beyond what is ancillary or incidental, or anything other than on a cost-recovery basis, would result in disqualifying an organization's net profits from tax exemption. Followed strictly, this rule means there would be little to no growth in capital to reinvest into the organization.

The plight of the sector is well-documented. The National Survey of Nonprofit and Voluntary Organizations (NSNVO) emphasized a collective problem that was already all too evident to those in the non-profit sector: "substantial difficulties in obtaining the appropriate financial and human resources needed to deliver their programs and services to Canadians" (Hall et al. 2003, vii). In the NSNVO survey, 66 per cent of BC organizations that received external funding cited problems with reductions in government support. Sixty-two per cent noted that external funders were unwilling to support core operations. The proportion of BC organizations that found reductions in governmental funding to be a "serious problem" was 8 per cent higher than the national average, 44 per cent compared with 36 per cent nationally (Murray 2006, 34). On average, governments provide 49 per cent of organizations' funds, while 35 per cent of reported revenue is earned income from non-government sources, membership fees, and sales of goods and services, and 13 per cent from gifts and donations from individuals, corporations, and other organizations (Hall et al. 2004, 23). Organizations noted that a number of external factors such as "the impact of government downloading and cutbacks in government funding, a greater emphasis on project funding instead of core funding, increasing competition for scarce resources, and mandated collaborations with other organizations" were significant challenges to non-profits maintaining financial viability (47). In particular, having a greater proportion of funding directed at specific projects influenced how organizations addressed their advocacy work. Canadian organizations surveyed in the Johns Hopkins Comparative Nonprofit Sector Project (CNP) reported that government funding has become "more short-term, more competitive, and less predictable" with little funding available to support overall organizational capacity (Hall et al. 2005, v). The NSNVO report stated that, "although the need for more money was often identified, organizations more frequently expressed a need for 'better money'":

> For participants, better money meant stable, longer-term funding that helps organizations plan and pay for core operating expenses, and gives them the autonomy to direct their services and programs to where they are most needed ... [F]unding is being increasingly restricted to direct program costs, making it difficult for organizations to pay for infrastructure, administration, and other organizational supports that they need to implement programs. (Hall et al. 2003, viii)

Many organizations also reported that funding is often accompanied by onerous demands for financial accountability, causing significant labour costs to be taken away from day-to-day operations and putting them under considerable strain.

The number of volunteers, donors, and monetary donations in Canada is declining (Hall et al. 2005, v). The latest Satellite Account found that while income in the sector increased that year, the pace of the increase was slower than in previous years (Statistics Canada 2009). In particular, individual donations decreased by approximately 3 per cent while investment income dropped by 20 per cent. The Johns Hopkins Project found that a major stumbling block in sector development was in the ability to deliver dual economic and social value, noting that "Canada is only beginning to understand how it can make the most of the civil society assets it has created," and posing two key questions: "What social and economic contributions is its nonprofit and voluntary sector best able to provide? And, how can it best be enabled to make these contributions?" (Hall et al. 2005, v). In his 2009 testimony to the House of Commons Standing Committee on Industry, Science, and Technology, Tim Draimin, executive director of the Social Innovation Generation, noted that restrictive tax regulations and capitalization options have become a serious challenge for NPOs and charities seeking access to capital and diversifying sources of operating income, stating "these financial barriers are unnecessary obstacles for a new breed of social entrepreneur[1] that is emerging and limits the potential impact of their innovations. The sector needs the flexibility to explore new forms of social finance."[2]

The non-profit dilemma is, of course, not isolated to Canada. Our southern neighbours have also struggled with the issue. Former American non-profit leader Dan Pallotta, author of the 2008 critically acclaimed book *Uncharitable*, has argued that society's "economic apartheid" of the for-profit and non-profit sectors "undermines our ability to eradicate great problems and, ironically, puts charity at a severe disadvantage to the for-profit sector at every level" (Pallotta 2010). His concerns stem from both legal and economic restraints as well as the cultural restraints that the public has placed on the non-profit sector. Pallotta argues that in five key areas – compensation, risk-taking, long-term vision, advertising, and capital investment – non-profits are stunted because there is a public expectation that every dollar donated should go directly to the needy. The anti-capitalist sentiment that pervades the non-profit sector (and particularly its donees) puts organizations in "a one-legged footrace with a competitor in a Ferrari" (43). Organizations cannot take innovative risks for fear of being wasteful, they cannot adequately purchase advertising over concerns they are being extravagant, they cannot raise capital or provide a financial return (leaving the for-profit sector monopolizing the capital markets), and leaders cannot be paid competitive compensation packages for fear of looking greedy (6). Pallotta argues that "[i]f we allow charity to use free-market practices, we will see an increase in the money being raised, more effective solutions, and a circular reinforcement that will further increase investment in solving the great problems of our time" (46). His argument is urgent and forceful, insisting that the limitations placed on the sector prevent the eradication of a great deal of human suffering, and are therefore immoral. Pallotta's book has been endorsed by several heads of prominent charities and NPOs, and highlights a level of unrest that seems to have been permeating the American non-profit sector for some time. The book offers a curious counterpoint to proponents who resist neoliberalism, since Pallotta and his supporters are arguing that their pursuit of greater public benefit is stunted by their inability to use economically liberalized policies.

Tightening regulations and decreasing financial resources are disheartening for the sector and a major concern is that these challenges directly affect the sector's effectiveness in advocacy. One reporter for Charity Village asks the poignant question, "Are charities apathetic or afraid?," citing several instances in which the Canadian government has increased its scrutiny of the political activities of charities, leaving charities less keen to pursue prominent advocacy roles for fear of jeopardizing their tax exempt status (Yundt 2012) (see also chapter 2). For NPOs and charities in general, dwindling resources have posed significant challenges for infrastructure and day-to-day operations, while increasing project-based funding can redirect goals and place time limits on achieving long-term solutions. It seems critical that organizations seek new and innovative ways to combat these challenges to maintain a strong voice within advocacy processes.

## GROWTH OF SOCIAL ENTERPRISES AND GLOBAL EMERGENCE OF HYBRID LEGAL STRUCTURES

There is considerable disagreement within and among nations as to the definition of "social enterprise." The term has generally been used quite broadly by organizations, which tend to encompass both

(1) enterprising non-profits, which can be considered as NPOs "exploring the development of business activities for the dual purposes of generating revenue and furthering their mission" (Centre for Social Innovation 2014) and (2) for-profit businesses whose primary purpose is the common good.[3] In the United States and the United Kingdom, the emphasis has been to focus on the latter definition as what comprises a social enterprise – NPOs and charities are not usually incorporated into the definition (Social Enterprise UK 2014). On the other hand, Social Enterprise Canada has elected to concentrate on the non-profit sector component, and define social enterprises more narrowly in that respect, calling them "businesses owned by nonprofit organizations that are directly involved in the production and/or selling of goods and services for the blended purpose of generating income and achieving social, cultural, and/or environmental aims" (Social Enterprise Canada 2014). None of the above organizations attempting to define social enterprises are governmental bodies, and indeed, several for-profit companies in Canada have chosen to identify themselves as social enterprises, despite not having an NPO/charity as a controlling shareholder. It is evident that the term is in its early stages, with little regulatory intervention or clarity, and that its usage continues to be treated differently among groups. The past decade has been one of rapid change as social enterprises and supporting organizations have begun to grow at a significant pace. Social Enterprise Canada (2010, 4) has offered four reasons for this: "(1) the general understanding that there are some needs the market will never meet on its own; (2) the opportunity for entrepreneurs to advance mission-related goals; (3) the diminished and changing nature of government funding; and (4) the promise of social enterprise as a vehicle for social innovation." Social enterprises are not fitting within the boundaries of the for-profit/non-profit divide, and many organizations within each sector have struggled to properly identify their dual mandates to funders, investors, and policy-makers. The increased ambiguity between for-profit and non-profit actors has led legislators to, among other things, create new corporate entities in order to address increasing demands for change.

A new generation of alternative legal entities is thus emerging on the global horizon. These corporate structures – called hybrids, blended enterprises, and socially responsible enterprises, among other names – combine traditional for-profit and non-profit legal characteristics in their design to enable businesses to pursue both economic and public benefit mandates. Each contain features that may be particularly attractive for those in either the for-profit or non-profit sectors. Legal entities such as the community interest company in the United Kingdom, and the benefit corporation and low-profit limited liability company in the United States, are alternative models for businesses that wish to have a governing infrastructure to support their public benefit output in addition to profit. Other countries, such as Belgium, Greece, Denmark, Japan, and South Korea, are also in the early stages of developing hybrids.[4] Some of these hybrids have been used extensively in their home nations, others have not. Restrictions on dividends, obligations on directors to consider community interests, and community purpose asset locks are only some of the unique governing features. The conceptual boundaries of the non-profit sector are being tested as hybrid structures become more recognized.

Figure 4.1 is a chart highlighting where current Anglo-American hybrid corporations are placed within existing corporate alternatives. On one end of the spectrum, charities are the most legally restrictive in terms of profit generation as their main purpose is to produce public benefit under certain heads of charity as defined in the ITA and any business activities must be linked and subordinate to the charity's charitable purpose. Charities thus receive the greatest tax advantages and ability to issue donation receipts. On the other end of the spectrum are for-profit corporations, which have a much debated corporate purpose in scholarship, but generally can be regarded as entities pursuing the singular objective of profit-making. Social gains resulting from corporate actions are considered ancillary, subordinate, and/or supporting this singular objective. The hybrids listed below are compared with each other within that spectrum, from the most profit-restrictive to the least profit-restrictive. If the entity only exists within a particular nation, then that nation's flag is shown.

The emergence of hybrid legal structures on the international stage suggests that a unique segment of the non-profit sector is beginning to form, but this assumption has not been tested. Legislators are responding to growing demands by social entrepreneurs, with little assurance as to how these hybrid entities will fare and whether they will bring an influx of private cash into the non-profit sector or alter the tone of public policy advocacy. Hybrids may be a key contributor in establishing critical infrastructure to help solve some of the

Figure 4.1 Anglo-American hybrid legal structures

most pressing social and environmental issues of our time, while lessening the pressure for funding sources within the non-profit sector and increasing the ability to have a voice in advocacy. Research on hybrids has received little scrutiny from scholars to date due to the fact that they are very new institutional phenomena.[5] The next section of this chapter explores the UK community interest company (CIC) (on which the BC model is almost wholly based), the differences between the UK and the BC models, and continued developments in social enterprise legislation in Canada.

## DEVELOPMENT OF NPO-ORIENTED SOCIAL ENTERPRISE LEGISLATION

### UK Community Interest Company

The community interest company was the very first of the new generation of hybrids. Implemented in the UK in 2005, CICs were established to trade goods or services for the community interest. The particular novelty of CICs is that they are able to do what NPOs/charities cannot, to raise equity capital in exchange for shares, thus encouraging the investment of private wealth through share capital into community projects. There is no special tax treatment for this hybrid.

To qualify for CIC status, interested parties must first pass a "community interest test" administered by the CIC Regulator, a public official who has "a continuing monitoring and enforcement role" over CICs (UK Companies Act 2004 s. 27, s. 35, and Schedule 3). An interested party submits a declaration to the CIC regulator that it is not an excluded company engaged in political activity, as well as a "community interest statement" stating that the company will carry on its activities for the benefit of the community and how those activities will create a benefit (UK Companies Act, s. 35(6); CIC Regulations, Reg. 6). There is little doubt that advocacy is welcome, and indeed, can play a central role in the purpose of this model. The CIC regulator may elect not to allow a party to become a CIC if a reasonable person might consider that the activities only benefit the members of a particular body or the employees of a particular employer (CIC Regulations 2005, Reg. 4). The stated community purpose of the CIC becomes a primary focus for CIC directors.

The most noteworthy features in the CIC are its asset lock and dividend cap. The asset lock means that CIC assets and profits are restricted from being either transferred for full fair market value (to ensure the CIC continues to retain the value of the assets transferred), or transferred to another CIC that is subject to an asset lock or a charity, or otherwise made for a community benefit (UK Companies Act, s. 30, 31; CIC Regulations, Part 6). This feature helps to ensure that assets, which are intended for community benefit, remain in that realm. Entrepreneurs interested in establishing a CIC, therefore, need to pay particular attention to this feature because once a business is established as a CIC there are permanent consequences. The dividend cap means that dividends on CIC shares and interest on bonds are limited to ensure that profits are either retained by the CIC or used for a community benefit purpose. Placing a cap on the amount of dividends investors may receive – which is set by the regulator (UK Companies Act, s. 51.94) – purports to ensure that there is an ongoing reasonable balance between the interests of shareholders and the community interest.

CICs also have annual reporting requirements to account for how their hybrid has benefited the community and engaged stakeholders (UK Companies Act, s. 8.1.1). A "stakeholder" is any person, group, or organization that has an interest in or is affected by an organization. Specifically, section 172(1) (a)–(f) of the UK Companies Act states that a director of a company must act in the way he or she, in good faith, considers to be most likely to promote the success of the company for the benefit of its members as a whole, and in doing so has regard to (a) the likely consequences of any long-term decision; (b) the interests of the company's employees; (c) the need to foster the company's business relationships with suppliers, customers and others; (d) the effect of the company's operations on the community and the environment; (e) the desirability for the company to maintain a reputation for high standards of business conduct; and (f) the need to act fairly as between members of the company. Stakeholder interests are prominent in the CIC model. CICs are recommended to form stakeholder advisory groups for the CIC's benefit and each CIC crafts its own individualized stakeholder process. The CIC is required to describe its stakeholder efforts in an annual report, which is placed on a public register at Companies House and reviewed by the CIC regulator, who can reject a CIC's report or require revisions before it is accepted.

The CIC regulator plays a key role in administering and maintaining CICs in the UK. That role is seen as one with "light touch regulation and an emphasis on proportionality" (Regulator of Community Interest Companies 2012, 15). In addition to having the power to investigate complaints, the regulator may also act if a CIC is found to be violating its community purpose or asset lock provisions, change the makeup of the board, or even terminate a CIC when necessary. Along with ensuring that CICs are properly registered and regulated, the regulator also addresses big picture issues. In the CIC 2011/2012 annual report (7), the regulator identified public concerns that CICs were taking away resources and business from the charitable sector, noting fears in these early years of "private sector intrusion into public service delivery." These concerns may be a challenge that will need to be consistently addressed in these nascent years of hybrid development.

Research on the CIC model is limited. Hybrids are faced with attempting to balance financial interests and enforceable rules to integrate social mandates, but frequently each seems to trade off against the other. Legal scholar Brakman Reiser (2010, 654) notes that the CIC form "faces the most serious obstacles to enhancing financing, by virtue of the dividend cap and asset lock ... Yet, the very same ... mechanisms endow the CIC with the staunchest commitments to social good of all the forms." In addition to these mechanisms, shareholders and the CIC regulator have the ability to hold CICs accountable to their dual mandates, making the CIC a particularly unique corporate form.

The CIC tends to be more attractive for those in the non-profit sector, as the legal characteristics of the model may come across as too limiting for many in the for-profit sector. The asset lock and dividend cap disrupts the market for corporate control, and entrepreneurs who envision broader market reach by way of larger corporations acquiring these companies will not clamour for this model. Since a CIC structure allows capital to be raised by issuing shares, it creates economic opportunities that have traditionally been closed to NPOs/charities while also opening the door to economically liberalized principles. A CIC structure may also be more attractive to individuals or groups wanting to start community projects or programs but who have little interest in member-based structures such as those found in a cooperative ownership model.

The number of CICs has doubled in the last two years (to 2013), and its numbers continue to grow. As of June 2014, there were over 9,500 registered CICs (Office of the Regulator 2014), with over 2,000 created in each of 2013 and 2012 (Regulator of Community Interest Companies,

15) and many CICs have survived the three-year mark. In comparison to the cooperative model, sources indicate that as of 2012 there were over 5,933 independent cooperatives in the UK, with a UK cooperative economy at £35.6 billion (approximately CAD$60.2 billion), and approximately 13.5 million members (Co-operatives UK 2014). There are no equivalent statistics available for CICs' monetary contributions to the UK economy, the average size of CICs, or total members. But if it is simply a numbers game, certainly over 9,500 CICs after nine years in existence is impressive.

## BC Community Contribution Company

The surge of CICs in the UK since its beginnings in 2005 caught the attention of Canadian social entrepreneurs and led to several public consultations and inquiries at both the federal and provincial levels, as to whether such a model would be feasible in Canada. In 2009–10, the House of Commons Standing Committee on Industry, Science and Technology conducted a review of the Canada Business Corporations Act (CBCA) (R.S.C., 1985, C.C–44) and explored the issue of special incorporation structures for hybrids. The committee recommended that the government broadly consult with the public within two years as to whether the CBCA should be amended and a separate regulator created to support a special kind of hybrid with both profit-making and non-profit goals, noting that the hybrid could be similar to an American low-profit limited liability company or a UK CIC (Statutory Review 2010, 25). Alternatively, the committee questioned whether such an enterprise could already be created under the existing CBCA.

Likely in reaction to these federal inquiries as well as in response to growing demands from local social enterprises in both the for-profit and non-profit sectors, the BC provincial government created an advisory committee in 2010 to explore the possibility of creating a new hybrid form within the province. Members from these consultations included representatives from several NPOs, including a number of charities, one for-profit corporation – Tyze Personal Networks, Ltd., a self-identified social enterprise that was majority-owned by an NPO – Plan Institute for Caring Citizenship (Tyze),[6] and a small number of lawyers. Following these meetings, in January 2011, the Ministry of Social Development and Social Innovation created the BC Social Innovation Council to make recommendations "on how best to maximize social innovation ... with an emphasis on social finance and social enterprise."[7] Council members were "drawn from government, Aboriginal and community organisations, and business agencies with an interest in social entrepreneurship, including credit unions, foundations, academics, local and/or provincial government, business, investors, social entrepreneurs and innovators" (BC Social Innovation Council 2012, 2). It should be noted that two of Tyze's board members (each of whom were also heavily involved in non-profit work) became members of the council. The council reported that it received feedback from individuals and organizations in the community and the non-profit sector as well as youth, academic, business, and government stakeholders.

In March 2012, the British Columbia government announced the creation of a new hybrid model, the community contribution company (C3). That same month, the council presented eleven action items, one of which stated that the provincial government should complete the work to establish C3s as a new corporate structure. The council noted that the C3 "could have widespread application in BC ranging from environmental service companies to business development platforms for Aboriginal and rural communities" (11). The C3 hybrid was made available to the public in July 2013. The new structure, in combination with the increased development of a social and policy framework to maximize social innovations, gave BC a reputation as "Canada's Social Silicon Valley" (Marcoccia 2013).

Nova Scotia has since followed suit, announcing the adoption of a hybrid similar to the C3 in November 2012 (Nova Scotia Canada 2012). These provincial hybrids are each modelled after the UK CIC: they are designed to allow traditional NPOs/charities the ability to make a profit while keeping their public benefit mandate intact through stringent limitations on how they distribute their capital. The federal government has also begun to consider following this international trend. On 11 December 2013, following up recommendations from the House of Commons Standing Committee, Industry Canada opened a review of some provisions within the CBCA for consultation, including a specific request for comments on adopting a federal version of the BC C3 model (Industry Canada 2013). The comment period for the CBCA public consultation closed on 15 May 2014. As of December 2015 there has been no announcement from Innovation, Sciences and Economic Development Canada on next steps.

The BC C3 hybrid has several noteworthy similarities to the UK CIC, particularly its asset lock, dividend cap, and annual reporting requirements. Like the CIC, the legal characteristics of the C3 make it particularly attractive for those in the non-profit sector – probably a significant number – who need to raise money through share capital rather than traditional funding sources. C3s may appease social investors seeking to ensure that the social purpose of their investment vehicle cannot be removed. The model will allow those previously in the non-profit sector to freely act as social entrepreneurs and use the market as an engine to disseminate goods and services without being restricted from purposely generating a profit, all the while ensuring that social mandates remain intact.

The differences thus far in the BC version of the CIC are mainly administrative. The provincial government indicated at the start of the legislative process that it had no funding to promote the C3 model to the public, or educate the public, something opposite from the substantial rollout produced at the start of the UK CIC. Furthermore, the provincial government has elected not to include the accountability mechanism of a regulator dedicated to the hybrid form, as found in the UK, citing cost concerns. Rather than passing a community interest test with regulatory approval, interested parties can become a C3 through unanimous shareholder approval (BC Business Corporations Act, s. 51.97). A C3 is required to state in its articles of incorporation that it is a C3 "and, as such, has purposes beneficial to society" (BC Business Corporations Act, s. 51.911). This somewhat vague terminology may prove challenging if the C3 were to significantly gain in numbers. Because of the restrictive nature of the asset lock, legislators want to ensure that all shareholders (including non-voting shareholders) are aware of the legal restrictions in the C3 model and approve of them. This requirement is atypical for for-profit corporations, whose usual practice is to require a majority or supermajority of voting shareholders to approve amendments to a company's articles. That means that no minority shareholder can be forced into a C3 model. Table 4.1 outlines some of the key features embodied within the BC C3.

While it is still early in the process for BC, and as of July 2015 only thirty-three C3s had been created, there is a question as to whether the lack of a regulator to monitor C3 compliance will be problematic if the model were to become more widely adopted. The C3 is only required to publish its annual report in the same way that companies are required to publish financial statements and auditors' reports, under the applicable provincial acts for standard corporations (BC

Table 4.1 Features of the BC Community Contribution Company

| Name | Must have in its name either "Community Contribution Company" or the abbreviation "CCC." |
| --- | --- |
| Community purpose | Required to have a community purpose that is beneficial to either the society at large or a segment of the society that is broader than those persons who are related to the C3. Purpose must be set out in its Articles, and its Notice of Articles must contain a specific statement making it clear that it is a C3, and outlining the asset lock and dividend cap restrictions. |
| Board of directors | Minimum of three (3) directors are required. Directors are required to act with a view to the community purposes of the company as set out in its Articles. |
| Asset lock | Restricted from transferring its assets for anything less than fair market value, unless the transfer furthers its community purposes, is to a qualified donee as defined in the ITA, or is to a community service cooperative as defined in the BC Cooperative Associations Act. Transfer of assets to a person that is related to the company is also prohibited. In essence, the idea is that the assets cannot go to an organization that is not otherwise subject to limitations on how its assets may be transferred. |
| Dividend cap | Maximum annual dividend currently set at 40% of profit of the organization according to GAAP principles (plus any portion of the unpaid dividend amount for any previous year). This restriction does not apply to shareholders that are registered charities and other qualified donees as defined in the ITA. There is no cap on bonds (differing from the UK CIC). |
| Reporting requirements | Required to annually publish a Community Contribution Report detailing certain activities including: (1) the total amount of dividends declared on all classes of shares; (2) the identity of shareholders receiving dividends; and (3) remunerations exceeding $75,000. |
| Tax status | No additional tax benefits. Not exempt from income tax and cannot issue income tax receipts for gifts or donations to the C3. |
| Dissolution | 60% of its assets on dissolution must go to another entity under a similar asset lock, such as another C3, or a qualified donee as defined in the ITA, or a community service cooperative as defined in the BC Cooperative Associations Act. |

Business Corporations Act, s. 51.96). It remains to be seen how the BC version will evolve in comparison with the UK CIC, despite having less regulatory infrastructure and governmental oversight, and no official to contact directly. In comparison, the UK CIC regulator's office has three full-time and four part-time staff members, and reported that in 2012 there were over 7,000 emails and 3,000 phone calls to their office (Regulator of Community Interest Companies, 13). C3s are required to adhere to provisions set forth in the BC Business Corporations Act and accompanying regulations, but do not have this same level of support. Some foreseeable risks with having less regulatory infrastructure and governmental oversight include confusion among the public, minimal or improper adherence to regulations, eroded credibility in the model, and a lack of focus on big picture issues.

The above concerns may, however, be non-issues given the slow pace at which the C3 model is being adopted, and some of the regulatory void may be filled by other sources. For example, in anticipation of the C3, the BC Centre for Social Enterprise (2014) provided several free workshops to educate interested parties in the details of the C3 model. Another example is Accelerating Social Impact CCC (2014), a newly formed C3 in BC that assists and advises social impact businesses on a variety of matters, including legal options. Other organizations may also step up. Furthermore, there is nothing preventing the government from establishing more regulatory support down the road if the development of BC C3s becomes as expansive and significant as it has in the UK.

UK CICs have only existed since 2005, and research on the CIC model is limited. In the early years of the UK CIC's development, one scholar noted that the model "assumes [there is] a pool of investors with an appetite for wedding financial and social return and sufficient brand awareness and confidence to appeal to them ... [It also] however, requires these investors to be especially devoted to the blended enterprise concept by substantially limiting the upside of their investments" (Brakman Reiser 2010, 649). While it seems that this has not posed a problem for the UK CIC given its numbers, the note of caution is also warranted for the C3 in these embryonic years of hybrid growth. The growth of impact investing in BC and Nova Scotia suggests that there are social investors who can balance these economic and social interests to sustain the C3 model, and, presumably, legislators would not have pursued hybrid legislation if they had not been assured there was a means to support it, but one can only surmise.

Given how few NPOs used the C3 model in its first year of existence, some explanation seems to be warranted. Some industry leaders have suggested that BC NPOs and charities contemplating a conversion to the C3 form may find the requirement to produce an annual community contribution report costly and onerous. Mason notes that "given the additional flexibility accorded to qualified donees by the legislation, [the Community Contribution Report] would be the most significant difference to using a business corporation for a social enterprise and while certainly providing a 'brand' advantage, it may not provide any significant financial advantage" (2013, 1). The lack of a tax benefit may also cause NPOs/charities to question whether it's worth it to convert – the ability to raise equity capital must outweigh the NPO tax advantage. To date, it seems that BC social entrepreneurs and existing organizations are not finding the C3 model as innovative an alternative as the social entrepreneurs who eagerly adopted the similar model in the UK, but it is unclear if this is a conscious choice or if many BC organizations have simply not heard of it. The UK has promoted, provided public education, and regulated the CIC model effectively, as well as providing early incentives, including an initial pool of social finance to gain a critical mass of early adopters. Similar incentives may be necessary for the C3 model to catch on in BC. The BC government's lack of financial support beyond drafting the legislation may in time be shown to be fundamentally detrimental to C3 development in the province; however, due to a lack of research in the area, speculation as to why there has been little interest in adopting the C3 form is thus far only that – speculation.

With those cautionary notes, it is important to emphasize that the creation of the C3 could be a positive development for Canada. There may be hidden benefits in BC's late start. Canadian legislators and regulators would be wise to translate the eight to nine year lead from the UK CICs into a latecomer advantage and identify where BC can benefit from the UK's experience, such as in determining valuation tools for setting dividend caps, or whether there have been actual tensions between the new CIC form and existing NPOs/charities in the sharing of resources, if at all. As put by Joel Solomon, chair of Vancouver-based Renewal Funds, "The devil is in the details. New models require testing and refinement, along with extra support of early adopters, or they are simply a public relations exercise ... time will tell if it's a symbolic gesture or if there is real commitment to social goods" (Bouw 2013). Further research will be crucial for optimal results in implementing hybrids in Canada – if indeed other provinces follow suit – as well as ongoing support from both corporate and individual leaders in the for-profit and non-profit sectors.

## POTENTIAL RISKS AND BENEFITS FOR PUBLIC POLICY ADVOCACY

As a dynamic and evolving phenomenon, it has still not been determined whether hybrids will have any significant role in the evolution of the non-profit sector in general, and in public policy advocacy specifically. There are potential ripple effects with any new innovation. The intermingling of profit and advocacy may immediately give many within the sector pause – setting aside the fact that business advocacy is already prevalent in the policy-making process. Encroaching onto a traditional non-profit space may prove controversial down the road – and several unforeseen and unforeseeable variables need to be considered.

The current environment suggests that boundaries may be blurring in public policy advocacy. From the private sector, trends in the marketplace and in regulation will likely increase dialogue between the private sector and a multitude of stakeholders. The notable growth of corporate social responsibility in business has led scholars to predict that the sustainability or "Green" movement is becoming an "emerging megatrend" that may soon "force fundamental and persistent shifts in how companies compete" (Lubin and Esty 2010, 2). Public–private dialogue is catching on within the private sector, and whether it is "structured or ad hoc, formal or informal, wide-ranging or focused on specific issues," the process can increase public benefit and significantly contribute to shaping private sector development (Herzberg and Wright 2006, 11). The International Charter of Good Practice in Using Public Private Dialogue for Private Sector Development, established in 2006 with the support of the Department of International Development (DfID), OECD Development Centre, and World Bank, among others, is a valuable guide to the collective expectations of public–private dialogue across multiple stakeholders (Public Private Dialogue 2014). The Charter recognizes that "reforms designed to improve the business climate are more effective when dialogue between the public and private sectors involves the ultimate beneficiaries of those reforms in diagnostics, solution design, implementation and monitoring" (1). Efforts to include the public sector in discussions on private sector development seem to be growing within certain organizations, making the need to establish and maintain a strong voice from the public sector all the more critical.

But how does the non-profit sector fit within this dialogue? Will the growth of public–private dialogue naturally draw participation from NPOs/charities and hybrids, or will it entrench the exclusion of the sector from public policy making? The long-standing scepticism within the sector on the infiltration of business into public policy development, and the underlying promotion of a neoliberal agenda, suggests that some may meet hybrids with great resistance. While hybrids may further advocate for healthier public policy, their social entrepreneurship may also distract others from engaging in social advocacy. The effect on public-sector decision-making from private sector lobbying is already heavily lopsided in the private sector's favour, and hybrids, by design, have features that reflect that sector. Given that NPOs and charities are already struggling to be heard, some may argue that there is a real risk that implementing hybrids will only further dampen these voices. The issue is complex and messy – it seems fitting to strive for public-private–non-profit dialogue to increase public benefit while shaping the development of each sector, but internal and external power dynamics, financial pressures, and other socio-economic factors cannot be ignored. Depending on the circumstances, the prescription for a tripartite dialogue may not always be warranted or worthwhile, but the concern lies in how to ensure that those in a less powerful economic or political position are not marginalized and can retain a meaningful voice in the dialogue.

The overarching issue that is transforming the NPO/charity landscape is power, and who holds it. While the BC C3 is one model that seems to be geared toward those in the non-profit sector, other hybrids are addressing those in the for-profit sector. Some of these hybrids – such as the benefit corporation in the United States – have all the same economic liberties as for-profit corporations. Joel Bakan, in a speech at the Canadian Centre for Policy Alternatives, has spoken passionately about "reclaiming the public sector" and not allowing the private sector to dictate needs within the public sphere. While Bakan's disdain for corporate social responsibility as a whole begs for some disagreement given the significant environmental improvements that have come from the sustainability movement, he certainly has legitimate concerns about the increased private intrusion into the public sector, and what that means for a democratic society (2013). Who is involved in deciding what kind of society we want to live in? The ability of large corporations to marshal their power means voices from smaller organizations and everyday citizens are easily drowned out. Therefore, the converse argument for those in the non-profit sector who are pushing back on hybrid development is that they need to quickly innovate to combat corporate power in the public policy arena. The unanswered question as to whether hybrids will (1) become a positive development that paves the way for increased NPO/charity involvement in public policy advocacy; (2) be irrelevant; or (3) dampen existing sector voices and do more harm than good, is frustrating during these early years of hybrid growth, both within BC, across Canada, and globally.

For now, it seems that the C3 model in BC is more at risk of simply becoming irrelevant to the discussion – thirty-three reported C3s do not a movement make. There is, unfortunately, a precedent for unused – and therefore irrelevant – hybrid models. Another BC hybrid, which seems virtually unknown, the community service cooperative,[8] has only twelve registered entities since it was created in 2007. Whether or not C3s will be headed in the same direction is yet to be determined. The likelihood that there will be changes to the status quo in advocacy processes due to hybrid development seems low at this stage in BC's non-profit sector history. However, the intensity with which hybrids are emerging on a global scale and how hybrids may be more positively received in public policy advocacy because they fit within the overarching goals of neoliberalism (such as privatization and less government spending), means that the potential for hybrids to change the future dynamic of advocacy in the provinces and Canada cannot be discounted, although it will be continuously questioned.

## NPOS AND CHARITIES REPURPOSED AND REIMAGINED

It is critical to consider the potential risks associated with the onslaught of hybrids, but the risks in maintaining the status quo should be equally considered, as well as the potential upside that may be realized from this global trend. It is quite understandable that most scholars regard the development of hybrids as simply addressing a niche sector of the market – it is highly probable that hybrids will operate more as a small supplement to the common NPOs and charities rather than as one that may one day overtake the sector. On the other hand, the global hybrid phenomenon is serving as a live experiment putting ongoing research to the test by telling business leaders that long-term vision, sustainable purposes, and multi-stakeholder collaboration are essential for the long-term success of the firm (Barton and Wiseman 2013; Eccles, et al. 2011). Hybrids are providing opportunities for entrepreneurs seeking to affirm that "the independence of social value and commercial revenue creation is a myth" (Battilana et al. 2012, 52).

Investors in hybrids will be made aware of the social mandates embodied within these entities and the particular legal limitations of the financial upsides, if any, meaning that hybrid investors will be, by nature, social investors. While charities have advocacy limitations under the CRA, they also have significant tax benefits. NPOs in general may well have certain tax advantages. C3s, on the other hand, have no tax benefits because they are treated under the CRA as though they are for-profit corporations. They have no advocacy restrictions other than they must have a community benefit and not be a statutorily excluded company engaged in political activity. Many UK CICs, for example, are created with social advocacy in their mandate. There is therefore no reason for C3 hybrids to limit their engagement in advocacy – indeed it can play a central role, providing a positive aspect for public policy advocacy in Canada. This approach is different from recent history wherein "advocacy chill" was pervasive and heavily documented in both scholarly and community literature (DeSantis 2010, 26). Considering this, NPOs and charities contemplating the future structure of their organizations to maximize their potential impact on public policy advocacy may want to seriously consider the C3 option.

In summary, many potential issues arise within any jurisdiction that introduces a new hybrid into the roster of alternatives. Hybrids may funnel away resources traditionally used by charities and NPOs, such as corporate donations (Regulator of Community Interest Companies, 7). There is the risk that mainstream corporations may feel they have little obligation to consider marginalized societal issues (e.g., social or environmental issues), now supposedly left for hybrids and NPOs/charities to address. Some corporations may already hold the view that social and environmental concerns should be resolved solely by the public sector and the non-profit sector, among other reasons. Regulators may also hold similar views. Hybrids may end up satisfying a niche market that, once saturated, is ineffectual in promoting any significant social change. There is considerable ambiguity about how to measure the community benefit of hybrids, which may prove to be advantageous to entrepreneurs but detrimental to overall public benefit. Others may argue that corporations have no place in addressing social needs in the first place – profit motivations may skew intentions, bolstering a neoliberal agenda rather than a search for the common good. The discussions that are just beginning to take shape among industry leaders and scholars about the hybrid phenomenon are multifaceted, nuanced, and oftentimes based, in these early years, more on conjecture than on probative empirical research.

Nevertheless, hybrids on an international scale are beginning to fill a driving legal need to house social purpose businesses and enterprises. Collaborative efforts among legislators and those in both the for-profit and non-profit sectors must examine the environment and design hybrids that significantly differentiate them from other alternatives, consider whether new hybrids can provide meaningful legal features to ensure dual economic and public benefit mandates, and also meet the particular needs of social entrepreneurs to make the model attractive. With proper strategic implementation, hybrids may become the new legal tool that fosters the growth of social innovation within the non-profit sector. In addition to the models that have been described in this chapter, there is considerable space for nations to contemplate establishing new yet-to-be-seen forms of hybrid structures to better address growing demands from both the for-profit and non-profit sectors. Such ideas for innovative new models are already being circulated (Dudek and Zieba 2012).

There is untapped potential in the strategic implementation of hybrids within a nation's NPO/charity landscape. While there is the potential that hybrid development may empower traditional NPOs and give them a stronger voice in the advocacy process, there are several big picture issues that need to be addressed in future research, including:

- how these hybrids are situated within local and global social economies;
- how they are balanced alongside other existing legal options;
- how they are to be treated as subsidiaries in corporate groups;
- whether and why they gain any traction in corporate practice;

- whether the existence of certain hybrids takes away from resources needed elsewhere or if instead they create a new source of private cash for the non-profit sector and
- whether tax and other laws should be adjusted to accommodate these models, and if so, how?

All these factors play roles in how hybrids will affect the future of advocacy. Further research in these areas is essential.

The next few decades will be telling as to the success or failure of hybrid legal structures, whether they gain any footing from players currently in the non-profit sector, and what their effects will be on public policy advocacy, if any. Paul Martin, Canada's former prime minister, commenting on the increase in social enterprises, noted: "Government policy hasn't caught up ... I think Canada is ready for it. I think Canada is looking for it" (Wingrove 2010). Hybrids are beginning to play an important role in challenging the non-profit model and forcing legislators to contemplate the legal limitations within that model – and indeed, hybrids may be integral in growing the sector and significantly enhancing its advocacy role in the policy-making process. The potential for hybrids to come up with solutions to some of the nation's most pressing social and environmental issues cannot be discounted.

## NOTES

1 "Social entrepreneur" is a term that is increasingly being used within both the for-profit and non-profit sectors. Gregory Dees (2001, 4) has taken concepts from Jean-Baptiste Say, Joseph Schumpeter, Peter Drucker, and Howard Stevenson to provide an "idealized" definition of the term, describing social entrepreneurs as change agents in the social sector that: (1) adopt a mission to create and sustain social value (not just private value); (2) recognize and relentlessly pursue new opportunities to serve that mission; (3) engage in a process of continuous innovation, adaptation, and learning; (4) act boldly without being limited by resources currently in hand; and (5) exhibit heightened accountability to the constituencies served and for the outcomes created, while recognizing that social entrepreneurs will exemplify these characteristics "in different ways and to different degrees."
2 Testimony of Tim Draimin, Social Innovation Generation, to the Standing House of Commons Committee on Industry, Science and

Technology, Meeting No. 43, 40th Parliament, 2nd Session, 16 November 2009, at 15:40. Employment and Social Development Canada defines "social finance" as "an approach to mobilizing private capital that delivers a social dividend and an economic return to achieve social and environmental goals. It creates opportunities for investors to finance projects that benefit society and for community organizations to access new sources of funds." Employment and Social Development Canada, "Social Finance," accessed 28 August 2014, http://www.esdc.gc.ca/eng/consultations/social_finance/index.shtml.

3 The Social Enterprise Alliance suggests the following basic working definition of a social enterprise: "an organization or initiative that marries the social mission of a non-profit or government program with the market-driven approach of a business." Social Enterprise Alliance, "What is a Social Enterprise?," accessed 28 August 2014, https://socialenterprise.us/about/social-enterprise/.

4 For more on Belgium, Greece, and Denmark, see Tineke Lambooy and Aikaterini Argyrou, "Improving the EU Legal Environment to Enable and Stimulate Social Entrepreneurship as a New Economic Structure" *European Company Law* (April 2014) 11, vol. 2: 70–5. Japan and South Korea have indicated an interest in the UK CIC; Regulator of Community Interest Companies, "Annual Report 2012/2013," accessed 28 August 2014, https://www.gov.uk/government/uploads/system/uploads/attachment_data/file/243869/13-p117-community-interest-companies-annual-report-2012-2013.pdf.

5 Of the few scholarly articles addressing hybrids, a significant majority are listed within this chapter. See e.g., Battilana et al., 2012; Brakman Reiser, 2010 (who has also authored several articles on "blended enterprises"); Lambooy and Argyrou, 2014, etc.

6 The author of this article attended the meeting as a representative of Tyze. Discussions from the meeting are bound by confidentiality agreements.

7 "Social innovation" is described by the BC Social Innovation Council as "a means to achieve better results, deliver more effective solutions and to lower the human and financial costs of our social and environmental problems" (3).

8 The BC government describes the community service co-operative as follows: "an association that must include in its memorandum: (1) a provision that the association is a community service cooperative; (2) that the association does not authorize the issuance of investment shares; and, (3) that the purpose of the association is a charitable

purpose or is otherwise to provide health, social, educational or other community services." BC Registry Services, "What Is a Community Service Cooperative," accessed 28 August 2014, http://www.bcregistryservices.gov.bc.ca/bcreg/corppg/coop-faq.page.

REFERENCES

Accelerating Social Impact CCC. Accessed 28 August 2014. http://asiccc.ca.

Bakan, J. 2013. "What's Left? Reclaiming the Public Sphere." Speech to the Canadian Centre for Policy Alternatives, 13 March. Accessed 28 August 2014. https://www.youtube.com/watch?v=yRdPVSbcqmQ (Part 1) and https://www.youtube.com/watch?v=BNDxcI_loyw (Part 2).

Barton, D., and M. Wiseman. 2013. "Focusing Capital on the Long Term," Address to the Institute of Corporate Directors, 22 May. Accessed 28 August 2014. http://www.cppib.ca.

Battilana, J., M. Lee, J. Walker, C. Dorsey. 2012. "In Search of the Hybrid Ideal." *Stanford Social Innovation Review* 51–5:52.

BC *Business Corporations Act* [SBC 2002], C 57.

BC Centre for Social Enterprise. "Community Contribution Companies Are Coming." Accessed 28 August 2014. http://www.centreforsocialenterprise.com/community-contribution-companies/.

BC Social Innovation Council. 2012. "Action Plan Recommendations to Maximize Social Innovation in Canada." Accessed 28 August 2014. http://tamarackcci.ca/files/social-innovationbc_action_plan.pdf.

Bouw, B. 2013. "B.C.'s New Business Model Makes It Easier to Make Money and Give Back," *The Globe and Mail*, 9 August.

Brakman Reiser, D. 2010. "Governing and Financing Blended Enterprise." *Chicago-Kent Law Review* 85:619-655.

Centre for Social Innovation. "Enterprising Non-Profits Toronto." Accessed 28 August 2014. http://socialinnovation.ca/enp.

Community Interest Company Regulations 2005, SI 2005/1788 [CIC Regulations].

Co-operatives UK, "About Co-operatives." Accessed 28 August 2014. www.uk.coop/co-operatives.

Dees, G.J. 2001. "The Meaning of Social Entrepreneurship." Accessed 28 August 2014. Center for ASE at Duke, http://www.caseatduke.org/documents/dees_sedef.pdf.

Department of International Development, the World Bank, the IFC and OECD Development Centre, "Charter of Good Practice in using Public

Private Dialogue for Private Sector Development." Accessed 28 August 2014. www.publicprivatedialogue.org/charter/.

DeSantis, G.C. 2010. "Voices from the Margins: Policy Advocacy and Marginalized Communities." *ANSERJ Canadian Journal of Nonprofit and Social Economy Research* 1:23–45.

Dudek, J., and A. Zieba. 2012. "The Deliberate Corporation: Moving Beyond Social Business." Accessed 28 August 2014. http://www.truevaluemetrics.org/DBpdfs/Initiatives/DeliberateEconomics/The-Deliberate-Corporation-by-Deliberate-Economics-May-2012.pdf.

Eccles, R.G., I. Ioannou, and G. Serafeim. 2011. "The Impact of a Corporate Culture of Sustainability on Corporate Behavior and Performance." Harvard Business School Working Paper No 12–035. http://dx.doi.org/10.2139/ssrn.1964011.

Hall, M.H., A. Andrukow, C. Barr, K. Brock, M. de Wit, D. Embuldeniya, L. Jolin, D. Lasby, B. Lévesque, E. Malinsky, et al. 2003. *Capacity to Serve: A Qualitative Study of the Challenges Facing Canada's Nonprofit and Voluntary Organizations*. Canadian Centre for Philanthropy. ISBN 1-55401-054-3., vii.

Hall, M.H., C.W. Barr, M. Easwaramoorthy, S. Wojciech Sokolowski, and L.M. Salamon. 2005. *The Canadian Non-Profit and Voluntary Sector in Comparative Perspective. Johns Hopkins Comparative Nonprofit Sector Project*. Ottawa: Imagine Canada.

Hall, M.H., M.L. de Wit, D. Lasby, et al. 2004. "Cornerstones of Community: Highlights from the National Survey of Nonprofit and Voluntary Organizations." Ottawa: Minister of Industry. Statistics Canada catalogue no. 61-533-XPE, 23.

Herzberg, B. and M. Wright. 2006. "The Public-Private Dialogue Handbook: A Toolkit for Business Environment Reformers."

Industry Canada. 2013. "Consultation on the *Canada Business Corporations Act*." Accessed 28 August 2014. www.ic.gc.ca/eic/site/cilp-pdci.nsf/eng/h_cl00867.html.

Lambooy T., and A. Argyrou. 2014. "Improving the EU Legal Environment to Enable and Stimulate Social Entrepreneurship as a New Economic Structure." *European Company Law* 11 (2):70–5.

Lubin, D.A., and D.C. Esty. 2010. "The Sustainability Imperative." *Harvard Business Review* 88(5):2.

Marcoccia, P. 2013. "Innovation Gathering in Canada's 'Social Silicon Valley'" *Axiom News*, 21 November. Accessed 28 August 2014. www.urbanmatters.org.

Mason, M. 2013. "British Columbia's Innovation: Community Contribution Companies" Charity Talk: Newsletter of the National Charities and Not-for-Profit Law Section of the Canadian Bar Association.

Murray, V. 2006. *The Nonprofit and Voluntary Sector of British Columbia: Regional Highlights from the National Survey of Nonprofit and Voluntary Organizations*. Imagine Canada.

Nova Scotia Canada, Service Nova Scotia and Municipal Relations. 2012. "New Opportunities for Social Entrepreneurs," 28 November. Accessed 28 August 2014. http://novascotia.ca/news/release/?id=20121128010.

Office of the Regulator of Community Interest Companies. 2014. Twitter @cicAssociation, tweet on 30 June 2014.

Pallotta, D. 2010. *Uncharitable: How Restraints on Non-Profits Undermines Our Potential*. London: Tufts University Press.

Public Private Dialogue. "Charter of Good Practice in using Public Private Dialogue for Private Sector Development." Accessed 28 August 2014. www.publicprivatedialogue.org/charter/.

Regulator of Community Interest Companies. 2012. "Annual Report 2011/2012." Accessed 28 August 2014. https://www.gov.uk/government/uploads/system/uploads/attachment_data/file/215265/12-p117-community-interest-companies-annual-report-2011-2012.pdf.

Statistics Canada. 2009. "Satellite Account of Non-profit Institutions and Volunteering." Catalogue No. 13-015-XIE. Ottawa, Ontario.

Social Enterprise Canada. 2010. *The Canadian Social Enterprise Guide*, 2nd ed. Accessed on 28 August 2014. www.socialenterprisecanada.ca.

Social Enterprise Canada. "What is a Social Enterprise?" Accessed 28 August 2014. www.socialenterprisecanada.ca.

Social Enterprise UK. "What are Social Enterprises?" Accessed 28 August 2014. www.socialenterprise.org.uk.

Statutory Review of the Canada Business Corporations Act. 2010. Report of the Standing House of Commons Committee on Industry, Science and Technology, Meeting No. 43, 40th Parliament, 3rd Session, 25.

UK Companies (Audit, Investigations and Community Enterprise) Act *2004 (UK), c 27* [UK Companies Act].

Wingrove, J. 2010. "Marc and Craig Kielburger's Do-gooding Social Enterprise." *The Globe and Mail*, 19 March.

Yundt, H. 2012. "The Politics of Advocacy: Are Charities Apathetic or Afraid?" Charity Village, 1 October. Accessed 28 August 2014. https://charityvillage.com.

# 5

# Saskatchewan Disability Income Support Coalition: Advocacy for a New Disability Benefit Program

KATHLEEN THOMPSON AND BONNIE MORTON

INTRODUCTION

This chapter describes how the Saskatchewan Disability Income Support Coalition (DISC) recently led a successful collaborative advocacy initiative. DISC members include individuals living with disabilities and a cross-section of over forty disability and anti-poverty non-governmental organizations (NGOs) from across Saskatchewan. As partners in a non-partisan coalition, DISC members joined together to speak as one voice for a distinct and separate income support system for people with disabilities built upon a common vision and principles that provide respectful, dignified, and adequate income support. DISC focused on advocating the Government of Saskatchewan to establish a separate financial support system for people with disabilities.

DISC has achieved many milestones in its partnership with the Government of Saskatchewan. The Saskatchewan Assured Income for Disability (SAID) was established in 2009 under existing social services legislation. SAID is considered a major achievement for the provincial disability and anti-poverty sectors as well as for the provincial government, and seemingly at odds with the neoliberal era described by DeSantis and Mulé (see chapter 1). Since its beginning in the fall of 2009, almost 15,000 provincial residents have been enrolled in SAID (Government of Saskatchewan 2014). In addition to being moved off welfare, SAID recipients initially received extra funds, approximately $200 more per month for single people living independently, than they would have received on welfare. At the same time the government committed to increasing that amount annually by $50 for the next three years.

This chapter summarizes of the collaborative advocacy model DISC used for the joint government/community Disability Income Task Team to develop the recommended design options for SAID. This collaboration between self-advocates, disability and anti-poverty community groups, and the provincial government represented an unprecedented level of participatory public policy development in Saskatchewan (similar to what is discussed in chapter 8). Provincial politicians and senior officials have said that the success of the collaboration between DISC and the Government of Saskatchewan represents a new form of participatory policy development. The chapter also highlights the importance of public education and support for achieving DISC's goals and notes that the challenges for DISC in continuing its advocacy role, including the effect of cuts from 2013 to 2015 to federal funding for DISC's administrative support. The chapter also describes the future challenges of implementing the SAID program and of ensuring that SAID meets the primary principle of providing an adequate income for beneficiaries. Residents on the Saskatchewan Assistance Plan (SAP) are considered recipients whereas residents on SAID are considered beneficiaries.

## Inadequate Income Supports

Proponents of an income support model for people with disabilities emphasize that welfare has become the reality for many Canadians with disabilities even though the welfare system was not designed to be a disability income support program (Stapleton, Tweedle, and Gibson 2013). This chapter focuses on income supports for people living with disabilities and also discusses concepts about welfare. The definition of welfare or social assistance is that it is a program of last resort for individuals and families who cannot meet the basic costs of living (Government of Saskatchewan 2014). Welfare is a system whereby the government undertakes to protect the health and well-being of its citizens, especially those in financial or social need (Merriam Webster nd). However, for people living with significant and enduring disabilities, the emphasis is on *income supports*. The term is intended to refer to both the common costs of basic living expenses as well as the extra monthly and occasional costs of living with a serious and persistent disability.

Throughout history, people with disabilities have had to depend on the charity of the church and the state to support and provide for their basic needs. In Canada, the welfare system became the state's main mechanism for providing support to people with disabilities. Various aspects of social welfare have been the responsibility of municipal, provincial, and federal governments. In July 1966, the Canada Assistance Plan was put in place (Osborne 1985), a federal, provincial, and territorial agreement for sharing the cost of all social programs to help unify them across the country. Welfare fell under this new agreement.

Welfare was never intended to be a long-term financial solution for anyone, but it became the default program for many people with disabilities in this province. People with disabilities in Saskatchewan who had no other resources for support found themselves dependent on welfare to cover their basic and exceptional needs. People with disabilities who found themselves dependent on this program also found themselves, in many ways, having to function under the same rules as people on welfare who did not have disabilities.

Many people live with disabilities that are chronic, and for some, debilitating. A major concern about whether it was appropriate for people with disabilities to have to follow general welfare rules was about proving their need for assistance. People on welfare have to do annual reviews to prove continued entitlement. For people with disabilities this means they have to continually prove that their medical conditions are either the same or worse. Also, the funding under welfare was not adequate for people with disabilities and did not provide the compensation needed for their extra costs, such as those for dietary and health needs and equipment requirements, among others (Saunders 2006). Occasional and extenuating costs may range from equipment and technology, such as wheelchairs, to modifying homes or vehicles (Australian Federation of Disability Organizations 2009).

## THE DISABILITY INCOME SUPPORT COALITION (DISC)

The Disability Income Support Coalition or DISC, formed in 2006, is made up of people living with disabilities who identify themselves as self-advocates and family members of people living with disabilities. DISC also comprises members from disability and anti-poverty organizations.

The coalition uses the consensus model of working together. Early in its formation, DISC members agreed to focus on one issue: creating an income support program separate from welfare for provincial citizens living with significant and enduring disabilities. The group only focuses on income support issues. It does not work on other issues, such as housing or transportation. When work needs to be done, the members form working groups within the coalition. Working groups include a media committee, a regulation/policy committee, etc. DISC members also sit on committees with government officials and are actively involved in implementing SAID.

Philosophically, DISC adopts a social justice lens, with an emphasis on a *social determinants of health* orientation (Mikkonen and Raphael 2010), which acknowledges that health is affected by a broad range of interrelated factors, such as ethnicity, income, education, employment and working conditions, unemployment and job security, housing, social inclusion, gender, disability, early life, food insecurity, and a social safety net (Raphael 2009).

The primary vision of DISC is to see an income system that offers both an adequate baseline income for people with disabilities and a user-friendly mechanism to address individual financial needs based on how much of an impact the disability has on their life (DISC 2013). The key principles that DISC advocates for in an improved income support system are:

- ADEQUACY – People with disabilities should have an adequate income that truly meets their individual needs, not just basic needs.
- HOPE AND SECURITY – People with disabilities must have financial accommodations so that they can live their lives with hope, respect, and dignity.
- PERSON-CENTRED AND USER-FRIENDLY – A disability income program should be easily accessible with consistent, respectful SAID specialists who have the mandate and discretionary power to respond quickly to individual needs.
- HIGHER INCOME EXEMPTIONS – Income exemptions need to be increased to eliminate disincentives to employment and independence. Rapid reinstatement needs to be a working

principle that allows people with disabilities to feel secure as they move in and out of employment.

CONSISTENT IMPLEMENTATION – People with disabilities should be able to expect a portable and flexible income system.

DISC's work encompasses multiple disabilities, called cross-disability, which means it is an approach that does not distinguish between different types of disabilities (DISC 2013).

## Collaborative Advocacy

DISC's activities are collaborative, using a consensus approach to decision making.

Collaboration is defined as a well-defined and mutually beneficial relationship between two or more organizations to achieve common goals. The level of collaboration organizations achieve varies based on variables such as the complexity of the issues, the scope of the project, and the intensity of the relationships. A systematic review of literature on collaborative mechanisms in public policy development found that a number of common process and contextual factors emerged as common success factors for building and maintaining collaborative mechanisms: sufficient resources (human, financial, and time); diverse and appropriate representation; clear and manageable roles, responsibilities and structures; having a shared vision, readiness, and context; engagement and connection with the community and effective leadership (Alberta Health Services 2011).

A public policy advocacy model that describes DISC's approach is collaborative advocacy. This model also fits solidly with the authentic interest in community engagement that the Government of Saskatchewan has exemplified while it has established and implemented SAID. Collaborative advocacy is a model that promotes positive intergroup relations between disenfranchised, previously competing stakeholders (Johnston 2010; Sherraden, Slosar, and Sherraden 2002; Bartunek, Foster-Fishman, and Keys 1996). Within this model, cooperative communications occur at the group level. The focus is on each group and each individual being heard, and each individual being supported and valued (Bartunek, Foster-Fishman, and Keys 1996). The goal of this model is to promote collaborative policy development while simultaneously encouraging the underlying goals of intergroup

Table 5.1 The underlying process goals, intervention, and outcomes of collaborative advocacy

| Critical Underlying Process Goals | Collaborative Advocacy Interventions | Outcomes |
|---|---|---|
| INTERGROUP COOPERATION | Identify common themes | Accomplish the mission |
| GROUP CO-EMPOWERMENT | Value subgroup diversity | Maintain subgroup goals |
| MEMBER EMPOWERMENT | Foster member inclusion in decision making | Perceived member influence |

Bartunek, Foster-Fishman and Keys 1996, p. 705.

cooperation, group empowerment, and individual empowerment, as depicted in Table 5.1.

*Intergroup cooperation* is the critical process of guiding diverse, even competing, advocacy issues into a unifying joint effort to achieve positive change (Bartunek, Foster-Fishman, and Keys 1996). Cooperative behaviour is more likely to occur if overarching goals can evolve that meet the needs of all of the participants (Sherif and Sherif 1953). *Co-empowerment* refers to the mutual simultaneous empowerment of each member group (Bartunek, Foster-Fishman, and Keys 1996). No one group should dominate or subordinate the voice of another group (Bond and Keys 1993). The significance of co-empowerment to successful collaborative advocacy cannot be understated. Groups that feel they have an active, respected voice in decision-making processes are more likely to feel their concerns are treated respectfully and to remain committed to the group (Bartunek, Foster-Fishman, and Keys 1996). Each group is legitimized through co-empowerment which enhances collaborative efforts (Pasquero 1991).

Achieving the two parallel process goals of intergroup cooperation and co-empowerment creates positive relations among previously divergent groups who traditionally have different access to power and resources (Bartunek, Foster-Fishman, and Keys 1996). Part of this process involves accepting disagreement and intergroup give and take (Deutsch 1993). *Individual member empowerment* refers to enhancing personal control and addressing the power differences between individual members of organizations and society in general. Involving and including group members in the decision-making

Table 5.2 Activities included in collaborative advocacy interventions

INTERVENTION 1: IDENTIFY COMMON THEMES

- Develop a supportive membership base
- Enhance group cohesion
- Foster intergroup awareness
- Emphasize shared concerns
- Develop superordinate shared goals
- Encourage informal socialization
- Hold celebratory rituals

INTERVENTION 2: VALUE SUBGROUP DIVERSITY

- Sponsor an inclusive strategic planning retreat
- Develop an inclusive strategic plan
- Encourage dissent
- Develop an active subcommittee structure

INTERVENTION 3: FOSTER MEMBER INCLUSION

- Identify and provide for member participation needs
- Access and use the talents of all members
- Actively involve all members in the decision making process

Bartunek, Foster-Fishman, and Keys 1996, 708.

process is a primary means of achieving empowerment in a collaborative advocacy model (Bartunek, Foster-Fishman, and Keys 1996). Achieving the three process goals of collaborative inquiry, intergroup collaboration, and co-empowerment and individual empowerment creates productive relationships. Table 5.2 provides a summary of how collective advocacy interventions can be carried out. DISC has achieved an effective collaborative advocacy initiative, as the following sections of this chapter outline.

## BACKGROUND

### *International and Federal Attention to Disabilities*

In the 1980s and 1990s, a number of key international and Canadian federal initiatives drew attention to the realities facing people living with disabilities. In 1976, the General Assembly of the United Nations declared 1981 the International Year of Disabled Persons (General Assembly of the United Nations 1976). In 1986, the Government of Canada introduced the Employment Equity Act, designating

Canadians with disabilities as one of four priority groups for increased inclusion in the federally regulated labour market. In 1996, the federal, provincial, and territorial governments identified Canadians with disabilities as a national priority for social policy renewal at a First Ministers' Meeting, and the Federal Task Force on Disability Issues published *Equal Citizenship for Canadians with Disabilities*. It recommended federal government leadership to ensure the full inclusion and participation of citizens with disabilities.

In 1998, the Canadian Human Rights Act was amended to add a statutory duty, short of undue hardship, to accommodate employees with disabilities (Employment and Social Development Canada 1998). In 1998 and 2000, the federal, provincial, and territorial ministers responsible for social services released framework documents outlining a vision for disability issues and a report that looked at individual stories, indicators, effective practices, and opportunities for progress (Federal, Provincial and Territorial Ministers Responsible for Social Services 2000; 1998). The documents addressed income, including the value of separating eligibility for disability supports from eligibility for income support programs. People from the Saskatchewan disability community and the Saskatchewan provincial government were among those who contributed to the federal policy process. The international emphasis on persons with disabilities, the changes to human rights, and the reports at the federal level were useful tools in advancing disability issues in Saskatchewan. When people participated in the process, it enhanced the networks of Saskatchewan people addressing disability issues with those addressing disability issues elsewhere in Canada (Saskatchewan Voice of People with Disabilities 2007). Collaborating in the 1990s with colleagues in other Canadian jurisdictions also helped foster the sharing of knowledge about best practices for providing adequate income supports to people living with disabilities that could be considered for Saskatchewan (Parliament of Canada 2006).

### The Impact of the Provincial Interagency Network on Disabilities (PIND)

The international and national collaboration that elevated the rights of people with disabilities was a precursor to the formation of the Saskatchewan Provincial Interagency Network on Disabilities (PIND) in 1995. This network laid the groundwork for disability groups to work collaboratively with both elected officials and government staff. In an interview on the historical significance of PIND, a former executive director of a non-governmental organization (NGO) that was active with PIND explained that it took decades of struggle for people with disabilities and groups representing people with disabilities to fight for fair, respectful treatment of people with disabilities (Duncan 2013). PIND's focus was to ensure that people with disabilities have the same opportunities for transportation, housing, and employment as those who do not live with disabilities. PIND's formation allowed individuals and groups struggling on their own to determine the common issues they could work on in partnership. This was the beginning of collaborative advocacy work in Saskatchewan on housing, transportation, and other issues of critical importance to citizens living with disabilities.

The efforts of PIND in meeting with elected government representatives and government staff led to some new developments in government. In January 1998, the provincial government announced the creation of a disability strategy. Part of the strategy was the creation of the Saskatchewan Council on Disability Issues, reporting to the minister responsible for disability issues. The council was intended to "provide advice on issues affecting individuals with disabilities, to obtain direct input from individuals with disabilities on issues related to government programs, policies and priorities and to assist in the development of a government-wide Disability Action Plan" (Saskatchewan Council on Disability Issues 2001). The plan was developed from a review of documents, council discussions, and consultations with individuals with disabilities, their families, and support networks. Direct input was obtained through a series of community forums held in the spring of 2000. The government also set up the Office of Disability Issues (ODI) in March 1998 as "a vehicle for collaboration and partnership with the disability community" (Ministry of Social Services 1998). One of the first tasks of the ODI was to create and provide support to the Saskatchewan Council on Disability Issues' work by developing a provincial action plan on disabilities and providing feedback to the government. This coordination involved extensive cross-departmental work within government. The government and the provincial disabilities community collaborated in hiring the first executive director of the ODI.

It was also about this time that some individuals and organizations within the Saskatchewan disability community and anti-poverty sectors were starting to call for a disability benefit program that would be separate from welfare, and that would get rid of the welfare stigma. This call for a separate program did not seem to be taken seriously so several disability organizations got together in 1999 and developed and sent out about 5,000 postcards calling on the government to address very specific social and economic issues, and asking that the postcards be sent to the leaders of all provincial political parties. The postcards created such a backlash that the NDP government set up a reference group. The community assumed that the reference group was set up to fail from the start: the government bureaucrats and officials came to the table with all the excuses as to why such an income support program for people with disabilities would not work, and had little or no vision for the program (Duncan 2013).

## Disability Action Plan

In June 2001, the Saskatchewan Council on Disability Issues released the document *Saskatchewan's Disability Action Plan*, reflecting the council's discussion and consultations with the disability community. The plan was developed with the assistance and involvement of individuals, community groups, organizations, government officials, and the Office of Disability Issues and included a significant discussion on income support. The plan's vision stated that individuals with disabilities were eligible for disability income support that was separate from social assistance. It also called for programs that would recognize and provide income support for costs incurred by individuals with disabilities and their families. Other key components of the report included recommending program and policy responses that addressed the effect and the costs of living with a disability and provide supports based on individual needs. Other recommendations from the action plan included measures to make it easier for individuals with disabilities to move into the labour market, separating training allowances and wages from income support, and developing a quality of life/disability supplement outside of social assistance for individuals with disabilities who may not have been able to participate in competitive employment.

The provincial government was also encouraged to find ways within the tax system to help offset the direct and indirect costs of disability incurred by individuals with disabilities and their families, and to work with the federal government to explore options for addressing the extra costs of disability. The report also recommended that the Saskatchewan Assistance Regulations be amended to allow money to be put into a trust either from an inheritance (established by a will) or in a living trust for a beneficiary with a disability so that the trust would not affect their social assistance eligibility or benefits. Many advocates had high hopes for quick action from Saskatchewan's Disability Action Plan, but changing government programs is not usually a quick process, due to the extent of discussion and development required and competing priorities in government. Progress occurred on some but not all items and not necessarily with the speed desired (Duncan 2013).

Along with the support from the disability community, it should be noted that anti-poverty organizations had been calling for an independent financial benefit program for people with disabilities since the mid-1970s. Two such groups were the Downtown Chaplaincy, established in 1971 (now the Regina Anti-Poverty Ministry), and the Regina Welfare Rights Centre, established in 1982. These two anti-poverty advocacy organizations were working in isolation from each other, as were the many other groups that were struggling with the same social and economic issues. The experience of the anti-poverty groups was very similar to those of the disability community (Duncan 2013). It was clear to both sectors that the NDP government, at that time, was not committed to developing an independent financial benefit program for people with disabilities that would be separate from welfare. A growing frustration with the lack of response by government to community calls for an independent financial benefit program for people with disabilities led to the formation of DISC in 2006.

## Changing Relations with Government

In June 2007, the NDP minister responsible for disability issues released the document *The Disability Inclusion Policy Framework: Government's Response to the Saskatchewan Council on Disability Issues' Disability Action Plan* (Government of Saskatchewan 2007). The framework was a combined effort of the Saskatchewan Council on Disability Issues and the departments of Social Services, Health, Learning, Advanced Education and Employment, Justice, Corrections and Public Safety, and the Public Service Commission. This was an example of government working across departments to develop the broader strategy. Progress had been made on a number of income-related recommendations from the *Disability Action Plan*, but the report did not contain a clear statement about a separate income support program for people with disabilities.

In the November 2007 Saskatchewan election, the political landscape changed and the Saskatchewan Party was elected as the new provincial government. DISC started calling upon the new government leaders, particularly the Minister for Social Services. Meetings were held between DISC and the new minister and shortly afterwards the new government and DISC had a working relationship.

This working relationship was in the form of the Disability Income Program Task Team, which included eight members from DISC and eight members from the provincial government (Ministry of Social Services 2009). On the DISC side, the team included six representatives of DISC, one representative of the Saskatchewan Abilities Council, and one representative of PIND. On the government side, it included a representative from the Ministry of Social Services and Office of Disability Issues. Officials from the Ministries of Health and from Advanced Education, Employment, and Labour participated on an as-needed basis. A government member and a community member co-chaired the task team. Because they were focusing on a more specific issue, the membership on these committees was reduced to a smaller number of government departments than was previously used in developing the broader strategies and approaches to disability issues, such as the Disability Action Plan or The Disability Inclusion Policy Framework. The Ministry of Social Services took over the disability strategy on behalf of the Government of Saskatchewan. The aforementioned ministries continued to be involved in advancing the strategy on an as-needed basis. Figure 5.1 shows the event timeline for the establishment of DISC and SAID.

The government announced its commitment to having a separate program for people with disabilities on 23 October 2008 (Government of Saskatchewan 2008), the task team was formed in December 2008, and its report to the minister was made public on 13 May 2009. The task team developed initial design options for a new disability income program to begin implementation in 2009–10. It also developed a discussion guide on the recommended options and consulted with people living with disabilities and others to develop a vision for what this new program would look like and how it should function.

To ensure that this collaborative relationship would continue to function amiably, it was important for DISC to set out ground rules. The main ground rule was to focus on income support and to not dilute

1995–2000: PIND Established – 1995; Office of Disability Issues (ODI) opens & provincial disability strategy announced – 1998; Early advocacy with postcard mailout – 1999; Community forums held – 2000

2001–2005: Saskatchewan Council on Disability Issues releases Saskatchewan Disability Action Plan – 2001; Early, pre-DISC meetings and advancement of PIND

2006 – DISC formation

2008 – Task team and recommendations created

2009 – SAID launched

2010–2015 Implementation tasks

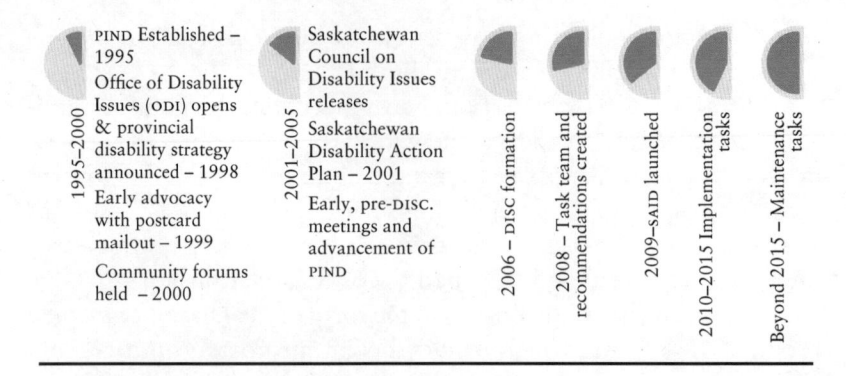

Beyond 2015 – Maintenance tasks

Figure 5.1 SAID event timeline – 1995–2015

DISC's message by taking on multiple issues. Other primary ground rules involved the process of working together using a collaborative, consensus model designed to hear all coalition voices, especially the voices of people with lived experience of disabilities. Developing the capacity to work collaboratively came about after DISC failed to provide a focused message at its first meeting with the Minister of Social Services. The minister kindly listened to the multiple, mixed messages from DISC and invited the group to focus on an issue the ministry could act upon before booking another meeting. This failure resulted in DISC hiring a consultant, who helped DISC members learn to openly exchange information with one another and to develop a message with a focus that the minister could act upon. The consultant was critical in helping the group establish ground rules for staying on message and for creating an authentic collaboration among the varied DISC partners (see chapter 7 for similar details about funding to do advocacy). Table 5.3 provides a list of the DISC partner organizations. Most of the organizations involved in DISC are registered charities.

The work of the task team in establishing a vision for the new program was an important part of this process. Just like the structure of DISC, the partnership between government and DISC has benefited greatly from setting out rules, working together, coming together on a common vision for this new program, and implementing it.

### 2009 *Task Team Recommendations*

Based on consultations with the community, the task team set out fifty recommendations in the report *The Final Recommendations of the Task Team of Income Support for People with Disabilities*

Table 5.3 List of DISC partner organizations

| | |
|---|---|
| 1. AIDS Saskatoon | 26. People First of Saskatchewan |
| 2. ALS Society of Saskatchewan | 27. People with Disabilities |
| 3. Arthritis Society – Saskatchewan Division | 28. Phoenix Residential Society |
| 4. Autism Resource Centre | 29. Regina and District Association for Community Living |
| 5. Autism Services | 30. Regina Anti-Poverty Ministry (RAPM) |
| 6. Brownstone Consulting | 31. Regina Welfare Rights Centre |
| 7. Canadian Association for Williams Syndrome | 32. Saskatchewan Association for Community Living (SACL) |
| 8. Canadian Deafblind Association – Saskatchewan Chapter Inc. (CDBA) | 33. Saskatchewan Association of Rehabilitation Centres (SARC) |
| 9. Canadian Mental Health Association (Saskatchewan Division) Inc. | 34. Saskatchewan Brain Injury Association (SBIA) |
| 10. Canadian Paraplegic Association (Saskatchewan) Inc. | 35. Saskatchewan Cerebral Palsy Association |
| 11. Community Service Centre | 36. Saskatchewan Council on Aging |
| 12. CNIB | 37. Saskatchewan Down Syndrome Society |
| 13. DAWN – RAFH Saskatoon | |
| 14. Epilepsy Saskatoon | 38. Saskatchewan Deaf and Hard of Hearing Services |
| 15. Equal Justice for All – Saskatoon | |
| 16. FASD Support Network of Saskatchewan Inc. | 39. Saskatchewan Families for Effective Autism Treatment (SASKFEAT) |
| 17. Federation of Saskatchewan Indian Nations (FSIN) Disability Working Group | 40. Saskatchewan Seniors Mechanism |
| | 41. Saskatchewan Voice of People with Disabilities |
| 18. Gary Tinker Federation for the Disabled Inc. | 42. Saskatoon Anti-Poverty Coalition |
| 19. Grassroots Alliance | 43. Saskatoon Housing Coalition |
| 20. IDEA Regina | 44. SaskTel Employee Network on Disabilities (SEND) |
| 21. Métis Family and Community Justice Services of Saskatchewan | 45. Schizophrenia Society of Saskatchewan |
| 22. Métis Nation Saskatchewan | |
| 23. Muscular Dystrophy Canada (SK) | 46. South Saskatchewan Independent Living Centres (SSILC) |
| 24. Neil Squire Society | |
| 25. North Saskatchewan Independent Living Centre (NSILC) | 47. Spina Bifida and Hydrocephalus Association of Saskatchewan North |

Source: Disability Income Support Coalition 2015.

(Government of Saskatchewan 2009) and presented them to the Minister of Social Services in May 2009. The Government of Saskatchewan supported all fifty of the recommendations.

These recommendations started by outlining the principles that should be adopted as the guide for developing the new disability income program. They included principles that directly involved people with disabilities and their representative organizations in policy development. The principles also included DISC's principles, articulated earlier in this chapter: adequacy, hope, and security; person-centred and user-friendly; higher income exemptions; and consistent implementation. Other principles included in the task force recommendations ensured that SAID beneficiaries receive high-quality services: treating beneficiaries with dignity, respect, and empowerment; offering non-intrusive services that minimize interferences in their lives; and finally, offering services that are simple to administer, explain, and understand; flexible, timely, individualized, and transportable; easily accessible; and separate from the welfare system.

Other recommendations focused on the leadership and management of SAID from a long-term sustainability perspective, ensuring that SAID is impact-based, with an emphasis on the impact of disability on a person's daily life, not just the medical diagnosis; that the system is fair, transparent, and accountable; and that SAID is aligned with other supports and services that help people with disabilities to be involved in their communities (Ministry of Social Services 2009).

Along with the principles outlined, the remaining recommendations address who the target population will be, and broadly set out the policy goals and eligibility criteria of this new program. Eleven recommendations deal with disability assessment and how to maintain disability eligibility and reporting. Other recommendations

- highlight the need for a simple and easy to understand income-testing procedure and when this procedure should happen;
- state that benefits should provide a living income, a disability income, an exceptional needs income, and supplementary health coverage, and should also be portable;
- include a commitment to index these benefits once they are at a socially acceptable level; and
- address earned income exemptions as well as asset exemptions, service delivery, appeals, and transitioning social assistance clients to the new program. (Ministry of Social Services 2009)

The report also discusses the collaborative approach for the community and the government for future work on SAID and for other areas of policy and program development in sections 47 to 50.

47. The collaborative approach between community and government representatives that was used to develop these recommendations should continue as more detailed program planning takes place.
48. Consideration should be given to creating an ongoing consultative role for members of the disability community in the ongoing administration of the program.
49. The knowledge, learnings and relationships developed in the community/government task team should continue to be drawn upon in some advisory or steering committee capacity.
50. The task team approach offers a collaborative model that should be considered by government in other areas of policy and program development (Government of Saskatchewan 2009, 17).

DISC members and government officials involved in the creation of the fifty recommendations felt that if the recommendations were truly used as the guiding tool for developing this program, with social and economic policies built into it, it would result in the best disability benefit program in the country. The feeling at the time was that creating Canada's strongest disability income support program would be a social policy achievement that people with disabilities, the disability and anti-poverty communities, and the government would be proud of (Duncan 2013). In late 2009, the Program Implementation Advisory Team (PIAT) for the SAID program was established to assist in planning for SAID for: reduced reporting requirements; revised benefit structure; staff training; new service delivery approaches; and a new program name and separate identity (Government of Saskatchewan 2009). At that point, the program had not been formally named.

Initially, PIAT was composed of eight DISC members nominated by DISC and appointed by the Minister. The Minister also appointed a person representing the Saskatchewan Abilities Council, a non-government organization. At DISC's recommendation, the committee has now evolved to having DISC nominate all members. Subcommittees were developed according to the needs at the time, such as developing the assessment tool. Currently, PIAT has two joint subcommittees: the Benefits Subcommittee, which works on benefit levels (basic living allowances, asset and earning exemptions, exceptional need costs, etc.), and the Service Delivery Subcommittee, which works on all aspects of the assessment process and the implementation of the new program.

## SASKATCHEWAN ASSURED INCOME FOR DISABILITY: A NEW SOCIAL SERVICE PROGRAM

Through meaningful participation and discussion with elected and senior officials of the Ministry of Social Services, the beginning of the SAID program was announced on 13 May 2009 (Government of Saskatchewan 2009). Saskatchewan citizens began to be enrolled in the program starting 1 October 2009. When the SAID program began, there were no benefit increases, and only people who were living in care homes and who required the highest level of care living outside of care homes were transferred from welfare to SAID.

In early 2012, a process was started to assess people on welfare with disabilities who had not previously been put into the program. These were people who were living independently (i.e., not in a care home or facility). It should be pointed out that this process was completely voluntary for those being assessed. The assessment application, in the beginning, was very long and took approximately two to three hours to complete. Members of DISC volunteered to help people fill out these applications. This lengthy process was difficult for many who were being assessed, and in some cases the assessment application took a couple of days to fill out as the individual was either not able to sit that long or was not able to stay focused for long periods of time.

By June of 2012, those individuals living independently on welfare, and who had been assessed and found to have an enduring and significant disability, were moved over to the SAID program. Almost 15,000 provincial residents are now beneficiaries of SAID (Government of Saskatchewan 2014). The number of provincial citizens coming onto SAID is significant: the number of Saskatchewan residents on social assistance declined six per cent from 1995 to 2005. In 1995, there were 82,200 recipients of SAP in Saskatchewan. In 2005, there were 48,700 (National Council of Welfare 2006).

The government committed to raising average SAID benefits over four years by $100 per month for individuals in residential care, $350 a month for singles living independently, and $400 per month for couples, with the first increases taking effect in June 2012. On 1 June 2013, monthly benefits for single individuals in independent living arrangements rose by $50. Couples received a $60 monthly increase, and the benefit for persons in residential care rose by $20 per month. The funding available to people on SAID, although still not amounting to what would be considered socially acceptable for an individual, is more than an individual would receive on welfare. A single person living in Regina or Saskatoon on SAID receives $300 more than people on the provincial assistance plan. The basic rates cover rent, basic needs (food, clothing, personal and household needs, and travel), a small disability amount, and telephone. Some special needs can also be accommodated. The actual costs of utilities such as water, power, and energy are covered. Benefit rates vary in relation to residential and marital status.

Under SAID, how people and their disabilities are identified in delivering services has also changed. In the general welfare program, a social worker is referred to as a "worker," but within the SAID program that person is referred to as a "SAID specialist." If a person is on welfare, he or she is referred to as a "client," whereas on SAID, a person is identified as a "beneficiary." This change in language is helping to combat stigma.

## HOW DISC ADVOCATED FOR CHANGE – COLLABORATING WITH GOVERNMENT

To people in the community, it had appeared impossible to get government support, particularly under the previous provincial government, for changes that were necessary. DISC's goal was to ensure that people with disabilities did not continue to lag behind others socially, economically, or in dignity. It became very clear to DISC members, after struggling for so many years, before and after the creation of DISC, that a new approach was needed.

While developing strategy, it was evident that the general population needed to be educated to gain the public support and pressure needed to be put on the government so it would take the need seriously, and call for a new, and separate, program for people with significant and enduring disabilities.

In the beginning, coalition members provided public education by continually doing public speaking on the issues and DISC's goals, in particular; newspaper and radio ads about who was on welfare and how meagre the funding was on welfare. DISC also developed a social media strategy that has been very beneficial in maintaining a public education presence as well as reaching many people at little or no cost.

Along with public education, DISC continued to meet with the Minister of Social Services and other government officials. At these meetings, self-advocates were able to educate government officials based on their firsthand experience about what it was like living on welfare with less than enough to cover their daily living needs, as well as not being able to meet the real cost of their disability needs.

The people with direct experiences, that is, First Voices, are very important in DISC. They have the lived experience of surviving under public policies that do not meet their needs, and people need to hear that reality. Public support for an independent income program for people with disabilities grew and continues to be strong. Public education has not stopped just because DISC is now working with the government. DISC continues to provide public education so that all people with disabilities can hear about the new benefit program, and so that the public understands the importance and relevance of such a program. After all, how effective is public policy if the public is not involved in pushing for it and continually ensuring it is still doing what it was intended to do? That can only be done through an informed public, and that requires having information and education that is easily available.

DISC has used a collaborative approach from the beginning. From PIND, disability groups had learned the value of working together on very specific issues and they carried that experience forward into DISC. The community of DISC is made up of people with the experience of living with disabilities, and members and staff of disability and anti-poverty organizations. To be able to work collaboratively, it has been important for all members to remember and respect everyone's input, particularly that of the self-advocating members. They help the members of DISC, government officials, and the general public who do not live with disabilities to understand why this program is so important and what the new program should encompass. Self-advocates are not token members of DISC; they are essential members of this coalition, who actively participate in discussions within DISC meetings and meetings with the Minister of Social Services and other government officials, committees within DISC, and members of the joint community-government committees. DeSantis and Mulé note, in chapter 1, that people's participation in these processes can ebb and flow for a variety of reasons – this did not happen with DISC.

From the initial meetings with the Minister of Social Services, it was clear the minister was very willing to carry on this collaborative approach, in which members of the Minister's office and other government officials would work with DISC members, in partnership, in developing and implementing a new benefit program for people with disabilities. The former Minister of Social Services and senior ministry staff worked collaboratively with DISC starting in 2010, championing benefit increases and increases to asset and exemption limits.

The members of the joint Program Implementation Advisory Team's (PIAT) subcommittees, the benefits subcommittee and the service delivery subcommittee, also sit on the main PIAT committee and feed the information back to PIAT. DISC also has a benefit and a policy/regulations committee that feeds information, concerns, and requests to the PIAT benefits subcommittee. If there are any recommendations coming from DISC, or the two subcommittees, they go to PIAT, which takes them to the government. Thus, this process is driven from the bottom up. Effective collaborative advocacy involves productive intergroup collaboration. The process with DISC has proven this to be true, although realizing progress in some areas has been slow given the complexity of the machinery of government and collaborative decision-making processes.

## Critical Analysis about Current SAID Outcomes

The work of implementing SAID has just begun. The program is nowhere near being the program envisioned by DISC, or as outlined in the fifty recommendations that the Saskatchewan Party government supported. The service delivery subcommittee of PIAT continues to address how the program operates and policy and regulations dealing with non-monetary matters. The benefits subcommittee is still working to ensure that SAID is a program that provides socially acceptable benefit levels. One task that needs to be done is addressing the methodological difficulties of quantifying the costs associated with disabilities. There is still a long way to go. In many ways, SAID still looks like SAP, and much work needs to be done to make this a truly stand-alone program. This program needs to function differently than SAP; it should not be just a name change that hides the fact that most of the program still resembles welfare. DISC is advocating for separate legislation and regulations for SAID.

There are substantial challenges with the service delivery of SAID. In Saskatoon, people on SAID still have an individual worker to contact if they need to, but in Regina, the government, without DISC's knowledge, initiated a pilot project without any designated workers. When a beneficiary called in, they spoke to whoever may have been on the phone at that time. The problem with that model was that if a person needed to phone back, they may have talked to someone else. When these frontline SAID specialists answered the calls, they did not say who they were and many people would not ask for names, so beneficiaries would not be able to say who they had spoken to last. Every contact and conversation was supposed to be noted on the beneficiary's computer file. But there were cases in which conversations with the beneficiary and their advocate were not documented. DISC members heard from SAID beneficiaries in Regina who were not happy with this way of dealing with their needs or their files. A review of this pilot project occurred in 2014. As a result, beneficiaries now have the option of staying on a generalized caseload or having their own SAID specialist. Although some changes have occurred, based on the DISC principle of achieving a person-centred and user-friendly system, to date advocacy has not brought about the needed changes to service delivery in the organizational culture of government.

Work still needs to be done to create a first-contact process that is suitable for all beneficiaries. This program should be flexible. If a person does not want to have a specific worker, then they should be able to speak to anyone when they call in, but if another person wants to have a specific person to speak to when they need to discuss their needs, then that should be accommodated too. For some individuals living with complex and multiple disabilities, it is important to experience consistency with service delivery through an established relationship with a SAID specialist. Having to re-explain one's complicated needs multiple times to multiple SAID specialists can be frustrating for someone with limited energy or who has hearing or verbal limitations. DISC maintains that SAID cannot be a one size fits all, or it will be as ineffective in meeting the needs of people with disabilities as welfare is. It is a struggle trying to incorporate flexibility into this program but that does not mean it cannot be accomplished.

Welfare is a program that does not, and cannot be flexible enough to meet the individual needs of everyone. SAID was intended to be just that, a flexible program that would address individual needs.

DISC needs to be ever-vigilant in each phase of the implementation of SAID, particularly in the development of assessment tools, frontline interaction between specialists and beneficiaries, policy and regulations, the benefit levels, and indexation.

Although SAID was supposed to be separate from welfare, it does not appear that it is at this time. When the program was launched, many of the welfare policies and regulations were moved over to SAID and became the new rules. Both DISC and government officials are working to change this, but at this time the majority of SAID policies and regulations still read like those of welfare. At this point, the most positive aspects of SAID are the substantially increased benefit levels and that there is a joint working relationship between the government, their officials, and DISC. Thus, it is fair to conclude that the structural change that DISC envisioned has yet to be fully realized in the implementation of SAID.

In 2010, DISC commissioned a literature review to explore the international research on the costs associated with disabilities and how benefit levels in other countries allow for the cost of disability (Watts 2010). The review found that there is no broad general consensus on the methodology to measure the extra costs of disability or to take into account the real costs of living with a disability (Stapleton, Protiuk, and Stone 2008; Tibble 2005).

Using both subjective and Standards of Living approaches, DISC members were surveyed in the summer of 2012 on the monthly, occasional, and social inclusion costs of living with a disability. The survey found that the monthly income that SAID recipients receive does not meet the adequacy principle that DISC and SAID are founded upon (Thompson et al. 2014). DISC funded the disability costs study so that it could deepen its understanding of the experiences of DISC members on SAID.

DISC later funded a 2013 study on the impact of SAID on SAID beneficiaries (Thompson, James, Bender, and Hembroff 2014). The 2013 study involved 112 interviews with SAID beneficiaries. The findings were that SAID positively affected the lives of 66 per cent of the interviewees. On the adequacy of benefit levels, the responses were mixed: 48 per cent of interviewees indicated that SAID benefit levels were adequate for meeting basic monthly needs whereas 47 per cent indicated that benefit levels were inadequate. Responses on service delivery were also mixed: just over half of interviewees (51 per cent) reported positive service delivery experiences whereas

43 per cent rated service delivery as neutral, poor, or very poor. More than one-fifth (21 per cent) of interviewees reported service delivery as being poor or very poor. A number of stories emerged during the inquiry about instances where service delivery was either concerning or problematic (Thompson et al. 2014). DISC feels that it is important to conduct research that is independent of the government so that it can generate independent evidence on the realities facing SAID beneficiaries.

### The Shifting Terrain: Critical Challenges Facing DISC

DISC's future challenges will thus be to make SAID a program that is truly separate from the Saskatchewan Assistance Plan. The establishment of SAID through the meaningful participation of DISC has led to substantive policy and program successes. Since the formation of DISC, its membership has risen from twenty organizations to forty-seven. The original groups are still with DISC, and as this coalition has grown in support so has the commitment to the work that needs to be done, whether within DISC (i.e., working committees) or, more broadly, with PIAT and its subcommittees. At no time has the commitment of DISC members wavered.

However, DISC's implementation advocacy process faces challenges in 2013 and beyond. A complicating factor facing DISC as it moves into the challenging implementation phase of SAID is a cut in federal funding. To date, the activities of DISC have been coordinated and funded through a Saskatchewan-based NGO, using federal government funding. DISC counted on these funds to pay a designated staff person to coordinate all the advocacy work. Within the staff person's job duties, DISC was a priority. The federal government announced in the spring of 2012 that the NGO coordinating DISC activities was losing all of its federal funding over two years, starting in the spring of 2013. This meant that DISC had to regroup and figure out another strategy to survive. As a result, DISC now requires fundraising both from its membership and from the provincial, philanthropic, and private sectors. Some of DISC's members have started to contribute and commit funds to DISC, but they will probably not be able to fund this work at the level it has been for the past few years.

Some DISC members have expressed concerns that the input of DISC in the establishment of SAID seems to have been less substantive during 2015 than in previous years. The Ministry of Social Services continues to encourage the participation of DISC members in PIAT and its subcommittees. The initial years of establishing SAID were intense and the perceived reduction in engagement could be part of the regular ebb and flow of public policy advocacy.

Although the federal funding for DISC was important, it is important to note that organizations have also been contributing staff time to DISC meetings and DISC working groups, and in PIAT and its subcommittees. From time to time, some organizations have contributed funding for special projects such as research or public awareness campaigns. There is a definite commitment to seeing the development of SAID through and ensuring that it is the program envisioned by DISC and people with disabilities as outlined within the *Final Recommendations of the Task Team on Income Support for People with Disabilities*.

Another challenge for DISC will be the work required to keep public and political support for this program alive until the SAID program is fully developed as envisioned, so that people with disabilities have a respectful and dignified program that is socially and economically acceptable, is separate from the Social Assistance Plan, and is indexed so that people with disabilities will no longer live in chronic poverty. During the 2011 provincial election campaign, Premier Brad Wall expressed the goal "to make our province the very best place in Canada to live for those with disabilities" (Saskatchewan Party 2011). Maintaining public support to sustain the political will to promote the quality of life for persons with disabilities will continue to be essential as the provincial government adjusts to significant declines in oil revenues and prepares for the 2016 provincial election. We are hopeful that a strong collaborative working relationship between the government and DISC will lay the foundation for future advocacy work around disability issues. Only time will tell how the collaborative work in this important area will evolve into the future. An authentic collaboration is dependent on both parties working together during good times and during times of struggle.

## SUMMARY AND CONCLUSIONS

Although government and community continue to collaborate on making SAID realize the vision of DISC's principles, many factors have contributed to the nature of the collaborative process between DISC and the Saskatchewan government. Preliminary evidence shows that the collaboration between government and DISC has been effective. However, the outcomes of future collaborative work will ultimately determine the success or failure of DISC's collaborative advocacy and the development of SAID. In summary:

a) The existence of international agreements, inclusion of disabilities in Canadian human rights legislation, and federal initiatives related to disabilities drew attention to disability issues, helped create a knowledge base about disability issues, and also created opportunities for Saskatchewan people concerned with disabilities to make connections with people in other locations and identify effective practices that could be used in Saskatchewan.

b) The Provincial Interagency Network on Disability initiated meetings with government elected officials and staff that provided an example of collaboration. Having the government mechanisms of an Office of Disability Issues and a Minister Responsible for Disability provided a focal point in government. Such a focus always needs to be balanced with the need for involvement across departments for dealing with complex issues. This extended involvement has been seen at various stages in the journey.

c) The public education efforts undertaken by DISC helped to create and sustain the interest of the general public and political will of elected officials and government staff. In addition, the direct personal experience of elected officials with friends and family living with disabilities contributed to their personal commitment to address disability issues.

d) Essential to the process were the provincial government's willingness to engage in a collaborative process with the joint Disability Income Support Task Team and the Program Implementation Advisory Team (PIAT) for SAID and the government's commitment to undertake the difficult process of creating a new program to respond to the request from the community. Also of great importance were the public consultations held by the previous and new governments that involved people in the disability community, their families, and disability-sector organizations.

e) Finally, focusing specifically on designing a provincial income assistance program for people with disabilities, instead of dealing with multiple issues, also contributed to effective collaborative advocacy and helps keep DISC focused on future efforts to strengthen SAID.

f) One of the pivotal issues going forward is DISC's desire to see separate legislation and regulations created to ensure that SAID is different than SAP and that it cannot be easily cut by future governments.

DISC and its members have contributed to the process of developing SAID in many ways: in discussions and committees within DISC, as task team and PIAT members, as public educators, as assistants to people applying for SAID, and as interviewees for research assessing economic needs. This work has been supported partially by disability and anti-poverty non-governmental organizations who have donated staff and volunteer time and resources, and by the volunteer efforts of individual members. The efforts by DISC to ensure that the first voices of self-advocates were heard within their own organization and at the table with the government have been an essential part of the whole process. DISC's continued willingness to help identify areas needing improvement and then working on resolving the problems have contributed and will continue to contribute to SAID working toward its intended, original vision.

In Canada, in recent years, a critical difficulty has been created by cutbacks to funding for advocacy and non-governmental organizations (for more details about funding cuts, see chapter 3). DISC is not immune to this as federal funding cuts led to the loss of current funding for DISC's administrative coordinator and DISC's researcher. Energy that may be needed to raise additional funds from DISC members, foundations, or other sources will take away from the time available to address disability issues, to conduct research and for further advocacy.

Although SAID has positively affected many lives in Saskatchewan, unintended consequences of the implementation of SAID affect some citizens negatively. Individuals on SAP whose disabilities are not severe and enduring enough to qualify for SAID are potential losers. Establishing and implementing SAID has taken and continues to take substantial time for the Ministry of Social Services as well as the DISC membership. Other programs or individuals might be unintentionally neglected, given the realities of implementing a new income support program.

To conclude, some of the groundwork for the SAID program was laid by previous policy work at the federal and provincial levels, and a collaborative approach used historically by PIND. The direct approach taken by DISC in working with the provincial government, government's willingness to engage in collaboration and take some action, and DISC's work in maintaining public education and thus political interest, were key to the adoption of the SAID program. Another essential element was the knowledge, experience, and dedication of people in the disability and anti-poverty communities to persistently work to create positive change.

This chapter has provided an example of effective collaborative advocacy by DISC. The success of DISC shows that collaborative models should be promoted to guide research, public policy development, and practice both by community organizations and by governments. Collaboration is an approach that can help activist groups and organizations serve their self-interests while at the same time "help move our democratic societies away from confrontation and divisiveness to more collaborative cultures" (Grunig 2000, 45).

### REFERENCES

Alberta Health Services. 2011. *A Literature Review of Collaborative Mechanisms of Healthy Public Policy Advocacy. Healthy Public Policy Report*, November. Edmonton: Alberta Health Services.

Australian Federation of Disability Organizations. 2009. *A Social Inclusion Rights Based Understanding of the Costs of Living with a Disability and the Need for a Disability Inclusion Allowance.* Melbourne, Australia: AFDO.

Bartunek, J.M., P.G. Foster-Fishman, and C. Keys. 1996. "Using Collaborative Advocacy to Foster Intergroup Cooperation: A Joint Insider-Outsider Investigation." *Human Relations* 49 (6): 701–33. http://dx.doi.org/10.1177/001872679604900601; http://hum.sagepub.com/content/49/6/701.

Bond, M., and C. Keys. 1993. "Empowerment, Diversity, and Collaboration: Promoting Synergy on Community Boards." *American Journal of Community Psychology* 21 (1): 37–57. http://dx.doi.org/10.1007/BF00938206.

Deutsch, M. 1993. "Educating for a Peaceful World." *American Psychologist* 48 (5): 510–7. http://dx.doi.org/10.1037/0003-066X.48.5.510.

Disability Income Support Coalition. 2013. DISC *Factsheet*. Saskatoon: DISC. http://www.saskdisc.ca/.

Duncan, B. 2013. Former Executive Director of the Saskatchewan Voice of People with Disabilities, Interview by B. Morton, 24 2013, Regina, Saskatchewan.

Employment and Social Development Canada. 1998. *Eighth Report of the Standing Committee on Human Resources, Skills Development, Social Development and the Status of Persons with Disabilities*. http://www.hrsdc.gc.ca/eng/disability/arc/eighth_report.shtml.

Federal, Provincial, and Territorial Ministers Responsible for Social Services. 1998. *In Unison: A Canadian Approach to Disability Issues: A Vision Paper*. SP-113-10-98E, MP43-390/1998E. Ottawa, Ontario: Human Resources Development Canada 1998. Listed at http://www.publications.gc.ca/site/eng/79880/publication.html.

–2000. *In Unison 2000: Persons with Disabilities in Canada*. 2000. SP-182-01-01E, MP43-390/2000E. Ottawa, Ontario, Canada: Human Resources Development Canada. http://www.publications.gc.ca/site/eng/95017/publication.html.

General Assembly, United Nations. 1976. *31/123, International Year of Disabled Persons*. http://www.un.org/en/ga/search/view_doc.asp?symbol=A/RES/31/123.

Government of Saskatchewan. 2007. *The Disability Inclusion Policy Framework: Government's Response to the Saskatchewan Council on Disability Issues' Disability Action Plan*. Regina, Saskatchewan: Government of Saskatchewan.

Government of Saskatchewan. 2008. *Province Announces $76.9 Million Investment and New income Plan for People with Disabilities*. Regina, Saskatchewan: Government of Saskatchewan News Release – October 23.

Government of Saskatchewan. 2009. *The Final Recommendations of the Task Team on Income Support for People with Disabilities*. Regina, Saskatchewan: Government of Saskatchewan

Government of Saskatchewan. 2014. *Current Total Number of Individuals on Saskatchewan Assured Income for Disability*. Regina, Saskatchewan: Saskatchewan Ministry of Social Services.

Grunig, J.E. 2000. "Collectivism, Collaboration and Societal Corporatism as Core Professional Values in Public Relations." *Journal of Public Relations Research* 12 (1): 23–48. http://dx.doi.org/10.1207/S1532754XJPRR1201_3.

Johnston, K.A. 2010. "Community Engagement: Exploring a Relational Approach to the Consultation and Collaborative Practice in Australia." *Journal of Promotion Management* 16 (1–2): 217–34. http://dx.doi.org/10.1080/10496490903578550.

Mikkonen, J., and D. Raphael. 2010. *Social Determinants of Health: The Canadian Facts*. Toronto, Ontario: York University School of Health Policy and Management. http://www.thecanadianfacts.org/The_Canadian_Facts.pdf.

Ministry of Social Services. 1998. *Disability Issues*. Regina: Government of Saskatchewan. http://www.publications.gov.sk.ca/details.cfm?p=50351.

Ministry of Social Services. 2009. *Final Recommendations of the Task Team on Income Support for People with Disabilities*. Regina, Saskatchewan: Government of Saskatchewan. http://www.gov.sk.ca/adx/aspx/adxGetMedia.aspx?mediaId=814&PN=Shared.

National Council of Welfare. 2006. "Number of People on Welfare." Welfare Incomes 2005 Fact Sheet #9. Ottawa: National Council of Welfare.

Osborne, J.E., and the Special Adviser on Policy Development, Department of National Health and Welfare. 1985. "The Evolution of the Canada Assistance Plan." In *Service to the Public – Canada Assistance Plan.*, 1–5. Ottawa, Ontario: Government of Canada; http://www.canadiansocialresearch.net/capjack.htm.

Pasquero, J. 1991. "Supraorganizational Collaboration: The Canadian Environmental Experiment." *Journal of Applied Behavioral Science* 27 (1): 38–64. http://dx.doi.org/10.1177/0021886391271003.

Parliament of Canada. 2006. "Standing Committee on Human Resources, Social Development and the Status of Persons with Disabilities." Number 038, 1st Session, 39th Parliament. Ottawa, Ontario: Parliament of Canada.

Raphael, D. 2009. *Social Determinants of Health: Canadian Perspectives*. 2nd ed. Toronto: Canadian Scholars' Press.

Saskatchewan Council on Disability Issues. 2001. *Saskatchewan's Disability Action Plan*. Regina, Saskatchewan. http://saskvoice.com/wp-content/uploads/2011/05/SkDisAP.pdf.

Saskatchewan Party. 2011. *Premier Announces Plan To Improve Quality of Life for Persons With Disabilities*. Regina: Saskatchewan Party.

Saskatchewan Voice of People with Disabilities. 2007. "Prairie Voice: Provincial Interagency Network on Disability (PIND)." Regina, Saskatchewan: Saskatchewan Voice of People with Disabilities. http://saskvoice.com/wp-content/uploads/2011/05/fall-2007-2.pdf.

Saunders, P. 2006. *The Costs of Disability and the Incidence of Poverty*. Sydney, Australia: The Social Policy Research Centre, University of South Wales. https://www.sprc.unsw.edu.au/media/SPRCFile/DP147.pdf.

Sherif, J., and C. Sherif. 1953. *Groups in Harmony and Tension: An Integration of Studies on Intergroup Relationships.* New York: Harper.

Sherraden, M.S., B. Slosar, and M. Sherraden. 2002. "Innovation in social policy: Collaborative policy advocacy." *Social Work* 47 (3): 209–21. http://dx.doi.org/10.1093/sw/47.3.209.

Stapleton, D., A. Protiuk, and C. Stone. 2008. *Review of International Evidence on the Cost of Disability,* Department for Work and Pensions Research Report No 542. London, England: Mathematica Policy Research, Inc. on behalf of the Department for Work and Pensions. https://www.google.ca/webhp?sourceid=chrome-instant&ion=1&espv=2&ie=UTF-8#.

Stapleton, J., A. Tweedle, and K. Gibson. 2013. *What Is Happening to Disability Income in Canada: Insights and Proposals for Further Research.* Winnipeg: Council of Canadians with Disabilities.

Tibble, M. 2005. *Review of Existing Research on the Extra Costs of Disability,* Department for Work and Pensions Working Paper No. 21. London, England: Department for Work and Pensions.

Thompson, K., J. James, K. Bender, and C. Hembroff. 2014. "Summary Report of the 2012 Study on Disability Costs and the 2013 Study on the Impact of SAID." Saskatoon: Disability Income Support Coalition (Internal Report).

Watts, R. 2010. DISC *"Adequacy" Research Project.* Saskatoon, Saskatchewan: Robb Watts Consultant.

# 6

# Who Is Minding the First Nations during the Flood?: Failing Advocacy at Every Policy Turn during a Human/Environmental Crisis

MYRLE BALLARD

### INTRODUCTION

This chapter presents the story of a provincial government-managed flood that was started by unprecedented high water volume in May 2011, destroying a once thriving and sustainable community in Lake St Martin First Nation (LSMFN) – a community with deep ancestral ties to the land – and forcing the evacuation of hundreds of my people. It is also a story about the invisibility and incapacity of the non-profit sector during an era of neoliberalism and an enduring process of colonialization. I lived in this community located in the Interlake Region of Manitoba, focused my PhD dissertation on this crisis, and attest to the devastating effects of the evacuation on the social, cultural, political, environmental, and economic well-being of the Anishinabek. Today, most of the Anishinabek are vulnerable, disempowered, displaced, homeless, and landless. Since becoming homeless and landless in 2011, with most of our Anishinabek members living in hotels in urban centres and other areas of the province during these years, the summer of 2015 saw the breaking of sod for the building of our new community. Over those five years, families have been displaced and many have lost track of one another.

This story is also an account of the many decisions made by governments, First Nation (FN) organizations, and non-FN non-profit organizations during the flood and its aftermath. Both federal and provincial government policies operated to both control and silence LSMFN; these policies affected the degree to which the community was entitled to participate in decisions that directly affected them. Worse still, LSMFN was caught between different government jurisdictions that have had profoundly damaging impacts on our well-being. Further, the non-profit-sector response, both in terms of service delivery and collective advocacy, was impotent, and thus ineffective. The lack of collective advocacy during the crisis has left LSMFN in turmoil. The question remains as to why there was a lack of advocacy during the great flood of 2011. All of this led us into a more marginalized state of existence without an opportunity to participate, our human rights denied, and no access to justice (see chapter 11). Public policy advocacy, the need for humanitarian intervention during a time of crisis when people desperately needed it, and the apparent apathy toward the evacuation and displacement of LSMFN people, are the focus of this chapter.

### Lake St Martin First Nation Ojibway Community

Lake St Martin First Nation (LSMFN), an Ojibway (Saulteaux) community of 2,394 people (AANDC 2012), was situated in the Interlake region of Manitoba, as shown in Figure 6.1. The main services, such as the band office, health centre, school, and a child and family agency, were funded by the government. There were three churches in LSMFN, which are registered charities that served as gathering places for our community residents. The other church was an Anglican church that was operated by non-resident priests, but it shut its doors decades ago. The churches were locally run with local congregations but they were also forced to evacuate and had no power to assist other members of our community. There were no individual proprietors or any other business ventures in our community. The people of my community have lived in this area since the late 1800s when treaties were signed and the federal government created reserves (Ballard and Thompson 2013).

Traditionally, our people of Lake St Martin were mainly fishers and buffalo hunters, although they pursued other hunting and agricultural activities. Women would get together to prepare the fishing nets and men made canoes for travel and fishing. In 1871, Lake St Martin took part in Treaty 2, leading to the creation of

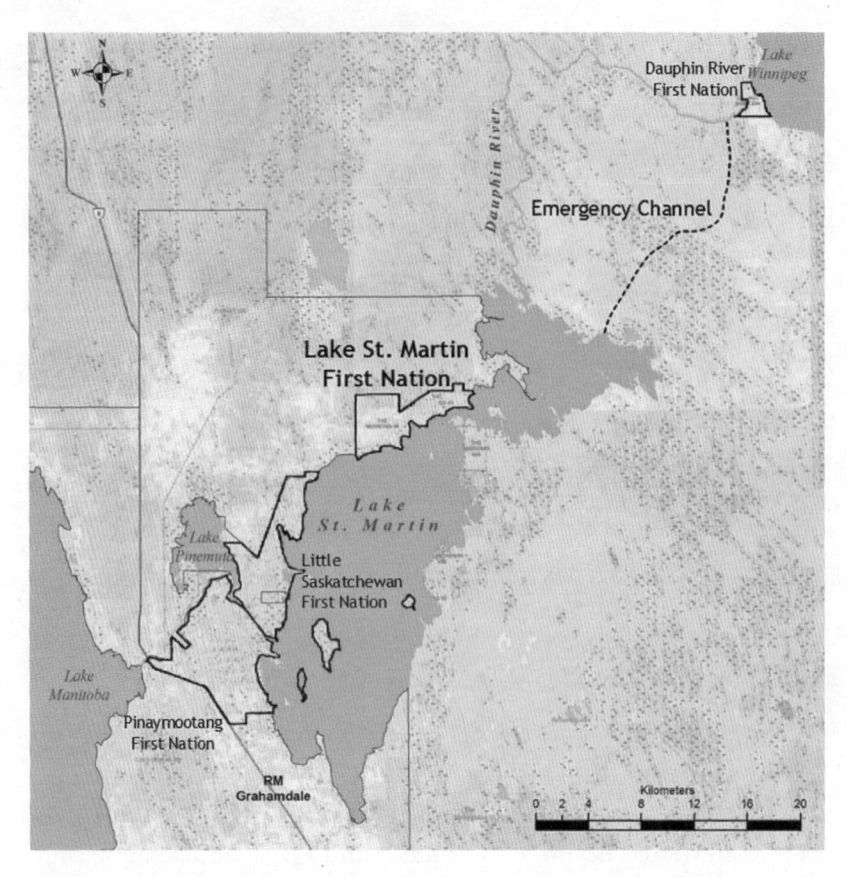

Figure 6.1 Lake St Martin is located in the Interlake region of Manitoba between Lake Manitoba and Lake Winnipeg.

Reserve No 49, and Treaty 5, leading to the creation of Reserve No 49A ... After settlement started in the mid-1850s, fishing, apart from being an important source of sustenance, provided an income for the Anishinabek peoples. Despite diminishing resource access due to settlers' superior technology and their ability to overharvest for export, and by settlement that reduced wildlife populations, the community of Lake St Martin FN adapted to their new circumstances, retaining their language, having a day school rather than a residential school, and practising agriculture to maintain their food self-sufficiency (45).

The community was permanently displaced in May 2011 by a devastating flood, nicknamed the "superflood." The superflood was considered the largest spring runoff in the province's history (Galloway 2012), whose geographical scope and duration surpassed previous provincial records (Province of Manitoba 2013a). The Manitoba provincial government elevated the water levels by using water control structures. This resulted in the displacement of people with a deep ancestral and spiritual connection to the land, while protecting cottages and agricultural land used by settler people with only an economic and recreational interest (Ballard, Klatt, and Thompson 2012). It is noteworthy that other FN communities living along the shores of the lake were also displaced, but this chapter focuses on my LSMFN community.

### Anishinaabe Pimatiziwin and Pimachiiywin

Before going further, it is essential to offer a brief overview of Anishinaabe people's philosophy because it helps to explain the severe personal trauma created by the forced relocation. In the Anishinaabe understanding, each person has specific gifts and a specific role to play on earth that is sacred and given from spirit. Anishinaabe "pimatiziwin" refers to the "life" or "being" of a person. It connotes a sense of how a person lives or their well-being. "Pimachiiywin" refers to the ability to sustain yourself – to be able to live sustainably as well as the ability to have a sustainable livelihood. If people cannot participate in life with their gifts and cannot fulfill their assigned roles in life, they lose their vision, their purpose, and their understanding of why they are here. They start to live in a state of chronic depression, hopelessness, powerlessness, despair, and grievance that leads to dysfunctional and self-destructive behaviour. This occurred when the Anishinabek of LSMFN were displaced from our community in May 2011. The elderly evacuees stated that because they were unable to move around and were confined to the small space of a hotel room, they began to feel depressed and found it difficult to walk and move around. The nurse for LSMFN confirmed that one of the signs of depression is the inability to move (Helm 2011).

The Anishinabek were given the land with everything on it by the Creator to create healthy lives and communities for ourselves. Land given by the Creator is since time immemorial. The Anishinaabe kwek (women) know that we were given the responsibility to protect and care for the land so that it will always provide for future generations. This understanding is so central to Indigenous peoples around the world but not to the rest of society. This is a fundamental core sacred value to Anishinaabe peoples, as expressed in the Anishinaabe ways. The Anishinaabe Elders (Ballard 2012) talk about:

> 'Muntoo kaki iizi miininung' to refer to language, the way of life, and everything that God or Muntoo created for the Anishinabek to use and to be part of Anishinaabe pimatiziwin. It is important to note that there are no Anishinaabe words for 'rights.' However there is a word that refers to our land, and that for the Anishinaabe speaker to refer to 'du kiinan' carries a lot of weight. 'Du kiinan' means 'our land'. Anishinaabe words are direct descriptions of their relationship with the land and with their everyday life – feelings and emotions. When Anishinaabe people speak of 'du kiinan' it is used in conversation with an outsider and refers to the Anishinaabe collective ownership of the land. 'Ki du kiinan' is used when talking with other Anishinabek or neechi Anishinabek. 'Ka tusii pi madiizhiyang' also signifies that the land is our base; the basis of our sustenance, health and culture, and this is where we live. However the translation is not enough, as the English language cannot accurately describe the full extent of these Anishinaabe words. (134)

The flood of 2011 had a significant impact on the pimatiziwin and pimachiiywin of the Anishinabek of LSMFN. When the flood happened, it was at the expense of the downstream users, who are the poor and marginalized. The LSMFN Anishinabek no longer have land, and without a land base, our pimatiziwin is disappearing.

There is no word for "advocacy" in the Anishinaabe language. However, the term "wiichiitiwin" is used to refer to the Anishinaabe way of life of helping one another. And when dealing with government agencies and other bureaucratic organizations, "kiigitoo tumawaa" refers to someone who will speak for you and help you. "Advocacy" refers to "the act or process of advocating or supporting a cause or proposal" (Merriam-Webster Dictionary 2016). Both of these terms illuminate key elements of the term "advocacy."

## HISTORIC PUBLIC POLICIES UNDER WHICH FIRST NATIONS PEOPLES ARE FORCED TO LIVE

In the nineteenth century, government legislation for Indians sought to assimilate, disempower, and destroy the Native way of life (Voyageur 1998). It was expected that we would be assimilated, meaning that we would give up our own culture, languages, and beliefs, and live and act like the settlers. Despite these attempts, we had no intention of giving up our culture. Some legislation and policies that were enacted by the British colonial government, and lately by the federal government, to control FNs are outlined in Table 6.1.

The main purpose of the Indian Act of 1876 was to assimilate, civilize, and control the Indians. The Indian Act essentially made "Status Indians" wards of the Crown, and regulated our lives. Indian status was regarded as a temporary stage on the road to assimilation. Restrictions ranged from rules about how we would elect leaders to how our children would be educated and how our estates would be dealt with after death. We were allowed virtually no self-governing powers. Forced assimilation meant the forced removal of children from our homes and into residential schools, but at the same time, it stripped any Indian who obtained a university education or ordination of his/her rights under the Act. The Act made it illegal for us to sell or produce goods without the written permission of the local Indian agent. We also had to get written permission from the Indian agents if we wanted to leave the reserve for any reason. The Indian agent became the de facto ruler of Indians on reserves.

Treaties were signed, land was shared with the settlers, and we were placed on reserves. The numbered treaty territories span the Prairies, yet we have no say or control over our treaty lands and resources. To this day the Indian Act, which has created bureaucratic control and dependency, still regulates our lives. Further, because we are wards of the Crown, other governments or agencies "pass up" the responsibility of "managing the Indians," such as is the case with the 2011 flood.

Today, these and other government policies validate the removal of Indians from lands needed for development by the province or corporations. In many instances, development is in the name of progress and to serve the economy, but, sadly, it is often the Indians who are at the mercy of development. Treaties that were made are not being honoured. For example, the promise was made that "as long as

Table 6.1 List of select legislation under which first Nations are forced to live

| Year | Policy/Event | Significance |
|---|---|---|
| 1000 | Vikings sail to "Americas" | Vikings are met by Beothuk Tribe. |
| 1492 | Columbus "discovers" America | Columbus sets foot on land that has inhabitants. |
| 1763 | Royal Proclamation of 1763 | Though the Act assumes the colonial right to take over the continent, it also assumes that the indigenous inhabitants are autonomous political bodies with basic rights. The Act establishes a colonization pattern in which settlers cannot simply take over Indigenous lands without first obtaining some form of surrender or cession of the land. |
| 1857 | Civilization of Indian Tribes Act | The Act was the first of many seeking to encourage FN Peoples to relinquish their land, language, culture, and existing rights in exchange for full British/Canadian citizenship. The law said that if an Indian man learned to read and signed a pledge to "live as a white" he was allowed to vote and own property. |
| 1867 | British North America Act | Transferred responsibility for Canada's First Peoples from the British to the Canadian government, granting the government sole authority to negotiate treaties with the Indians, purchase their land, and look after the Indians' best interests. It was a huge conflict of interest that led to many abuses. |
| 1869 | Purchase of Rupert's Land | The Dominion of Canada purchases Rupert's Land from Hudson's Bay (becomes final in 1870) |
| 1870 | Manitoba Act | Creates the province of Manitoba (the northern part of the province was added in 1912) to become part of Canada. |
| 1871 | Treaty #1 signed | Signed at Upper Fort Garry. This treaty covers much of southern Manitoba. |
| 1871 | Treaty #2 signed | Signed at the northwest shore of Lake Manitoba, the signatories included ten Ojibway tribes, including LSMFN. One of the Treaty provisions includes 160 acres for each family of five persons, or in the same proportion for a greater or smaller number of persons. |
| 1873 | North West Mounted Police | Created as a result of the sudden shift of authority from the sale of Rupert's Land, and to quell the resultant uncertainty and unrest among the inhabitants of the region. Order was needed if the Canadian Northwest was to attract settlers. (Became the Royal Canadian Mounted Police in 1905). |

| Year | Policy/Event | Significance |
| --- | --- | --- |
| 1876 | Indian Act | Passed with the purpose of assimilation, in which Aboriginals would be encouraged to leave behind their Indian status and traditional cultures and become full members of the broader Canadian society. |
| 1876–1950 | Some key amendments to the Indian Act include: | Between 1876 and 1950, the purpose of the amendments to the Indian Act was to strengthen the philosophy of civilization and assimilation underlying the first Act. Changes to the Act granted powers to move FNs and expropriate their lands for the purpose of non-FN use. |
| 1880 | Department of Indian Affairs | Bureau created to manage "affairs of Indians" and still exists today. |
| 1880s–1996 | Indian Residential Schools | More than 140 church-run schools operated by the Government of Canada which developed a policy called "aggressive assimilation." The premise was that children were easier to mould than adults and boarding schools would prepare them for mainstream society. |
| 1894 | Amendment to Indian Act | Removed band control over non-Aboriginals living on reserves. This power was transferred to the Superintendent General of Indian Affairs. |
| 1905 | Amendment to Indian Act | Power to remove FN peoples from reserves near towns with more than 8,000 people. |
| 1911 | Amendment to Indian Act | Power to expropriate portions of reserves for roads, railways, and other public works, as well as to move an entire reserve away from a municipality if it was deemed expedient. |
| 1918 | Amendment to Indian Act | Power to lease out uncultivated reserve lands to non-Aboriginals if the new leaseholder would use it for farming or pasture. |
| 1927 | Amendment to Indian Act | Prohibited anyone (Aboriginal or otherwise) from soliciting funds for Aboriginal legal claims without special license from the Superintendent General. It granted the government control over the ability of Aboriginals to pursue land claims. |
| 1930 | Natural Resources Transfer Act | Control of Crown Lands and natural resources is transferred from Federal to Provincial Governments. |
| 1960 | First Nations' right to vote in federal election | FN people finally gain the right to vote. |
| 1960 | Fairford Dam constructed | Constructed to control outflows. Downstream are FNs inhabitants. |

*(Continued)*

Table 6.1 (Continued)

| Year | Policy/Event | Significance |
|---|---|---|
| 1969 | White Paper | Pierre Trudeau's Minister of Indian Affairs, Jean Chrétien, releases a proposed policy, the "White Paper," to abolish the Department of Indian Affairs, and eliminate special status for Indian peoples and lands as part of assimilation. |
| 1971 | Portage Dam is constructed | Constructed to save City of Winnipeg from flooding. Outflow into Fairford Dam. |
| 1982 | Canadian Constitution | Patriation of the Canadian Constitution, which includes the Charter of Rights and Freedoms that recognizes Aboriginal and treaty rights. |
| 1990 | Meech Lake Accord | Prime Minister Brian Mulroney's Accord is defeated, in part by Elijah Harper's famous stand in the Manitoba Legislature. |
| 1990 | Oka Crisis | Plans to create a golf course on Aboriginal burial grounds lead to the Oka Crisis in Quebec |
| 1991 | Aboriginal Justice Inquiry | The Aboriginal Justice Inquiry is created by the Government of Manitoba to investigate the deaths of Helen Betty Osborne and J.J. Harper. |
| 1991–1996 | Royal Commission on Aboriginal Peoples | Federally created, this becomes the longest and most expensive royal commission in Canadian history, which was established to address the many issues of Aboriginal peoples. |
| 1992 | Charlottetown Accord | Prime Minister Mulroney's national referendum is defeated. The Accord promises to recognize the "inherent right to self-government" of aboriginal people. |
| 2004 | Wuskwatim Hydro Dam construction starts | The Manitoba Government gives Manitoba Hydro the green light to construct the Wuskwatim Hydro Dam in northern Manitoba. It is the first new dam in Manitoba since Limestone, which was completed in 1990. |
| 2005 | Kelowna Accord | With the Kelowna Accord, the minority Liberal government commits $5 billion over ten years to improve education, employment, and living standards for Aboriginal people. The Conservative government that follows chooses a different path. |
| 2011 | Emergency Measures Act (EMA) | The Manitoba Government uses its power and implements EMA, citing an artificial flood to permanently flood out LSMFN without consultation. |
| 2011 | Superflood in Manitoba | Flooding leads to the evacuation and permanent displacement of LSMFN, and the evacuation of other First Nations communities. |

the sun shines, the river flows and the grasses grow," Indians would be on that treaty land. Waldram quotes a FN person who gave testimony for the Manitoba Hydro Easterville brief:

> We want to tell a story, our story, of what can happen to Indian people when their land is flooded by a hydro project and their way of life is forced to change ... It is only ten years since we left the home we had chosen about one hundred years ago when the white men first came into our country and told us that we must give up our land and settle down to live on a reserve which we chose at that time. We were told that this reserve would be our home as long as the sun shines, the river flows and the grasses grow.

The question is, what happens to the promise "as long as the rivers run," when the rivers no longer flow or they are disrupted by flooding? Waldram (1993, 3) asks if flooding constitutes breaking of the treaties: "When Indian reserve land has been flooded, has the spirit of the treaties been broken?" I answer that it does.

## A BRIEF HISTORY OF THE FLOOD PROBLEM

The Anishinabek have lived in despair for over half a century, since the early 1960s when the first dam became operational. "At Lake St. Martin FN, people lived sustainably until the mid-1960s when a water control structure increased water levels and flooded their land." Our livelihoods, culture, and community life have also been deeply affected by the 2011 flood. The flood has destroyed the very core of pimatiziwin and pimachiiywin, which is interconnected with the land. If this interconnectedness is fractured or broken, then our people are fractured and broken (Ballard and Thompson 2013, 45).

Since time immemorial, the rivers, lands, and lakes were occupied and used by the original peoples of Canada, believing that the waterways were given to them by the creator (Waldram 1993). To FN peoples, water is considered life and the rivers are considered the veins of Mother Earth. In addition to our Aboriginal and treaty rights, FN peoples have riparian rights (Notzke 1994). Riparian rights are the "legal right of owners of land bordering on a river or other body of water, and any law that pertains to use of the water for that land" (Beausoleil First Nation 2014, 3). Riparian rights have great significance, notably because many of the reserves provided for in the treaties are located on the shores of lakes and rivers (Notzke 1994). In this instance, LSMFN is named after the lake: Lake St Martin and the community are located on the shores of Lake St Martin. However, the Province of Manitoba and its utilities have taken the view that waterways are a common property resource and that FN peoples have no special rights to them. Thus, dams are developed to create hydroelectricity for the "common good" (Ballard and Thompson 2013).

Many other FN communities in Manitoba have been flooded due to hydro damming. The community of South Indian Lake FN was displaced when the Nelson River was dammed, causing it to reverse its flow and increase water levels. The ability of FN peoples to live off the land has been compromised at South Indian Lake FN and other communities, with South Indian Lake fishers reporting catching four tubs of fish with forty nets, where before they had caught forty tubs with four nets (Thompson et al. 2011).

Undoubtedly, the flood of 2011 was unprecedented: "[the] water [at Lake St. Martin] peaked at 806 feet, almost 3 feet higher than the historic peak of 1955" (KGS Group and AECOM 2011), which flooded the three reserves adjacent to Lake St Martin, but hit LSMFN the hardest. The spring precipitation was two to three times the norm. Every watershed in southern Manitoba flooded. The resulting crisis mobilized a vast workforce of volunteers, contractors, and the army. Thousands of acres of farmland went underwater but the most significant flood damage was in the vicinity of Lake Manitoba and Lake St Martin. Hundreds of people lost their homes and cottages, lost their businesses, lost their incomes, suffered long-term damage to their farms, and were, or continue to be, displaced. A detailed account of the flood, water levels, and affected communities can be found in *Flooding Hope and Livelihoods: Lake St. Martin First Nation* (Ballard and Thompson 2013).

Although the people on the shores of Lake Manitoba, Lake St Martin, and Dauphin River were all subject to the same flood waters, the communities downstream were hit the hardest. The divergent experiences and interests in this region are defined in part by the hydraulic relationship between these bodies of water.

Figure 6.2 LSMFN members claimed Site #9 between Grahamdale and Moosehorn for their new community.

Lake Manitoba is a large lake compared with Lake St Martin. Small changes to water levels on Lake Manitoba can result in much larger changes downstream on Lake St Martin and the Dauphin River. Finding a water management approach acceptable to all locations and people requires concessions by everyone (Province of Manitoba 2013a).

First Nations people who live around Lake Manitoba have a very clear idea of what they would like to see in terms of lake levels and control structures (Province of Manitoba 2012). In particular, there is a strong demand for another outlet to deal with inflows from the Portage Diversion. The people of LSMFN have had an unfortunate and much longer history of flooding; we have been on the receiving end of altered flows from Lake Manitoba since the Fairford River Water Control Structure began operating in 1961. The flood of 2011 just compounded an already bad situation.

## ANALYSIS

### Different Ideology about Water

To settlers, water is a commodity, but for FNs, water is an important part of our broad and holistic perspective, which recognizes the interrelationships among all aspects of Creation (McGregor 2009). To FNs, water goes beyond human and ecosystem needs (Cave, Plummer, and de Loe 2013): it is used in ceremonies, cleansing, and in growing foods and medicines necessary for survival. The degradation of water quality has threatened the survival of FNs (McGregor 2009); similarly, the anthropogenic impact of water level alterations also threatens the survival of FNs. Commodifying water via large dams has become a key instrument of economic development in the past century (Richter et al. 2010). In Canada, water governance is treated as a solely provincial matter. The provincial government has the authority and mandate to manage water resources within watersheds. Thus, the province's water governance has controlled the water and developed dams and water control structures for hydroelectricity for the "common good" of all, but the "common good" turns bad for downstream users – and the inequity falls on FN communities. Provincial guidelines for operating dams privilege residential property and agricultural land over FNs communities, who have a deep and long-term connection to the land.

### Good Governance, but for Whom?

When it comes to FNs, does the province practice "good governance"? Is the province's action on LSMFN considered to be "good governance"? The trade-offs made by the province in handling LSMFN water management and displacement issues are compared and described in Ostrom's (2005) four measures of good governance evaluation criteria: *economic efficiency, equity, accountability*, and *adaptability*.

First, let us consider *economic efficiency*. Economic efficiency was achieved when the province made a profit on hydroelectricity from

Table 6.2 Summary of DFAA eligibility on First Nations reserves

| Scenario | Reimbursement of on-reserve costs | Reimbursement of off-reserve costs |
|---|---|---|
| Off-reserve costs over provincial DFAA threshold | DFAA fully compensates a province for all eligible expenses (including incremental administrative costs) for the reserve. | Off-reserve costs are subject to normal DFAA cost-sharing formula. |
| Off-reserve costs under provincial DFAA threshold | INAC fully compensates the province for all eligible expenses (including incremental and administrative costs) for the reserve. DFAA does not apply. | Province is responsible for off-reserve costs since DFAA does not apply. |
| Damage limited to reserve (whether above or below DFAA threshold) | INAC fully compensates the province for all expenses for the reserve (including incremental administrative costs). | Not applicable. |

*Source*: Public Safety Canada 2013.

high water levels and avoided costs for damage to provincial property by channelling it to FNs communities. Economic efficiency was also achieved by diverting the water through the Portage Diversion to keep the City of Winnipeg safe and dry. FNs are a federal government responsibility, so money that flowed from the federal government for LSMFN damages and expenses became a provincial economic investment – essentially, the flood generated economic development. Despite the millions of dollars injected into the local economy, the City of Winnipeg has yet to say thank you to LSMFN for sacrificing its traditional lands so the City of Winnipeg can be safe and dry.

Second, there are serious *equity* issues. The flow of federal government money generated by the 2011 flood was staggering. But the money did not reach the FNs, who have yet to be compensated *equitably* regardless of residency. Public Safety Canada, through the Disaster Financial Assistance Arrangement (DFAA), provides financial assistance in the event of a large-scale natural disaster to provincial and territorial governments (Public Safety Canada 2013). But the DFAA has different criteria for FNs living on-reserve. These criteria are discriminatory and inequitable.

Table 6.2 provides a list of some of the DFAA criteria for FN reserves. The multiple layers of bureaucracy and money filtering from DFAA and Aboriginal Affairs and Northern Development Canada (AANDC) to the province, and then again to the Manitoba Association of Native Fire Fighters (MANFF) is immense. For each transfer of money, an administration fee is charged. One is left to wonder where the efficiency, equity, and accountability are in this maze of money exchanges that is the result of jurisdictional wrangling. A recent article in the *Winnipeg Free Press* (2013) reads "Value of federal flood aid to First Nations questioned." The article states

> The federal government provided more than $84 million to Manitoba First Nations communities flooded out in 2011 but admits it doesn't know how effective the emergency aid was. An Emergency Management Assistance Program (EMAP) report released this week by Aboriginal Affairs and Northern Development Canada (AANDC) finds the program helped with immediate safety issues but the government says it can't assess the effectiveness of long-term safety issues and permanent flood protection. (Moore 2013)

The article further states that its emergency assistance program was ineffective, and highlights the government's limited ability to address long-term and systemic issues faced by FN communities during natural disasters.

Third, the *accountability* criterion was problematic. In addition to section 35 of the Canadian Constitution, which states that there is a duty to consult FN on matters that affect our treaty rights, FN peoples elect provincial representatives in provincial elections and those elected officials should be *accountable* and responsible to them. However, when the LSMFN chief and council, as well as community members attended the press scrum after the legislature debates in November 2012, the New Democratic Party (NDP) premier, Greg Selinger, and Members of the Legislative Assembly refused to meet with them. When a reporter asked if the premier would meet with the community, the premier halted his press scrum and walked away, never addressing or talking to the community or chief who were present. This ongoing failure of the provincial government to consult FNs, who form a large percentage of the province's population, shows a lack of accountability. The province has well-developed institutional capacities that should be able to embrace consultation and respond to risks to both FNs and non-FNs as well as learn from the past mistakes of flooding communities.

*Accountability* was questioned, when in April 2013, MANFF was under scrutiny about how flood management on reserves was being handled. MANFF was retained by AANDC (formerly INAC) to administer the funding for the 2011 FN evacuees. The media (CBC 2013a) reported that restaurant and hotel bills were not being paid. In December 2013, the Red Cross signed a formal agreement to oversee aid for the evacuees and transfer of responsibility was complete by February 2014. The Red Cross took over the administration of evacuee services from the MANFF, which was audited by Ottawa following accusations of squandering money meant for evacuee administration and inappropriate hiring practices (e.g., hiring relatives), to name but two of many problems.

In another situation, the lack of *accountability* was again evident when beleaguered FN evacuees received an unsigned letter with no letterhead in September 2012 stating that their daily food allowances would be drastically cut as of 1 October 2012, from $23.40 to $4 for adults, and $18.70 to $3.20 for children. The province later admitted (though not publicly) that the letter had come from the province and AANDC. There was no warning that the letter was forthcoming and no opportunity given to FN peoples to plan ahead and budget.

Finally, the *adaptability* criterion requires explanation. First Nations people are more deeply affected by crises because they have fewer financial and human resources to cope with them. In addition, floods disrupt FNs' deep emotional and ancestral attachment to the land. The inadaptability of FN people made the effect of dislocation more profound. The fact that this dislocation has persisted over so many years adds to the depth of the trauma. It is morally reprehensible to target FN people with floods to save the economic and recreational interests of cottagers and agricultural land. It may be concluded that the province failed FNs people on the basis of these four evaluation criteria of good governance.

## A Community Disempowered

Lake St Martin FN members have had little influence over policies, programs, and development. Charities, non-profits, and cooperatives from the surrounding areas did not rise up to assist our community in our crucial time of need. The Fairford House of Prayer provided a gathering place for wake services for LSMFN people who died. The local charities and churches at LSMFN were affected as well since their pastors and congregation were evacuated and displaced. We faced the impacts of the flood alone (Ballard 2012). The Assembly of Manitoba Chiefs, Assembly of First Nations, and Southern Chiefs Organization supported us and provided media releases to make the public aware but they lacked capacity and funding to provide other supports.

The evacuees were dispersed throughout the province, with a majority of them sent to live in hotels and private accommodations in Winnipeg. A temporary band office was set up for them in Winnipeg to administer social assistance services and health programs. Disconnected from our land and from each other, and without finances, the people of Lake St Martin were rendered incapacitated and disempowered. The federal government's structure for FN governance has created a state of marginalization for FN people (Cook 2003). This structure has created an invisible wall that separates FNs from receiving the same services or treatment as a non-First Nation from other levels of governments and non-profit organizations, even in an urban setting. This is so systemic and tolerated that no one questions it – especially during this neoliberal era.

## Health, Life, and Death

The LSMFN evacuees were placed in hotels at the onset of the evacuation. In 2015, many were still living in hotels. Diabetes is rampant among First Nations, and LSMFN is no different, yet the hotels made no special provisions for diabetic dietary or other diet needs. Evacuees stated that they were eating foods that were too spicy and rich in sauce that they were not accustomed to (Ballard and Thompson 2013; and AANDC 2014a). Medical transportation was also problematic for evacuees who chose not to live in the service centres, where medical transportation was available. Evacuee coordinators and FN community staff were overworked and stressed. Workers who were dealing with stress had no place to turn for help.

There have been suicides and people passing on without ever returning home. FNs culture honours life and death. Evacuees have been unable to put their loved ones to rest. Traditionally, death is followed by certain customs. People gather at the home of the deceased to offer condolences and support to the relatives, but for those living in hotels, this is not so simple. In the final days of her life before passing on from terminal cancer, one elderly evacuee was sent back to her hotel room from the hospital to die. Another elderly evacuee who has since passed on, wept in despair, "It hurts when I think of Lake St. Martin. I get very lonely ... I want to cry all the time" (Ballard, Klatt, and Thompson 2012). The elderly evacuee, who has since passed on, died of cancer at a temporary resettlement site. She required health care during her last days at her temporary home, including someone to change her bandages and clean her feeding tubes. The temporary site is not a reserve, but because LSMFN evacuees are living there temporarily it is treated like a reserve because its residents are all FNs. Due to the systemic nature of the "invisible boundary" of the reserve and the wrangling over responsibility, the elder fell between the cracks. The provincial health care system should have stepped in to provide the health care that was required for the elder, regardless of her race.

Wake services after a death are also part of First Nations culture. However, evacuees cannot have wakes in our own community, which further creates stress. The neighbouring community of Pinaymootang First Nation has been gracious in allowing wake services to be held at their church as well as burials for those wishing to bury their loved ones in the Pinaymootang cemetery rather than LSMFN. Evacuees who attended wake services in Pinaymootang had to find transportation to get there and overnight accommodation in the area. Many times, evacuees attending wake services ended up sleeping inside the church overnight because there was nowhere else to sleep. Hotel rooms were not an option because they were not affordable. Provisions should have been made to provide hotel accommodations at least to immediate members of the family when their loved ones died.

## Non-Profit-Sector Humanitarian Responses

Beyond these government policy and program problems, LSMFN people were not well-served by surrounding area non-profit-sector organizations either. It appears that systemic barriers exist within this sector too. For example, during the Christmas season, charitable organizations such as the Winnipeg Cheer Board made it difficult for evacuees to obtain Christmas food hampers because FNs lacked permanent addresses. Many evacuees simply did not have the proper identification that was required for living and doing business in the city.

The LSMFNs approached the Mennonite Central Committee (MCC) as a possible NPO to assist us as a host for money that the FNs wanted to raise to purchase the resettlement land it needed. Our FN is not a registered charitable organization, and we were not able to manage finances due to AANDC's imposed third-party management. Our FN needed a registered charitable organization for fundraising. After MCC said they would take it to their board of directors, they never provided an answer. We were left wondering why they did not provide an answer.

The Winnipeg Humane Society (WHS) offered to rescue pets that were left behind during the evacuation but it did not notify LSMFNs that they would be rescuing our pets. The WHS posted pictures of pets on their website about a month after the evacuation in 2011, asking evacuees to claim them. Many of the evacuees did not have access to the Internet in their hotel rooms, nor did they know that WHS was posting pictures of our pets. However, WHS only offered to house our pets for a certain period of time. The evacuees were living in hotels, thus how could they expect evacuees to rescue their pets and move them to hotels? Many of the pets were unclaimed. WHS then blamed the evacuees for not taking care of and abandoning their pets on the reserve. Unfortunately, evacuees had only been given a few days' notice to evacuate and were told to take only a few days' worth of clothing, therefore they assumed that they would be gone for only a few days. A breakdown in communication between the WHS and LSMFN led to misdirected blame. Why were the evacuees blamed for a system that failed to accommodate both evacuees and their pets?

The Canadian Red Cross is heralded for its humanitarian relief efforts. However, it does not provide assistance to FN communities unless the chief and council or AANDC request their services. The lack of will to deliver the same type of services to FNs shows how deeply entrenched systemic discrimination is. Legislation that applies only to FNs such as the Indian Act creates jurisdictions that are barriers to service delivery and advocacy.

## No Social Justice for Housing or Possessions

Governments and other organizations do not recognize FNs' home ownership on reserves because the government gives money to the band to build homes for its members. As is the case for most reserves, housing is in the form of band housing that is provided by AANDC. Homeowners live in houses provided by the band, therefore they are not considered the owners of the houses by outside agencies. Even if they were to purchase a house, homeowners on reserves cannot own the land their house is on, because the land is held in trust by the Crown, which means FNS cannot get normal bank mortgages because the property cannot be seized. However, FNS consider their homes as their own and invest money in them, fixing and upgrading their property by building extensions, garages, fences, landscaping, and so forth.

Evacuees were ineligible for compensation for their property that was destroyed by the flood because government did not consider it their property. An elderly woman expressed her frustration when she went to the Emergency Measures Organization office to ask if she would get reimbursed for her damaged belongings, furniture, and property. The office person asked her to give them proof and provide photographs to show that her house was under water. This type of treatment by the province shows complete disrespect and lack of empathy toward the evacuees. As of the summer of 2015, the LSMFN has not been compensated for our lost homes or our possessions. The province must replace all the homes it destroyed due to the 2011 flood.

## Environmental Advocacy

Environmental and advocacy groups offered support to LSMFN. Kairos North East Justice and Peace Speaker Series invited me to make a presentation about the LSMFN evacuees to help create awareness in the larger community. Kairos said they wanted to have a community dinner for the evacuees. Project Peacemakers invited me to speak to their board as well; they provided a voice for the evacuees by influencing their MLAS. One church also said that they want to host a community dinner and event for the evacuees, however, due to conflicting schedules, the dinner did not happen. Environmental groups generated public awareness of the LSMFN catastrophe and are working to ensure that the issue does not go away. The video – *Flooding Hope: The Lake St. Martin First Nation Story* (Ballard et al. 2012) – was shown at some film festivals, the universities of Manitoba and Winnipeg, at various community events, and discussed on the radio.

## A Systemic Public Policy Quagmire: Failing Advocacy

A root cause of the origin and evolution of this humanitarian crisis has to do with the social, economic, physical, and constitutional location of the LSMFN people and the accompanying quagmire of public policies that render us unable to influence our situation and advocate for our own well-being. Two of these locations are particularly poignant given the attendant multiple and overlapping public policies. Physically, LSMFN is located in the province of Manitoba and falls under provincial land, water, and flood policies. Constitutionally though, we have been placed within the jurisdiction of the federal government generally, and what was then called the Indian Act in particular. Advocacy is particularly difficult in this policy quagmire because successful advocacy requires a mix of strategic policy analyses, social networks, volunteer time, financial resources, and legal expertise – all of which our FNS communities have very little of because of our forced dislocation. What follows in this section is an explanation of some of these multiple and overlapping public policies that make this situation overwhelming and advocacy a serious challenge.

Although the federal government did not explicitly target the FN, what role did the federal government play in the LSMFN flooding? The Government of Canada is responsible for FN governance through the Indian Act. The Indian Act gave the federal government authority to create elected band chiefs and councils to maintain financial and regulatory control over FN political, administrative, and service structures. However, under Canada's constitution, the federal government has a fiduciary responsibility for the health and safety of FNS communities, including the effect of floods. The Government of Canada, through AANDC, provided $63.6 million for flood protection and recovery costs for FNS affected by the flooding in Manitoba. The Honourable John Duncan, Minister for AANDC at that time, stated: "This year's flood has had a significant impact on First Nations communities in Manitoba. Ensuring the safety of First Nations residents has been our highest priority. We have also worked to protect property and infrastructure on reserves. The funding provided to date has gone to important preparedness and response activities such as dikes, sandbagging, as well as emergency planning" (Public Safety Canada 2011). The federal government bore the cost of the evacuation, but it is uncertain whether LSMFN will ever be fully compensated for all the damages.

Governments have a duty to consult and accommodate First Nations, as shown by court cases such as the Haida and Taku River Decision in 2004 (Hunter Voith 2005), and the Mikisew Cree Decision in 2005 (Supreme Court of Canada 2005). Meaningful consultation of FNs never occurred for LSMFN at the federal level. This is an important area of public policy. The duty to accommodate applies when an action or policy adversely affects potential or established Aboriginal or treaty rights, which would include being flooded from treaty land as well as replacement land. Although the federal government claims that "consulting is an important part of good governance, sound policy development and decision-making" and a way "to strengthen relationships and partnerships with Aboriginal peoples and thereby achieve reconciliation objectives" (AANDC 2011, 5), its action toward LSMFN was contrary to these goals. Without consultation, "the government spent $1.5-million to buy 3,200 acres for a new reserve site that community leaders reject" (Galloway 2012). This area, referred to as the "Halaburda site," is adjacent to the current reserve land and is also prone to flooding. The chief explained that he found out about the purchase from the seller, rather than the federal government, after, not before, money had changed hands to purchase the new reserve site. Worse still, the location the federal government chose was not even considered in earlier discussions about an interim community site. This lack of consultation is unconstitutional; LSMFN members should have been consulted and should have a voice about where we want our new community. The Anishinaabe people of LSMFN knew where they wanted their community to be relocated but they have been systematically ignored.

If the FNs had been consulted and listened to during the lakes and rivers policy development stages, would the FNs have ended up flooded, or would better public policy have been developed that considered the interests of everyone living along the shores of the lakes and rivers? First Nations considerations are strangely absent from provincial water and water diversion policy documents. For example, nowhere do the operating guidelines of the Portage Diversion mention FNs in their explanation: "The Portage Diversion operating guidelines allow it to be used for three objectives: minimizing the volume of water diverted to Lake Manitoba, protecting the city of Winnipeg, and preventing ice from jamming on the Assiniboine River east of Portage la Prairie" (Province of Manitoba 2013b, 1).

The operating guidelines of the Fairford Dam are to "maintain suitable levels on Lake Manitoba upstream of the dam and on the Fairford River, Lake St Martin and Dauphin River downstream of the dam ... It was recommended that the lake be allowed to fluctuate more like it would have in a state of nature in order to benefit aquatic habitat along the lake shore" (Province of Manitoba 2014, 1). Clearly, the guidelines manage water levels to reduce effects on residential property and on agricultural land that is on provincial land, but this narrow focus excludes FN communities, where currently 85 per cent of the LSMFN reserve has been ruled unsuitable for construction or rebuilding, due to the risk of being flooded. The FNs live downstream of the Fairford Dam, and the exclusion of FNs in its operating guidelines is disrespectful to the original inhabitants. The flood of 2011 on LSMFN has ruined the land, rendering the FNs homeless and landless.

Provincial governments have policies about "the duty to consult" and Aboriginal peoples have a right to consultation on development that affects our treaty rights. Despite these rights and the duty of the provincial government to consult, our community was not meaningfully consulted or fully involved in deliberations about water levels before or after the Fairford control structure was set up. LSMFN and other reserves nearby opposed drawing down Lake Manitoba water by way of Lake St Martin flooding. To channel more water into Lake St Martin, the province applied the Emergency Measures Act to override the requirement for an environmental assessment and the duty to consult on the 2011 $100-million water channel from Lake St Martin to Buffalo Marsh, Big Buffalo Lake, and into Buffalo Creek, although it borders their reserve and traditional territory. The FNs living downstream of the water control structures – the Portage Diversion, the Fairford Dam, and the emergency channel – were not meaningfully consulted about how the water should be managed. First Nations living downstream from water control structures have a legal right to be meaningfully consulted about water management yet the provincial government used a higher-level public policy tool against the FN and effectively silenced them.

These provincial water decisions were not the only areas where there was a lack of meaningful consultation by the province. The Anishinabek of LSMFN were actively engaged and participated before, during, and after the flood in offering solutions but we were systematically ignored by governments, non-profits, and non-FNs people of Manitoba and Canada. Our community voted in favour of a permanent settlement site, referred to as "site 9," immediately after the flood to bypass a temporary settlement and instead move directly toward permanent resettlement. The community members gathered at site 9 for a campout in August 2011 to demonstrate that we were serious about the land we wanted and to send a message to the government and the rural municipality; after all, site 9 is on Treaty 2 territory. The community members erected a sign that said "Welcome to Obushkudayang Treaty #2 Anishinaabe Nation," as shown in Figure 6.2, which signified that we were claiming site 9. But the next morning someone had vandalized our sign with expletives and racist language. We also held peaceful demonstrations on the highway near site 9 (Ballard et al. 2012). We invited the media to come to our camp to generate publicity about the land we wanted. We wanted to demonstrate that we were squatters on our own ancestral homeland and traditional territory. However, someone advised the media that the campout was cancelled, so no media arrived. Consequently, there was no public support for us when we claimed site 9 during the campout, other than some nearby FN community residents.

We also held peaceful demonstrations outside the Manitoba Legislative building, as shown in Figures 6.3 and 6.4, on several occasions that attracted the media. However, there was no support from the non-profit organizations or non-FNs communities. Our community had negotiated with the landowners for a fair price for site 9 of less than $2 million. However, it ended there because our FN had no money to buy our chosen land. Further, according to the federal and provincial governments, our FN had no right to choose our own land (Galloway 2012). If the land is purchased it has to be converted into reserve status that requires approval from the Government of Canada. The land would be an "Addition to Reserve," which is "a parcel of land that has been added to an existing reserve. Upon being added, the legal title also becomes vested in Her Majesty and is set apart by Her Majesty for the use and benefit of the Indian band that made the application. Funding has not been provided to LSMFN to acquire the lands we need. Should funding be provided, LSMFN should be given the option of asking the Government of Canada to transfer land they have acquired into reserve status, thus creating an Addition to Reserve (AANDC 2014b).

Figure 6.3 LSMFN members took part in many peaceful protests but their voices were not heard.

Figure 6.4 LSMFN members' protests for a new community and wanting to go home were ignored.

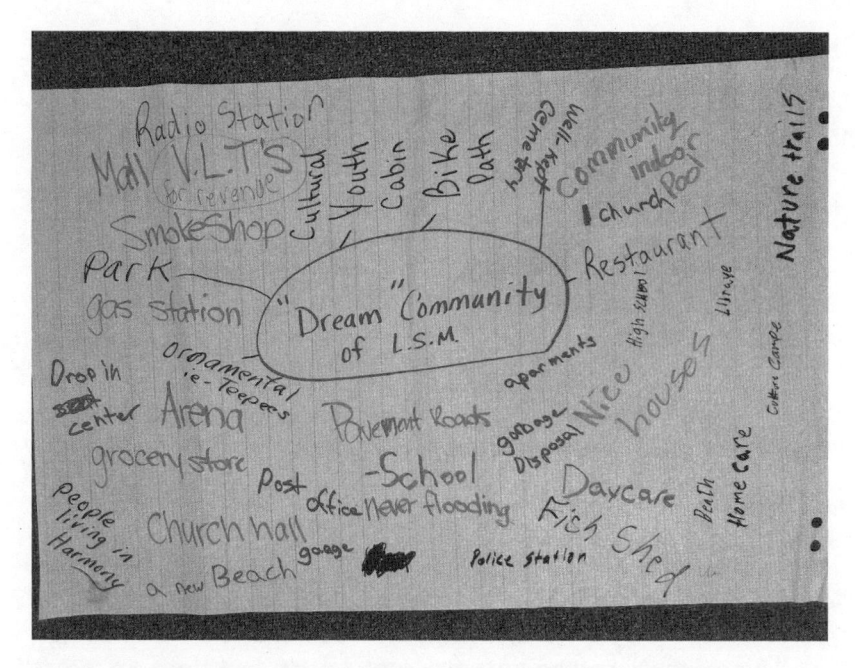

Figure 6.5 LSMFN members were asked what they wanted to see in their new community during a planning meeting.

In summary, a public policy quagmire exists for FN peoples in Canada which influences how advocacy is carried out. It is clear that we wanted to be part of decision-making processes – and had a legal right – regarding our property claims, new land, and in all aspects of water management, but federal policies such as the Indian Act still control our daily lives as FNs peoples. Our displacement from our ancestral land is the result of provincial policies that control the land and water and federal policies that control FN peoples.

## LAKE ST MARTIN FIRST NATION UNDERTOOK COMMUNITY DEVELOPMENT WORK

During all of this, we had high hopes and aspirations about the new community we knew we needed. As shown in Figure 6.5, we undertook our own community development work in an effort to take control and design our own community. We proved we have the capacity to do this work. We developed a community plan for a walkable and self-sufficient eco-community producing economic development, energy, and food; a community that would be sustainable. However, the province made a unilateral decision on a temporary site (for a similar account of a lack of democracy on the part of a provincial government, see chapter 9). The provincial government invested $14 million of the federal government's money for LSMFN for temporary housing in 2011 at an unacceptable location called the "radar base," an abandoned military base. Rather than start development on a permanent site, site 9, which would have been cheaper, the province developed the radar base as a temporary site. The province reasoned that there was no infrastructure on site 9 and that a road would have to be built. Oddly, the same reasoning proved true for the radar base. In March 2014, LSMFN evacuees occupied only ten of the approximately sixty homes on the radar base. First Nations members refused to move to this abandoned military base because it was only a temporary site and there were few services, including no piped water, no piped sewage, no schools, no community centre, no church, and no store. Once again, no organizations advocated for the LSM Anishinabek. In summary, attempts at exercising our democratic rights and responsibilities failed at every turn during and after the flood. The failure to engage and listen to LSMFN is evidence that democracy is failing in Canada.

The community needs a permanent land base now and wishes to be reunited in one location to rebuild its culture, family, and social bonds as quickly as possible. Under the stress of having no land base over such an extended time, the community felt increasingly pressured to accept the remote Halaburda site, which has few economic development opportunities. The Halaburda site, which was previously rejected by the LSMFN leadership and FNs, was the site of a sod turning ceremony in the summer of 2015 to mark the construction of the "new" community. Construction started in the summer of 2015 by draining water from the "new" site. The elders of LSMFN have warned LSMFN leadership that the proposed "new" site is a swamp. The province and/or AANDC did not consult with LSMFN members, nor did they hold a referendum before the construction started. The displacement and disempowerment of the community is taking its toll on the community. The common sentiment among the LSMFN members is "I just want to go home." At a recent workshop, our

LSMFN community created a vision statement for the next five to fifteen years:

> This Anishinaabe community is strong, sustainable and healing from the trauma of flooding and displacement on land free from flooding through empowering lifelong education, health and recreational services, abundant economic opportunities, rich cultural programming, healthy housing, state-of-the-art infrastructure and reconnecting to their ancestral lands. (Lake St. Martin First Nation Elders 2012)

We have articulated what we need and are prepared to work toward those goals but are prevented by governments that thwart our aspirations.

## CONCLUSIONS

From a sustainable and thriving community a century ago, LSMFN community members have, since the flood, been homeless, landless, and impoverished for many years. This was layered on top of the vulnerability context created by colonization and the post-colonial policies of present-day governments and the discriminatory practices of non-profit organizations. Government institutions and public policies played major roles in determining the degree of risk that LSMFN was forced to endure as well as the degree to which we were entitled to participate in decisions that directly affected us. In Canada, the provinces govern and manage water resources but the federal government is responsible for FN communities – this is where jurisdictional problems arose that profoundly and negatively affected the well-being of our FN community. Further, non-profit organizations appear to have followed the lead set by the provincial and federal governments when it comes to dealing with FNs: systemic barriers to human services and discriminatory assumptions became evident during the crisis and its aftermath. The federal and provincial governments, as well as non-profit organizations, made unilateral decisions without involving FNs, often under the guise of advocating for FNs' best interests. Given all of this, strategic policy analysis and collective advocacy was impossible.

There are government policies that state that LSMFN should have a say in where we want our new community to be. The lack of consultation is unconstitutional; the "duty to consult" requires governments to consult with First Nations about decisions affecting them. LSMFN voted for site 9 as our permanent reserve because it provided the opportunity to meet our economic, social, and cultural goals. The regional municipality where site 9 is located supported this choice after hearing about our plans to create an eco-community there. But none of this mattered.

Despite all of this, First Nations are persevering and have no intention of giving up our rights or special status. We have formed political organizations at the provincial and the national levels, and in fact, our political power, advocacy, and national voice have increased over the past few decades. For example, Idle No More formed in 2012 to confront the alleged abuses of treaty rights and the federal government's omnibus Bill C-45.

Within the wider society, the Anishinabek people have been relegated to the underclass. Access to resources and supports are moderated by formal and informal institutions such as laws and local systems of resource governance and policies (Tough 1997) that were built to support the settler society and take away land and resources from FNs. The Anishinabek are particularly vulnerable as a result of these existing structures and processes. Our FNs communities exist on the margins of society, dominated by a neoliberal agenda, where we have no opportunity to participate, where our human rights are denied, and where we have no access to justice. This is oddly different from the successes experienced by other First Nations and their non-profit organizations' advocacy work for telecommunications services in Canada's North (see chapter 10).

Our Anishinabek people are caught between federal government, provincial government, and NPO policies, leaving the Anishinabek with a triple challenge in trying to launch and move our advocacy work forward. Taken together, these governments and non-profit organizations have many systemic barriers, and in some cases operationalize systemic racism. This has resulted in a shuffling of responsibilities and jurisdictional excuses that lead us to the question, "Who is minding the First Nations during the flood?"

## REFERENCES

AANDC, Aboriginal Affairs and Northern Development Canada. 2011. "Aboriginal Consultation and Accommodation: Updated Guidelines for

Federal Officials to Fulfill the Duty to Consult," Government of Canada: Minister of Aboriginal Affairs and Northern Development Canada.

– 2012. *Aboriginal Peoples and Communities*. Accessed 19 November 2012. http://pse5-esd5.ainc-inac.gc.ca/FNP/Main/Search/FNRegPopulation.aspx?BAND_NUMbER=275&lang=eng.

– 2014a. *Manitoba Floods 2011 – First Nations Recovery Needs Assessment*. Accessed 19 August 2014. https://www.aadnc-AANDC.gc.ca/eng/1387391495840/1387392049811.

– 2014b. *Treaty Land Entitlement*. Accessed 5 June 2014. http://www.aadnc-AANDC.gc.ca/eng/1100100034819/1100100034820.

Ballard, M. 2012. *Flooding Sustainable Livelihoods of the Lake St Martin First Nation: The Need to Enhance the Role of Gender and Language in Anishinaabe Knowledge Systems*. PhD dissertation. Winnipeg: University of Manitoba.

Ballard, M., R. Klatt, and S. Thompson. 2012. *Flooding Hope: The Lake St. Martin First Nation Story. Documentary film directed by Myrle Ballard*. Winnipeg, MB: University of Manitoba.

Ballard, M., and S. Thompson. 2013. "Flooding Hope and Livelihoods: Lake St. Martin First Nation." *Canadian Journal of Nonprofit and Social Economy Research* 4 (1): 43–65.

Beausoleil First Nation. 2014. *Beausoleil First Nation Land Code*, June 16, 2014 – Draft. Accessed 17 August 2014. http://www.chimnissing.ca/landsdocs/LAND-CODE-DRAFT-JUNE2014.pdf.

Cave, K., R. Plummer, and R. de Loe. 2013. "Exploring Water Governance and Management in Oneida Nation of the Thames (Ontario, Canada): An Application of the Institutional Analysis and Development Framework." *Indigenous Policy Journal* 23 (4): 1–27.

CBC. 2013a. Hotel Bills For Manitoba Flood Evacuees Going Unpaid: Manitoba Association of Aboriginal Fire Fighters Received Funds for Invoices, Bills Remain Unpaid. Accessed 10 December 2013. http://www.cbc.ca/news/canada/manitoba/hotel-bills-for-manitoba-flood-evacuees-going-unpaid-1.1325274.

Cook, C. 2003. *Jurisdiction and First Nations Health and Health Care*. Master of Science thesis. Winnipeg: University of Manitoba.

Galloway, G. 2012. "Flooded Out to Save Winnipeg, Lake St. Martin Resident Now Feel Forgotten." *Globe and Mail*. Accessed 24 November 2012. http://www.theglobeandmail.com/news/national/flooded-out-to-save-winnipeg-lake-st-martin-residents-now-feel-forgotten/article5621936/?page=all.

Government of Canada. 2016. The Indian Act, R.S.C., 1985, c. 1-5. Retrieved http://laws-lois.justice.gc.ca/eng/acts/i-5/FullText.html.

Helm, D. 2011. *Personal communication*. Nurse, Lake St. Martin First Nation.

Hunter Voith. 2005. Consultation with First Nations and Accommodations Obligations. Accessed 21 August 2014. http://www.litigationchambers.com/pdf/JJLH%20Paper%20Compensation.pdf.

KGS Group and AECOM. 2011. *Analysis of Options for Emergency Reduction of Lake Manitoba and Lake St. Martin Levels Report from KGS Group and AECOM*. Winnipeg, MB: Province of Manitoba.

Lake St. Martin First Nation Elders. 2012. *Lake St. Martin Elders' Workshop*. Brokenhead, MB.

McGregor, D. 2009. "Honouring Our Relations: An Anishinaabe Perspective on Environmental Justice." In *Speaking for Ourselves: Environmental Justice in Canada*, edited by J. Agyeman, P. Cole, R. Haluza-Delay, and P. O'Riley, 28–41. Vancouver, BC: University of British Columbia Press.

Merriam-Webster Dictionary. 2016. http://www.merriam-webster.com/dictionary/advocacy.

Moore, H. 2013. *Value of Federal Flood Aid to First Nations Questioned*. CBC News posted: 15 August 2013. http://www.cbc.ca/news/canada/manitoba/value-of-federal-flood-aid-to-first-nations-questioned-1.1387070.

Notzke, C. 1994. *Aboriginal Peoples and Natural Resources in Canada*. Concord, ON: Captus Press.

Ostrom, E. 2005. *Understanding Institutional Diversity*. Princeton, NJ: Princeton University Press.

Province of Manitoba. 2012. Flood Outlook Forecast Map. Accessed 19 November 2012. http://www.gov.mb.ca/mit/floodinfo/floodoutlook/forecast_centre/lakes/lake_levels/2010/lake_st_martin_levels_2011-12.pdf.

– 2013a. *Manitoba 2011 Flood Review Task Force Report*. Winnipeg: Province of Manitoba. https://www.gov.mb.ca/asset_library/en/2011flood/flood_review_task_force_report.pdf.

– 2013b. *Media Bulletin February 27, 2013. Province Issues 2013 February Flood Outlook: Minor to Moderate Flooding Likely Along Red, Souris, Pembina, Assiniboine Rivers and in the Interlake*. Accessed 5 April 2013. http://news.gov.mb.ca/news/print,index.html?archive=&item=16814.

– 2014. *Fairford Dam Operation*. Accessed 21 August 2014. http://www.gov.mb.ca/mit/floodinfo/floodoutlook/forecast_centre/reservoirs_dams/general_dam_inform_operation_targets/fairford_dam.pdf.

Public Safety Canada. 2011. "Government of Canada assists Manitoba with 2011 unprecedented spring flood." News Release 21 November 2011. Accessed 10 December 2013. http://www.publicsafety.gc.ca/cnt/nws/nws-rlss/2011/20111121-eng.aspx.

– 2013. *Disaster Financial Assistance Arrangements (DFAA) – Revised Guidelines*. Accessed 5 April 2013. http://www.publicsafety.gc.ca/prg/em/dfaa/.

Richter, B., S. Postel, C. Revenga, T. Scudder, B. Lehner, A. Churchill, and M. Chow. 2010. "Lost in Development's Shadow: The Downstream Human Consequences of Dams." *Water Alternatives* 3 (2): 14–42.

Supreme Court of Canada. 2005. *Mikisew Cree v. Canada*. Accessed 21 August 2014. http://iportal.usask.ca/docs/ICC/MikEnglish.pdf.

Thompson, S., A. Gulrukh Kamal, M. Ballard, D. Islam, V. Lozeznik, and K. Wong. 2011. "Is Community Economic Development Putting Healthy Food on the Table?: Food Sovereignty in Northern Manitoba's Aboriginal Communities." *Journal of Aboriginal Economic Development* 7:14–39.

Tough, F. 1997. *As Their Natural Resources Fail: Native Peoples and the Economic History of Northern Manitoba, 1870–1930*. Vancouver: UBC Press.

Voyageur, C.J. 1998. "Contemporary Aboriginal Women in Canada." In *Visions of the Heart: Canadian Aboriginal Issues*, 2nd ed., edited by D. Long and O. Dickason, 81–106. Scarborough: Nelson.

Waldram, J. 1993. *As Long as the Rivers Run: Hydroelectric Development and Native Communities in Western Canada*. Winnipeg, MB: University of Manitoba Press.

Winnipeg Free Press. 2013. Fed Order Analysis of Flood Management: Native Group Under Fire Over Unpaid Evacuee Bills. Accessed 10 December 2013. http://www.winnipegfreepress.com/local/feds-order-analysis-of-flood-management-201576061.html.

# 7

# Poverty Free Ontario: Cross-Community Advocacy for Social Justice

CHRISTA FREILER AND
PETER CLUTTERBUCK

### INTRODUCTION

The virtual elimination of poverty among elderly people (from 37 per cent to 5 per cent in twenty-five years) is often cited as one of Canada's social policy success stories (Struthers 2006). The formula for success was the combination of a principled and tenacious champion, Senator David Croll, and a responsible and responsive federal government that acted quickly to introduce a new income program. Such a combination, however, is rare. While there are still champions within government, serious government action on poverty has been sporadic rather than sustained. The refusal of senior levels of government to make a serious commitment to tackle poverty has placed a "particular responsibility" on advocacy organizations (Wharf 1992, 22). This, together with the advent of neoliberalism in the 1970s, generating successive waves of austerity and tax-cutting, have made policy advocacy by non-profit organizations more important than ever before in the struggle to end poverty.

This chapter examines the policy debates, the advocacy dynamics, and the different roles played by advocacy groups in Ontario's poverty reduction strategy from 2007 to 2013. In particular, we explore the challenge of maintaining a strong and consistent social justice approach to public policy advocacy when there is pressure for political accommodation within a community advocacy coalition. In Ontario, this produced strategic and ideological divisions that led to the formation of Poverty Free Ontario by the Social Planning Network of Ontario (SPNO),[1] a province-wide network of local social planning and community development organizations.

## The Ontario Poverty Reduction Strategy

In the months leading up to the 2007 Ontario election, there was considerable advocacy activity by the SPNO and other advocacy groups, some of which had been engaged in anti-poverty advocacy for many years. Just days before the election, then Premier Dalton McGuinty pledged to produce a poverty reduction strategy in the first year of a new mandate, which was welcomed by a wide range of community advocacy organizations.

Following the Liberals' re-election in October 2007, Premier McGuinty announced a cabinet committee to develop a Poverty Reduction Strategy (PRS) by the end of 2008. The advocacy community came together to organize itself to influence the shape of the PRS. The SPNO allied itself with the 25 in 5 Network for Poverty Reduction (25 in 5), a broad-based community advocacy coalition, made up of provincial and Toronto-based advocacy organizations. The coalition fashioned a two-pronged strategy: (1) ongoing consultation and negotiation with senior public policy officials, undertaken by 25 in 5 leadership who had strong government connections; and (2) province-wide mobilization of community voices of support coordinated by the SPNO. This "inside/outside" strategy appeared to have promise but it also produced problems. While they can be effective, insider strategies have their limitations and challenges because of the constraints placed on insiders to "toe the party line." As Lang (2013, 8) points out, those who "are invited to sit at the table are most likely to have agendas in accordance with the government's." Insider strategies can also limit democratic access and participation.

After a year of working together, tensions began to appear in the community advocacy coalition (see also chapters 6 and 9 for other similar challenges) shortly before the government announced its PRS. These differences were put aside while the coalition responded collectively to the government's PRS report released in December 2008. At the time, it was considered a major achievement to keep a coalition of provincial and cross-community partners together for fourteen months of strategy development and consultation. Sustaining that effort through the implementation of the government's poverty reduction plan would prove more challenging than could be managed.

Coalition members were unanimous in their disappointment at the government's failure to commit adequate resources to the PRS. However, internally, they disagreed on how and whether to address the shortcomings of social assistance, in particular how urgent it was for government to address the deep poverty experienced by people on social assistance. It soon became obvious that different approaches to public policy advocacy and to addressing poverty were at play: a) a social justice approach committed to community advocacy and structural strategies to eradicate poverty, beginning with urgent action on ending deep poverty and ensuring income adequacy; and b) poverty alleviation approaches focused on more incremental changes, often through insider access to government, to reduce the incidence of poverty among vulnerable populations. At the beginning, these differences were moderated by a shared commitment to advocate for "timelines and targets" for eradicating poverty over three stages – a 25 per cent reduction in five years, a 50 per cent reduction in ten years, and eradication in a final push after that.[2] Getting the government to commit beyond the first 25 per cent reduction target proved to be impossible, ending any hope of moving beyond reduction to eradication. The resistance within the coalition to push government to take serious action on deep poverty and income adequacy for social assistance recipients turned out to be the breaking point.

Although attempts were made to keep the network together, in the end the differences proved irreconcilable. The SPNO dissociated itself from the 25 in 5 coalition and, in 2009, formed Poverty Free Ontario, a cross-community network of activists and organizations, to move beyond poverty reduction to poverty eradication as an explicit advocacy goal.

## THE LEGACIES OF ANTI-POVERTY POLICY AND ADVOCACY STRATEGIES SINCE THE 1960S

"Poverty is the great social issue of our time" began the 1971 report of the Special Senate Committee on Poverty chaired by Senator David Croll (Senate of Canada 1971). Just as Michael Harrington's *The*

*Other America* (Harrington 1962) reminded Americans that poverty existed in the United States, the Senate report almost ten years later awakened Canada to the reality of poverty in this country. The Committee on Poverty did not have the same effect as Senator Croll's earlier Committee on Aging (Senate of Canada 1966), which resulted in the dramatic reduction of poverty among the elderly. It did, however, make a substantial contribution by focusing attention on poverty as an issue of national urgency and importance. The Senate Poverty Committee attracted over 800 people to its ninety-three cross-Canada public hearings and, for the first time, the voices of people living in poverty were heard. This later translated into a more powerful voice when the civil servants on the National Council of Welfare (NCW) were replaced by people living in poverty (O'Neal 1994).

It is noteworthy that a schism in the Poverty Committee's process resulted in a minority report, *The Real Poverty Report* (Adams et al. 1971), by four of the Senate Committee's staff who had resigned in frustration. The *Real Poverty Report* argued that, because poverty was a structural issue resulting from how the Canadian economy normally worked, it required structural solutions. The Senate report had placed less emphasis on the economy, employment, and the tax system (Grady 1972). The minority report, as well as the work of both Senate committees, serve as important backdrops to advocacy efforts and Canadian public policy aimed at eradicating poverty.

## Policy Shifts to More Comprehensive, Structural Approaches

Public policy advocacy, like public policy itself, is not born in a vacuum. Social justice advocacy, and the issues that divided the advocacy sector after the release of Ontario's PRS, have their roots in the anti-poverty work that began in the 1970s and 80s. The emergence of cross-community mobilization strategies and the shifting focus on research into the structural causes of poverty highlight the fact that shifting policy contexts can generate different forms of advocacy, ranging from social benevolence to poverty alleviation to social justice advocacy. Here we look at the advocacy and policy influences of the child and family poverty movement and others in keeping poverty on the public agenda for the past thirty years.

In Ontario during the 1960s, economic growth contributed to the expansion of social services and public housing and a modest reduction in poverty levels (Novick 1985). But from 1975 to 1985, economic stagnation and rising deficits led to cuts in social spending, particularly for income support programs. This, combined with a recession in the early 1980s, caused significant increases in both unemployment and Ontario's poverty rate (Maxwell 2009). Ontario's non-profit social services sector responded by providing support services to alleviate the effect of poverty on individuals and by working to empower the poor to act on their own. A pre-1960s' model of charity returned to Ontario with the opening of the first food bank in 1983 and, with it, the emergence of "social benevolence" advocacy marked by food drives and other charitable initiatives. At the same time, advocates called for increased funding for social services to support Ontario's most vulnerable citizens.

In the 1980s, the Social Planning Council of Metro Toronto (SPCMT), a registered charity, and the Child Poverty Action Group (CPAG) helped reframe the policy debate to focus on structural issues and on ending poverty, not just on lessening its impact on people, as important as that is. The SPCMT's research and advocacy activities included major reports on unemployment, income security, and social assistance reform (Wharf 1992; McGrath 1999). Calling itself a "public interest" advocacy organization, CPAG did not purport to speak on behalf of low-income families. Its attempts to build a cross-community base were limited both because it did not have the resources to support a membership and because it chose to work through other organizations with community memberships. A non-registered NPO under the auspices of the SPCMT, CPAG consisted of a Toronto-based steering committee of about ten to twelve people – social workers, community workers, researchers, social policy professors, nurses, teachers, and other professionals. It frequently worked with a broader circle of "community supporters" that included people with lived experience of poverty.

CPAG's 1986 declaration, "A Fair Chance for All Children," proposed a "bold" policy agenda to end child poverty. CPAG framed child poverty as "the national neglect of children" and the lack of support for parents. It called for a comprehensive strategy for the *elimination* – not merely *reduction* – of child poverty by means of structural strategies such as: a commitment to full employment; a major restructuring of the tax system; and a significant extension of public education, housing, and child development programs. The centrepiece of CPAG's agenda was a National Income Program for

Children that included a universal child benefit delivered through the tax system (CPAG 1986).

On the provincial government front, in 1988, Ontario's Social Assistance Review Committee (SARC) released its report, *Transitions*, widely hailed as the most comprehensive review of welfare in North America (Wharf 1992). The committee, appointed by the Liberal government of David Peterson and chaired by George Thomson, a former family court judge, consisted of twelve members representing a diversity of experiences and perspectives, including labour, business, non-profit and religious leaders,[3] and people from disability and First Nations communities. Although not explicitly calling for the elimination of poverty, SARC's analysis and far-reaching recommendations addressed the deeper roots of poverty.

Understanding that failings in other systems drove people onto social assistance, SARC extended its proposals beyond the welfare system to address the shortcomings of the federal income security, unemployment, and tax systems. Linking welfare reform to the growing national shame of child poverty, *Transitions*' vision included a national child benefit. Significantly, "adequacy" was one of the first principles articulated by *Transitions*: "All residents of Ontario who are in need must receive a fair and equitable level of social assistance, adequate to meet their basic needs for shelter, food, clothing, and personal and health care" (Government of Ontario 1988, 13). At a time when American and British welfare policies were introducing workfare-type reforms, SARC rejected the argument that the "spur of poverty" was essential to make people leave social assistance and move into the labour market (Klassen and Buchanan 2006). Research and anecdotal evidence convinced SARC that most people wanted to leave social assistance and that, "moreover, the payment of insufficient benefits is profoundly counter-productive" to transitioning to independence (Government of Ontario 1988, 13). Taking a strong stand on adequacy was particularly prescient and progressive given that attacks on social assistance (on both benefits and recipients) continue to this day and were fundamental to the tensions that arose within the 25 in 5 coalition twenty years later.

## Shifting to Community Advocacy and Mobilization

Since the late 1970s, shifting policy demands to more comprehensive, structural proposals were accompanied by shifting advocacy strategies –

from centralized, top-down mobilization to more horizontal organizing efforts across communities. Both centralized elite and horizontal community mobilization strategies were employed in the advocacy efforts that followed the release of the SARC report. A private foundation funded an advocacy plan under a coalition called the SARC-Public Awareness Campaign (SARC-PAC) to push for provincial government action on implementing the recommendations. One part of the action plan was a letter to the premier signed by social policy and business leaders, including Conrad Black and members of the Bronfman family, as well as politicians, including the mayor of Toronto, and media dignitaries, such as Pierre Berton (Wharf 1992). The use of "blue chip" supporters or committees was a type of vertical mobilization that is still used but may no longer have the effect that it did several decades ago.

SARC-PAC's advocacy organizing also reached out into Ontario's regions and urged local community leaders and groups to express their support for SARC's recommendations to the Ontario treasurer, premier, and MPPS. SARC-PAC appealed for donations from individuals and organizations to produce a full-page ad in *The Globe and Mail* and in selected regional newspaper dailies to call for a major investment in social assistance reform in the 1988 provincial budget, and was successful. Ontario Treasurer Robert Nixon included the advocacy community's demand for a $415 million increased allocation in the 1989 provincial budget for social assistance reform (Nixon 1989).

CPAG's advocacy strategy was also expanded to include outreach to national organizations with cross-Canada networks, thereby broadening its horizontal reach and influence across the country. In the late 1980s, CPAG stimulated the emergence of an active coalition of organizations advocating nationally and provincially to end child poverty in Canada (Baker 1997; McGrath 1997). In 1989, on the occasion of Ed Broadbent's retirement as federal leader of the New Democratic Party, the House of Commons passed an all-party resolution "to seek to achieve the goal of eliminating child poverty by the year 2000." That this happened was in no small part the result of the advocacy work of CPAG and its collaborators (Hay 1997; McGrath 1999).

In 1990, CPAG and several other organizations with long histories in child poverty work decided to broaden their coalition beyond a handful of national organizations and develop a network of grassroots community-based groups under the banner of Campaign 2000. They realized they could "create an echo effect ... if local organizations across the country clearly committed to the same goal regardless of their provincial or sector affiliations" (Popham et al. 1997, 251). Early in 1991, Campaign 2000 held policy soundings in thirteen Canadian communities to build the network of community partners and forge agreement on a national policy agenda and action strategies. The founding declaration still guides the advocacy and policy work of Campaign 2000, a non-registered NPO under the auspices of Family Service Toronto, a registered charity. It has grown to 120 national, provincial, and community partners, including organizations from the social policy, faith, labour, disability, First Nations, health, and housing communities.

The annual Child Poverty Report Card is a good example of horizontal community advocacy. Just as National Campaign 2000 produces a report card for Canada, community partners across the country simultaneously release their own report cards, thereby linking local advocacy and research with the larger cross-Canada movement to end child poverty. In addition, compelling and credible discussion papers have provided community advocates with the intellectual confidence to present strong advocacy positions that can be publicly defended. For example, the Campaign 2000 report, *Crossroads for Canada* (Campaign 2000 1996), demonstrated the capacity of advocates to address cross-national fiscal issues, propose major social investments in a national child benefit system, and call for the development of a comprehensive system of early development and child care in every community across Canada. The 2007 report, *Summoned to Stewardship* (Campaign 2000 2007), introduced themes that would become core parts of Ontario advocacy – a target to reduce child poverty in Ontario by 25 per cent as the first step to eradication, a minimum wage that would enable a full-time/full-year earner to live out of poverty, and a call for raising social assistance incomes for families and adults to 80 per cent of the income poverty standard.

As attention to child poverty and the living conditions of social assistance recipients came into focus in the 1980s, community advocacy, connected across localities and regions, became much more proactive and sophisticated and increasingly used research evidence, including cross-national and economic data, to support its arguments.

## ANTI-POVERTY ADVOCACY IN THE NEW MILLENNIUM: THE SUCCESSES AND LIMITS OF COALITION WORK IN ONTARIO

Much of the progress in advancing structural policies to end poverty was undone by the severe economic recession of the early 1990s, and the neoliberal strategies of downloading and deficit-fighting that were employed federally and provincially. In the mid-90s in Ontario, this took a particularly harsh form when the Conservative Mike Harris government (1995–2002) demonized people on social assistance Fernando and Earle (2011, 1) contend that the Common Sense Revolution not only stigmatized people living in poverty, but also redefined "the policy approach to social investment and thus poverty reduction in the province in accordance with the vilification of low income Ontarians." The neoliberalism of the Harris era created a policy environment that "was hostile to structural responses to poverty reduction" (33) – an environment that prevailed in 2008 when the McGuinty government released its Poverty Reduction Strategy.

On 4 December 2008, a little more than a year after the premier's pledge to frame a poverty reduction strategy, the Hon. Deb Matthews, Minister of Children's and Youth Services, released *Breaking the Cycle: Ontario's Poverty Reduction Strategy* (Ontario 2008). The strategy passed several tests applied by the 25 in 5 Network for Poverty Reduction, but not some important others. The breakthroughs included the government's commitment to setting clear targets and timetables for poverty reduction and the adoption of the internationally-used Low Income Measure (LIM) as the primary way to mark progress, both demands of 25 in 5. The PRS, however, was limited to reducing *child* poverty, not *all* poverty, as the community coalition had advocated. There was no specific action on social assistance incomes, and policy statements for sustaining employment, liveable incomes, and supportive communities were more in the realm of gestures and studies than clear and firm initiatives, as had been proposed by 25 in 5 (Maxwell 2009).

The PRS did not signal any commitment to a serious initial investment on poverty reduction in the 2009 budget beyond accelerating the implementation of the already announced Ontario Child Benefit (OCB). Although the community coalition had not yet released its expectations for the 2009 budget, its own estimates of the needed down payment on poverty reduction to launch a three-four year sustained plan was $2.3 billion in the first year (25 in 5 2009). Nevertheless, the 25 in 5 Network received the strategy enthusiastically, as an important first step to "turning the corner on poverty" and "laying the foundation for action" (25 in 5 2008c). Notably, the government invited the many coalition members to assemble at Queen's Park for a briefing on the PRS before the release. Premier McGuinty, who was out of town at the time, phoned into the meeting to thank the coalition members for their support.

## Building a Province-wide Coalition

The advocacy community's response to the PRS was the culmination of a year-long campaign to mobilize community support from across the province under the 25 in 5 banner and behind a unified, coherent, and compelling set of policy demands for poverty reduction. Although 25 in 5 had initially formed among provincial advocacy groups, Toronto-based foundations, and the City of Toronto before the provincial election in the fall of 2007, it did not coalesce into a truly province-wide initiative until late 2007 when the challenge of shaping the government's PRS presented itself (Hudson and Graefe 2011).

The SPNO had organized its community base in the summer/fall of 2007 to have an impact on the provincial election campaign. Its particular strength lay in its strong network of local social planning and community development bodies in more than twenty communities across the province. Social planning councils had a long history of policy development and community advocacy for low-income people (Wharf 1992). The SPNO's report identifying Ontario as "the child poverty centre of Canada" (SPNO 2007) had caught the attention of the Premier's Office during the election campaign (*Toronto Star* Sept. 2007).

Other advocacy groups had also mobilized to get poverty on the provincial election agenda, including: the Interfaith Social Assistance Reform Coalition (ISARC), which had been calling for serious welfare reform since the SARC report in 1988; Ontario Campaign 2000, which had been reporting annually on child poverty since the 1990s; and the Income Security Advocacy Centre (ISAC), an independent, non-profit organization specializing in poverty law reform in the province's community legal clinic system. In the run-up to the election, all of these groups, along with the United Way, food banks, self-advocacy groups, and private charitable foundations, were calling for a provincial commitment to reduce poverty. (Figure 7.1 illustrates the many groups, organizations and coalitions involved in the Poverty Reduction Strategy process for the period 2007–13.)

Many of these primarily Toronto-based groups organized themselves into the 25 in 5 Network during the summer of 2007. Post-election, the SPNO joined them in a meeting called by the Atkinson and Metcalf Foundations to discuss how to follow up on the government's commitment to develop a poverty reduction strategy over the next year. All were motivated to collaborate for the chance to have a major impact on public policy to reduce poverty. The SPNO was charged with canvassing activist groups across the province on their expectations of the PRS. After interviewing leadership in thirteen communities and twenty-three provincial organizations, the SPNO returned to the larger advocacy table to propose three broad themes for a province-wide mobilization campaign on the PRS, which became the centrepiece of the 25 in 5 Network's Declaration on poverty reduction:

> We are asking our government for a plan to reduce Ontario poverty levels by 25% in 5 years and by 50% before 2018 ...
> Ontario's poverty reduction plan should address three priorities:
>
> 1. Sustaining employment means assuring a living standard above poverty for any adult who works full time throughout the year. It means fair pay and stable working conditions for all Ontarians.
> 2. Livable incomes mean dignity for all Ontarians – including those unable to work.
> 3. Strong and supportive communities mean affordable housing, early learning and child care; public education and community programs that help people connect (25 in 5 April 2008a).

Since several of the 25 in 5 participants had well-established relationships with both senior policy bureaucrats and key political representatives in the Liberal government, they initiated a regular conversation on the development of the PRS, essentially an "insider" channel to the policy-makers.

The SPNO's role in the community coalition was to engage community leadership across the province and to mobilize province-wide support for the three themes adopted in the policy framework, which became the "outsider" or cross-community advocacy strategy. It should be noted that the terms "insider" and "outsider" are used here as terms to describe strategy, not status (see Maloney et al. 1994). For both 25 in 5 and the SPNO, initially the insider/outsider approach was a deliberate and mutually-supportive strategy. Funded by the Atkinson Foundation, SPNO took the policy framework on the road in the winter months of 2008, visiting more than fifteen communities across the province, some several times. Community assemblies received the policy themes enthusiastically and local media coverage was extensive (SPNO 2008b).

All of this activity was occurring before any government outreach for community input. Internally, Minister Matthews was convening her cabinet committee to begin the policy development process. But leaders in 25 in 5 maintained regular communication with the minister and her officials and with senior policy staff in the Premier's Office. The minister's first major public engagement on poverty reduction occurred at a 25 in 5 forum in April 2008, attended by 500 community leaders from across the province, where the 25 in 5 Declaration was publicly unveiled. Although the minister made no commitments at that time, she did urge the community to continue to advocate and contribute to the development of the PRS (Monsebraaten 2008).

The Minister's own outreach plans, however, were for only a limited number of community consultations. The community coalition proposed a more open and inclusive consultation. In early May, when Minister Matthews encountered community resistance and negative media coverage in her first consultations in two small eastern Ontario cities, she turned to 25 in 5 for assistance with the rest of her consultation schedule (*Peterborough Examiner* 2008). 25 in 5 leaders called on the SPNO to help prepare more inclusive community invitation lists and to encourage citizens to participate constructively in the Minister's consultations.

Beyond assisting the Minister's outreach, the SPNO led the coalition's cross-community strategy for a much broader independent consultation process. Between May and August, more than seventy local consultations were conducted across Ontario, with the results reported at a media conference at Queen's Park on 8 September 2008 (SPNO 2008a). Community input reinforced support for the Declaration, which by late fall would accumulate more than 1,500 endorsements from organizations and individuals across the province.

A very tangible sense of hopefulness was suddenly stalled by the global financial crisis that struck in the fall of 2008. Premier McGuinty mused in late September that the PRS might need to be delayed in light of an impending recession (Gillespie 2008). A strong and united insider/outsider response by engaged communities vis-à-vis their local MPPs and by 25 in 5 leaders lobbying the premier's office renewed the government's resolve. Premier McGuinty reaffirmed a commitment to the PRS in a letter to the SPNO co-chair of 25 in 5 (McGuinty 2008). In a speech to the Canadian Club, Finance Minister Duncan asserted, "We could no more abandon our efforts to reduce poverty than we should abandon working with our business community to increase productivity" (Duncan 2012; 25 in 5 2008b). The insider/outsider strategy had worked well for the community coalition to avert the loss of a year's momentum toward the PRS.

## Fragmentation in the Coalition

Although the coalition had accomplished much through the year, tensions began to surface within 25 in 5 in its final push to influence the PRS in October–November of 2008. The SPNO developed a framework specifying policy initiatives for action on the three themes of the Declaration. Called the *Blueprint for Poverty Reduction* (25 in 5 2009), it was taken into the field by the SPNO with meetings in more than twenty communities and was endorsed at a large "cross-community" assembly of leaders from across the province in mid-November. A number of key partners in the 25 in 5 coalition, however, resisted a key proposal in the policy framework – the Healthy Food Supplement (HFS), which proposed a $100/monthly increase to the basic welfare rate to begin to alleviate chronic cycles of hardship and hunger as social assistance recipients ran out of money at the end of each month (25 in 5 2008a). Arising from the SPNO's consultations with low-income people, public health officials, and community leaders across the province, the HFS was presented as a first step on the path to adequate livable incomes for social assistance recipients. This would be the first increase in the real income of welfare recipients since the 21.6 per cent rate cuts in 1995 by the Harris government.[4]

Several 25 in 5 leaders, most notably those carrying the coalition's insider strategy with the government, opposed the HFS. Increasing benefits by using the existing social assistance system did not fit into their vision of overhauling income security altogether.

The tensions between the different visions of poverty reduction and of advocacy within the coalition became much clearer. An internal struggle ensued over a number of meetings among coalition partners in late 2008 and early 2009. Frustrated at SPNO's persistence on the HFS, the Atkinson Foundation, which was both a funder of the SPNO's cross-community mobilization work and an influential insider advocate for specific policy initiatives, most notably all-day kindergarten, abruptly discontinued funding the SPNO's work in March 2009.

The decision to pull the SPNO's funding increased the distance between the cross-community anti-poverty work and the 25 in 5 steering committee (Hudson and Graefe 2011). More limited resources also presented a serious problem for the SPNO in advancing advocacy work for the HFS. Nevertheless, the SPNO managed to build a campaign called Put Food in the Budget (PFIB). By the spring of 2009, the SPNO and its cross-community partners had secured the endorsement of fifteen public health departments and more than twenty communities for the HFS. Grounded in the lives and voices of people on social assistance and with strong community allies across Ontario, the PFIB campaign efforts continued through 2013. Notably, the 2012 Review of Social Assistance in Ontario, by Commissioners Frances Lankin and Munir Sheikh, recommended a $100/month increase to social assistance rates, acknowledging the broad community support for the HFS, including resolutions passed by twenty-five municipal councils across the province as a result of PFIB campaigning (Lankin and Sheikh 2012).

Active community mobilization by the 25 in 5 Network was scaled down after the spring budget of 2009 and the introduction of Bill 152, the Poverty Reduction Act, which committed the government to a review of its poverty reduction strategy and targets every five years (Statutes of Ontario 2009 C.10). 25 in 5 maintained a watching brief and reported annually on its assessment of progress with the PRS. It re-engaged for input into the work of the Social Assistance Review commissioners and several 25 in 5 leaders who had been part of the 25 in 5 insider strategy joined the commissioners' research and outreach staff during the review process.

The SPNO maintained an active presence and connection with the twenty-five communities it had engaged in the 2008–09 PRS advocacy campaign by forming Poverty Free Ontario to promote moving beyond poverty reduction to poverty eradication (SPNO 2010). Poverty Free Ontario was an advocacy network of local community anti-poverty leaders and non-profit organizations in thirty communities across the province that had become mobilized during the cross-community advocacy for the PRS. During the 2011 provincial election, SPNO/PFO joined with ISARC (Interfaith Social Assistance Reform Coalition) to mount a coordinated cross-community advocacy campaign called "Let's Vote for a Poverty Free Ontario." The PFIB campaign also continued to press for the $100/month HFS with a range of public awareness and advocacy actions that engaged thousands of Ontarians from 2009 through 2013. Government action, however, was discouraging as the reign of austerity introduced by the government-commissioned Drummond Report not only precluded any serious anti-poverty measures but led to additional cuts to services to the most vulnerable populations (PFO 2012; Drummond 2012).

By the time of Premier McGuinty's resignation in the fall of 2012, poverty reduction was not being reported as part of the legacy for which he would be known. Although the new premier, Kathleen Wynne, assumed office in February 2013 declaring herself the

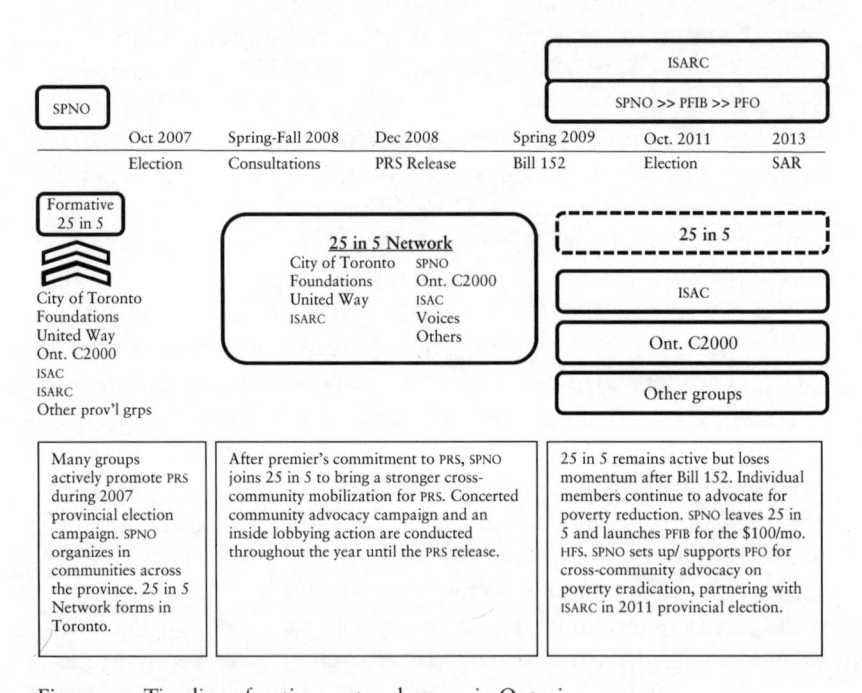

| | | | | | | |
|---|---|---|---|---|---|---|
| | | | | | ISARC | |
| SPNO | | | | | SPNO >> PFIB >> PFO | |
| | Oct 2007 | Spring-Fall 2008 | Dec 2008 | Spring 2009 | Oct. 2011 | 2013 |
| | Election | Consultations | PRS Release | Bill 152 | Election | SAR |

| Formative 25 in 5 | | 25 in 5 Network | 25 in 5 |
|---|---|---|---|
| City of Toronto Foundations United Way Ont. C2000 ISAC ISARC Other prov'l grps | | City of Toronto — SPNO<br>Foundations — Ont. C2000<br>United Way — ISAC<br>ISARC — Voices<br>— Others | ISAC |
| | | | Ont. C2000 |
| | | | Other groups |

| Many groups actively promote PRS during 2007 provincial election campaign. SPNO organizes in communities across the province. 25 in 5 Network forms in Toronto. | After premier's commitment to PRS, SPNO joins 25 in 5 to bring a stronger cross-community mobilization for PRS. Concerted community advocacy campaign and an inside lobbying action are conducted throughout the year until the PRS release. | 25 in 5 remains active but loses momentum after Bill 152. Individual members continue to advocate for poverty reduction. SPNO leaves 25 in 5 and launches PFIB for the $100/mo. HFS. SPNO sets up/ supports PFO for cross-community advocacy on poverty eradication, partnering with ISARC in 2011 provincial election. |

Figure 7.1 Timeline of anti-poverty advocacy in Ontario 2007–13

"social justice" premier, she demonstrated no particular passion on that front in the first months of her administration (*Toronto Star* 2013; PFO 2013).

### DIFFERENT APPROACHES TO ANTI-POVERTY ADVOCACY

#### Understanding the Fault Lines

Sometimes conflict and division can produce even greater clarity and coherence. Withdrawing from the 25 in 5 Network offered the SPNO a chance to reflect, to understand the divisions, and to re-conceptualize its mission, objectives, and mobilization model. Using the formation of Poverty Free Ontario as a case study we examined the differences between the social justice and poverty alleviation approaches to anti-poverty advocacy. Although there can be overlaps in the two approaches, it became clear that the fault lines that emerged were both strategic and ideological.

#### Strategic Differences: Insider versus Community Advocacy

25 in 5's inside/outside strategy, albeit deliberate, proved to be a double-edged sword. While it opened some doors, it closed others and, in the end, led to divisions and political accommodation. Hudson and Graefe (2011, 9) note that some coalition members were concerned "that pursuing an [insider] strategy of greater political influence along the lines of individual organizational policy expertise risked both government co-optation and 25 in 5's poverty reduction strategy dwindling into pet projects." This concern proved to be well-founded.

Although perspectives differ on some aspects of inside/outside strategies, there is agreement on two things: a) that insider strategies can be effective, and b) that success is achieved at a price, whether that is co-optation, political accommodation, or organizational mission drift (Lang 2013; Chandler 2004; Maloney et al. 1994). At its most extreme, insider strategies can lead to the exclusion of some groups and growing insider relations between government and other groups. Under these circumstances, insider strategies become a serious threat to democracy and inclusion (Chandler 2004). While this worst-case scenario did not materialize, what the insider approach delivered did not prove to be highly effective (see chapter 5 for delivery limitations). Granted, there were some "wins" as a result of the insider strategy, but they were either minimal or produced policies that the government had previously committed itself to that were now being presented as part of the Poverty Reduction Strategy, namely the Ontario Child Benefit and the full-day early learning initiative (Hudson and Graefe 2011; see also chapters 5, 8, and 10, for varying outcomes).

In NGOs, *Civil Society and the Public Sphere*, Lang (2013, 7) draws a distinction between institutional advocacy, "the attempt to influence by gaining some degree of insider status with governments," and public advocacy, which "attempts to achieve policy success by engaging broader publics, actively stimulating citizen voice and engagement." Lang observes that NGO advocacy has become more institutionalized as advocacy organizations increasingly seek insider status by working with governments as partners. This is not a problem in and of itself since "both institutional and public advocacy are necessary for a democratic culture." In this chapter, we use the terms "insider" and "community" advocacy to reflect Lang's distinction between "institutional" and "public."

Insider advocacy becomes an issue when political accommodation becomes the norm (i.e., when only those who share the government's agenda are accepted as insiders). This was the case with the PRS process. Often insiders are put in the difficult position of having to sell government policies to others in the broader coalition. Not surprisingly, the "outsiders" see the deal as "caving in" and setting the bar too low. In the worst examples, the insiders are reduced to becoming apologists for government policies vis-à-vis their coalition partners. Some, who were not part of the "insider" group, felt that this was the case with the PRS process.

Public advocacy is also not without its problems. According to Lang (2013, 8), public advocacy can become anti-democratic when advocacy *organizations* become the "proxy public" or "hollow stand-ins" for communities. The SPNO played an important role in making sure that this did not occur during the PRS process by connecting the 25 in 5 Network to communities throughout the province, which supplemented the government-organized consultations with more than seventy community meetings for input on poverty reduction. ISARC, with its province-wide network of faith groups, also brought the broader public perspective to the 25 in 5 table. Indeed, the SPNO and ISARC frequently expressed frustration to the 25 in 5 steering committee that there was not enough direct regional input in the central strategy development and decision-making.

The leaders of the "outsider" strategy were concerned about a lack of transparency because of the insider knowledge of government thinking. While the cross-community work was openly planned, reported, and discussed at the 25 in 5 steering committee table, there was less than full disclosure of insider discussions with government officials on the grounds that these channels would close if the insiders shared information too widely with all members of the coalition. This aspect of the inside strategy can erode trust among partners in a coalition as worries about concessions, deals, and co-optation arise among those not part of the chosen insiders. In this way, "insider" and "outsider" transform from describing a strategy that is mutually agreed upon to a status that is externally assigned (Maloney et al. 1994).

Lang (2013) identifies another important difference between insider and community advocacy that is particularly relevant to the PRS context. While insider advocacy may be effective in some situations, only community advocacy can "generate citizen engagement and voice" (Lang 2013, 7). SPNO's horizontal approach to advocacy highlighted the community context of poverty and gave a voice to community members who would otherwise not have been heard. Further, the trust between engaged community leadership and the SPNO, which provided support and coordination, enabled an ongoing cross-community advocacy capacity to be maintained, as reflected in the transition to Poverty Free Ontario.

The SPNO's ongoing relationship with the network of more than twenty-five anti-poverty community leadership groups across the province was consensual, rather than contractual. Communities looked to the SPNO for its policy leadership and its strategic guidance in social justice advocacy. The SPNO respected community leadership for knowing what would work on the ground and recognized that authentic and effective advocacy depended on local community engagement, commitment, and action on an agenda, which communities helped shape and which they knew was shared in solidarity with other communities across the province.

## Policy Differences: The Urgency of Addressing Income Adequacy to End Deep Poverty

Adequacy became the flashpoint for division in the community advocacy coalition. Although the $100/month HFS was incorporated in the 25 in 5 Blueprint because of its province-wide support among social assistance recipients, public health officials, faith leaders, social planning councils, and other community advocates, it was never enthusiastically supported by the Toronto-based leaders with the insider track to the Liberal government. After a heated debate at the steering committee table, 25 in 5 decided not to release the proposed blueprint budget that included a $400 million first-year amount for the HFS until two months after the PRS was released, in February 2009.

Hudson and Graefe (2011) explain the Toronto-based "social liberals'" opposition to a rate increase as fear that it would generate a public backlash plus incur a heavy upfront cost, which would deter any political will for the longer-run transformation of income security policy. In promoting a transformed income security system, the coalition's insider leadership argued that the current social assistance system should be replaced with a "different income security architecture" (13).

Since the SARC report of the late 1980s, advocates have agreed that social assistance has to be re-thought and re-designed. The need for a transformed income security system in the long term was never under dispute. The SPNO, however, argued for a two-track approach in the PRS. It acknowledged that long-term reform of social assistance was required but that the immediate relief of the hardship and hunger of social assistance recipients via a significant rate increase was a moral imperative after fifteen years of no increases in recipients' real incomes. Further, the HFS would be a breakthrough recognition of the importance of moving social assistance rates toward adequacy. The SPNO feared that the proposed transformation would fall seriously short of meeting basic living needs, noting that the housing benefit model under consideration for the new income security architecture would reach only 200,000 low-income people in a province with 1.7 million living in poverty (PFO 2011a). Finally, given the extended time needed to design and implement an overhauled income security system, the SPNO and PFIB called for the government to clearly show its good faith by immediately implementing the Healthy Food Supplement.

Advocates of the HFS were not insensitive to the concern about the possible public reaction and political resistance to what amounted to a rate increase, which is why they never talked about rate increases, certainly never in terms of percentage increases. For strategic and communications reasons, the HFS was intentionally framed as providing access to food for relieving hunger and improving health. A compassionate public could understand the connection between monthly income levels below $600 and the inability to buy adequate and healthy food after paying the rent. Food bank usage rates rising annually at record levels only reinforced the point (Food Banks Canada 2009). Support for the HFS by public health departments across the province and twenty-five municipal councils was evidence enough for the Social Assistance Review Commissioners to recommend the $100/month increase in their final report (Lankin and Sheikh 2012).

Recognizing the urgency of addressing adequacy for all at the lowest end of the income scale, Poverty Free Ontario proposed:

i) Ending deep poverty in calling for a 2–3 year government action program to increase social assistance rates so that no one in Ontario lives below 80% of the official income poverty line and bringing the overall poverty rate below 5%; and
ii) Ending working poverty by committing to a 2–3-year timetable to raise the minimum wage so that a full-year, full-time worker's earnings bring him/her to 10% above the official income poverty line.[5]

### Advocacy Goal: Poverty Reduction/Alleviation versus Poverty Eradication

For more than thirty years, Ontario's poverty level had struggled to dip below double-digit numbers. By 2009, it was at 13.1 per cent (PFO 2011). Good economic times and supportive social programs helped to lower Ontario's poverty rates to 8 per cent or 9 per cent several times, but getting below the 5 per cent that many Scandinavian countries had achieved during the same period was not within reach without concerted action on both decent employment and adequate income support (LaRochelle-Coté and Dionne 2009).

Poverty Free Ontario committed itself to poverty eradication, not with the expectation of achieving and sustaining zero per cent poverty levels, but poverty rates comparable to the lowest rates in the industrial world, which others had demonstrated could range between 3 and 5 per cent and which had been achieved with seniors' poverty in Canada. The "targets and timelines" strategy adopted by 25 in 5 originally aspired to eliminate poverty. The coalition called for a 25 per cent reduction target in five years as the first stage, to be followed by a 50 per cent reduction over ten years, and a final push to end poverty after that. The 25 in 5 Network however, did emphasize *poverty reduction*, and obfuscated the coalition's clear commitment to poverty elimination.[6]

In the end, however, the fault line is not between those who are in favour of poverty eradication and those who are not. The dividing line is around different notions of what is "realistic," with some believing that the most Canada can aspire to is poverty alleviation or reduction, and others being convinced that we can do better. Based on research evidence from Canada and other jurisdictions and insights acquired from four decades of anti-poverty advocacy, the clear lesson is that poverty is political and that governments always have fiscal options even during hard times. "Being realistic," as became apparent during the PRS process, has become code for "capitulating to current conditions." Keeping the focus on poverty eradication and structural strategies, Novick (2011, 10) contends, "is central to committed advocacy that creates new realities of social justice and human dignity for all."

## CONCLUSION

There are two ways to assess the advances made in addressing poverty since the 1989 Commons resolution and since the 2007 Ontario commitment to poverty reduction. The simplest way is to determine just how much levels of poverty have been lowered during this period. Child poverty in Canada was above 10 per cent in 1989, and is still at this level twenty-five years later. Ontario did not meet its commitment for a 25 per cent reduction in child poverty by 2014, a commitment that would have meant 103,000 fewer children living in poverty. By 2012, less than half that target had been met (Blackstock and deGroot-Maggetti 2013).

A second approach is to look at advances made in strengthening the prospects for advocacy. Since the 1980s, there has been a far greater understanding of the structural dimensions of poverty and, in many communities, less willingness to accept political accommodation as inevitable. The PRS process revealed that the ideological fault lines between advocates and political leaders and among advocates themselves are becoming more pronounced.

There are, however, two serious and interrelated challenges to advocacy aimed at eradicating poverty in Ontario and the rest of Canada: a) the neoliberal agenda, and b) the trend toward cautious, insider advocacy. Neoliberalism promotes a rigid world view that does not allow other perspectives even in the face of overwhelming evidence to the contrary. The unrelenting promotion of tax cuts and wage erosion are good examples. There is little serious evidence that lower taxes contribute to decent work and prosperity for all (Piketty 2014; Yalnizyan 2011) but the impact of neoliberal doctrine on the persistence of poverty is profound. Most people living in poverty, including single adults and parents on social assistance, are employed at some point during the year. Minimum wages keep full-time earners in poverty. Social assistance incomes keep single adults in regular cycles of hunger and hardship when food money runs out well before the end of each month.

Neoliberalism's rigid world view can affect both the policy and funding environment, thereby weakening the prospects for strong, independent advocacy, particularly by organizations that rely on government funding. This has resulted in the trend toward cautious, insider advocacy, which is becoming well-documented (Kamizaki 2013; Lang 2013; chapter 3).

There are other serious reasons for the trend toward insider strategies besides the impact of neoliberalism. According to Sabine Lang (2013, 208), insider advocacy is "more predictable, more immediately gratifying, and reputation-enhancing" than working with communities and other publics. Worse still, few funders provide financial support for community advocacy and when they do, it is in accordance with their agendas. Lang suggests this is as true of private foundation funders as it is of government. Notably, SPNO, one of several strategic partners for poverty reduction funded by the Atkinson Foundation, lost its funding for cross-community mobilization when it did not agree with the advocacy agenda being advanced by the insider position of the 25 in 5 coalition. A study of insider advocacy under Britain's New Labour government after years of Thatcherism also has sobering lessons for Ontario. The post-Thatcher policy environment that Craig, Taylor, and Parkes (2004, 223) describe is similar to the Ontario of Dalton McGuinty after years of Mike Harris's Common Sense Revolution, i.e., a government that is much more likely to listen; that draws organizations into "partnerships"; and that has "permeable boundaries" between the government and those who want to influence it. Their research reveals a number of troubling risks and outcomes for advocacy organizations and their policy agendas. These include power imbalances being subsumed or buried under notions of "partnership"; co-optation into governmental agendas; "pressure to self-censorship, with organizations trading the ability to critique with the ability to influence." (225). The UK government's perception that some advocacy groups were pushing for what government players considered to be "lost causes" became a major challenge. Like most governments, New Labour would have preferred advocacy groups to focus on government objectives, rather than on their own agendas. Unfortunately, in Ontario's PRS experience, addressing social assistance adequacy and focusing on poverty eradication were also considered to be lost causes by the provincial government and some advocates.

Poverty eradication will not be achieved through insider advocacy strategies that conform to the limited perspective on social change held by institutional elites, particularly given the current political and policy context. Only bold strategies that challenge neoliberal, low-tax, low-wage dogma, and are rooted in and shared across communities, will end poverty. Communities across Ontario remain deeply committed to this goal. There is recognition of the need to move away from a charity model of social provision, as reflected in recent calls to close food banks (Power 2011; Yarema 2013). The urgency to increase levels of social assistance for single adults is becoming accepted (Mendelson 2013). The momentum is starting to shift from poverty alleviation, which takes a limited view of what is possible, to the promise of social justice and poverty eradication.

## DEDICATION

We wish to dedicate this chapter to the late Marvyn Novick in acknowledgment of his important contribution in helping us to establish the historical continuity of the latest community anti-poverty advocacy with developments thirty years ago in Ontario and Canada and to identify the shifts underlying various approaches to advocacy that have taken place since the mid-1980s. Marvyn passed away suddenly in June 2016. A retired professor in social policy at Ryerson University and one of the founders of CPAG and Campaign 2000, Marvyn was a recognized leader in community advocacy for social justice and for the eradication of poverty in Ontario and Canada.

NOTES

1 The Social Planning Network of Ontario (SPNO) is a non-profit organization (NPO). It does not have registered charitable status although many of its local organizational members do. Poverty Free Ontario is an informal, unincorporated network of community-based organizations organized and supported by the SPNO in the campaign to end poverty in Ontario.
2 Eradication was always recognized and was defined in community meetings as ensuring no one lived in "deep poverty" (below 80 per cent of the poverty line) and getting overall poverty rates down to the 3 or 4 per cent rates that some European jurisdictions had achieved.
3 This welfare reform initiative sparked the formation of the Interfaith Social Assistance Reform Coalition (ISARC), made up of multi-denominational faith groups in Ontario, which has remained a major advocacy voice for low income people for more than twenty-five years.
4 The Liberal government had made cost of living adjustments of 1–2 per cent in the Basic Needs Allowance since 2003, but these were to adjust for inflation and did not amount to an actual increase in the real incomes of social assistance recipients.
5 http://www.povertyfreeontario.ca/policy-agenda-overview/.
6 Notably, in discussions with government officials on Bill 152, Network advocates encountered resistance to a firm legislative commitment to poverty elimination on the grounds that the advocacy community had already achieved a government commitment to what it was striving for, as evident in its very name, "25 in 5."

REFERENCES

25 in 5 Network for Poverty Reduction. April 2008a. *25 in 5 Founding Declaration.* Toronto: 25 in 5 Network for Poverty Reduction.
– October 20 2008b. *Countdown to a Poverty Reduction Strategy.* Toronto: 25 in 5 Network for Poverty Reduction.

- December 4 2008c. "Poverty plan lays foundation for action". Media release. Toronto: 25 in 5 Network for Poverty Reduction.
- 2009. *A Blueprint for Economic Stimulus and Poverty Reduction in Ontario*. Toronto: A Report for the 25 in 5 Network for Poverty Reduction, 22.

Adams, I., W. Cameron, B. Hill, and P. Penz. 1971. *The Real Poverty Report*. Edmonton: Hurtig.

Baker, M. 1997. "Advocacy, Political Alliances and the Implementation of Family Policies." In *Child and Family Policies: Struggles, Strategies and Options*, edited by J. Pulkingham and G. Ternowetsky, 158–71. Halifax: Fernwood Publishing.

Blackstock, S., and G. deGroot-Maggetti. 2013. "Poverty Reduction Key to Fairer, More Prosperous Ontario." *Toronto Star*, 4 December.

Campaign 2000. 1996. *Crossroads for Canada*. Discussion Paper. Toronto: Campaign 2000 / Family Service Toronto.

Campaign 2000. 2007. *Summoned to Stewardship*. Discussion Paper. Toronto: Campaign 2000 / Family Service Toronto.

Chandler, D. 2004. "Building Global Civil Society 'From Below'." *Millennium* 33 (2): 313–39. http://dx.doi.org/10.1177/03058298040330020301.

Child Poverty Action Group. 1986. *A Fair Chance for All Children: The Declaration on Child Poverty*. Toronto: Social Planning Council of Metro Toronto.

Craig, G., M. Taylor, and T. Parkes. 2004. "Protest or Partnership? The Voluntary and Community Sectors in the Policy Process." *Social Policy and Administration* 38 (3): 221–39. http://dx.doi.org/10.1111/j.1467-9515.2004.00387.x.

Drummond, D. 2012. Chap. 8 in Commission on the Reform of Ontario's Public Services. Toronto: Queen's Printer.

Duncan, D. 2012. *Ontario Finance Minister Dwight Duncan, Remarks to the Economic Club of Canada. 13 February 2012*. Ontario: Ministry of Finance.

Fernando, S., and B. Earle. 2011. "Linking Poverty Reduction and Economic Recovery: Supporting Community Responses to Austerity in Ontario." *Canadian Review of Social Policy* 65/66:31–44.

Food Banks Canada. 2009. Hunger Count 2009. Toronto.

Gillespie, K. 2008. "Poverty Slips on McGuinty's Agenda." *Toronto Star*, 22 September.

Government of Ontario. 1988. *Transitions: Report of the Social Assistance Review Committee*. Toronto: Queen's Printer for Ontario.

Harrington, M. 1962. *The Other America, Poverty in the United States.* New York: Simon and Schuster.

Hay, D.I. 1997. "Campaign 2000: Family and Child Poverty in Canada." In *Child and Family Policies: Struggles, Strategies and Options*, edited by J. Pulkingham and G. Ternowetsky, 248–72. Halifax: Fernwood Publishing.

Hudson, C.A., and P. Graefe. 2011. "The Toronto Origins of Ontario's 2008 Poverty Reduction Strategy: Mobilizing Multiple Channels of Influence for Progressive Social Policy Change." *The Canadian Review of Social Policy/Revue canadienne de politique sociale* 65/66: 1–15.

Kamizaki, K. 2013. *Linking Community Organizing with Policy Change Initiatives: Implications for Future Community Practice in Toronto.* Toronto: Social Planning Toronto.

Klassen, T.R., and D. Buchanan. 2006. "Ideology, Policy and Economy: Liberal, New Democratic and Conservative Reforms of Ontario's Welfare Program." *Journal of Canadian Studies. Revue d'Etudes Canadiennes* 40 (3): 186–210.

Lang, S. 2013. *NGOs, Civil Society, and the Public Sphere.* New York: Cambridge University Press.

Lankin, F., and M.A. Sheikh. 2012. *Brighter Prospects: Transforming Social Assistance in Ontario.* Toronto: Commission for the Reform of Social Assistance in Ontario.

LaRochelle-Coté, S., and C. Dionne. June 2009. "International differences in low paid work." *Perspectives*, Statistics Canada, Catalogue no. 75-001.

Maloney, A., G. Jordan, and A. McLaughlin. 1994. "Interest Groups and Public Policy: The Insider/Outsider Model Revisited." *Journal of Public Policy* 14 (1): 17–38. http://dx.doi.org/10.1017/S0143814X00001239.

Maxwell, G. 2009. "Poverty in Ontario – Failed Promise and the Renewal of Hope." In *Poverty Reduction, Policies and Programs in Ontario. Social Development Report Series*, edited by K. Scott, 1–30. Ottawa: Canadian Council on Social Development.

McGrath, S. 1997. "Child Poverty Advocacy and the Politics of Influence." In *Child and Family Policies: Struggles, Strategies and Options*, edited by J. Pulkingham and G. Ternowetsky, 172–187. Halifax: Fernwood Publishing.

– 1999. "The Politics of Truth: A Case Study of Knowledge Construction by the Social Planning Council of Metropolitan Toronto, 1957–1988." Unpublished doctoral dissertation.

McGuinty, Premier Dalton. October 1, 2008. Correspondence to Peter Clutterbuck, 25 in 5 Co-Chair.

Mendelson, M. September 2013. "A Note from the Caledon Institute on Poverty Reduction in Ontario." *Caledon Commentary*. Ottawa: Caledon Institute of Social Policy. http://www.caledoninst.org/Publications/PDF/1017ENG.pdf.

Monsebraaten, L. 2008. "Ontario Wary of '25 in 5' Poverty Plan." *Toronto Star*, 15 April.

Nixon, R.F. 1989. *1989 Ontario Budget*. Toronto: Queen's Printer.

Novick, M. 1985. "Social policy: The Search for a New Consensus." In *The Government and Politics in Ontario*. 3rd ed., edited by Donald C. MacDonald. Scarborough: Nelson Canada.

– 2011. "Campaign 2000 Retrospective: Dealing with the Structural Challenges." Round Table Presentation to Child Care Canada (23 November). http://childcarecanada.org/sites/default/files/Campaign%202000%20retrospective%20-%20Marvyn%20Novick.pdf.

O'Neal, B. 1994. *Senate Committees: Role and Effectiveness*. Political and Social Affairs Division.

*Peterborough Examiner*. 2008. "Behind Closed Doors; Public Media Not Allowed to Enter Poverty Meeting." 6 May.

Piketty, T. 2014. *Capital in the Twenty-First Century*. Harvard University Press. http://dx.doi.org/10.4159/9780674369542.

Poverty Free Ontario. 19 September 2011a. Getting the Housing Benefit Right. PFO Bulletin #8.

– 2011b. "Human Dignity for All: Working for a Poverty Free Ontario." PDF of Community Presentation, Spring 2011.

– 16 June 2011. 2009 Figures Show Growth Rate of Poverty in Ontario. Toronto: PFO Bulletin #2.

– 24 October 2012. Commissioners Show Constraints of Austerity Climate. Media release.

– 19 February 2013. Ontario Speech from the Throne: Fair Ontario Still a Faint Hope for People in Deep Poverty. Media release.

Power, Elaine. 2011. "It's Time to Close Canada's Food Banks." *Globe and Mail*, July 25.

Senate of Canada. 1966. *Final Report of the Special Senate Committee on Aging*. Ottawa: Information Canada.

– 1971. *Poverty in Canada. Report of the Special Senate Committee on Poverty*. Ottawa: Information Canada.

Social Planning Network of Ontario (SPNO). September 2007. Ontario Children Living in Poverty Comparative Provincial Levels 2000 and 2005. Toronto.

- 2 May 2010. A Poverty-free Ontario. Proposed Strategy & Action Plan, 2010–11. Presented to SPNO Spring Conference, Subury, Ontario.
- September 2008a. Summary Report: Ontario Poverty Reduction Strategy Consultations (March–August 2008). Toronto.
- 10 June 2008b. Cross-community Engagement Strategy, February through May, 2008. Unpublished report on activity to Atkinson Foundation.
- May 2011. Poverty Free Ontario. Unpublished overview.

Struthers, J. 2006. "Framing Aging Through the State: Canada's Two Senate Committees on Poverty, 1963–1966 and 2006–2009." *Canadian Review of Social Policy* 68/69:1–9.

*Toronto Star.* 2013. "Ontario Liberal Leadership Candidate Kathleen Wynne; 'I Want to Be the Social Justice Premier'," 15 January.

Wharf, B. 1992. "Reforming Income Security in Ontario." In his *Communities and Social Policy in Canada*, 63–94. Toronto: McClelland & Stewart.

Yalnizyan, Armine. 2011. "Five Reasons to Say No to More Tax Cuts." *Globe and Mail* Blog, 28 January.

Yarema, M. 2013. "Take Time on October 17th to Think Beyond Food Banks." Ottawa: Dignity for All, 17 September.

# 8

# The Québec Act to Combat Poverty and Social Exclusion: A Case of Democratic Co-construction of Public Policy

YVES VAILLANCOURT AND
FRANÇOIS AUBRY[1]

INTRODUCTION

The literature on Québec public policy initiatives over the last two decades, has sometimes stated that most of the initiatives are the result of the neoliberal orientations of successive governments. For example, some researchers and social movement leaders argue that Premier Lucien Bouchard's Parti Québécois (PQ) government, in office from 1996 to 2000, introduced a socioeconomic policy inspired by the zero deficit objective adopted at the March 1996 Summit on the Economic and Social Future of Québec, which generated a series of negative effects in the fields of education, health, social services, and social policy. Mouterde (2012, 13) writes: "Think simply of the neoliberal economic regulation mode that finally dominated Québec especially from the middle of the nineties with Lucien Bouchard and his zero-deficit policies."[2] Other authors defend a similar position (Piotte 1998; Lamarche 2007; Greason 2013).

In contrast, a progressive trend in the literature, of which we are participants, argues that in the last two decades, the Québec government, often pressured by social movements and civil society, has introduced – alongside neoliberal initiatives – a number of very progressive public policy measures (Jenson 2002; Klein et al. 2010; Levesque 2003; Noël 2013). Among these, we find

- the AccèsLogis program in the area of social housing (Ducharme and Vaillancourt 2012);
- the recognition and support of autonomous community organizations (Jetté 2008);
- the institutionalization of the Carrefours Jeunesse Emploi and other networks of community-based organizations whose mission is to help vulnerable people integrate into the labour market (Larose et al. 2005);
- the introduction in 1996 of "a proactive law on pay equity" which permitted the government, in 2006, to reach "a comprehensive pay equity agreement with its own employees" (Noël 2013, 269);
- a new family policy whose goal, among others, is to develop a universal network of low-cost daycare centre spaces for pre-school children (Noël 2013, 266–8);
- a local and regional development policy that has led to the creation of a provincial network of local development centres (Comeau et al. 2001);
- the recognition and support of the social economy (Vaillancourt 2009); and
- the anti-poverty policy adopted in December 2002.

These public policy reforms represent social innovations (Vaillancourt 2012a). They are the product of government intervention, but not only of government intervention. Indeed, they were put in place with the participation and advocacy practices of civil society actors and organizations that were well aware of the reality of poor and marginalized people. In other words, these reforms have been democratically co-constructed (see some similarities with chapter 5 as well as chapter 10).

In this chapter, we have chosen to consider and analyze Bill 112, the Québec Act to Combat Poverty and Social Exclusion (Government of Québec 2002), as a case of democratic co-construction of public policy. Updating earlier studies and working papers (Aubry 2010 and 2012; Vaillancourt and Aubry 2014), this chapter is divided into five parts. Part one focuses on our conceptual framework, where we compare the concept of advocacy used in this book with our concept of how civil society participates in the co-construction of public policy. The second part presents the grassroots mobilization campaign leading to the emergence of Bill 112 (1995–2002) and highlights the interactions between grassroots organizations and government and political actors. The third part examines the content of Bill 112 – an Act focusing on poverty and social exclusion, which is a marginalized societal issue – adopted in December 2002, with an emphasis on the elements influenced by the dynamics of co-construction. Part four centres on the implementation of the bill from 2003 to 2013. The final part analyzes the content presented in the previous sections using the theoretical lens presented in part one with a special focus on the conditions that have contributed to reconciling advocacy and the democratic co-construction of public policy.[3]

## THEORETICAL FRAMEWORK

The theoretical framework used in this chapter is the outcome of a dialogue developed on the concept of advocacy, which is central in this book, and the concept of democratic co-construction of public policy, which is central in our recent writings.

Before addressing these two concepts, note that we will not dwell on other aspects of our analytical framework that are part of the theoretical tradition of Laboratoire de recherche sur les pratiques et les politiques sociales (LAREPPS) and on which we have dwelt at length in our previous writings (Vaillancourt and Jetté 1997; Jetté et al. 2000; Vaillancourt and Tremblay 2012; Vaillancourt 2006, 2009, 2012a, and 2012b). Within the LAREPPS legacy, we pay attention to the following elements:

- The *development of social policy*, and more broadly of public policy, implies the interplay between four categories of social actors: the state, the private enterprise sector, the third sector, and the family (informal sector).
- In this chapter, we use the term *third sector organizations (TSOs)* and we acknowledge the existence of several similar concepts. We use alternatively the concept of Social and Solidarity Economy – grouping together market and non-market components, including non-profit community-based organizations – and the concept of third sector organizations. We conceptualize these alongside the "European tradition" as opposed to the "US tradition" so we can include cooperatives and mutual

companies, as well as non-profit organizations (NPOs), including community-based organizations. We also acknowledge the "moving frontiers" between the welfare state and TSOs (Evers and Laville 2004; Vaillancourt 2006).
- We are conscious of the polysemy of the concept of *civil society* used in the literature. We use it with a meaning slightly broader than the one given to third sector: "The sphere of ideas, values, institutions, organizations, networks, and individual that are ... located between the family, the state, and the market" (Anheier quoted in Vaillancourt 2013, 129–30). This broader meaning makes room for old and new social movements.
- The LAREPPS perspective blends well with that of the "proactive social investment state," particularly with "the social democratic version" of this model conceptualized by Evers and Guillemard (2013) in the concluding chapter of their recent work *Social Policy and Citizenship. The Changing Landscape.* "Under the more social democratic version – as opposed to the liberal or neoliberal version – the state coordinates and orients investment in human capital, and oversees the equality of distribution" (375). This new democratic variant of the social investment state "implies a different form of welfare governance. The state is no longer alone in offering a wide range of benefits and services to citizens. More and more parties are involved. The 'pillars' of welfare ... namely, the state along with the market place, the various organizations that represent the third sector such as civic associations, non-governmental organizations, and voluntary agencies, and finally families and communities – are increasingly interconnected through partnership" (368). In line with the LAREPPS' theoretical tradition, we particularly favour a renewed partnership between the state and TSOs. Let us now examine the concepts of lobbying, advocacy, and democratic co-construction.

## *Lobbying*

Before we consider the interfaces between advocacy and co-construction, and in order to identify the specificity of advocacy, we need to examine the concept of lobbying, which is sometimes incorrectly used as a synonym for advocacy. At first glance, the concepts of lobbying and advocacy share a common core. They both refer to a process whose aim is to influence decisions made by government officials. These decisions may concern the adoption of a new bill or the distribution of grants or fiscal privileges, or any other advantage. The lobbyists and the advocates both intervene to influence decision-making processes on behalf of a group of citizens, an organization, a corporation, a coalition, etc. Both may be paid or not for their services.

But by carefully examining the concept of lobbying, more particularly its historical evolution,[4] we find some differences with the concept of advocacy. The word lobbying has a pejorative connotation attached to it, in spite of the legislation adopted in some societies to regulate it. In some circles, lobbying seems to refer more to the efforts made to influence decision makers behind closed doors to advance the particular interests of a specific group or organization rather than the general interest. We refer to professional lobbyists (sometimes former politicians or bureaucrats) as those who use their political experience and networks to put forward corporate interests like those of the oil and gas industries.

### Advocacy

For the concept of advocacy as it relates to social policy, we begin with the definition provided by DeSantis (2010, 25–6): "*Social policy* advocacy consists of those intentional efforts *of* NPOs (Non-profit Organizations) to change existing or proposed *government* policies on behalf of or with groups of *marginalized people*." The words in italics suggest that DeSantis (2010) is narrowing a broader definition to use it in a particular research context. This suggests that the author is examining specific advocacy practices which:

- are developed in the social policy domain;
- aim to create public policy changes (either by amending a former policy, or by creating a new policy);
- imply the intervention of TSOs;
- are done on behalf of or with groups of marginalized people.

In narrowing the definition of advocacy in this way, DeSantis (2010) acknowledges that other forms of advocacy could: (1) apply to domains other than social policy; (2) produce outcomes other than public policy changes; (3) imply the participation of stakeholders other than TSOs; (4) be done on behalf of or with people other than those who are marginalized.

### Advocacy and Democratic Co-construction of Public Policy

In our recent conceptual work on the theme of "democratic co-construction of public policy" (Vaillancourt, 2009, 2012a, 2012b, and 2013), referring to the four parameters used by DeSantis, we have studied socioeconomic initiatives, which (1) are in the public policy domain (which is broader than the social policy domain); (2) aim to create public policy reforms; (3) imply the participation of TSOs and also of other social actors in civil society, and (4) are done with the participation of marginalized people and other groups of people.

The DeSantis advocacy approach and our own approach thus share some common elements. But there are also differences. In our theoretical and empirical research work in the area of social and public policy, we have focused on the *participation* of third-sector actors *in the democratic co-construction of public policy*. Let us explain briefly.

1. When we focus on *the participation of TSOs*, we assume that they are often marginalized in public policy development and that their participation can enrich the contents of public policy and democratize the decision-making process.
2. We agree with Evers (2013), who argues that some authors who favour the participation of TSOs in welfare state reforms too often focus on the only participation of TSOs in the delivery of goods and services and only rarely on the contribution of TSOs that advocate in favour of citizen's rights. Both categories of TSOs – *provider organizations and advocacy organizations* – should participate in the public policy co-construction process to make it richer and more democratic.
3. We use the concept of *co-construction of public policy* to raise the issue of how civil society stakeholders can participate in designing public policy. Co-construction calls for a process of co-decision by civil society actors and state actors. We also make an important distinction between co-construction and co-production of public policy. In the co-production of public policy, citizen participation is limited to the implementation

stage of public policies constructed by state actors alone or in partnership with other non-state actors. But, in the co-construction of public policy, citizen participation contributes directly to the creation of policies. It is much more than citizen consultation.

4. We refer to *a democratic* co-construction of public policy as opposed to *non-democratic* forms of co-construction. For example, we can encounter a *corporatist co-construction* of public policy when some civil society stakeholders, those who enjoy more economic and political capital, participate in the political decision-making process, while other stakeholders, who enjoy less economic and social capital, are excluded. A good example is the pre-budget consultation process at the provincial and federal levels in which business and union organizations are systematically consulted while associations representing marginalized groups are often ignored. Alternatively, in a democratic process of public policy co-construction, a broad diversity of stakeholders participate in *democratic deliberation* permitting the development of public policy consensus and decisions that reflect the general interest. In other words, citizen participation alone is not enough to achieve democratic co-construction of public policy. Indeed, in our societies we often encounter very real citizen participation, for example in parliamentary commissions, that does not lead to democratic public deliberation and decision-making processes.

5. As we have explained elsewhere (Vaillancourt 2009), we may encounter non-democratic co-construction of public policy even in cases in which marginalized people and TSOs, normally excluded from the political decision-making process, participate. Indeed, we can imagine co-construction scenarios in which particular groups of marginalized people, allied with specific TSOs, are capable of doing efficient *lobbying* and *advocacy* with government actors, but are not participating in a democratic deliberation with other stakeholders directly concerned by the socioeconomic problem in question. In other words, it is possible to encounter *lobbying* and *advocacy* practices in which, because of the some stakeholders are excluded, the end result is not a democratic co-construction but a corporatist co-construction of public policy (Vaillancourt 2012b). Our concern here is not to devalue the importance of developing

efficient lobbying and advocacy practices. It is to reconcile it with the aim of democratically co-constructing public policies. It is to harmonize a *bilateral process* of advocating with the state in favour of some specific marginalized social groups with a *multilateral process* of integrating this initiative within a broader democratic deliberation process that includes a diversity of other stakeholders.
6. In addition, to avoid all ambiguity, we acknowledge that elected political representatives have the last word in the decision-making process.

We now turn to the long and intense mobilization campaign that led up to the unanimous adoption of Bill 112 by all political parties represented at the Québec National Assembly.[5]

### EMERGENCE OF BILL 112 (1995–2002)

In this section, we summarize the history of the mobilization of civil society over the seven years leading up to the enactment of Bill 112 in 2002.

The Québec Act to Combat Poverty and Social Exclusion, named Bill 112 before its adoption in December 2002, was born from a grassroots movement that spread over several years and which brought together community organizations, faith-based organizations, women's groups, disability associations, trade unions, and citizens motivated by the desire to lay the foundation for a poverty-free Québec (see similarities in chapter 3). Resulting from exceptional participation and a well-structured consultation process, with which representatives of people living in poverty have been associated when concerned, this Act provided ample room for the concerns that Québec community groups had brought for more than a decade.

The movement began in 1995, when hundreds of women walked to Québec City to defend their claims aimed at fighting poverty and violence against women. Organized by the Québec Women's Federation, this march, called Du Pain et des roses (Bread and Roses March) marked the historic starting point of Bill 112. On 4 June 1995, hundreds of women from all regions of Québec, after walking over 200 kilometres to express their desire to end poverty, arrived at the Québec National Assembly, greeted by a crowd of thousands of supporters. Their message to the National Assembly was in the form of nine demands, including an important increase in the minimum wage and increased investments in social housing.

Although the immediate response of the Jacques Parizeau PQ government fell short of the objectives of the organizers, many of their demands rapidly received a positive answer. It is important to consider that the approaching referendum on the independence of Québec (30 October 1995) created a context favourable to the coming together of the sovereignty movement and progressive social movements, which, in the following years, contributed to the emergence of many progressive social policy reforms (Vaillancourt 2012a). One year later, after the narrow defeat of the referendum, the Québec government, led by Lucien Bouchard, organized the Economic and Employment Summit. For the very first time in an event of this importance, community organizations were invited by the government to actively participate alongside employer and union organizations. At the summit, the women's movement and community organizations advanced the idea of establishing a zero poverty policy as opposed to the zero deficit policy put forth by the government on that occasion.

In the fall of 1997, while participating in a popular movement against the government's regressive social welfare reform proposal, the faith-based organization Carrefour de pastorale en monde ouvrier de Québec (CAPMO) and a few other organizations decided to try an alternative global approach to welfare reform by demanding that the Québec government adopt a law aimed at eliminating poverty, to be drafted by the people and organizations representing the poor and the excluded. To draft such a law, a people's parliament sat in session for one month in the Esplanade Park facing the parliament building.

The CAPMO proposal consisted of a constructive and ambitious project that solicited TSOS, many small and stretched, who had historically mobilized against rising poverty only to obtain modest gains, simply preserve limited benefits, or suffer setbacks. At the outset, the project was designed as an "open book," which meant it had to be collectively defined through a broad and inclusive process of public deliberation.

In January 1998, a formal organization was established to promote the project: the Collective for a Law on the Elimination of Poverty.[6] The ten founding organizations of the Collective included CAPMO and other faith-based groups, the Québec

Women's Federation, the Québec Coalition of People on Welfare, the Confederation of National Trade Unions, the Québec Teachers Union, and the Québec Association for Mental Health Alternative Resources. Later, several other groups joined the Collective, including international development non-governmental organizations, student federations, a nurse's federation, disability associations and civil rights organizations. Some groups, for example the Mouvement d'éducation populaire autonome du Québec (MEPACQ), initially opposed the project. Some militants just did not believe that poverty could be eliminated by adopting a law while the same government was simultaneously weakening social programs and public services through its zero deficit objective (Greason 2004). Lamarche (2007) draws attention to the fact that there were internal debates and tensions within the coalition. According to her, some human rights activists and organizations were bound to a legal approach based on a "human rights framework" influenced by United Nations covenants while other anti-poverty activists and organizations were bound to an ethical approach based on values of dignity and social justice (Lamarche 2007, 146–7).

The Collective opted for a strategy based on "citizenship and popular education" to encourage citizens to participate directly. The goal was to rally as many people as possible around the project and, especially, to allow people living in poverty to participate. From the start, the focus was as much on the process as on the outcome.

Over a period of two years, from the fall of 1998 to the fall of 2000, the Collective carried out an operation that took place across the Province of Québec, one of the largest mobilizations in Québec social action history. From the start, the Collective worked on two fronts.

On one front, it launched an ambitious project of collective action and public deliberations. The Collective undertook an extensive consultation, gathering more than 20,000 comments and 5,000 suggestions. These were used to produce, with the help of legal experts, a first version of the bill, which was made public in front of the Montréal Stock exchange in December 1999. This draft was then discussed in all regions of Québec and modified through some 200 sessions of the "people's parliament." The bill garnered the support of more than 1,800 community organizations – some were registered charities while others were not.[7] Finally, in the spring of 2000, the Collective adopted the final proposal for a law on the elimination of poverty, written in the form of a conventional bill and submitted to the PQ government, to representatives of all the political parties and to all members of the National Assembly.

Simultaneously, on the other front, the Collective circulated a petition in favour of adopting a law on the elimination of poverty. On 22 November 2000, the petition, which had collected 215,316 signatures, was submitted to the National Assembly by a member of each of the three sitting political parties.

On that same day, the National Assembly voted on a resolution asking the government to adopt a comprehensive strategy to fight poverty, taking into account certain principles put forward by the Collective. For the next two years, the Collective conducted an intense campaign to advance its proposed legislation.

In March 2001, Premier Lucien Bouchard resigned and was replaced by Bernard Landry who, upon taking office, announced that the fight against poverty would be a priority of his government. He named a minister responsible for this initiative and later made the government's strategy public in a document entitled *Nobody Left Behind!* The government launched a consultation process in each of Québec's seventeen regions, where more than 1,000 organizations participated.

In June 2002, the government published *The National Strategy to Combat Poverty and Social Exclusion* and tabled Bill 112 – An Act to Combat Poverty and Social Exclusion. The bill was studied by a Parliamentary Commission from 1 October to 19 November 2002. Nearly 135 people, groups, and organizations from different sectors[8] were heard, and 166 written reports were tabled. During this period, the Collective multiplied its actions so it could amend the government's proposal. Its methods of communication with parliamentarians included writing to them as often as necessary, keeping them informed, and confronting them when possible, but always in a non-partisan way.

With some amendments to improve its scope, Bill 112 was finally passed unanimously by the National Assembly on 13 December 2002 and entered into force on 5 March 2003. The bill was adopted as the PQ government was living its last months in power. In April 2003, the Liberal Party of Québec led by Jean Charest was elected.

## ARCHITECTURE OF THE QUÉBEC ANTI-POVERTY ACT

Although the proposed Anti-Poverty Act[9] fell short of the objectives of the Collective, many of its aspects constituted important steps forward on which the Collective decided it could build. The first was the statement that the poor and excluded should be the first to act to change their situation. The second pertained to the final objective of the law, which was to work toward a Québec without poverty. There were many other interesting aspects of the Anti-Poverty Act on which the popular movement could build, including the reference to the Québec Charter of Rights, the importance that the law gave to the participation of the poor and excluded in the strategy, the obligation to produce an action plan, and an assessment of its results.

The Québec Anti-Poverty Act is a framework law that defines a number of general principles and obligations and gives the Québec government the responsibility to implement it. The Act (Government of Québec 2002) comprises a preamble and eight chapters. The preamble and the first two chapters deal with the principles and objectives of the law. The ensuing six chapters (3 to 8) deal with the institutions and the means conceived to carry out these principles and objectives.

### The Preamble, Purpose, and Definition of the Act

The preamble of the law establishes its major principles by referring to the Charter of Human Rights and Freedoms. After stating that "persons living in poverty and social exclusion are the first to act to improve their situation and that of their families and whereas such improvement is linked to the social, cultural and economic development of the entire community," the preamble then affirms "the desire of Québec society as a whole to act in a coordinated manner and pursue a course of action designed to combat poverty and social exclusion." Further, the desire to recognize the role and responsibility of Québec society as a whole, not just government, in finding and implementing solutions to poverty and exclusion is clearly outlined in the definition of the main object of the Act which is "to guide the Government and Québec society as a whole towards a process of planning and implementing actions to combat poverty, prevent its causes, reduce its effects on individuals and families, counter social exclusion and strive for a poverty-free Québec" (Art. 1). Article 2 of the Anti-Poverty Act then defines poverty broadly and inclusively. It states that poverty "means the condition of a human being who is deprived of the resources, means, choices and power necessary to acquire and maintain economic self-sufficiency or to facilitate integration and participation in society."

### National Strategy against Poverty and Social Exclusion

The Act institutes a national strategy against poverty and social exclusion (Art. 3) that "is intended to progressively make Québec, by 2013, one of the industrialized nations having the least number of persons living in poverty, according to recognized methods for making international comparisons" (Art. 4). At the heart of the Act is the creation of a national strategy against poverty and social exclusion which "shall consist of a set of actions implemented by the Government, its socio-economic partners, regional and local communities, community organizations and other social stakeholders to counter poverty and facilitate social inclusion. In that respect, the Government shall solicit citizen participation, particularly the participation of persons living in poverty" (Art. 5).

The National Strategy goals are the following (Art. 6):

1. to promote respect for and protection of the dignity of persons living in poverty and combat prejudices in their regard;
2. to improve the economic and social situation of persons and families living in poverty and social exclusion;
3. to reduce the inequalities that may be detrimental to social cohesion;
4. to encourage persons and families living in poverty to participate in community life and social development;
5. to develop and reinforce the sense of solidarity throughout Québec so that society as a whole may participate in the fight against poverty and social exclusion.

So that society as a whole may participate in the fight against poverty and social exclusion as specified in goal number 5 above, the bill specifies that actions "must provide for the inclusion of stakeholders representative of the broader Québec community" (Art. 11). These actions must:

1. favour citizen participation, particularly that of persons living in poverty and social exclusion and the organizations representing them;
2. support specific local and regional initiatives for the achievement of the goals set out in the National Strategy;
3. recognize the social responsibility of enterprises and include the labour market partners; and
4. recognize the contribution of volunteer and community action (Art. 11).

(Government of Québec 2002) Implementation of the Anti-Poverty Act (2003–13)

It is important to note that although Bill 112 was adopted by a PQ-led government, the Anti-Poverty Act was implementedunder successive liberal governments, from 2003 to 2014, except for an 18-month minority PQ government between 2012 and early 2014. In this section, we examine the implementation of the new act. First, we will pay attention to the two action plans and the new obligations placed on the government; second, we examine the roles and composition of three new institutions created by the Act.

## Two Government Action Plans

To implement the national strategy to combat poverty and social exclusion, Chapter III of the Act specifies that the government, before 5 May 2003, had to establish an action plan setting forth a set of measures the government planned on carrying out to achieve the goals (Art. 13).

The first action plan, *Reconcile Freedom and Social Justice: A Challenge for the Future* (*Concilier liberté et justice sociale: un défi pour l'avenir*), covers the years 2004 to 2010 and was finally unveiled on 2 April 2004 (MESS 2004). The plan was based on two principles: employment is the first solution to ensure economic security and social inclusion, and better protection for people with significant employment limitations is required (8). The first action plan contained several measures that aimed to support people with disabilities (Aubry 2010).

The plan consisted of four main objectives with a set of forty-seven measures representing investments of $2.5 billion over the next five years (MESS 2004). Most of these measures had been announced in the 2004–05 budget speech. The four objectives of the first plan were to:

- improve the well-being of people living in poverty;
- prevent poverty and social exclusion by developing each person's potential;
- involve society as a whole. The measures proposed for this objective supported the development of solidarity with disadvantaged communities and groups through local and regional actions and collective efforts against poverty and social exclusion;
- ensure consistent, coherent action; This last goal provides tools to coordinate the efforts of various concerned departments and agencies, to involve citizens in the efforts and to assess the impacts on poor people and families.

Reactions to the first Action Plan were mixed (Noël 2004). The Collective reacted in a positive but moderate way. It characterized the Plan as "a commendable effort to comply with the obligations contained in the law but limited by serious omissions that will allow the situation of the poorest people to deteriorate further" (Collectif pour un Québec sans pauvreté 2004). Other reactions went from critical – by those who believed that the Plan was too populist, gave too much importance to the poor to the detriment of the middle class, and did not respect the conservative electoral program of the newly elected Liberal government – to very positive, by those who considered the plan to be progressive and innovative (Noël 2004; Dufour 2004).

To put a national and regional consultation process on the contents of the second action plan in place, on 3 November 2008, pressured by the Collective, the minister responsible for the implementation of the Anti-Poverty Act announced a one-year extension of the first action plan. A national consultation forum was held in Québec City in June 2009. Participation was very limited and by invitation only, leading many community organizations to call for a boycott.

However, the Collective decided to participate because it initially considered that the empty chair policy was a bad strategy to advance its cause. The meeting gave rise to the confrontation of viewpoints concerning the content of the plan. Displeased with the intentions of the government, the Collective and many member groups left the meeting in protest. Notwithstanding the Collective's stance at the national meeting, public consultation meetings were held in every region in the fall of 2009 in which community organizations and ordinary citizens expressed their dissatisfaction with the government's orientation (Collectif pour un Québec sans pauvreté 2013).

Launched in June 2010, the second five-year action plan, entitled *Government Action Plan for Solidarity and Social inclusion 2010–2015: Québec's Mobilization against Poverty* (*Plan d'action gouvernemental pour la solidarité et l'inclusion sociale 2010–2015: le Québec mobilise contre la pauvreté*) set out four main objectives:

- Review our standard practices and make local and regional communities key players in the decision-making process;
- Acknowledge the value of work and foster the self-sufficiency of individuals;
- Foster the economic self-sufficiency of underprivileged individuals;
- Improve the living conditions of low-income individuals and families.

The second action plan provided $1.3 billion in new investments over five years. The Plan included six components, including a solidarity tax credit to compensate for the increase in the Québec sales tax, a full cost of living adjustment of social assistance benefits, and the creation of Solidarity Alliances in each region to coordinate regional action plans.

The Collective received this new action plan negatively. There were many reasons for this: the plan proposed a piecemeal approach with few new measures and no long-term direction; the plan did not respect the guidelines contained in the Anti-Poverty Act (Art. 6) because it placed more and more responsibility on the shoulders of the poor and excluded; the plan promoted territorial cooperation in lieu of structural measures to redistribute wealth and a national approach to combat poverty (Collectif 2013; RIOCM 2010).

### Three New Institutions

The Anti-Poverty Act also created three new institutions to support the implementation of the Act: (1) the Advisory Committee on the

Fight Against Poverty and Social Exclusion, which was activated in March 2006; (2) the Poverty and Exclusion Research Centre, which began its activities in 2005; (3) The Québec Social Initiative Fund, which was established in 2002 and is dedicated to financing initiatives to combat poverty and social exclusion (Art. 46).

## DISCUSSION

In this section, we critically analyze the empirical facts presented in the preceding sections, using the conceptual framework introduced in the first section. We argue that the Québec Anti-Poverty Act constitutes a remarkable innovation in terms of the political process that produced it (see chapter 7 in this collection for a contrasting example). We are conscious that some authors do not share our viewpoint. Some even argue the opposite, suggesting ironically that the Québec Anti-Poverty Act was not a "made in Québec" process and content, because some of its features were influenced by neo-liberal patterns imported from other OECD countries (Lamarche 2007; Lamarche and Greason 2008; Greason 2013). With other researchers (Noël 2004 and 2007; Dufour 2004), we believe that the Québec Anti-Poverty Act was innovative principally during the emergent years (1995–2002), and, to a lesser degree, during the implementation years (2003–13).

### Co-construction Initiated in Civil Society

Bill 112 is an example, perhaps unique in Québec, of a bottom-up legislative approach. Usually, new legislative bills are initiated and prepared within the government, and then are presented by the government in the form of proposed legislation. The proposed legislation is then reviewed by a Parliamentary Commission where political and civil society organizations give their points of view. In this process, the state is the main designer of public policy, although it consults civil society actors during the process. However, the genesis of Bill 112 illuminates an alternative model. In this case, the project was initiated in civil society. At the end of the emergence period, from the fall of 2000 to the fall of 2002, public deliberation involved not only civil society actors, but also political actors and bureaucrats.

## A Rich Laboratory of Advocacy Practices

During the first years of the emergent process, civil society actors attempted to construct the bill on their own. At the outset, the bill's objective was to eliminate poverty and exclusion completely, rather than to combat them. From 1995 to 2000, little energy was spent to initiate a dialogue with government and political party representatives. It was more an advocacy process to educate and mobilize Québec civil society, than a traditional lobbying process to convince the decision makers within the government. The idea was to create a popular movement within civil society, a movement that would one day be capable of pressuring political decision makers. In that context, a vast array of advocacy practices were imagined and enacted: the introduction of the concept of "zero impoverishment" to counter the concept of zero deficit; the idea of a law aimed at eliminating poverty in the fall of 1997; the creation of a people's parliament; the launching of a "citizenship and popular education" campaign; and the writing of a draft bill on the elimination of poverty circulated for discussion to all regions of Québec. All these practices were part of an innovative advocacy movement.

## In Harmony with the Independent Living Movement Paradigm

In the second, third, and fourth sections above, we saw that one basic principle characterizing the emergence, design, and implementation of the Anti-Poverty Act is that "persons living in poverty and social exclusion [and their associations] are the first to act to improve their situation." But if we look at the available literature on the Anti-Poverty Act, some writers, surprisingly, do not seem convinced of the importance of the participation of the poor and their associations as a central part of a law aimed to combat poverty. For Greason, the responsibility of social actors, beginning with the poor and excluding themselves, to participate in the fight against poverty is seen as a neoliberal government plot whose aim is the "de-responsabilization of government as the principal agent for fighting poverty" (2013, 4). However, this point of view is not at all convincing. It ignores key philosophical advances of the last thirty years in the anti-poverty and disability movements.

Indeed, citizen participation in resolving poverty and social exclusion problems through the co-construction of social policy reforms is very much a historical demand of the disability movement and associations at the international, Canadian, and Québec levels, during the last three decades. In English Canada and in Québec, and in many European countries, this philosophical and political vision embraced by the Independent Living Movement (ILM) was promoted by various disability TSOs in the late 1970s and the following decades (Prince 2009, 116, 120–2).

On the Québec scene, the ILM theoretical framework was present in a seminal paper, *On Equal Terms*, published in 1983 by the Office des personnes handicapées du Québec (OPHQ) and co-constructed by the disability movement and the Québec government (Boucher, Fougeyrollas, and Gaucher 2003, 152–3). This innovative vision has been reaffirmed many times in the last three decades and is at the heart of the new *À Part Entière* policy adopted in 2009 by the Québec government (OPHQ 2009). For the disability movement and the TSOs involved, the ILM paradigm has two concrete implications. First, the TSOs in the disability area must be "organizations controlled and run by people with disabilities" (Boucher, Fougeyrollas, and Gaucher 2003, 138–9). Second, people with disabilities and their network of TSOs are not only users but designers and co-constructors of social policy reforms.

On the broader Canadian scene, we observe that the ILM paradigm was making a breakthrough in the disability movement at nearly the same time (since the late 1970s) and in a similar manner. This new paradigm is well articulated in the following quotation from the Roeher Institute, an organization that promotes self-determination of people with disabilities: "In the current context, however, people and groups are demanding participation in more decision-making processes. They want to be involved in decision making in welfare state policies and programs, in labour market and other economic institutions" (Roeher Institute 1993, 18–19). It is easy to see the harmony between the self-determination principle of the disability movement and the desire to place the participation of the poor at the heart of the Anti-Poverty Act (see chapter 5 on disability advocacy in Saskatchewan).

*Participation of a Diversity of Stakeholders from Civil Society*

Within our framework of democratic co-construction, the participation of marginalized people is a condition, but not a sufficient condition, to develop democratic social policy reforms and avoid the corporatist co-construction described earlier. Indeed, other stakeholders of civil society also need to participate to permit a solidarity perspective within the co-construction process. The Anti-Poverty Act, in its preamble for example, focuses on the participation of the poor as well as that of other stakeholders. For us, this double participation is important for attaining democratic co-construction. If those who are living in poverty and their associations do not participate in designing the anti-poverty strategy, something essential is missing for "reducing poverty and enabling citizenship." In addition, if a diversity of other stakeholders is not participating in the development of "action plans" for example, the co-construction process becomes narrower and less democratic. In the case of the preparation and implementation of the Anti-Poverty Act, it is obvious that the participation of many social movements (e.g., labour, feminist, disability, seniors) and other stakeholders (e.g., church-based social justice associations, alternative medias, family organizations, civil rights organizations, student federations) was a decisive factor in broadening the coalition and making it more democratic and politically influential. In other words, the co-construction process was more than a short list of "interest groups" working in a corporatist way to secure new legislation.

## Participation of a Diversity of Political Actors

As we have stated earlier, authentic democratic co-construction of public policy implies not only the participation of civil society, but also of those in the political realm – the executive and legislative branches and the bureaucracy – to deliberate and decide together. For a few years, from 1995 to 2000, the anti-poverty organizations and their allies in civil society were almost alone in constructing a bill to eliminate poverty. The anti-poverty coalition was busy developing advocacy campaigns to promote understanding and secure support from the public in general, knowing that these initiatives would eventually help their efforts to gain the support of politicians and bureaucrats.

At the end of 1999, when the Collective and the anti-poverty coalition released their own version of a bill to eliminate poverty, a double dynamic ensued. On the one hand, the coalition continued its work within civil society by making sure that the bill was largely known and discussed in all regions of Québec. On the other hand, the coalition multiplied its interactions with various political actors it tried to convince of the relevance of the project. From that moment on, the government and all the political parties sitting in the National Assembly talked of combating poverty, while the coalition continued to talk about eliminating poverty. The internal and external efforts made by the coalition continued throughout 2001 and 2002. They intensified with the arrival of the Landry government in March 2001 and reached their peak from June to November 2002, when the government was working internally on its own strategy to fight poverty. In June, Bill 112 was tabled and a parliamentary commission was announced to discuss it. During this time, the coalition continued to consolidate its support in civil society, to multiply interactions with political actors and to obtain amendments to Bill 112. We consider the above process as a genuine co-construction of public policy, regardless of the differing goals of the coalition (i.e., a goal of eliminating poverty) and the government (i.e., a goal of combating poverty), because of the increased interactions among civil society and political actors.

The investment of energy in the legislative and the executive arenas by the Collective and its allies for the elimination of poverty therefore became very important at the end of the emergent period. The lobbying and advocacy practices developed in 2001 and 2002 were concerned not only with the rules of participative and direct democracy, but also with the rules of representative democracy. Civil society and political actors deliberated and worked together to secure an anti-poverty project. The leadership of the anti-poverty movement was capable of working not only with the political party in power, but also with the political parties in opposition. This was instrumental in preparing the unanimous adoption of Bill 112 on 13 December 2002, on the one hand, and in the survival of the Anti-Poverty Act after the defeat of the PQ government in April 2003, on the other.

### The Architecture of the Anti-Poverty Act Favours Co-construction

Some might argue that an anti-poverty act is not very important because any government could refuse to implement its objectives if they are not in harmony with its own philosophy. This consideration is justified in some respects, but not all. Of course, when a new political party is elected and has to cope with specific policies or pieces of legislation that contradict its own convictions, it may be tempted to ignore, modify, or repeal them. However, we must recognize that a new government would find this easier to do if it is dealing with a policy that had not been democratically co-constructed.

Contrary to many fears, the Charest government was incapable of seriously weakening many innovative public policy reforms – including the Anti-Poverty Act – which had been co-constructed under the former PQ governments from 1994 to 2003. To explain this situation, we share some hypotheses put forth by Alain Noël (2007 and 2013). To analyze the political practices of the Charest governments from 2003 to 2012, it is important to take into account not only the "partisan dimension," but also the "cross-partisan dimension" that influenced both the PQ and the Liberal governments over the last twenty years. The resilience of the Anti-Poverty Act during the Charest Liberal years – and of some other socioeconomic policy reforms initiated by the PQ government – was made possible because of this "cross-partisan dimension" (Noël 2007), which is also called "coalition politics" or "coalition engineering" by Noël (2013, 262–6), and democratic co-construction by us. In other words, "partisan politics certainly played a role" (263) both in the PQ and Liberal governments' decisions, but it was not the principal factor. The participation of civil society in the design and implementation of some public policy reforms, such as the Anti-Poverty Act, explains why these reforms have a social-democratic character, in spite of the scarcity of Québec social-democratic premiers.

In the end, the three Charest governments were not able to ignore the obligations of the Anti-Poverty Act. This does not mean that the leadership of these governments was in a hurry to pay attention to them. On the contrary, the political will to develop the first action plan in 2004 and the second in 2008, as we described earlier, was feeble or absent. Fortunately, the co-constructed architecture of the Act offered levers to civil society and opposition parties to defend the democratic principles and mechanisms of the Act. The Anti-Poverty Act contains various mechanisms that ensure the effective enforcement and coordination of government actions: the government must present its Action Plan at a specific date; each minister with a legislative or regulatory proposal must analyze the anticipated effects on those living in poverty; the government must annually publish a report on the activities carried out within the framework of the action plan; and the CEPE (Poverty and Social Exclusion Research Center) must publish a progress report on the evolution of poverty each year. In addition, the participation of anti-poverty network activists and allies in the new institutions, such as the Advisory Committee and the CEPE, have contributed, in a difficult political context, to breathing life into the provisions of the bill, even if it was not done with the intensity that activists and their allies had wished.

## CONCLUSION

In this chapter, we have presented the case study of the Québec Anti-Poverty Act, focusing on the review of the democratic process that led to its adoption rather than on the analysis of the results obtained in the fight against poverty. We have distinguished two phases in the history of the legislation which spans nearly twenty years, that of its genesis (1995–2002) and that of its implementation (2003–13). We examined the role of TSOs, especially those involved in improving the situation of the poor and excluded people, from two perspectives: first, did these TSOs deploy advocacy practices and, second, did they participate in the democratic co-construction of the anti-poverty policy? In our framework, the deployment of advocacy practices by TSOs must be combined with their participation in the democratic co-construction of policies to produce sound social policy reforms. "Put simply, there is hardly any chance of good social policy in a 'spoiled democracy'" (Evers and Guillemard 2013, 381).

For the advocacy practices of TSOs, as numerous and original as they are, to be consistent with the perspective of democratic co-construction, the requirements of participatory democracy must accompany those of representative democracy. This implies that a diversity of actors of civil society, including TSOs working with persons who live in poverty, debate with a diversity of political actors to define policy content. Co-construction does not exist if civil society alone or those in the political realm alone develop the policy. Co-construction may exist, but it cannot be described as democratic if it only concerns certain actors of the political realm (e.g., those of the executive branch but not of the legislative branch) and certain actors of civil society (e.g., certain dominant players but without the poor and excluded and their network of TSOs). In sum, the participation of TSOs in the democratic co-construction of policies is an exacting process, rarely encountered in public policy reforms.

In fact, the philosophical foundations of the Québec Anti-Poverty Act presented in the second section are in harmony with the features of a democratic co-construction process of public policies that were presented in the first section. We can summarize these foundations of the fight against poverty and exclusion as follows:

- It is not solely the responsibility of governments;
- It recognizes the responsibility of the poor and the excluded to act to improve their and their families' situations;
- It is also the responsibility of partners in the labour market;
- It is also the responsibility of Québec society as a whole.

This emphasis on identifying civil society actors aims to make it clear that the fight against poverty is not only the responsibility of governments and the state as proposed in certain state-focused visions which can come from the left or the right of the political spectrum. However, it is still essential that a diversity of actors of the political realm participate in a democratic co-construction process. In the political sphere, democratic co-construction involves not only the participation of elected officials in the executive branch of government, but also of members of various political parties who sit in legislative bodies and committees, as was the case throughout 2002 during deliberations preceding the adoption of the law. To summarize, democratic co-construction means that, in certain decisive moments, there must be dialogue between civil society and the political realm, a dialogue that is not without compromise, such as that which emerged in 2002 when the anti-poverty coalition accepted a law that aimed to *combat* rather than *eliminate* poverty and exclusion.

Our chapter demonstrates that in the history of the Québec Anti-Poverty Act, the TSOs of the anti-poverty coalition, those who defend human rights as well as those who deliver alternative human services, participated in a plethora of original advocacy practices as well as democratic co-construction activities.

The frequency and intensity of these practices have fluctuated over the years and advocacy is accepted and sometimes even funded by the provincial government (see endnote 7):

- Advocacy practices were constant throughout the emergent stage (1995–2002), but were less frequent and intense during the implementation stage. They reappeared at the time of the

preparation of the two Action Plans in 2003–04 and 2008–10;
- The democratic co-construction process peaked at the end of the emergent period, from November 2000 to December 2002, and appeared more timidly during the preparation of the Action Plans;
- Advocacy practices helped to prepare the phases of democratic co-construction. Thus, from 1995 to 2001, the TSOs of the anti-poverty coalition devoted their energies to raising awareness and mobilizing civil society and to preparing their own bill to eliminate poverty, giving the impression that they did not care about making concessions with political actors;
- These advocacy practices were a challenge to the political realm, hence the turning point at the end of 2000. The institutions and actors of the political realm then began to respond to the demands resulting from the mobilization of civil society. For a time, in 2001, it seemed that two approaches to developing a draft anti-poverty law coexisted in the form of two solitudes – one in civil society and the other in the political realm;
- And then, at the end of 2001, a public debate was initiated and bridges appeared between social mobilization and political mobilization. It is here that the process that we have labelled democratic co-construction began.

In closing, can the concept of democratic co-construction of public policies used in certain circles of social action and research be considered as "shifting discourse"? We believe so, while at the same time we recognize that social movements and research communities are currently debating this concept within Québec and across Canada.

## NOTES

1 The production of this paper was made possible by the support of the Community-University Research Alliance (CURA) "Disabling Poverty and Enabling Citizenship" coordinated by Michael Prince of the University of Victoria and Yvonne Peters of the Council of Canadians with Disabilities (CCD). We also wish to thank Lucie Dumais and Léonie Archambault, our colleagues of the Laboratoire de recherche sur les pratiques et les politiques sociales (LAREPPS), for their useful comments and suggestions.
2 Authors' translation.

3 In this chapter we focus on the process and not on the results of the anti-poverty legislation. For an analysis of the effect of the legislation, see our research report, available on the CCD website (Vaillancourt and Aubry, 2014). http://www.ccdonline.ca/fr/socialpolicy/poverty-citizenship/demographic-profile/research-report-quebec-act-to-combat-poverty-and-social-exclusion.
4 Originally, the concept referred to individuals or groups who met public officials in the lobby of the Parliament of Westminster in the 1830s with the aim of influencing coming decisions.
5 Québec considers itself a nation and thus has a "national" assembly, which differs from other provinces/territories, which have "provincial/territorial" assemblies. Further, and for example, Québec adopted *The National Strategy to Combat Poverty and Social Exclusion*, which refers to a province-wide strategy, not a Canada-wide strategy.
6 The name of the Collective changed a few years later to become: Collectif pour un Québec sans pauvreté.
7 Among these 1,800 community organizations, some were part of the Réseau québécois de l'action communautaire autonome (RQACA), whereas others were not. Also, some were registered charitable organizations according to federal legislation, whereas others were registered non-profits without charitable status. The RQACA is funded by the provincial government and represents about sixty umbrella organizations, representing 4,000 local and regional organizations/bodies across Québec. It advocates across government departments and throughout Québec for a more just society, without fear of funding loss. It is noteworthy that this independent community advocacy structure, funded by the provincial government, exists in Québec but does not appear to exist elsewhere in Canada.
8 Including employer organizations and chambers of industry and commerce.
9 In the rest of our paper, we refer to the Anti-Poverty Act to mean the Québec Act to Combat Poverty and Social Exclusion.

REFERENCES

Aubry, F. 2010. *The Québec Act to Combat Poverty and Social Exclusion: How Does it Tackle the Situation of People with Disabilities*. Winnipeg: Council of Canadians with Disabilities. http://www.ccdonline.ca/en/socialpolicy/poverty-citizenship/income-security-reform/quebec-law-poverty-exclusion.

– 2012. *The Fight Against Poverty and Exclusion in Québec: Mixed Results, Including for Persons with Disabilities*. Winnipeg: Council of Canadians with Disabilities. http://www.ccdonline.ca/en/socialpolicy/poverty-citizenship/income-security-reform/fight-poverty-exclusion-quebec.

Boucher, N., P. Fougeyrollas, and C. Gaucher. 2003. "Development and Transformation of Advocacy in the Disability Movement of Québec." In *Making Equality. History of Advocacy and Persons with Disabilities in Canada*, edited by D. Stienstra and A. Wight-Felske. Concord, Ontario: Captus Press Inc.

Collectif pour un Québec sans pauvreté. 2004. *Communiqué: Une loi appliquée… avec de graves omissions*, Québec, 2 avril. http://www.pauvrete.qc.ca/?Une-loi-appliquee-avec-de-graves.

– 2013. *Historique critique et bilan dans le cadre du dixième anniversaire de la Loi visant à lutter contre la pauvreté et l'exclusion sociale*. http://www.pauvrete.qc.ca/IMG/pdf/Historique_critique_et_bilan_Loi.pdf.

Comeau, Y., L. Favreau, B. Lévesque, and M. Mendell. 2001. *Emploi, économie sociale, développement local: les nouvelles filières*. Sainte-Foy: Presses de l'Université du Québec.

DeSantis, G.C. 2010. "Voices from the Margins: Policy Advocacy and Marginalized Communities." *Canadian Journal of Nonprofit and Social Economy Research / Revue canadienne de recherche sur les OSBL et l'économie sociale* 1 (1): 23–45.

Ducharme, M.-N., and Y. Vaillancourt. 2012. "The *AccèsLogis Québec* Program: 15 years of Partnership." *Canadian Review of Social Policy / Revue canadienne de politique sociale* 1: 16–29.

Dufour, P. 2004. "L'adoption du projet de loi 112 au Québec: le produit d'une mobilisation ou une simple question de conjoncture politique?" *Politique et Sociétés* 23 (2–3): 159–82. http://dx.doi.org/10.7202/010888ar.

Evers, A. 2013. "The Concept of 'Civil Society': Different Understandings and their Implications for Third Sector Policies." *Voluntary Sector Review* 4 (2): 149–64. http://dx.doi.org/10.1332/204080513X667800.

Evers, A., and J.-L. Laville, eds. 2004. *The Third Sector in Europe*. Cheltenham, UK: Edward Elgar. http://dx.doi.org/10.4337/9781843769774.

Evers, A., and A.-M. Guillemard, eds. 2013. *Social Policy and Citizenship. The Changing Landscape*. New York: Oxford University Press.

Government of Québec. 2002. *L.R.Q. chapter L-7: An Act to Combat Poverty and Social Exclusion*. Québec: Éditeur officiel du Québec.

Greason, V. 2004. "La loi 112 – un pas en avant ou un pas en arrière pour le pouvoir citoyen?" *Actes du Colloque du MEPAQ 2004 – précis de la présentation en atelier.* http://www.socialrightscura.ca/documents/Quebec/La%20lutte%20contre%20la%20pauvret%C3%A9.pdf.

– 2013. "Poverty As a Human Rights Violation." CURA on "Social Rights in Canada" coordinated by J. Jackman and B. Porter. www.povnet.org/node/5107.

Jenson, J. 2002. "Against the Current: Child Care and Family Policy in Québec." In *Child Care Policy at the Crossroads. Gender and Welfare State Restructuring*, edited by Sonya Michel and Rianne Mahon, 309–30. London: Routledge.

Jetté, C. 2008. *Les organismes communautaires et la transformation de l'Etat-providence. Trois décennies de coconstruction des politiques publiques dans le domaine de la santé et des services sociaux*. Québec: Presses de l'Université du Québec.

Jetté, C., B. Lévesque, L. Mager, and Y. Vaillancourt. 2000. *Économie sociale et transformation de l'État providence dans le domaine de la santé et du bien-être. Une recension des écrits (1990–2000)*. Sainte-Foy: PUQ.

Klein, J.-L., J.-M. Fontan, D. Harrisson, and B. Lévesque. 2010. "L'innovation sociale dans le contexte du 'modèle québècois': acteurs, composantes et principaux défis." *Philanthropist* 23 (3): 93–100.

Lamarche, L. 2007. "The 'Made in Québec' Act to Combat Poverty and Social Exclusion: The Complex Relationship between Poverty and Human Rights." In *Poverty: Rights, Social Citizenship, and Legal Activism*, edited by M. Young, S. Boyd, G. Brodsky, and S. Day, 139–61. Vancouver, Toronto: UBC Press.

Lamarche, L., and V. Greason. 2008. "Poverty Impact Analysis (PIA) and Governmental Action: 'Made in Québec' … Again?" http://www.socialrightscura.ca/documents/publications/margot/LamarcheGreason.pdf.

Larose, G., Y. Vaillancourt, G. Shields, and M. Kearney. 2005. "Contribution de l'économie sociale au renouvellement des politiques et des pratiques dans le domaine de l'insertion socioéconomique au Québec, de 1983 à 2003." *Canadian Journal of Career Development / Revue canadienne de developpement de carrière* 4 (1): 11–28.

Lévesque, B. 2003. "Fonction de base et nouveau rôle des pouvoirs publics: vers un nouveau paradigme de l'État." *Annals of Public and Cooperative Economics* 74 (4): 489–513. http://dx.doi.org/10.1111/j.1467-8292.2003.00232.x.

Ministère de l'emploi et de la solidarité sociale (MESS). 2004. *Plan d'action gouvernemental en matière de lutte contre la pauvreté et l'exclusion sociale Concilier liberté et justice sociale*. Québec: Gouvernement du Québec.

Mouterde, P. 2012. "Sur les traces du virage à gauche latino-américain." *Relations* 754 (février): 13–4.

Noël, A. 2004. "Lutte contre la pauvreté ou lutte contre les pauvres." *Administration et politique publique*, 504–13. http://www.omiss.ca/activite/pdf/noel/pdf.

– 2007. "Québec's Law Against Poverty and Social Exclusion." *Perception* 29 (1–2): 16–7.

– 2013. "Québec's New Politics of Redistribution." In *The Fading of Redistributive Politics: Inequality and the Politics of Social Policy*, edited by K. Banting and J. Myles, 256–84. Vancouver: UBC Press.

Office des personnes handicapées du Québec (OPHQ). 2009. *À part entière: pour un véritable exercice du droit à l'égalité*. Québec: OPHQ.

Piotte, J.-M. 1998. *Du combat au partenariat. Interventions critiques sur le syndicalisme québécois*. Montréal: Nota Bene. http://classiques.uqac.ca/contemporains/piotte_jean_marc/du_combat_au_partenariat_livre/du_combat_au_partenariat.pdf.

Prince, M. 2009. *Absent Citizens. Disability Politics and Policy in Canada*. Toronto: University of Toronto Press.

RIOCM. 2010, 6 juin. *Plan de lutte à la pauvreté: Des organismes communautaires de Montréal refusent le marché de dupes proposé par Québec*.

Roeher Institute. 1993. *Social Well-Being. A Paradigm for Reform*. Toronto: The Roeher Institute.

Vaillancourt, Y. 2006. "Le tiers secteur au Canada, un lieu de rencontre entre la tradition américaine et la tradition européenne." *Canadian Review of Social Policy/Revue canadienne de politique sociale* 56 (Fall): 23–39.

Vaillancourt, Y. 2009. "Social Economy and the Co-construction of Public Policy." *Annals of Public and Cooperative Economics / Annales de l'économie publique, sociale et coopérative* 80 (2): 275–313. http://dx.doi.org/10.1111/j.1467-8292.2009.00387.x.

Vaillancourt, Y. 2012a. "The Québec Model of Social Policy, Past and Present." In *Canadian Social Policy. Issues and Perspectives*. 5th ed., edited by Anne Westhues and Brian Wharf, 115–44. Waterloo: Wilfrid Laurier University Press.

Vaillancourt, Y. 2012b. "Third Sector and the Co-construction of Canadian Public Policy." In *New Public Governance, the Third Sector and Co-Production*, edited by V. Pestoff, T. Brandsen, and B. Verschuere, 79–100. New York & Abingdon, UK: Routledge.

Vaillancourt, Y., and C. Jetté. 1997. *Vers un nouveau partage des responsabilités dans le réseau des services sociaux et de la santé. Rôles de l'État, du marche, de l'économie sociale et du secteur informel*, Cahiers du LAREPPS, Montréal: LAREPPS, SAC.

Vaillancourt, Y., and L. Tremblay, eds. 2012. *Social Economy: Health and Welfare in four Canadian Provinces*. Halifax: Fernwood Publishing.

Vaillancourt, Y. in collaboration with P. Leclerc. 2013. "The Co-construction of Public Policy: The Contribution of the Social Economy." In *Innovation and the Social Economy: The Québec Experience*, edited by M.J. Bouchard, 127–57. Toronto: University of Toronto Press.

Vaillancourt, Y. and F. Aubry. 2014. *Research Report on The Québec Act to combat poverty and social exclusion, a case of democratic co-construction of public policy*, for the CURA Disabling Poverty/Enabling Citizenship.

# 9

# Reinventing Democracy through Public Advocacy: The Case of the Anti-shale Gas Movement in New Brunswick

SUZANNE DUDZIAK AND MARK D'ARCY

INTRODUCTION

This chapter presents a case study in participatory democracy that has emerged in response to the issue of shale gas exploration in New Brunswick. In its quest to transform New Brunswick's status as a "have not" province, recent governments under the Liberal and Conservative premiers Lord, Graham, and Alward have aggressively pursued policies of resource extraction in their quest for economic "self-sufficiency." While the accelerated development and sell-off of natural resources has far-reaching environmental, economic, and social impacts, it is shale gas exploration that has provoked immediate threats to local communities and prompted a grassroots movement to stop hydraulic fracturing, or "fracking," in New Brunswick. Fracking is a form of natural gas extraction that involves pumping millions of gallons of pressurized, chemically treated water into shale formations or coal beds. The fluid, injected deep into the ground, creates or widens cracks in the rocks, releasing methane gas from the underground (CTV News, 20 Oct. 2013).

Shale gas exploration is occurring primarily in rural communities in New Brunswick and it is these communities that have mobilized to protect their environments, specifically the underground and surface water sources threatened by fracking. Thus, unlike many other public policy advocacy initiatives, which tend to be urban-centric, this movement is composed of citizens from small communities who have been marginalized politically, economically, and socially. In the context of New Brunswick politics, where half of the population is still considered "rural,"[1] the anti-fracking movement represents a significant political awakening and challenge to the elite-run, urban-dominated "politics as usual" in the province.

Many First Nations, including several communities in the province directly affected by shale gas exploration, have joined the movement as protectors of the land and the water for the sake of future generations. Most of New Brunswick is unceded territory so the onus on governments and corporations to consult and to seek the consent of First Nations before any development is very high. There has been an increase in recent years in Aboriginal and non-Aboriginal communities working together on environmental issues in Canada (Davis 2010) and that is an important feature of this movement. They share a common goal in calling for a moratorium on shale gas development in New Brunswick.

New Brunswick is surrounded by jurisdictions that have responded to public pressure and imposed moratoriums on shale gas development. They include Nova Scotia, Prince Edward Island, Quebec, Newfoundland, Vermont, and New York State. In contrast, New Brunswick has not held any public consultations on whether or not the province should move forward on shale gas. Instead, in 2012, the government issued draft regulations for the shale gas industry and held nine public meetings in small rural communities for public input on the regulations. These meetings were chaired by Dr Louis LaPierre, who has since been discredited for lying about his academic credentials. The Alward government cited industry data to back up its messaging to the public and to the media that shale gas can be developed safely and responsibly. The government ignored a growing list of reports from other jurisdictions and peer-reviewed academic studies that show alarming problems with water, air pollution, and human health effects that result from shale gas development (West Coast Environmental Law 2013; MacQuarrie 2014). The provincial government claimed that shale gas was the only way to build New Brunswick's economy and create jobs (Donkin 2014). The foreclosure of any public discussion and debate about energy policy, the imposition of an economic strategy based on the extraction of non-renewal resources, and the deregulation of legislative frameworks that protect the public interest are hallmarks of neoliberal policy making in Canada at the national level (Holmes 2013).

Echoing their federal counterparts, the same strategy has been advanced by the Progressive Conservative and Liberal parties when in power in New Brunswick and reinforced in the mainstream media. Public resistance to this strategy can and should be understood not only as a rejection of current economic and energy policy but also as a response to the democratic deficit created by such impositions. The anti-shale gas coalition has thus sought to articulate a different economic and energy future and to do so in a way that anticipates the possibility of a different politics, one that is both participatory and democratic. To understand the anti-shale gas alliance as an example of public policy advocacy in New Brunswick, we will examine its development, first by looking at the coalition's activities and evolution through several phases and turning points, as it has faced prevailing economic and political conditions in the province. We will follow this with a discussion of the contribution this public policy advocacy initiative is making to the process of democratizing New Brunswick politics, and the challenges that lie ahead.

## The Coalition, Its Strategies, and Activities

The coalition opposed to fracking in New Brunswick comprises over thirty community groups. The majority consist of concerned citizens who came together directly in response to the issue of shale gas exploration in their rural areas. Other groups in the coalition comprise local environmental groups that adopted shale gas as part of their agendas. Unless otherwise specified, the organizations listed below are not registered.

Ban Fracking NB
Concerned Citizens of Penobsquis
Corn Hill Area Residents Association of NB
Council of Canadians – Fredericton Chapter (registered non-profit at the national level)
Council of Canadians – Moncton Chapter (registered non-profit at the national level)
Council of Canadians – Saint John Chapter (registered non-profit at the national level)
Darlings Island Fracking Intervention Naguwigewauk

Federation of Rural New Brunswickers
Friends of Mount Carleton
Friends of UNB Woodlot
Friends of the Tantramar Marsh
Hampton Water First
Harvey Environmental Action Team
Kent South NO SHALE GAS Kent Sud (Cocagne)
Maliseet Grand Council
Memramcook Action
National Farmers Union in NB
New Brunswickers Against Fracking
Our Environment, Our Choice (Rexton)
Parents Against Everyday Poisons
Penniac Anti-Shale Gas Organization
Petitcodiac Watershed Alliance
Quality of Life Initiative
Sierra Club Atlantic (registered charity at the national level)
Stanley Area Action Group
Sustainable Energy Group
Tantramar Alliance Against Hydro-fracking (Sackville)
Taymouth Community Association
Transition Town Woodstock
Upper Miramichi Stewardship Alliance
Upriver Environment Watch (Bass River)
Water and Environmental Protection for Albert County (Hillsborough)

When working together in coalition, they are organized under the umbrella of the "Shale Gas Caucus," a subset of the New Brunswick Environmental Network (NBEN) and the New Brunswick Anti-Shale Gas Alliance (NBASGA). All of these organizations work together in their public advocacy activities.

DeSantis (2010, 26) states that "advocacy strategies include interactions with policymakers and politicians (e.g., amicable meetings, angry confrontations); media strategies to generate public awareness; and legal approaches through the courts (Cohen, de la Vega and Watson 2001; D'Aubin 2003; Dobson 2003; Hick and McNutt 2002; McCarthy and Castelli 2001)."

Based on DeSantis's framework, we have constructed a table (Table 9.1) that identifies the types of strategies pursued and the

Table 9.1 Advocacy activities of the New Brunswick Anti-shale Gas Movement (2011–14)

---

A) INTERACTED WITH GENERAL PUBLIC AND MEDIA TO GENERATE AWARENESS

Initiated public film screenings in communities in shale gas license areas
  *Gasland* (2011–12) and *Gasland 2* (2013);
  *Be Without Water* (2012) and sequel *Be Without Water 2* (2013) by New Brunswick documentary filmmaker Rob Turgeon

Initiated public presentations by experts and advocates opposed to shale gas
  Calvin Tillman, mayor of Dish, Texas (2012);
  Dr Anthony Ingraffea, Cornell University professor of fracturing technology (2012);
  Deborah Rogers, venture capitalist (2013);
  IdleNoMore co-founder Sylvia McAdam;
  Winona LaDuke, Anishinaabe activist and founder of Honour The Earth (2013);
  Maude Barlow, chair of Council of Canadians (2013)

Initiated shale gas information tables at markets throughout New Brunswick
  Fredericton, Sackville, Shediac, Taymouth, Hampton, Moncton (2011–14)

Initiated sale of anti-shale gas and pro-local economy signs throughout New Brunswick (NB)
  Created graphics to promote counter discourses: "NO SHALE GAS" with angry-waterdrop image; "Fracking. Health. Pick One." and "JOBS: You do the math!" lawn signs;
  "FOREST JOBS IN NB VS OTHER JURISDICTIONS" posters with comparative data;
  "Are You In The Frackzone?" poster and sidewalk stencils

Initiated citizen-led public meetings throughout New Brunswick
  Voice of the People Tour town hall meetings in 27 communities (March–June 2014);
  The Great Resource Giveaway public presentations in 7 communities (May–Sept 2014);
  All-Candidate Meetings in ridings across New Brunswick (August–Sept 2014);

Worldwide media coverage of New Brunswick shale gas protests
  Al Jazeera documentary *Elsipogtog: The Fire Over Water* on anti-shale gas protests in Kent County (December 2013);
  Michael Shade's *Nowhere Else to Go* documentary on anti-shale gas protests in Kent County (March 2014);

Initiated distribution of anti-shale gas information to households throughout New Brunswick
  *The Daily Glove Puppet* parody newspaper (dailyglovepuppet.com/) with 1,500 copies distributed in New Brunswick communities (Spring–Summer 2013);

---

*(Continued)*

B) INTERACTED WITH GOVERNMENTS

Created open educational opportunities for interactions among marginalized groups and governments in community settings
Shale Gas Public Debate held in Fredericton during provincial and municipal election. Governnment and industry representatives refused to attend (May 2012);
People's forum and rally at energy ministers' conference in Charlottetown, PEI (September 2012);

Attempts to initiate conversations with government
Legislature Opening rally in Fredericton with all parties invited to speak (29 Nov. 2012); IdleNoMore rally at Fishermans PowWow, Miramichi, and YouTube responses from NB Premier David Alward, Assembly of First Nations regional chief for New Brunswick-Prince Edward Island, and National Chief Shawn Atleo of the Assembly of First Nations (30 June 2013);
Longhouse and Sacred Fire on the Fredericton Green directly across the street from the Provincial Legislature (26 Oct. 2013–6 Nov. 2013);
Unity and Solidarity Rally at the Provincial Legislature and the Longhouse, Fredericton (5 Nov. 2013);

Brought marginalized people to participate in formal meetings organized by governments
9 meetings on proposed shale gas regulations held in only rural communities, chaired by Louis LaPierre and civil servants representing various departments (June–July 2012);
Energy Institute public presentation in Saint John (June 2014);

Public advocacy with governments
Petition signed by 20,000 NB citizens to impose moratorium on shale gas in New Brunswick and presented to Opening Legislature in 29 Nov. 2012;
Blue Ribbon Campaign asking people to vote for candidates who support a moratorium on shale gas, in communities across New Brunswick during Provincial Municipal Election (May 2012);
Shale Gas parade in downtown Fredericton during Provincial Municipal Election (May 2012); Petitions and letters by constituents demanding public meeting by MLAs to provide information and answer questions on shale gas (2013–present);
Media advisory and public outcry over censorship and accountability forced the government to release the health report on shale gas prepared by NB Chief Medical Officer Eilish Cleary (Sept. 2012);
Rally at Blackville, New Brunswick (Official 2013 NB Day Location) with Premier David Alward (August 2013);
Media advisory and public outcry over suspected fraud in the academic credentials claimed by Louis LaPierre (Sept. 2013);
Rally in front of Energy Minister Craig Leonard's constituency office in Fredericton (Nov. 2013); Unity and Solidarity Rally at the Provincial Legislature, Fredericton (Nov. 2013);

(*Continued*)

Table 9.1 (Continued)

> Rally at Cocagne, New Brunswick (Official 2013 NB Day Location) with Premier David Alward (August 2014).

C) CREATED EVIDENCE AND NETWORKED BEHIND THE SCENES

> Conducted or participated in research and wrote papers
>> Anti-Shale Gas Groups educated themselves about shale gas, climate change, and alternatives offered by local economies (e.g., clean energy, building efficiency, community forests, and value-added wood products, local food production);
>
> Networked with other groups, cross-fertilizing issues via meetings and teleconference calls
>> Picnic at Sacred Fire Site near Elsipogtog First Nation (July 2013);
>> Monthly teleconference calls with up to 20+ community groups (2012–present);
>> Call for a moratorium on shale gas by 20+ community groups, Conservation Council of New Brunswick, Community Forests International (Sackville), Council of Canadians – 3 NB Chapters, Maliseet Grand Council NB, Sierra Club, Atlantic, SikniktukMikmaq Rights Coalition NB, Wolastoqiyik First Nations Chiefs and Band Councils of NB, and the Maliseet Grand Council (October 2013);
>
> Networked with other groups, cross-fertilizing issues, using social media
>> Twitter hashtags used include #nbpoli, #Elsipogtog, #fracking, #shalegas;
>> Numerous Facebook pages and groups set up: Ban Hydraulic Fracturing (hydro-fracking) In New Brunswick, Canada (founded 2 Dec. 2011 and 3,448 likes as of 5 August \ 2014);
>> New Brunswick is NOT for Sale (closed group founded January 2011 and 1,990 members as of 5 August 2014);
>> SAY NO TO SHALE GAS IN NEW BRUNSWICK; Upriver Environment Watch (closed group founded January 2012 and 399 members as of 5 August2014);
>> Moncton Anti-Fracking (2 June =2013 and 9,453 likes as of 5 August 2014);
>> SHALE GAS ALERTS NEW BRUNSWICK (closed group founded June 2013 and 3,245 members as of 5 August 2014);
>> Council of Canadians – Fredericton Chapter (page founded 2013 and 140 likes as of 5 August 2014), Voice of the People Tour (page founded March 2013 and 600 likes as of 5 August 2014);
>
> Networked with other groups, cross-fertilizing issues, using alternative media
>> Charles Leblanc's blog (http://charlesotherpersonality.blogspot.ca/);
>> Charles Leblanc's YouTube videos (https://www.youtube.com/user/oldmaison333/videos);
>> Purple Violet Press (http://thepurplevioletpressnb.blogspot.ca/);
>> NB Media Co-op (http://nbmediacoop.org/);
>> New Brunswick Environmental Network (http://www.nben.ca/);

(Continued)

Graeme Decarie's blog "The Moncton Times@Transcript – Good and Bad" (http://themonctongrimes-dripdrain.blogspot.ca/).

Networked with municipalities

Call for a moratorium on shale gas by 12 English-speaking municipalities;

51 French-speaking municipalities of the Association francophone des municipalités du Nouveau-Brunswick (2012);

14 municipalities and local service districts of the Kent County Regional Service Commission (2013).

Networked with professional medical organizations

Call for a moratorium on shale gas by the New Brunswick Nurses Union (Dec. 2011), New Brunswick College of Family Physicians (April 2012), medical staff at Sackville Memorial Hospital (May 2012 and again in May 2013), medical doctors of the Moncton Hospital (June 2012), medical doctors at Georges Dumont Hospital, Moncton (Sept. 2012), and New Brunswick Lung Association (Nov. 2012).

Networked with unions, church groups, and associations

Call for a moratorium on shale gas by the NB National Farmers Union (March 2012);

Maritime Conference of the United Church of Canada (March 2012 and October 2013);

Canadian Union of Public Employees – CUPE with 30,000 members (April 2012);

The Federation of Rural New Brunswickers (August 2012);

Public Service Alliance of Canada – Atlantic Region (July 2013);

Really Local Harvest Cooperative – Southeast NB (Oct. 2013);

KAIROS – Saint John and area chapter (Oct. 2013);

Concerned Physicians of Rexton and Richibucto (Oct 2013);

UNIFOR – Canada's largest energy union with 300,000 members, called for a national moratorium on fracking (Nov. 2013); and

The New Brunswick Federation of Labour (March 2014).

D) PROTESTS AND DIRECT ACTION

Blockades and highway protests against seismic testing trucks in Stanley (August 2011), Norton (June 2011), Cornhill (October 2011), Rexton (Summer and Fall 2013);

Civil Disobedience Training sessions (2012–2014), setup communication alert systems (e.g., SHALE GAS ALERTS NEW BRUNSWICK closed group on Facebook set up as a clearing house for reports and/or photographs of water/air testing, surveying, and seismic testing; phone trees; e-mail contact lists), and provide transportation to peaceful protest events;

Frack Fries and Frack Cow costumes (2012–13);

Know Your Legal Rights Regarding Shale Gas Exploration with lawyer Michel Desneiges from New Brunswick Environmental Law Society (28 Jan 2012 in Bass River, NB);

*(Continued)*

Table 9.1 (Continued)

> IdleNoMore Flash Mob Round Dance with drumming and singing in Regent Mall food court, Fredericton (Dec. 2012) and Champlain Mall, Moncton (Dec. 2013);
> Daily protests in Kent County against the seismic survey testing on Highway 126 (June–July 2013);

E) LEGAL ACTION

> Successful petition to Court of Queen's Bench Judge by Green Party Leader David Coon to order release of shale gas contracts signed by NB government (May 2014);
> People's Lawsuit launched in response to SLAPP suit by shale gas company Southwestern Energy (June 2014, http://willinolanspeaks.com/shares/media-release-frack-back-peoples-lawsuit-launched-june-26-2014/);
> NBASGA Science Lawsuit launched in response to exploration licenses awarded to shale gas company Southwestern Energy (June 2014, http://www.noshalegasnb.ca/category/nbasga/).

initiatives undertaken to further the goals of the anti-shale coalition in New Brunswick. They constitute a wide range of activities created by citizens at the local level in what is essentially a grassroots movement that has engaged in advocacy consistently over a four-year period. We include the dates of activities in the table as a way of documenting the evolution and growth of this movement.

### KEY MOMENTS IN BUILDING A MOVEMENT

Anti-fracking advocacy in New Brunswick has used a multi-dimensional approach, focusing on government, the media, and the public, as evidenced from the activities identified in Table 9.1. In this first phase of public advocacy (Moyer 2001, 44–5), the alliance of anti-shale gas groups has educated themselves and others sufficiently to make shale gas, or fracking, a public issue; poll results have consistently shown that the majority of New Brunswickers are against or have serious concerns about shale gas development. The coalition undertook a second phase of public advocacy focused on understanding and promoting alternative economic solutions to shale gas development to counter the dominant discourse of the Conservatives that shale gas was the solution to New Brunswick's economic woes (Donkin 2014). Anti-shale gas advocates knew that without providing real solutions to job creation in the province the general public, despite their concerns, would be reluctant to speak up against the government and industry promotion of shale gas. The coalition highlighted the importance of local economic initiatives such as building efficiency, clean energy, community forestry, and local food production. Both public education phases were necessary to make a significant impact on citizens, including voter turnout and voter choice during elections.

## Gasland

Screenings of the documentary *Gasland* (Fox 2010) took place in more than fifteen communities throughout the province in late 2010 and throughout 2011. *Gasland* examined the shale gas industry in the US and exposed its negative health, environmental, and economic effects on local communities with footage and in discussion with experts and people directly affected. Directed by Josh Fox, it was nominated for an Academy award for best documentary in 2011. Screenings of the film were organized by the Conservation Council of New Brunswick (CCNB), one of the oldest, strongest, and most effective public advocacy organizations in the province. This was the first time most residents in New Brunswick had heard the terms "fracking" and "shale gas," and learned that shale gas companies had an exploration license covering 20 per cent of the province. Many in the environmental movement had been tracking the New Brunswick government's systematic dismantling of environmental protection. Upon learning of the shale gas industry emerging in New Brunswick, it became clear that these two concurrent events were not happening by coincidence but that the protection of wetlands and watersheds was being dismantled to make way for this industry. The shale gas industry requires an unregulated, unmonitored, and non-transparent environment in which to operate (Nikiforuk 2014).

*Gasland* sensitized local communities to the issue and in a few communities the Texas-based company Southwestern Energy, which had been given an exploration license, organized Open Houses. By the time exploration vehicles arrived in these communities several months later to start seismic testing, residents had mobilized road protests and blockades in four counties. One of the strengths of a rural-based movement is that it comprises smaller, close-knit communities, where family and friends quickly spread the word about issues of local concern. The spectre of ruined water sources and thumper trucks invading the local landscape had raised the alarm in these communities.

## IdleNoMore

In October 2012, the IdleNoMore movement responded to the systematic dismantling of environmental protection by the federal government that was contained in omnibus bills C-38 and C-45. The Harper government did so in response to lobbying by the oil and gas industry (West Coast Environmental Law 2013). Aboriginal peoples were concerned about the trampling of their treaty rights and the destruction of the environment that would result from lack of regulation. IdleNoMore leaders led rallies throughout New Brunswick and these were attended by anti-shale gas supporters, helping to grow the relationship and strength of solidarity between Aboriginal and non-Aboriginal communities opposed to shale gas development.

## Creating Alliances

The growth of the grassroots movement against shale gas in New Brunswick was helped significantly by several established organizations. The Conservation Council of New Brunswick, a registered charity, provided the initial and ongoing education campaign against shale gas. The New Brunswick Environmental Network (NBEN), a registered non-profit organization, takes a neutral position on issues but played a supporting role in bringing environmental groups together face-to-face, and over teleconference calls, to discuss issues and strategy related to watersheds, wetlands, forests, and shale gas. The Shale Gas Caucus operates under the umbrella of NBEN. While the vast majority of the groups in the Caucus are located in rural areas, in the three major urban centres of Moncton, Fredericton, and Saint John, community groups formed chapters of the Council of Canadians, a national registered non-profit organization, to provide them with more resources and opportunities to exchange information and strategy with chapters across Canada. All of these organizations work together in their public advocacy activities.

As evidenced in Table 9.1, while most of the groups in the coalition are grassroots and not formally registered as non-profit organizations, they have been very effective in enlisting the support of recognized social institutions such as church organizations, unions, and professional organizations, primarily in the health sector, in calling for a moratorium on fracking, thus greatly expanding their public reach and influence. Similarly, the strategy of pursuing formal endorsements for a moratorium from municipal governments in the province has proven effective in expanding their own legitimacy as a coalition and their political impact on the issue throughout the province.[2]

While much has been achieved in a few short years, the dilemma remains: How can a movement get the majority of the public not only to pay attention to the issue of shale gas, but also to support a paradigm shift in the model of economic development being pursued when most of the media are either controlled by one family or imposing their own censorship on reporting information brought forward by anti-shale-gas voices? This question points to the structural issues confronting any public advocacy group in the province. Issues raised pertaining to natural resources and economic strategy strike at the heart of neoliberal agendas advanced by the federal government under Stephen Harper and the Government of New Brunswick.

## A "CAPTURED" PROVINCE

### Evolution of Public Policies Away from Public Benefit but toward Corporate Benefit

The web of influence exerted by the corporate elite on the political process in New Brunswick is enormous. Good and McFarland (2005, 101) state that "since the nineteenth century, New Brunswick has followed a path of dependent development, relying heavily on externally controlled (British) merchant capital, and later industrial capital, to exploit its natural resource base. Many of these undertakings were arranged by invitation, with the political elite serving as facilitators." The concept of the role of the state as being in the service of particular capitalist interests, with the government aggressively aligning itself with specific companies, is a pattern familiar from the past (Good and McFarland 2005, 112). The fact that all the newspapers in the province, with two small exceptions, are owned by the Irving family shows an unprecedented degree of corporate concentration and control of the media in the province (Walker 2010; Jack 2012).

Bowser (2014) indicates that corruption of the state can operate on two levels: administrative corruption (bribes for services) and grand-scale political corruption (state capture). Bowser explains that "state capture" is a term developed by the World Bank to describe what happened in Eastern Europe and the former Soviet Union under the rapid privatization of those states in the 1990s and distinguishes it from ordinary political corruption in public administration. "Defined as the efforts of firms to shape the laws, policies, and regulations of the state to their own advantage, 'State capture' is exerting influence over the legal and regulatory framework which facilitates channelling funds or providing resources from public budgets de jure, i.e., legally." Applied to the New Brunswick context, Bowser explains that firms that hold a monopoly manipulate political and economic systems so that only they can access and benefit from natural resources, with the cooperation of a few public officials. In essence, the province's assets are "tunnelled out" by companies who write their own regulations.

Corporate control of the state by a few families or oligarchs ensures corporate control of the economy, including natural resources, control of access to information through media monopoly, and control of the political process through undue influence over politicians (Couture 2013). The population, often poor, unskilled, and semi-literate, is held in check through control over the workforce which is sustained both by promises of jobs and threats of loss of work. This is the case in New Brunswick.

The "tunneling out" of the province's assets, particularly in the area of natural resources, was an analysis developed by experts, including some former employees of the provincial government, and presented publicly in 2014 in a series of teach-ins called the "Great Resources Giveaway." Their analysis helps to explain why provincial governments in New Brunswick continue to make bad economic decisions, especially in the extractive resource sector, that result in losses paid for by the citizens and taxpayers of the province (Bowser 2014; Cumberland 2014; Theriault 2014). It also helps to explain why New Brunswick continues to be a "have-not" province in its ability to fund health, education, social, and public services, despite being rich in natural resources (Theriault 2014).

The timeline in Table 9.2 documents the systematic hollowing out of regulations and creation of policies that favour private sector

Table 9.2 Timeline of the dismantling of environmental regulations and policies (2005–14)

A) DISMANTLING OF WETLANDS PROTECTION

16 March 2011 – A "new" wetlands map and policy was introduced by NB Department of Environment, showing that more than 60 per cent of the wetlands in the province do not exist. Since the regulations remained unchanged, this new policy to protect only "regulated wetlands" (i.e., those shown on the map) violates the province's own legislation on wetlands protection. All wetlands not shown on the map can now be destroyed without a Watercourse and Wetland Alteration (WAWA) permit; the government now practises willful blindness and treats these "unregulated" wetlands as if they do not exist.

16 March 2011 – Environmental Impact Assessments (EIAS) not required for development projects that involve wetlands (larger than 2 hectares in size) that no longer exist on the "new" New Brunswick Government wetland map. Since the regulations remained unchanged, this new policy violates the province's own legislation on wetlands protection.

18 April 2013 – A WAWA permit was granted to Southwestern Energy (SWN) for shale gas seismic testing in wetlands and watercourses in a total of eight counties in New Brunswick, covering 20 per cent of the total area of the province. This is an unprecedented blanket permit, especially when WAWAs are normally granted on a case-by-case basis to individual wetlands and watercourses. This permit allows for wetland and watercourse alteration, including excavation, cut/fill operations, drilling, the installation of charges, and the cutting of vegetation. The only prohibited areas are those few wetlands designated as provincially significant wetland.

B) DISMANTLING OF WATERSHED PROTECTION

13 July 2011 – The water classification program was shelved after a decade of data collection by nineteen watershed groups around the province. These watershed groups were notified that their ongoing project work to develop a Water Classification Program was dropped because the regulations would be too difficult to enforce. This would have provided the framework for a watershed protection regulatory framework in New Brunswick.

25 Oct. 2011 – Environment Minister Margaret-Ann Blaney quickly dismissed any discussion of implementing watershed-based source water protection in New Brunswick. Watershed-based source water protection is the protection of drinking water based on watershed boundaries, and would allow for regionally-managed conservation areas that include First Nations, municipalities, watershed groups, etc. This was implemented in the Province of Ontario after the Walkerton tragedy.

Nov 2012 – The Saint John River is the only watercourse remaining in New Brunswick that is designated "navigable waters." The Navigable Waters Protection Act was rewritten as the Navigation Protection Act in Bill C-45 by the federal government to remove the government's obligation of public consultation and environmental assessment before it approves development projects near rivers and lakes.

(*Continued*)

Table 9.2 (Continued)

2012 – Canada's Fisheries Act removed protection against the destruction of "fish habitat" and replaced it with protection of fish that is part of "a commercial, recreational or aboriginal fishery." This will contribute to the loss of the mandatory consultation process before the approval of large industrial projects, thus affecting many watercourses.

2012 – The Canadian Environmental Assessment Act was replaced in Bill C-38 with CEAA 2012. Proposals for LNG (liquefied natural gas) plants for the export of shale gas would not trigger an environmental assessment by the federal government.

C) NEGLECT OF AQUIFER PROTECTION

2005–Present – There is no program for aquifer mapping in the Province of New Brunswick, even though large areas of the province have been designated for shale gas exploration, which requires huge withdrawals of water. For most aquifers in New Brunswick, there is no mapping data, i.e., baseline data, on our drinking water sources.

D) DISMANTLING OF AIRSHEDS PROTECTION

2009 – A change in the Clean Air Act means that the Minister of Environment now has discretion on the release of documents related to the approval process and monitoring of shale gas operations.

2011 – The NB Government announced a policy of a "phased-in" Environmental Impact Assessment for the approval of shale gas development. By breaking up the review process, shale gas wells would be approved on an individual or small-number basis. This policy will effectively mean that allowable emissions from the thousands or tens of thousands of eventual sources in one area of shale gas development would easily exceed that of a major new point source (e.g., oil refinery).

2013 – A seemingly innocuous change in Air Quality Regulation 97–133 of the Clean Air Act will be helpful to the shale gas industry, because it pertains to two emissions known to be low in this industry ($SO_2$ and particulate matter), while ignoring all the other shale gas industry emissions. The NB government is implementing "a permit by rule, or PBR" system of regulation, like the State of Texas. There will be little, if any, monitoring of volatile organic compounds such as benzene, many of which cause cancer, and no current regulation or monitoring of greenhouse gases such as methane and $CO_2$.

2013 – There will be no formal, public participation component in the approval process for the air emissions of shale gas operations. By basing the approval process on the volume of emissions known to be low in shale gas operations ($SO_2$ and particulate matter), this will ensure that shale gas operations have a low-class designation under the Air Quality Regulation of the Clean Air Act. Only the highest class designation, Class 1 sources (e.g., pulp mills, power plants, large manufacturing plants) would require a formal, public participation component in the approval process.

(*Continued*)

E) DISMANTLING OF THE PROTECTION OF HUMAN HEALTH

**May 2012** – Removal of "public health and safety" from the guiding principles for shale gas regulations. The provincial government discussion Paper on Shale Gas Regulations was released and "public health and safety" had been removed from their list of 12 guiding principles. Requirement 10 now refers to "security and emergency planning," leaving out any mention of public health.

**May 2012–2015** – The Chief Medical Officer for New Brunswick, Dr Eilish Cleary, stated publicly that she would have liked her recommendations on public health with respect to shale gas to be included in the proposed regulations. Issuing the Discussion Paper on Shale Gas Regulations before Dr Cleary's report was released, precluded incorporating any of her 30 recommendations into the discussion paper. To date, none of these recommendations have been implemented by the Province of New Brunswick.

**February 2013** – The "Rules for Industry" was released by the New Brunswick Government for shale gas development, with no reference to public health.

**July 2014** – Medicare in New Brunswick and Prince Edward Island will not cover the cost of tests for the detection of environmental toxins in a patient, even if signs and symptoms strongly indicate exposure to an environmental toxin.

**July 2014** – Baseline well-water testing now being conducted by the Rivers Institute of the University of New Brunswick is not testing for heavy metals and radioactive elements, both contaminants that are known to be naturally present in shale geology, and serious contaminants in fracking wastewater. This baseline water testing is funded by the government's Energy Institute of New Brunswick.

F) DISMANTLING OF THE ENVIRONMENTAL ASSESSMENT PROCESS AND ACCESS TO PUBLIC DOCUMENTS

**2010** – The Access to Information Act was amended to include the Right to Privacy Act. The majority of public documents that were released by the Minister under the previous Access to Information Act, are now subject to the Right to Privacy portion of the Act and are routinely denied. Corporations, not the minister, have the final say in whether or not many of these public documents are released.

**February 2013** – Removal of "public disclosure" of environmental requirements and environmental assessment data from the Rules for Industry document. For instance, sub-section 11.1 entitled "Publicizing the province's environmental requirements and standards for oil and gas activities" and subsection 11.2 entitled "Public disclosure of environmental assessment data," which were both present in the discussion paper, were excluded from the rules for industry.

G) DISMANTLING OF THE FEDERAL GOVERNMENT'S RESEARCH AND MONITORING OF OIL SPILLS, WATER QUALITY, AND CLIMATE CHANGE

**2010–2014** – The federal government dismissed scientists and significantly cut funding/closed research programs and facilities that monitor oil spills, water quality, and climate change. There are many examples, a few of which are listed below:

*(Continued)*

Table 9.2 (Continued)

**Feb 2010** – Layoffs at The Canada Institute for Scientific and Technical Information;

**Mar 2010** – Information restrictions enacted by the government have severely restricted the media's access to government researchers

**Jul 2011** – Budget cuts were made to Climate Change and Clean Air, Substance and Waste Management, Weather and Environmental Services, Water Resources and Internal Services, Action Plan on Clean Water, the Federal Contaminated Sites Action Plan, Chemicals Management Plan, the Clean Air Agenda, the Air Quality Health Index, Species at Risk Program.

**Dec 2011** – Withdrawal from the Kyoto Accord

**Mar 2012** – Closure of the Canadian Foundation for Climate and Atmospheric Sciences

**Mar 2012** – Substantial changes made to the Fisheries Act that will limit public consultation

**May 2012** – 1,000 jobs cut at Department of Fisheries and Oceans (DFO)

**Oct 2012** – Department of Fisheries and Oceans (DFO) Habitat Management Program cut

**Oct 2012** – Ozone Science Group falls victim to federal government cuts

**Apr 2013** – Closure of Department of Fisheries & Oceans libraries

interests over public sector interests in New Brunswick. It includes both federal and provincial government policies.

### A Broken Democracy

These structural changes have very real consequences for public advocacy in the province. A lack of transparency by government and lack of access to information ensures limited scrutiny and public debate. The lack of independent oversight means limited or no political accountability and few requirements for public engagement. The lack of a genuinely free media means that pertinent questions are not even asked in the first place (Couture 2013). As a key organizer has said, "democracy is broken in New Brunswick":

> Decades of corporate media and corporate control of our governments has caused many New Brunswickers to feel powerless and helpless to make change, and an abnormal

degree of resignation, even fear, has become entrenched in our society. Citizens do not have a voice in New Brunswick politics, citizens do not have the confidence to speak up about issues important to them, and citizens rarely have the opportunity to question their MLA politicians in a public forum. The result is that people cannot hear the exchange of ideas between their fellow constituents that are important in their provincial riding. This absence of meaningful public consultation reduces citizen engagement and is likely a significant factor in voter apathy and turnout. (Personal communication, 15 July 2014)

In the run-up to the provincial election in September 2014, the coalition created a strategy aimed at addressing two main concerns: the democratic deficit *and* shale gas development. The strategy consisted of three major initiatives: the "Voice of the People" tour, which consisted of twenty-seven town hall meetings held throughout the province; a series of "Great Resource Giveaway" teach-ins held in seven towns and cities; and All-Candidates Meetings held in several communities during the election period.

A coalition leader explains:

Why did we decide to go with this strategy when being ignored? It's like we have to re-learn how to ask questions. We were doing two things, reinvigorating democracy and providing input on shale gas that the government has refused to do themselves; for citizens to regain their confidence and to become more engaged. With Voice, to engage on shale gas and the alternatives to it and with All-candidates, once people are more confident, they can resolve to have the candidates answer and be accountable for their rhetoric, such as "the only way to rebuild the economy is through shale gas or a pipeline." (Personal communication, 10 July 2014)

"Voice of the People" was an important discourse and strategy aimed at "priming the pump for democracy." In the absence of meaningful public consultation, the town hall sessions presented research and data on shale gas and alternatives like clean energy, building efficiency, and local economies. The second half of each session was dedicated to questions from the audience and discussing what was important to their families and communities. What do you want in your backyard? Do you feel that you have a voice in our democracy? How do you want to create jobs and well-being for your family and your community? The citizens' comments were written down on large sheets of paper and a "Red-dot Poll" was taken at the end of each meeting. People in the audience were given five red-dot stickers and asked to put the dots on the issues/solutions most important to them, thus creating an accurate visual record of their collective priorities. The result of each red-dot poll was shared on the Web, including Facebook and other social media. The results of all town hall sessions were tabulated and used as a Voice of the People call-to-action document for future governments. This is participatory democracy operationalized.

As a follow-up to the Voice of the People tour, citizen organizers were encouraged to hold a non-partisan "Meet the Candidates Q&A – A Town Hall Meeting" in their ridings. These were citizen-led meetings with a strict format that ensured that the main portion of the meeting would be dedicated to constituents to ask questions directly from the floor.

Further, a series of public teach-ins called "The Great Resource Giveaway – Why New Brunswick is Poor" were organized by citizen groups and held in communities across New Brunswick. The presenters, experts in their fields, questioned the management of New Brunswick's resources, including Crown forests and shale gas. The new forestry deal affecting New Brunswick's Crown forests, and the shale gas exploration areas affecting private and Crown lands, which comprise 55 per cent and 20 per cent of the land mass of New Brunswick, respectively, are occurring at the same time and on such a massive scale that they may have been designed as a "Shock Doctrine" strategy by the government to overwhelm the public. Fortunately, the opposite effect occurred, with a large number of communities speaking up, including 184 professors, demanding a halt to the Crown Forest Policy.

All the above initiatives were intended to reinforce one another to provide citizens with a voice to discuss provincial issues important to them, to increase citizen engagement, and to increase voter turnout in the province. These are essential elements of a healthy democracy.

The Anti-Shale-Gas Movement is still at an early stage of development, like the shale gas industry itself in New Brunswick. The first phase of exploration to "test" for shale gas reserves in 20 per cent of the province ended in the fall, 2013. Southwestern Energy (SWN Resources Canada) was undergoing an environmental impact assessment to proceed with drilling and shale gas production in two counties in New Brunswick at the time of the provincial election in September 2014. Since then, newly elected premier Brian Gallant has announced a temporary moratorium on shale gas drilling.

## DISCUSSION

Our approach to policy advocacy, development, and analysis is based on social justice theory, which "espouses that people who are directly affected by a new or modified social policy should participate in deliberations about that policy" (Mullaly 1997, cited in DeSantis 2010, 24). When citizens who are affected by policy developments become involved in the process, policy advocacy can be seen as a form of civic participation (Salamon and Lessans Geller 2008), cited in DeSantis 2010, 24) which strengthens democracy. Schragge (2013, 130) observes that "one of the key roles of community organizing is to be part of a wider struggle for the redistribution of wealth and power. Organizations can provide the means for citizens to gain a voice."

When those citizens are from marginalized constituencies, as in this case study, it is all the more salient that their voices and perspectives be heard and considered in the policy-making process. Rural communities in New Brunswick may constitute half the population but their influence over policy deliberations is marginal at best (CBC News, 7 Nov. 2011).

### Public Advocacy

Lang (2012) draws a distinction between institutional advocacy, "the attempt to influence by gaining some degree of insider status with governments," and public advocacy, which "attempts to achieve policy success by engaging broader publics, actively stimulating citizen voice and engagement" (cited in chapter 7). In the case of shale gas development in New Brunswick, our analysis of the provincial government as a "captured" government means that the possibility of attaining "insider" influence and status is not an option. Government policy-makers have refused to engage in any public consultation on the issue, allowing only for limited input on the regulations post facto. Thus, in this instance, where no other avenue remains open, policy change must necessarily come through public education and advocacy.

While this points to structural issues with the political system, institutional advocacy also has its limitations. Lang states that a lack of transparency by government means that those privy to "insider" information often provide less than full disclosure on the grounds that these channels would close if information was shared too widely among stakeholder organizations. This can erode trust among partners in a coalition and raise concerns about co-optation. Lang concludes that while insider advocacy may be effective in some situations, only community advocacy can "generate citizen engagement and voice" (cited in chapter 7).

### Creating a Democratic Space

In this case study, "public advocacy" denotes a "public," open, democratic, transparent, community-based approach to policy making. The "outsider" status assigned by the ruling elite to the anti-shale-gas groups is being transformed into a credible voice of citizen opposition; rural constituents are being empowered on this issue with support from urban constituents. The coalition did not necessarily have that clarity at the beginning of the struggle in 2010 but it has become part of their analysis since: that the root of the problem on shale gas and other resource extraction issues in the province is the democratic deficit; "you can't fight the one without dealing with the other." This awareness became part of the movement's modus operandi.

Given the lack of any public consultation, democracy itself has become a key discourse and a strategy. As Schragge (2013, 130–1) observes: "Community development, in all of its incarnations, has as a core belief its potential to involve stakeholders in a democratic process ... Creating a "democratic space" in which those without power can have a voice is a starting point in creating social change." The coalition has moved beyond mere "informing the public" to actively engaging rural communities and interested urban groups in priority-setting exercises and democratic decision-making processes about their future. The positive experiences of the town hall sessions served to empower everyone involved.

As a result of these community deliberations, anti-shale-gas advocates became aware that the role of coalition was not just about stopping shale gas development but also about creating jobs in a viable, green, and locally-based economy. An interview participant states:

> Our learning initially focused on shale gas, the techniques and technology involved, the effects on human health and environment as seen in *Gasland*. People started to research climate change and the role of shale gas in hastening climate change contrary to the government claim that it was a clean burning transition fuel. We did this for two reasons: to counter the government's spin and because we were freaked out about our kids' future. Post tropical storm Arthur, people realize the immediate effects that climate change presents. The third learning is we've been against shale gas but what are we for: the clean economy, local sustainable economies. The more we researched, these were powerful arguments because they create long-lasting, better paying jobs and when we add in climate change, then we have no choice but to get off fossil fuels. The economic rationale is key. So we've changed our message to not just environmental, but also to address the economy. (Interview, 10 July 2014)

Thus, the second phase of research, education, and advocacy activities on economic development served to provide a long-term goal and perspective for the coalition. Developing and proposing practical, local, and green economic alternatives also served, in the short term, to undermine and challenge current government and corporate discourses about the number of jobs that would supposedly be created through shale gas and other resource extraction-driven policies. As Browne (2001) notes, exercises such as countering discourses and designing alternatives can provide "potential vehicles for the development of democratic capacities, of the ability to participate fully in society and to be self-governing – a process of cognitive and ethical transformation. They offer glimpses of a more democratic way of governance" (Schragge 2013, 131). In this regard, the need to implement alternatives to shale gas development became linked to the need to address the "democratic deficit" in the province. Voters demonstrated this in a key Fredericton riding during the September 2014 provincial election by defeating PC energy minister Craig Leonard, whose party slogan during the campaign was "Say Yes" to shale gas and instead, in a historic breakthrough, electing David Coon, leader of the Green Party, to the legislature.

In the context of a "captured" government and a broader neoliberal agenda, which is anti-democratic, public advocacy by the anti-shale gas coalition stands in contrast to the "advocacy chill" (DeSantis 2010) that pervades New Brunswick politics generally and the public sector specifically.[3] Striving to create a democratic space is one strategy for dealing with the dilemma of how to gain legitimacy when frozen out of formal politics and public policy making. Creating such a space is possible in part because the groups involved comprise grassroots actors and conservation and labour groups who are not beholden to government for their funding. In addition, DeSantis (2010) points out that non-profit organizations who provide services are often more compromised because of their duty to clients and because of restrictions the federal government has placed on advocacy activities that can be carried out by charitable organizations.

Perhaps in recognition of the greater freedom enjoyed by coalition activists, before the provincial election in September 2014, Elections New Brunswick posted a public ad attempting to restrict public discussion of policy issues on the basis that "you may be considered to be a third party engaging in election advertising" if "you intend to publicly promote or oppose a political party or the election of a candidate, or take a position on an issue with which a political party or a candidate is associated" (*Daily Gleaner*, 26 July 2014, A6). A number of people connected to the anti-shale coalition also received phone calls from Elections NB reminding them that to do so would mean being subject to additional rules and spending limits.

Expanding the democratic space in New Brunswick has also meant engaging with municipal governments (see Table 9.1 and endnote 2). Magnusson (1996) views the municipality as an especially significant space for political action. It is here, he says, at the local level, that critical social movements arise from everyday life, meet, find common ground, and develop joint projects (Marquardt 2007/2008, 24). As a result of rural empowerment through coalition activities, more than sixty municipalities in the province have endorsed a moratorium on shale gas development. In the context of a "captured" province, local governments asserting their rights to protect the water, health, and environment of constituents and communities is potentially a very powerful instrument. The Supreme Court of Canada has established the precedent for Canadian municipalities to do so with respect to pesticide use ([2001]2 S.C.R.241 paras 42 &42]); the door has been opened for local governments to create bylaws or community "bills of rights" to control and protect the health and safety of their citizens and the environment in their jurisdictions.

The rural–urban alliance represented in the coalition is a salient factor in the context of New Brunswick politics. The province remains highly dependent on resource extraction industries (fishing, forestry, and mining) for economic development where half of the province lives but where decisions are made in distant urban backrooms and boardrooms. The shale gas issue has helped to unite urban and rural voters, who experience a common threat and share a commitment to find an alternative model of economic development.

Some of the most forthright advocates in the coalition are members of the Wabanaki Confederacy, who come from both rural and urban First Nations communities in New Brunswick. Their involvement is empowering not only for themselves but also for others in the coalition (Personal communication, 10 July 2014). In defending their Aboriginal rights, they are also defending the rights of the land and the environment for all New Brunswickers. Their willingness to defend the land – whether through court injunctions, protest, or their insistence on their right to free, prior, and informed consent, before resource development proceeds – has had a real impact on halting shale gas exploration at times and will be a decisive factor in the future.

## CONCLUSION

In this chapter, we have presented a case study of public advocacy in New Brunswick that is focused on the issue of shale gas development. In outlining the evolution of the anti-shale gas movement and describing the multiple forms of advocacy that have been used, it is evident that a much deeper struggle has been enjoined. The refusal by the provincial government to engage in public consultation on the issue highlights the long-standing "democratic deficit" that exists in New Brunswick (see also chapter 6 on governmental communication failures in Manitoba). The explanation of New Brunswick as a "captured" state helps us to understand how this deficit is maintained to the detriment of those affected by many issues. Despite attempts at "advocacy chill," rural communities in New Brunswick, including First Nations, have educated themselves and voiced their opposition to being excluded from policy decisions affecting their lives and futures. The discourse of "voice" is particularly apt: gaining the confidence to speak up, overcoming fear to take a public stand, and learning how to take action with others who share the same concerns constitute the practices of democracy that are being learned and exercised as a new experience for many in the province.

The evolution of a large coalition incorporating numerous social sectors in both rural and urban areas of New Brunswick and Aboriginal and non-Aboriginal citizens not only indicates a rejection of the governing elite's current economic and energy policy, it also represents a response to the democratic deficit created by such impositions (see chapter 3 on coalition advocacy). While continuing to call for a moratorium on shale gas development, the coalition has sought to articulate an alternative model of economic development and to do so in a way that anticipates the possibility of a more inclusive, democratic, participatory politics.

In this vein, the coalition has sought to overcome the "democratic deficit" by creating "democratic space" in the province through new rural–urban, Aboriginal–non-Aboriginal alliances at the grassroots level and with the support of municipalities and organizations from many social sectors. Although the issue of shale gas development is still at an early stage and the final outcome is unknown, it is clear that public advocacy has played a crucial role in empowering citizens, encouraging public participation and reinvigorating democracy in New Brunswick.

## NOTES

1 After Prince Edward Island, New Brunswick has the largest percentage of rural population with close to 50 per cent of the population continuing to live in rural communities (Statistics Canada 2012).

2 List of organizations calling for a ban or moratorium on fracking (source: Shale Gas Caucus, NBEN):

New Brunswick College of Family Physicians – 700 members (April 2012)
Medical Doctors of the Moncton Hospital (June 2012)
Medical Doctors at Georges Dumont Hospital, Moncton (Sept. 2012)
New Brunswick Nurses Union – 6900 members (Dec. 2011)
Medical Staff at Sackville Memorial Hospital (May 2012 and again in May 2013)
New Brunswick Lung Association (Nov 2012)
Canadian Union of Public Employees – 30,000 members (April 2012)
NB National Farmers Union with 150 farms as members (March 2012)
Maritime Conference of the United Church of Canada (March 2012 and again in October 2013)
The Federation of Rural New Brunswickers (August 2012)
Public Service Alliance of Canada – Atlantic Region (July 2013)
Really Local Harvest Cooperative – Southeast NB (Oct 2013)
KAIROS – Saint John and area chapter (Oct 2013)
Concerned Physicians of Rexton and Richebucto (Oct 2013)
Unifor – Canada's largest energy union with 300,000 members, called for a national moratorium on fracking on 14 Nov 2013.
Fredericton and District Labour Council (Dec 2013)
Community Forests International (Feb 2014)
Elgin Eco Association (Feb 2014)
New Brunswick Federation of Labour (March 2014)
Public Service Alliance of Canada, Atlantic Region, (reissued) and Miramichi Regional Aboriginal People's Circle (March 2014)

Each of the following municipalities (and associations) has passed resolutions calling for a moratorium or ban on hydro-fracturing within their community (source: New Brunswick Anti-Shale Gas Alliance NBASGA):

Association francophone des municipalités du Nouveau-Brunswick (51 municipalities): these municipalities reaffirmed their position in October 2013, calling once again for a moratorium.
Kent Co. Regional Service Commission (14 municipalities)
Moncton
Hillsborough
Alma
Sackville
Memramcook
Hampton
Minto

| | |
|---|---|
| Stanley | Wolastoqiyik First Nations |
| Bathurst | Chiefs and Band Councils |
| Sussex Corner | of NB and the Maliseet |
| Quispamsis | Grand Council |
| Port Elgin | Dorchester |

3  DeSantis (2010) defines "advocacy chill" as follows: Despite the awareness on the part of NPOs across the country of the need for policy advocacy, there is clear evidence of "advocacy chill" in Canada. "Advocacy chill" refers to the inhibitory effect that government laws and funding regimes have had on NPO advocacy behaviour over the past few decades – a phenomenon that is, in essence, a form of "civic participation chill" (26).

## REFERENCES

Bowser, D. 2014. "New Brunswick: A Captured Province in 6 Easy Steps." *Public Presentation*, July 27. Fredericton, NB: The Great Resource Giveaway.

Browne, P.L. 2001. "Rethinking Globalization, Class and the State." *Canadian Review of Social Policy* 45 (Fall): 93–102.

CBC News. 7 Nov. 2011. "Province 'Bullying' Rural New Brunswick."

Cohen, D., R. de la Vega, and G. Watson, 2001. *Advocacy for Social Justice: A Global Action and Reflection Guide*. Bloomfield, CT: Kumarian Press for Oxfam America and the Advocacy Institute.

Couture, T.D. 2013. "Without Favour: The Concentration of Ownership in New Brunswick's Print Media Industry." *Canadian Journal of Communication* 38:57–81.

CTV News. 20 Oct. 2013. "What Is Fracking and Why Is It So Controversial?" Christina Commisso.

Cumberland, R. 2014. "Deer in the Kettle." Public Presentation, 27 July. *The Great Resource Giveaway*. Fredericton, NB.

D'Aubin, A. 2003. "We Will Ride: A Showcase of CCD Advocacy Strategies in Support of Accessible Transportation." In *Making Equality: History of Advocacy and Persons with Disabilities in Canada*, edited by D. Stienstra and A. Wight-Felske. Concord, ON: Captus Press.

Davis, L. 2010. *Alliances: Re/Envisioning Indigenous-non-Indigenous Relationships*. Toronto: University of Toronto Press.

DeSantis, G.C. 2010. "Voices from the Margins: Policy Advocacy and Marginalized Communities." *Canadian Journal of Nonprofit and Social Economy Research* 1 (1): 23–45.

Dobson, C. 2003. *The Troublemaker's Teaparty: A Manual for Effective Citizen Action*. Gabriola Island, BC: New Society Publishers.

Donkin, K. 2014. "Alward Hitches Hopes to Shale Gas." *Telegraph-Journal*, 22 August.

Fox, J. 2010. *Gasland*. Writer and Director. Documentary Film, 107 min.

Good, T., and J. McFarland. 2005. "Call Centres: A New Solution to an Old Problem?" In *From the Net to the Net: Atlantic Canada and the Global Economy*, edited by J. Sacouman and H. Veltmeyer. Aurora, ON: Garamond Press.

Hick, S. and McNutt, J., eds. 2002. *Advocacy, Activism and the Internet: Community Organization and Social Policy*. Chicago, IL: Lyceum Books.

Holmes, M. 2013. "Spinning Out of Control?". http://nbmediacoop.org/2013/04/28.

Jack, C. 2012. "Do Not Pass Go, Do Not Collect $200." http://nbmediacoop.org/2012/11/11

Lang, S. 2012. *NGOs, Civil Society, and the Public Sphere*. New York: Cambridge University Press. http://dx.doi.org/10.1017/CBO9781139177146.

MacQuarrie, D. 2014. "NB Anti-Shale Gas Alliance Takes Province to Court to Stop Shale Gas." http://nbmediacoop.org/2014/06/26.

Magnusson, W. 1996. *The Search for Political Space: Globalization, Social Movements, and the Urban Political Experience*. Toronto: University of Toronto Press.

Marquardt, R. 2007/2008. "The Progressive Potential of Local Social Policy Activism." *Canadian Review of Social Policy/Revue canadienne de politique sociale* 60/61.

McCarthy, J. and J. Castelli. 2001. "The Necessity for Studying Organizational Advocacy Comparatively." In *Measuring the Impact of the Nonprofit Sector*, edited by P. Flynn and V. Hodgkinson. New York, NY: Kluwer Academic/Plenum Publishers.

Moyer, B. 2001. *Doing Democracy: The MAP Model for Organizing Social Movements*. Gabriola Is., B.C. New Society Publishers.

Mullaly, B. 1997. *Structural Social Work: Ideology, Theory and Practice*. Don Mills, ON: Oxford University Press.

Nikiforuk, A. 2014. "Canada's 500,000 Leaky Energy Wells: 'Threat to Public'. Badly sealed oil and gas wellbores leak emissions barely monitored, experts find." TheTyee.ca, 5 June. http://thetyee.ca/News/2014/06/05/Canada-Leaky-Energy-Wells/.

Salamon, L., and S. Lessans Geller. 2008. Nonprofit America: A Force for Democracy (Communique No. 9). Baltimore, MD: Centre for Civil Society Studies, Institute for Public Policy, Johns Hopkins

University. Accessed 25 November 2009. http://ccss.jhu.edu/pdfs/LP_Communiques/LP_Communique9_Advocacy_2008.pdf.

Schragge, E. 2013. *Activism and Social Change: Lessons for Community Organizing*. 2nd ed.. Toronto: University of Toronto Press.

Statistics Canada. 2012. *Canada's Rural Population in Brief*. Ottawa: Statistics Canada Catalogue # 98-310-X2011003.

Theriault, C. 2014. "Is Our Forest Really Ours?" Public Presentation, 27 July, *The Great Resource Giveaway*. Fredericton, NB.

Walker, J.H. 2010. "The Once and Future New Brunswick Free Press." *Journal of New Brunswick Studies* 1:64–79.

West Coast Environmental Law. 2013. "The Smoking Gun: Who was the Real Author of the 2012 Omnibus Bills?" Environmental Law Alert Blog, 11 January. http://wcel.org/resources/environmental-law-alert/smoking-gun-who-was-real-author-2012-omnibus-bills.

# 10

# Canada's Northern Communications Policies: The Role of Aboriginal Organizations

ROB MCMAHON, HEATHER E. HUDSON,
AND LYLE FABIAN[1]

### INTRODUCTION

In this chapter, we[2] examine how various institutions and policies have shaped the development of information and communication technologies (ICTs) in Canada's northern regions. We also outline how Aboriginal non-profits have mobilized to advance policy and regulatory reforms. This activity often arises from conditions of scarcity, reflecting this anthology's consideration of social justice as encompassing full and equitable participation among all citizens in society. Bringing reliable ICT infrastructures and services to the remote and sparsely populated North presents both technological and financial challenges. In these regions, the market alone cannot support the development and ongoing operations of ICT resources that support core public services and economic development initiatives. But over the past four decades, the activities of Indigenous and northern residents not only supported ICT development, but also led to the formation of non-profit ventures that contributed to that process in significant ways. These actors have worked to shape public policies in ways that govern the development of ICT infrastructures and services to provide a basis for long-term economic and community development.

These efforts have been an ongoing struggle. The historical record points to the lack of formal opportunities for non-profit citizen and consumer groups to influence broadcast, telecommunication, and broadband policies (Babe 1990; Rideout 2003; Shade 2008). Challenges to the advocacy efforts of non-profit organizations[3] are increasing with the rise of neoliberal regulatory and policy discourses that favour the "free hand" of the market (McChesney 2013). But at the same time, they are not fixed. As Pickard (2013) points out, policy discourses can be changed, and play an important role in shaping whether and to what degree government intervenes in media and telecommunications markets (339). The structural frameworks of laws, policies, and regulations that shape the "rules of play" in these negotiations are sometimes subject to binding decisions resulting from the outcomes of regulatory hearings or legal cases (Carpentier, Dahlgren, and Pasquali 2013). At certain key moments, state institutions do provide formal opportunities for stakeholders to express their views. These opportunities reflect the agenda of the government in power, the changing policy and regulatory landscape, and the availability of funds, among other factors. In the specific context of Indigenous peoples in Canada, these activities are influenced by the unique relationship between Aboriginal peoples and the state, which is supported by the inherent Aboriginal and treaty rights enshrined in section 35 of the Canadian Constitution Act (1982) and expressed in different ways among a diversity of Indigenous groups (Borrows 2010). In leveraging the opportunities opened by these conditions, Aboriginal non-profit organizations can shift policy discourses to better meet the needs of their constituents.

The struggles that take place in these formal arenas are also informed by the activities of individuals and groups. In the context of northern development, the lack of private-sector ICT investment in their territories led Indigenous parties to undertake their own community-based projects, convincing some policy-makers to reshape policy discourses to support this work. In this chapter we frame these initiatives as examples of Indigenous ICT4D (information and communication technologies for development) (Unwin 2009; Heeks 2002, 2009; Kleine 2013). Initially encompassing radio, television, and telephony development, after the advent of the network society this process included the diffusion of networked digital infrastructures (Castells 2009). Scholars, including Hudson (1984; 2006; 2011), Valaskakis (1992), Alia (2010), and Roth (2005), have all examined how Indigenous peoples have helped develop telecommunication and broadcast systems. Using both formal and ad hoc avenues of participation, Aboriginal non-profits secured policy and regulatory outcomes to help them introduce new technologies and services in their communities.

Importantly, the technical characteristics of ICTs play a key role in these activities because they enable small, geographically-dispersed, and/or rural groups to connect with one another, and with policy-makers, quickly, cheaply, and over long distances (Hudson 2006; Löblich and Wendelin 2012). We suggest that recent activities associated with digital ICTs reflect a rearticulation of strategies deployed by Aboriginal groups in past efforts to assert ownership and control over broadcasting and telecommunications infrastructures (Whiteduck et al. 2012; O'Donnell et al. 2009). The emergence of new digitally-enabled services, social actors, and institutional frameworks all reflect the persistence of ongoing dynamics linked to long-term and ongoing projects of Indigenous self-determination.

## THE NORTHERN CONTEXT: PARTICIPATORY COMMUNICATION FOR RURAL AND REMOTE DEVELOPMENT IN CANADA

Northern and Aboriginal ICT policies should be considered within the context of the political economy of northern Canada. For the purposes of this chapter, our definition of Canada's "North" includes the three territories (Yukon, Northwest Territories, and Nunavut), and the northern regions of the provinces. Despite different geographies and political demarcations, these regions share characteristics that affect the diffusion and use of ICTs (Fiser and Jeffrey 2013). For example, in northern Ontario and Manitoba, thousands of lakes pepper the landscape, whereas northern Québec is isolated from the province's more populated south by hundreds of kilometres of wilderness. Yukon and northern BC (British Columbia) share mountains and forests, whereas communities in Nunavut are separated by vast stretches of tundra and ocean.

Factors other than geography shape the social conditions in these regions. Isolated northern communities range in size from a few hundred to several thousand residents. Many are located on the traditional lands of diverse Indigenous nations, such as the Inuit, Dene, Cree, Ojibway, and Gwich'in peoples. While small in absolute numbers, these populations are also young and growing rapidly. Demographic models show that these northern Aboriginal communities will continue to constitute a majority or significant minority of the residents of the northern territories of Nunavut and the Northwest Territories (NWT), and the remote regions of provinces such as Québec (Nunavik), Ontario, Saskatchewan, Northeastern Labrador (Nunatsiavut), and Manitoba.

Government policies of resettlement and containment, combined with the uneven development patterns of the majority society, have contributed to social problems in these communities, such as high levels of violence, suicide, family breakdown, unemployment, and household poverty (Palmater 2011). Although many villages are located near profitable sites of resource extraction, their residents often lack a significant share of revenues from these ventures or participation in the economic activities they generate (Jacobs, Berrouard, and Mirellie 2009). Communities also lack the transportation, electrical, and communications infrastructures that residents of the South take for granted.

While the diverse approaches taken by Aboriginal peoples in negotiating their relationships with the state are too complex to address here, many groups are advocating for increased participation and autonomy in jurisdiction over natural resource and economic development, education, and health care (see chapter 6 on failed advocacy in a natural resource context). In part, these negotiations link to the unique status of Aboriginal peoples, as expressed in the Canadian Constitution. As a result of historic and "modern" treaty negotiations – land claims agreements and other activities – the federal government has certain fiduciary responsibilities to the original inhabitants of the territories now known as Canada. Treaty and Aboriginal rights affect many services available in northern communities today, including health and education. Desire for self-government in the administration and delivery of these services – alongside other areas of self-determination like economic and community development – has led Aboriginal northerners to establish their own governing institutions and service providers.

As described below, these initiatives include the formation of non-profit Aboriginal communication societies, which have

Table 10.1 ICT4D in the Canadian North: Key stakeholders

| Indigenous Broadcasting | Indigenous Communications Organizations | Consumer Organizations | Government agencies |
|---|---|---|---|
| IBC | FMCC | CAC | CRTC |
| TNI | ECN (non-Aboriginal entity that includes First Nations) | NAPO PIAC | Canadian Heritage |
| Wawatay | KNET (for-profit entity with First Nations owners) | | Industry Canada / ISED |
| | NBDC | | CanNor |
| | | | Provincial and territorial governments |
| | | | CBC (Crown corporation) |

CAC: Consumers Association of Canada; CRTC: Canadian Radio-Television and Telecommunications Commission; FMCC: First Mile Connectivity Consortium; IBC: Inuit Broadcasting Corporation; ISED: Innovation, Science and Economic Development; KNET: Kuh-ke-nah Network; NAPO: National Anti-Poverty Organization; NBDC: Nunavut Broadband Development Corporation; PIAC: Public Interest Advocacy Centre; TNI: Taqramiut Nipingat Incorporated

played prominent roles in both advocating for and administering a variety of ICT4D projects and services (see Table 10.1). These organizations emerge from diverse Indigenous communities with defined powers of self-government and customary laws, institutions and practices. Indigenous governments leverage funding mechanisms established by the federal government's Indian Act (1985) and implemented by Aboriginal Affairs and Northern Development Canada (AANDC), as well as other federal agencies, to use ICTs to deliver public services and economic development opportunities. Their activities also include attempts to reform policy and regulatory frameworks created for more populous and southern regions. Aboriginal non-profits used these negotiations to advocate for reforms that better fit the unique contexts of the Canadian North, and to secure funding and material support for their initiatives.

## CANOR: CANADIAN NORTHERN ECONOMIC DEVELOPMENT AGENCY

*Changing Technologies and New Opportunities*

People living in remote and rural Indigenous communities historically transmitted messages in person as they travelled by canoe or kayak, on foot and by dog team. Later, they established more permanent transportation and communication links using technologies developed in the urban South. Often moved to action by the lack of corporate services, northern residents formed non-profit and commercial organizations to establish infrastructure and services in their communities.

*Radio and Television Broadcasting*

The path to regional Aboriginal ICT4D is linked to the introduction of northern satellite services in the 1970s. In 1971, researchers funded by the federal Department of Communications visited First Nations leaders from remote areas of the provinces, and the Yukon and Northwest Territories, to ascertain their communications needs and priorities (Kenney 1971). This study was undertaken in preparation for Canada's first communication satellite, Anik (for "little brother" in Inuktitut), launched in 1972. Aboriginal leaders said their first priority was reliable telephone service (to get help in emergencies, keep in touch with family and friends, contact government agencies, and so on) followed by radio and television broadcasting. At that time in the Far North, radio reception was restricted to the Canadian Broadcasting Corporation's (CBC) shortwave Northern Service, while residents in the northern parts of provinces could only receive AM radio from distant cities in Canada and the US at night. After reviewing these findings, the Department of Communications funded the Northern Pilot Project to introduce community-controlled High-Frequency (HF) radios and radio broadcasting stations in remote Northwestern Ontario and the Keewatin region of the NWT. The subsequent evaluation of this project highlighted community operation, training of Indigenous participants, and benefits for social and economic development, and informed a government green paper in the mid-1970s (Hudson 1974).

Other technological advances at that time included low-power FM radio stations, which brought the possibility of inexpensive local broadcasting. Northerners saw the potential of this technology to develop their own non-profit radio stations. For example, Taqramiut Nipingat Incorporated (TNI) or "Voice of the North" was a non-profit organization founded in Nunavik in 1975 to promote Inuit culture and language in that region. As community radio stations became established across the North, the CBC began to explore ways it could carry some of its news and public affairs programs. The solution adopted was to form a partnership between the CBC and the non-profit community radio stations. The CBC designated the northern stations as affiliates, which could receive the public broadcaster's content via satellite and rebroadcast it to their communities. This initiative included capacity-building benefits, as local staff received training in the legal and ethical requirements of licensed broadcasters. Formal agreements signed between the CBC and the radio stations outlined the terms of their arrangement, and their obligations as stations licensed by the federal regulator, the Canadian Radio-Television and Telecommunications Commission (CRTC) (Hudson 1977). In short, this initiative enabled northerners to gain experience in both the operational and the policy aspects of radio broadcasting.

Community radio has since flourished in the North and across Canada; as many as 120 Aboriginal community radio stations were operating in 2013 (Roth 2013). Northern residents listened to southern news, sports, and music; broadcast Aboriginal-language content; and relayed messages between communities and to people at fishing and hunting camps. These radio stations also supported public services. For example, in Ontario the Wawatay (originally Wa-Wa-Ta) Native Communications Society partnered with the Wahsa Distance Education Centre to deliver adult education courses over radio. Today, radio stations remain an important and popular channel for public dialogue within northern communities.

Television arrived in the north in the mid-1970s, as part of the federal government's Accelerated Coverage Plan (1974), which required the CBC to make its content available in every community in Canada with 500 or more residents. A few communities, including Igloolik in Nunavut, initially chose to reject television until more Inuktitut-language programming became available, given television's perceived negative effects (Savard 1998; Roth and Valaskakis 1989). Valaskakis (1992) identified several challenges stemming from Inuit exposure to the technology: non-Indigenous people acquired authority over

Inuit peoples through their control over knowledge of and access to media, and the media content they produced introduced political and economic ideologies that contributed to the erosion of community, social and political structures, and cultural values. However, many northerners embraced television, purchasing TV sets at local Hudson's Bay Company stores to watch hockey and other southern content (Hudson 1990).

Aboriginal leaders considered how to manage the diffusion of these new broadcasting services. The easiest option was simply to open the door to information and entertainment from the outside world. Yet there were still concerns that one-way transmission of English and French language programs would undermine Indigenous languages and cultures. The strategies taken by the Aboriginal non-profits to address these issues varied, reflecting a key aspect in the shifting terrain of ICT4D policy in northern Canada: the growing diversity of organizations and communities involved.

For example, in Northern Ontario, Wawatay focused on radio, because content was relatively easy and inexpensive to produce, and several community radio stations already existed in the region. The non-profit society chose to create regional Oji-Cree radio programming that could be fed to northern communities by satellite and transmitted through local stations. The federal Department of Communications (later part of Industry Canada) provided resources for this strategy, reflecting government engagement in and material support for this initiative. In 1975, the experimental Communications Technology Satellite (also known as Hermes) began transmitting Wawatay's regional Oji-Cree news programs for free to several community radio stations in northern Ontario. After this experiment concluded, high commercial tariffs for dedicated audio satellite channels led Wawatay to negotiate an agreement with TV Ontario to piggyback its audio signal on the southern network's transponders on the Anik B satellite. Inside the communities, the signal was split, with the TV component rebroadcast over a low-power TV transmitter, and the radio signal delivered to the community radio station, where it was retransmitted locally (Hudson 1990).

Elsewhere, Inuit non-profits focused their advocacy strategy on television. They believed that television could not be ignored and so aimed to harness it to deliver northern and Inuit content. This initiative reflected another collaboration among Aboriginal non-profits and the federal government. Inuit Tapirisat (now Inuit Tapiriit Kanatami), the major political organization representing the Inuit, used satellite capacity and funding provided by the government for video production and videoconferencing over the Anik B satellite. This project, called Inukshuk, linked six Inuit communities in three Arctic regions (with different dialects and time zones) in a one-way-video, two-way-audio teleconferencing network. During a nine-month period, Inukshuk produced more than 320 hours of programming, of which about half were interactive teleconferences. According to Hudson (1990): "The project not only fostered communication among Inuit across three regions about issues of land claims, education, and cultural identity, but also demonstrated to all – including the federal government, the Northwest Territories government, and the CBC – that the Inuit were capable of producing their own programs" (99).

Later, the Inuit used the experience and visibility gained from these satellite experiments to lobby government for funding for their own non-profit network, the Inuit Broadcasting Corporation (IBC), which was established in 1981. Other community-based media projects included an initiative in Igloolik, where local residents founded Isuma to create and distribute their own media content (Evans 2008; Roth 2014).

The success and visibility of community radio and TV projects became a key source of evidence that Aboriginal non-profits used to advocate for policy and regulatory support. Formal opportunities to contribute to policy formulation became platforms of mobilization where coalitions of Aboriginal non-profits secured several key reforms, including the Northern Native Broadcasting Policy adopted in 1990 and the recognition of the "special place" of Aboriginal peoples within Canadian society in the 1991 Broadcasting Act. Before discussing these policy reforms, we outline the role of Aboriginal non-profits in establishing telecommunications and Internet infrastructure in the North.

## Telecommunications and Internet Infrastructure

Northern telecommunications development reflects a similar dynamic to broadcasting: the extension of southern-based infrastructures into remote regions alongside community ICT4D projects undertaken by non-profit organizations. Although the focus is on transmission rather than content, development patterns echo similar strategies and challenges. Before telephone service was widespread in the North, most isolated communities only connected to each other and the outside world through unreliable high-frequency (HF) two-way radios that were often inaccessible to local residents, except in emergencies (Hudson 1974). Each community might have one or two HF radios at the nursing station and Hudson's Bay store. Some communities had local telephone service, but their link to the outside world was via HF radio.

Analogue telephone services arrived in the late 1970s and early 1980s as a result of regulations that required incumbent telecommunications providers to extend services in remote regions. To meet these requirements in smaller communities, the companies typically provided a single pay phone. Local exchanges linking households used outdated equipment, with periodic maintenance undertaken by fly-in technicians. Partly due to the lobbying efforts of Indigenous organizations, residential telecommunications services with external links via microwave and satellite became more widespread in the 1980s. In the 1990s, inadequate telecommunications infrastructure resulted in slow and congested circuits that restricted access to emergent applications like email and the Internet.

Compared with their early support for broadcasting technologies, policy-makers were initially sceptical of the need for high-capacity digital networks and services in remote northern communities because they did not anticipate the demand for high bandwidth applications like distance learning, telemedicine, and videoconferencing. However, Aboriginal non-profits used a strategy similar to that used for broadcasting: leveraging evidence from their community ICT initiatives to demonstrate to funders the benefits of applications like telemedicine and distance education (Whiteduck et al. 2012) (similar to chapter 3 on "evidence").

As with broadcasting, these projects reflect the diversity of the stakeholders involved. In the northern regions of provinces, Keewaytinook Okimakanak's KNET (the Kuh-ke-nah Network) was among the first Aboriginal non-profit service providers – although others are in place today, including the First Nations Education Council (FNEC) in Québec and the Atlantic Canada First Nations Help Desk (FNHD) (O'Donnell et al. 2009). Established by a tribal council set up by the chiefs of six remote First Nations in Northwestern Ontario (Keewaytinook Okimakanak), KNET has provided access and services to remote Cree and Ojibway communities in Northern Ontario (and

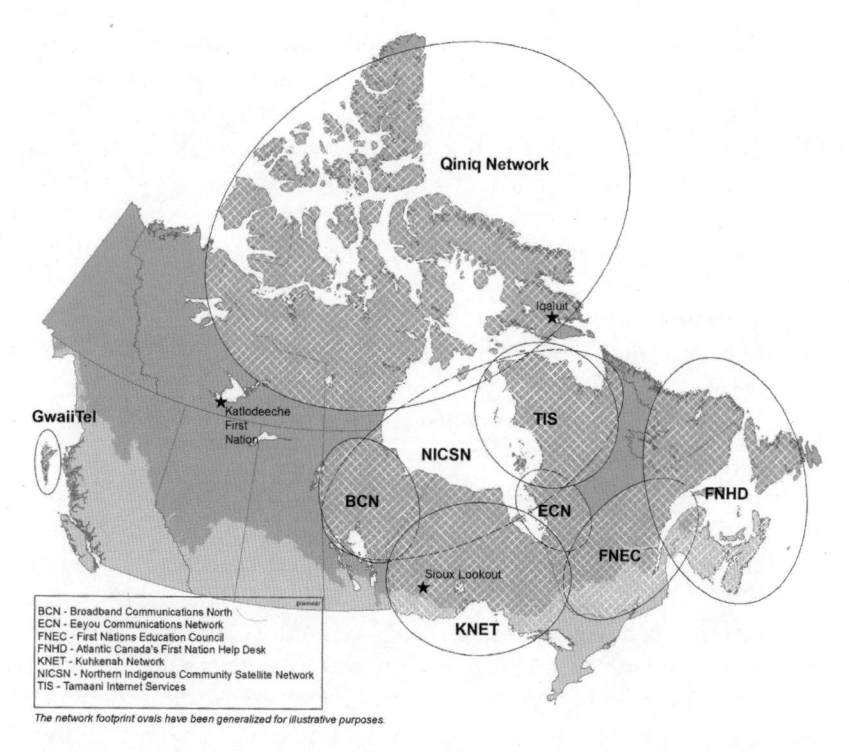

Figure 10.1 Indigenous non-profit networks discussed in this chapter
Source: Produced by J. Piwowar, University of Regina.

other communities across Canada) since 1994. The organization – which now operates on a for-profit basis but remits any profits to its owners, which are First Nations communities – also contracts with health care providers to provide telehealth networks and with the Ontario Ministry of Education to support an online high school (Potter 2010). It offers computer training and skills development, as well as videoconferencing, Internet telephony, and mobile telephone services (O'Donnell et al. 2010). KNET also engages in partnerships with other regional First Nations and Inuit providers. For example, it is one of three partners in the non-profit Northern Indigenous Community Satellite Network (NICSN), which services communities in the northern regions of Quebec, Ontario, and Manitoba (McMahon 2013). Although managed from Sioux Lookout, Ontario, each of NICSN's regional partners follows its own operational and development model. The network is financially sustainable in terms of operations and maintenance, but, like other satellite providers in the North, requires public funding to cover the high costs of bandwidth.

Another First Nations non-profit telecommunications operator, GwaiiTel, provides high-speed Internet service to residents of seven communities on the islands of Haida Gwaii in BC. GwaiiTel was formed by the Gwaii Trust, a non-profit organization established to enhance environmentally sustainable social and economic benefits to Haida Gwaii. It connects to the mainland over North America's longest over-water radio link for Internet transmission. GwaiiTel invested more than C$1 million to build infrastructure connecting the communities, with funding from the Gwaii Trust Society and a grant from Industry Canada's Broadband for Rural and Northern Development (BRAND) (GwaiiTel 2006).

First Nations community broadband projects also exist in the northern territories. For example, K'atl'odeeche First Nation was funded by the Canadian Northern Economic Development Agency (CanNor) to build its own fibre-optic network. The Band-owned KFN Community Network serves the community of approximately 325 people living near Hay River in the NWT. In 2009, the Band received funding from CanNor to build a 48-strand fibre network to interconnect facilities such as the administration office, school, health clinic, adult education centre, day care centre, and Elder-care facility. The community network still faces bottlenecks because of the aging infrastructure that connects its local network to "backbone" transport networks, but in 2010 an entrepreneur from the community began working on a project to address this challenge.

In Nunavut, residents established the non-profit Nunavut Broadband Development Corporation (NBDC) to identify the territory's broadband needs. With support from the BRAND program, NBDC contracted a commercial provider, SSi Micro, to build and manage broadband through public and private sector investment. This network, Qiniq (meaning "to search" in Inuktitut), began offering satellite-based commercial wireless broadband infrastructure to all twenty-five Nunavut communities in 2005. SSi Micro owns and operates Qiniq's infrastructure and pays a small commission to local agents, who distribute modems, manage billing, and assist with local troubleshooting (Mignone and Henley 2009). Connectivity remains a challenge, given the limited bandwidth, high costs, and latency problems associated with satellite broadband. Although it is a commercial enterprise, like other service providers in these regions Qiniq is dependent on public sector support to pay for bandwidth (Nunavut Broadband Development Corporation 2010). Other regional networks operating in northern Canada reflect both commercial (e.g., AirWare in the NWT – also managed by SSi Micro) and non-profit models (such as the Eeyou Communication Network or ECN in Quebec, which is a non-Aboriginal organization that includes First Nations members). Regardless of their ownership structure, these organizations are all dependent to some extent on government regulations and policies for capital and operational funding.

## INTERVENTIONS IN POLICY AND REGULATORY PROCEEDINGS: ENGAGING WITH STATE INSTITUTIONS

ICT policy is the responsibility of federal departments, primarily Innovation, Science and Economic Development (ISED) (formerly Industry Canada), whose portfolio includes telecommunications, trade and commerce, science and technology, and other industry-related fields. In 1996, the department absorbed the functions of the Department of Communications, which was established by the Trudeau government in 1968. The CRTC is responsible for regulating telecommunications and broadcasting. Several other federal agencies also play a role in northern ICT4D. For example, Canadian Heritage is responsible for broadcasting policy and digital media, while the Canadian Northern Economic Development Agency provides some infrastructure funding in the far North. Indigenous and Northern Affairs Canada (INAC) (formerly Aboriginal Affairs and Northern Development Canada, or AANDC), is responsible for most policies affecting Aboriginal peoples, and provides some funding for Aboriginal connectivity. For example, INAC administers the First Nations Infrastructure Fund (FNIF), which has been available to First Nations (but not Inuit) applicants since 2009 and includes broadband as an eligible expense. All FNIF projects involve public–private partnerships among government, private sector entities, non-profits, and First Nations organization. INAC also monitors broadband deployment in northern Aboriginal communities (AANDC 2012).

This summary illustrates how government policy to support broadband in remote and rural Indigenous communities is coordinated among many different departments and program areas (McMahon et al. 2014). Since 1996, a variety of regulations, funding initiatives, strategies, and projects have been put in place to support broadband development in these communities. However, these initiatives face tensions with market-oriented development models that fail to address the unique conditions and challenges present in northern regions. The road to changing policy and regulatory frameworks can be long and contorted. It often requires drafting legislation that may or may not be adopted, or persuading politicians or senior administrative officials to adopt new policies, set regulations, or release funds. The outcomes of proposals raised by advocacy groups are also subject to pressures from political and economic elites (Freedman 2008; Crawford 2013). The format of regulatory proceedings is also formidable. While public participation is encouraged and agencies like the CRTC have established funding and other support mechanisms, hearings tend to be formal, legalistic, and dauntingly complex. Government staff and well-resourced corporate stakeholders use technical and legal language that can be challenging for citizen and consumer groups to engage with, and can discourage advocates who lack professional advisers or legal counsel (see chapter 2).

Nonetheless, interventions in the formation of broadcasting and telecommunications regulatory frameworks do provide opportunities for interested parties to participate. The CRTC hosts public consultations, as laid out in its governing legislation. In contrast, ISED's consultation process is much less transparent, with fewer direct efforts to encourage public involvement (Shepherd, Taylor, and Middleton 2014). But the CRTC's decisions are not necessarily binding; they can be appealed to the courts, and the governor-in-council (Cabinet) can choose to "vary" (i.e., change or reverse) them. Yet there is a strong tradition of public advocacy in the form policies and regulations for Canada's communications system – see, for example, discussions about public service radio in the 1920s and 1930s (Raboy 1990).

In short, while they appear complex and legalistic, regulatory proceedings have the advantage of resulting in binding and enforceable decisions – at least compared with government policy statements or plans, which may never be enacted or funded. Public hearings also provide an opportunity for stakeholders to address policymakers directly, and to include their concerns and evidence in the public record. They also provide a means of obtaining information from incumbent telecommunications carriers about matters such as quality of service, costs of providing services, and plans for service expansion or upgrades that companies may not otherwise release. However, participating in this process requires that parties follow procedures and understand legal and technical terms that may be unfamiliar to community-based non-profit organizations.

Aboriginal non-profits provide many examples of strategic interventions in these processes. Their efforts are constrained by power imbalances and other inequalities. However, by forming partnerships, mobilizing community-held knowledge and resources, and using the opportunities to participate opened by government agencies, Indigenous actors have had many successes in this area. For example, they intervened with the Consumers Association of Canada in the 1970s, the National Anti-Poverty Organization in the 1980s, and, more recently, with the Public Interest Advocacy Centre. These coalitions provided capacity-building benefits for Aboriginal groups, who gained experience in preparing written testimony and appearing at hearings. At the same time, consumer organizations benefited from the Aboriginal groups' knowledge of their ICT requirements and issues affecting remote northern communities. In the next section, we explore these activities in detail, and provide examples of how over the past several decades, coalitions of Aboriginal organizations have influenced the regulatory and policy frameworks of ICT4D in the North.

## *Aboriginal Participation in Broadcast Policy and Regulation*

Aboriginal non-profit organizations worked with several federal agencies during the 1980s to obtain policy and regulatory support to produce and distribute their own media content. For example, the Northern Native Broadcast Access Program was established by the Department of the Secretary of State (now Canadian Heritage), with $40 million in federal funding between 1983 and 1987. By 1990, the program had funded thirteen non-profit Native Communications Societies (including Wawatay and TNI) to establish production facilities, train broadcasters, and produce and distribute Aboriginal content (Hudson 1990). This support led to a vibrant Aboriginal newspaper and radio sector across Canada (Avison and Meadows 2000).

The formation of the federal government's national broadcasting policy and regulatory framework – a process that culminated in an updated Broadcasting Act in 1991 – provided another opportunity for Aboriginal groups to mobilize and advocate for change. This activity was linked to a series of public hearings held by the CRTC focused on Northern Native Broadcasting, and the Federal Task Force on Broadcasting Policy (1986). A consortium of Native communication societies joined the CBC and territorial governments to propose a government-funded northern satellite distribution system. To support this proposal, the group gathered evidence demonstrating the success of community ICT projects (Roth 2005). In 1988, the federal government committed $10 million over four years to develop a northern regional broadcast network, and Television Northern Canada began broadcasting to ninety-six northern communities in January 1992. However, unexpected budget cuts during the 1990s forced nine of the Native Communications Societies to close down during that decade (Roth 2005).

Inuit and First Nations communication organizations leveraged the broadcasting and technical expertise built up through their involvement in these projects to advocate for the federal government's Northern Native Broadcasting Policy, issued in 1990 (Valaskakis 1990). This effort was informed by the CRTC and its Regulatory Framework for Aboriginal Broadcasting (1989). Through this process, Aboriginal groups articulated five key principles (described in Baltruschat 2004):

1. greater access to a range of programming choices in the North;
2. participation in the CRTC's decisions over the form, quality, and placement of programming broadcasted in Aboriginal communities;
3. access to broadcast distribution channels to maintain Aboriginal cultures and languages;
4. programming featuring Aboriginal issues, and content produced by Aboriginal peoples; and
5. regular consultations between Aboriginal representatives and government to develop broadcasting policies.

The new policy relaxed rules on content and advertising, so that some Aboriginal broadcasters could adopt a more commercial business model. As a result, they shifted their content to attract advertisers and expand to new regions, including southern Canada (David 2012).

These various developments culminated in reforms to the language of the 1991 Broadcasting Act (which significantly revised the 1968 Act). Several waves of community mobilization, public consultation, and regulatory intervention carried out by Aboriginal non-profits succeeded in adding language to the Act recognizing "equal rights, the linguistic duality and multicultural and multiracial nature of Canadian society and the special place of aboriginal peoples within that society" (Broadcasting Act, section 3(1)(d)(iii)). Once this language was incorporated in legislation, it was invoked in subsequent interventions from these parties. For example, during a CRTC hearing in 1997, Aboriginal groups used it in a proposal to develop their existing broadcasting system into the national Aboriginal Peoples' Television Network (APTN). A year later, APTN received Category 1 status from the CRTC, making it a "must carry" channel on basic cable packages across the country – a status the network retains today.

## Aboriginal Interventions in Telecom and Digital Policy and Regulation

Aboriginal non-profits also participated in policy debates and regulatory proceedings associated with telecommunications. For example, 1970s regulatory proceedings held by the CRTC to review carriers' requests for rate increases became a vehicle for First Nations subscribers to improve their services. In Northern Ontario, the incumbent's quality of service was often poor, with outages, billing errors, and no staff who could communicate with Indigenous subscribers. The Wawatay Native Communication Society partnered with the Consumers Association of Canada, with the assistance of expert witnesses and participants from northern communities, to intervene in the proceedings. Bell Canada stated that it was unable to find Indigenous-language speakers to hire for its regional offices and therefore could not provide services in those languages. Wawatay responded that bilingual interpreters could be located in the North and provide services by telephone. The CRTC subsequently approved the establishment of a service called "Translataphone," which northern customers calling Bell's customer service could use to reach a Native-language speaker. Bell was also required to fund a bilingual (English and Oji-Cree) version of the Northern Ontario telephone directory (CRTC 1978; Hudson 1984).

Aboriginal communication organizations built on this experience in 1984 and 1985. A coalition of groups – including Inuit Tapirisat, Taqramiut Nipingat Inc., and Wawatay – collectively intervened in CRTC hearings concerning rates in Bell Canada territory. As a result of these efforts, the CRTC ordered Bell Canada to publicize discounted inter-exchange rates that could be used by northern subscribers, and also ordered Bell not to increase the existing direct-dial long distance rates in the remote regions (CRTC 1985).

These early activities became the forerunners of Aboriginal advocacy for digital ICTs. In the mid-1990s, several First Nations nonprofits in Ontario (including KNET) formed a coalition to petition the CRTC to require incumbent carriers to extend digital infrastructure to communities located in so-called High Cost Serving Areas (HCSAs) (CRTC 2005). This group included Wawatay among its members – with the Ontario-based Native Communication Society providing key expertise in the process and format required in the CRTC's regulatory hearings. The coalition of northern and Indigenous non-profits argued that access to broadband (1.5 Mbps) be included as an "essential service" in the HCSAs, which had previously been exempt from universal service provisions. Although the incumbent carriers resisted the provision of 1.5 Mbps service, in 1999 the CRTC did establish a new definition of "basic service" that included a requirement for the carriers to provide digital switches that could connect lines for low-speed data transmission (56 kbps) at local rates (users had previously paid long distance charges) (Fiser 2010).

Parallel to these First Nations activities, Inuit groups also launched activities to improve connectivity in the far North. In 1994, the non-profit Inuit Broadcasting Corporation hosted consultations in twenty-seven communities, where Inuit debated issues of digital divides, the effects of connectivity on culture and language, capacity-building, maintenance and use of technologies, participation, and funding. Hundreds of people participated in these consultations using television, community meetings, fax machines, and phone-in sessions. The federally-appointed Nunavut Implementation Commission used the group's final report during the formation of the territory in 1995, arguing "the road to Nunavut is along the information highway" (Alia 2010). To this end, from 1999 to 2001, the Government of Nunavut's Department of Sustainable Development convened the Nunavut Broadband Task Force. Its 2002 report *Sivumuqpallianiq: Moving Forward: Strengthening our Self-Reliance in the Information Age* supported the creation of the Nunavut Broadband Development Corporation (NBDC), a non-profit organization tasked to manage connectivity solutions for the territory. NBDC then lobbied the federal government to obtain bandwidth and facilities for the for-profit Qiniq network. In 2008, NBDC released its five-year business plan, called *Managing Bandwidth – Nunavut's Road Ahead*, and the following year signed a five-year contribution agreement with Infrastructure Canada.

A key avenue for digital ICT4D advocacy opened in 1994, when Industry Canada established the Information Highway Advisory Council (IHAC) to direct national broadband development. At that time, non-profit groups from across Canada united to address public interest issues in the formation of digital policy, although the process remained dominated by corporate entities, commercial media, and telecommunications corporations (Moll and Shade 2013; Shade 2008). Among these actors were Aboriginal organizations, including KNET. However, although IHAC's action plan, *Building the Information Society: Moving Canada into the 21st Century* (1996), supported universal, affordable, and equitable access, it offered few concrete suggestions on how to address issues specific to remote, northern, and Indigenous communities (Bredin 2001). Despite these challenges, that same year, First Nation organizations began partnering with the federal government and carriers to extend Internet connections to schools (First Nations SchoolNet) and public Internet access sites (Community Access Program) (Moll 2012). The federal government provided funds and decentralized the management of these programs allowing Aboriginal non-profits to administer them. This approach provides an example of how these non-profit organizations helped the federal government achieve its policy objectives – for example, to connect First Nations schools – while benefiting from funding provided to carry out those tasks. These programs also laid the groundwork for future advocacy, through the federal government's *Connecting Canadians* suite of policy initiatives.

Seven years after IHAC, Industry Canada launched the National Broadband Task Force. As in earlier initiatives, most of this group's membership consisted of representatives from industry and government, with some involvement from non-profit organizations (including KNET). Nonetheless, in its final report, the Task Force concluded that broadband networks and digital ICTS could support social and economic goals, and that government could play a role in deploying infrastructure in regions that lacked a business case for private sector development – including in the North. Industry Canada implemented these goals through *Connecting Canadians*, which provided almost $600 million between 1998 to 2006 in seven broadband initiatives: the Community Access Program (CAP); SchoolNet/First Nations SchoolNet (FNS); Library-Net; VolNet (for charitable and not-for-profit organizations); SMART Communities; Canadian Content Online; and Government Online. While usage levels varied and they faced ongoing challenges to their long-term financial sustainability, these programs provided access, training, and economic development opportunities to residents in remote and Indigenous communities (Pacific Community Networks Association 2006; AFN Chiefs Committee on Economic Development 2010). For example, in 2002 a network of seven non-profit First Nations regional management organizations – including groups like KNET with past experience in ICT development and advocacy – gained control over FNS program design and delivery. These organizations formed a national coalition that regularly convened to discuss challenges, best practices, and strategic development (Whiteduck, T. 2010).

The Aboriginal non-profits associated with *Connecting Canadians* also leveraged several short-term funding programs targeting infrastructure development. These included the federal government's BRAND and National Satellite Initiative initiatives, which encouraged private-public partnerships between community intermediary organizations and incumbent telecommunications providers. Indigenous networks like KNET and NICSN, as well as for-profit networks like Qiniq, benefited from this funding and regulatory support.

Aboriginal Internet and broadband activities also faced many challenges and setbacks during this time. For example, in 2003, Aboriginal groups engaged with government departments to develop the (now defunct) Aboriginal Canada Portal (Alexander 2009).

However, despite the funding they provided, government departments, rather than Indigenous organizations, drove much of this work. Ironically, lack of infrastructure also meant that many northern residents could not access the portal's digital content. During consultations held by government to address this issue, participants at three Connecting Aboriginal Canadians forums from 2002 to 2004 concluded that while the federal government should support their work through appropriate funding programs, communities must drive development, and programs must include opportunities for local engagement (O'Donnell et al. 2010).

Around this time, the Aboriginal Policy Research Conference was established by several partners, including the University of Western Ontario (now Western University), the Strategic Research and Analysis Directorate of Indian Affairs and Northern Development Canada (now Indigenous and Northern Affairs Canada), and the National Association of Friendship Centres. Designed to build bridges between research and policy, the event was held three times – in 2002, 2006, and 2009 (Aboriginal Policy Research Consortium). Participants in these events identified the challenges that First Nations and Inuit groups continued to face, including limited planning capacity, few opportunities to participate in decisions, a lack of technical capacity, and conflicting jurisdictional responsibilities among government funders (AFN Chiefs Committee on Economic Development 2010). Some commentators pointed out that these state-led initiatives reflected the government's lack of awareness and/or appreciation for the challenges within Indigenous communities (Alexander 2001). For example, rather than support Aboriginal efforts, government programs often forced communities to compete with one another for scarce, short-term funding (see Gibson, O'Donnell, and Rideout 2007) (see chapter 11).

Motivated by the lack of an inclusive policy framework, the First Nations regional non-profits associated with *Connecting Canadians* mobilized to establish their own community-based ICT4D strategy (O'Donnell et al. 2010). Led by KNET, this "e-Community" initiative encompassed five broad themes: capacity building; broadband infrastructure and connectivity; human resources; information management; and service delivery. It was advanced as a resolution at the 2008 annual AFN chiefs' assembly, presented at the 2009 Aboriginal Policy Research Conference, and re-affirmed in AFN *Resolution 2011–09* (Whiteduck, J. 2010). As of 2013, several First Nations had begun to implement the model in their communities (Keewaytinook Okimakanak e-Community).

Several contextual factors shaped these activities, including a shift in federal administration. In 2007, the newly elected Conservative government introduced broadband policies intended to reduce digital divides and promote economic development opportunities. *Broadband Canada: Connecting Rural Canadians* carried out these goals by providing subsidies for private sector entities to build and operate infrastructure. However, critics argued that this undermined the sustainability of local networks and service delivery in remote and rural communities (Rideout 2008). The Aboriginal non-profits involved in this work also criticized these policy shifts, partly because they were not consulted during their planning or involved in their implementation. For example, Industry Canada's 2010 consultations on the national digital economy strategy did not include any mention of Aboriginal issues (McMahon 2011); although some First Nations and Inuit organizations submitted position papers and identified principles to drive the digital economy (see for example Nunavut Broadband Development Corporation 2010; Whiteduck et al. 2010). A research project conducted at that time confirmed that many staff in First Nations and Inuit technology organizations felt they lacked substantive opportunities to contribute to digital policy, and that funding from federal agencies remained short-term, uncoordinated, and lacking support for their ongoing operations and maintenance costs (McMahon et al. 2010).

This overview – summarized in Table 10.2 – demonstrates how, in the context of northern ICT4D, Aboriginal non-profits have emerged as mediators between local stakeholders and external entities such as

Table 10.2 Summary of Indigenous ICT4D initiatives in the Canadian North

| Decade | Government-driven Initiatives | Sector | Aboriginal/Non-profit-driven Initiatives | Sector |
|---|---|---|---|---|
| 1970s | Introduction of northern satellite services | B, T | Man in the North report: Arctic Institute of North America | B, T |
|  | Northern Pilot Project (NW Ontario; Keewatin region of NWT) | B, T | Low-power community FM radio stations | B |
|  | CBC licenses Aboriginal radio stations as affiliates | B | Regional Native Communication Societies (e.g., Taqramiut Nipingat Inc; Wawatay) | B, T |
|  | CBC Accelerated Coverage Plan | B | Cooperative projects (e.g., Wawatay works with TV Ontario) | B |
|  | Experimental satellite projects (Hermes, Anik B) | B, T | Wawatay intervention in CRTC Bell Canada hearings | T |
| 1980s | Northern Native Broadcast Access Program (1983) | B | Inukshuk Project: Inuit start video production and videoconferencing in 6 communities | B, T |
|  | Federal Task Force on Broadcasting Policy (1986) | B | Inuit Broadcasting Corporation (1981) | B |
|  | Regulatory Framework for Aboriginal Broadcasting | B | Aboriginal coalition secured discounted inter-exchange and long-distance rates at CRTC hearing | T |

| Decade | Government-driven Initiatives | Sector | Aboriginal/Non-profit-driven Initiatives | Sector |
|---|---|---|---|---|
| 1990s | Northern Native Broadcasting Policy (1990) | B | Consultations held by Inuit Broadcasting Corporation (1994) led to Nunavut Broadband Task Force (1999–2001). | B |
|  | *Broadcasting Act* revisions (1991) | B | Early telemedicine; distance education applications (e.g., Wahsa) | D |
|  | CRTC hearings on digital services in high-cost areas | T, D |  |  |
|  | Industry Canada's Information Highway Advisory Council | D | Forum for Inuit organizations to advocate for connectivity solutions in Nunavut | D |
| 2000s | National Broadband Task Force and *Connecting Canadians* policy initiatives (2001) | D | Telemedicine; distance education applications (e.g., Keewaytinook Internet High School; Keewaytinook Okimakanak Telemedicine) | D |
|  | Aboriginal Canada Portal | D | Government/Aboriginal events (e.g., Aboriginal Policy Research Conference & Connecting Aboriginal Canadians Forums) | B, T, D |
|  | Broadband Canada | D |  |  |
|  | First Nations Infrastructure Fund (includes broadband as eligible funding area) | D | Nunavut Broadband Development Corporation formed | D |
|  |  |  | Research and advocacy strategies among First Nation non-profits (e-Community; First Nations Innovation, First Mile) | B, T, D |
|  |  |  | Growth of Aboriginal operators and ISPS: KNET, NICSN, ECN, First Nations Education Council, Atlantic Canada First Nations Help Desk, KFN, GwaiiTel, etc. | T, D |

Sector: B: Broadcasting: radio, television
T: Telecommunications: telephony, teleconferencing
D: Digital ICTs: Internet, broadband

government funders. These organizations operate complex networks and applications while enabling their constituents to assert self-determined development goals. They reflect a diversity of organizational structures and strategies to match the conditions present in the regions they operate in, but collectively they reflect a strong focus on consultation and engagement with their membership of geographically dispersed, politically autonomous First Nations (McMahon et al. 2014).

Yet despite increased levels of policy engagement by these Aboriginal non-profits, conditions are not necessarily improving over time. In fact, during the previous federal government's administration engagement became more difficult in some areas, given that some federal funding for Aboriginal non-profits was cut due to the effects of government austerity measures. For example, between 2010 and 2015, the AFN suffered major cutbacks to its operational funding from the Harper government, as did First Nations technology organizations such as the First Nations Technology Council in BC. These pressures are accompanied by a growing demand for services among the Indigenous constituents of these organizations. These converging trends reflect deep challenges to the long-term sustainability of these organizations.

## CONCLUSIONS AND FUTURE DIRECTIONS

This chapter describes how over the past four decades, a growing and diverse collection of Aboriginal non-profits has joined with experienced consumer organizations, policy experts, and academics to shape ICT4D in Canada's Far North. These activities reflect the shifting field of policy discourse – shaped by technological and political change – as a platform of mobilization as well as a focus of advocacy. We suggest that such activities are part of a long and varied history. Canadians have been involved in grassroots participation in both media production and the use of ICTs for advocacy from the era of farm radio forums on the Prairies during the 1930s (Sandwell 2012) and the National Film Board's (NFB's) "Challenge for Change" programs in the 1960s and 1970s (Waugh, Winton, and Baker 2010). The dynamics of these initiatives reflect the persistence of common goals, strategies, and challenges alongside new avenues of participation opened by technological change.

This chapter has discussed how Aboriginal non-profits have increasingly contributed to, and in many cases, led these initiatives. A diversity of organizations established radio, TV, telecommunications, and Internet facilities and services across the North, and helped to shape policies to address their unique needs as northerners and as Indigenous peoples. The proof of their successes is reflected in funding programs, regulatory decisions, policy principles, and even the language of the Broadcasting Act (1991). Yet despite these efforts, many challenges persist – particularly in the area of digital ICTs.

Today, access to digital infrastructure in Canada's Far North remains limited. A significant and multifaceted digital divide – influenced by factors including availability, affordability, speed, and quality of service – persists (CRTC 2012). The federal government is taking some steps to address these challenges. For example, in 2013 the northern economic development agency CanNor announced funding to develop a strategic connectivity plan covering all three northern territories, and provided support for community broadband projects like the KFN Community Network discussed earlier (CanNor 2013). As well, in 2015 the CRTC launched a national review of what constitutes "basic telecommunications services" and encouraged the public, consumer groups, and Aboriginal communication organizations to participate (CRTC 2015). Nonetheless, the North still lacks adequate infrastructure and bandwidth for residents to fully use services such as e-health and distance education, e-services, e-commerce, e-governance, and cloud-based applications. Finally, the lack of capacity, resources, and operational subsidies undermine the sustainability of Aboriginal community networks – in spite of the clear benefits they offer to northern residents.

Policy and regulatory commitments can address some of these challenges, as demonstrated in the ICT4D initiatives discussed in this chapter. But without long-term guarantees of revenue-sharing or operational subsidies, Indigenous-led community networking projects will continue to struggle. In this context, Aboriginal non-profit organizations are involved in several projects aimed at reshaping policy discourses to better meet their needs. The "e-community" strategy that KNET first articulated in 2005 and which First Nations across Canada widely adopted is one promising initiative. Research projects like the First Nations Innovation project at the University of New Brunswick (First Nations Innovation) continue to collect and present evidence of Aboriginal communication organizations as providers as well as consumers of digital infrastructure and services. Such research initiatives highlight the successes of locally owned and operated Indigenous digital infrastructure, while also describing ongoing challenges.

These activities are accompanied by efforts to reshape policy discourses. One organization engaged in this activity is the First Mile Connectivity Consortium (FMCC), which was founded in 2010 by a coalition of university-based researchers, First Nations regional technology organizations, and individual First Nations.[4] The FMCC was formally incorporated as a non-profit association in 2014. Its membership extends across Canada, but is concentrated in rural and remote regions. The organizations that belong to the coalition are diverse but share a common interest in showcasing how community-driven broadband policy can support development, highlight local innovation, and overcome digital divides. The FMCC frames locally-driven broadband infrastructure projects as an alternative to the "last mile" link from service providers to subscribers (see Strover 2000; Paisley and Richardson 1998). The concept of the First Mile provides language that proponents can use as shorthand in policy discourses to stress the need for rural and remote user communities to generate and operate their own infrastructures. In the context of Indigenous communities, it provides a way to reframe broadband policy and regulatory frameworks to better fit diverse Indigenous laws, customs, values, and institutional arrangements (McMahon et al. 2011).

In 2013, the FMCC intervened in a CRTC consultation concerning services provided by Northwestel (the incumbent telecommunications carrier in the three northern territories) (McMahon, Hudson, and Fabian 2014). Focusing on issues of access, affordability, and the potential for infrastructure development in the North to support community and economic development, the group argued that northern residents should be offered opportunities as producers as well as consumers of telecommunications services. In its decision, the CRTC recognized that broadband Internet access is, more than ever, an important means of communication for northern Canadians, and is needed to achieve a number of social, economic, and cultural objectives. The Commission agreed with the FMCC's position that the North lacks competitive markets. It recognized the special conditions and challenges in the North, and that market forces alone are not addressing them. In 2014, recognizing that many isolated northern communities remain dependent on satellite connectivity, it launched an inquiry into satellite transport services and in 2015 began a national review of the Basic Service Objective (including whether broadband should be considered a basic service available to all Canadians, like telephony).

At the time of writing, the CRTC had just released its decision to declare broadband a basic service, with a new $750 million fund to extend infrastructure to under-served regions of Canada.[5] The FMCC, as well as other Indigenous organizations, participated in these proceedings with the goal of continuing to highlight the need for communities to contribute to the development and provision of networked digital services. While the long-term impacts of this regulatory decision remain uncertain, the involvement of Indigenous peoples in the process leading up to it is but one example of how they are continuing to strategically participate in opportunities to shape Canadian communication regulations and policies.

## NOTES

1 This chapter was made possible thanks to the support of the First Nations Innovation project (http://fn-innovation-pn.com), which receives in-kind contributions from Keewaytinook Okimakanak, the First Nations Education Council, Atlantic Canada's First Nation Help Desk, and the University of New Brunswick, and by a grant from the Social Sciences and Humanities Research Council of Canada (SSHRC). The authors thank our friends and colleagues at these organizations and in these communities. We also acknowledge the dedication of the community practitioners and public servants involved in this work. We hope this history accurately captures some of their efforts.
2 Disclosure: the authors are members of the First Mile Connectivity Consortium.
3 Some of the non-profit organizations referred to in this chapter have since become for-profit cooperation/social enterprise organizations. These organizations are owned by communities and return any revenues to community stakeholders. Since these are collective organizations that continue to provide benefits to community members, and also given the sheer number of organizations and extensive time period covered, we do not make these distinctions.
4 For more information, please visit: www.firstmile.ca.
5 The CRTC decision is available at: http://www.crtc.gc.ca/eng/archive/2016/2016-496.htm.

## REFERENCES

Aboriginal Affairs and Northern Development Canada (AANDC). 2012. *Connectivity and Partnerships Website*. Ottawa: AANDC. Accessed 4 April 2013. http://www.aadnc-AANDC.gc.ca/eng/1343229993175/1343230038242.

Aboriginal Policy Research Consortium. Accessed 14 Dec 2013. http://www.aprci.org.

AFN Chiefs Committee on Economic Development. 2010. *Overcoming the Digital Divide: An Historical Overview of First Nations Connectivity. DRAFT*. Ottawa: Assembly of First Nations, Chiefs Committee on Economic Development paper.

Alexander, C.J. 2001. "Wiring the Nation! Including First Nations? Aboriginal Canadians and the Federal E-government Initiatives." *Journal of Canadian Studies. Revue d'études canadiennes* 35:277–96.

– (with Adamson, A., Daborn, G., Houston, J., and Tootoo, V.) 2009. "Inuit Cyberspace: The Struggle for Access for Inuit Qaujimajatuqangit." *Journal of Canadian Studies. Revue d'études canadiennes* 43:220–49.

Alia, V. 2010. *The New Media Nation: Indigenous Peoples and Global Communication*. New York, Oxford: Berghahn Books.

Avison, S., and M. Meadows. 2000. "Speaking and Hearing: Aboriginal Newspapers and the Public Sphere in Canada and Australia." *Canadian Journal of Communication* 25:347–66.

Babe, R.E. 1990. *Telecommunications in Canada: Technology, Industry and Government*. Toronto: University of Toronto Press.

Baltruschat, D. 2004. "Television and Canada's Aboriginal Communities." *Canadian Journal of Communication* 29:47–59.

Borrows, J. 2010. *Canada's Indigenous Constitution*. Toronto: University of Toronto Press.

Bredin, M. 2001. "Bridging Canada's Digital Divide: First Nations' Access to New Information Technologies." *Canadian Journal of Native Studies* 2:191–215.

Broadcasting Act. 1991. *Broadcasting Act of Canada*. Ottawa: Government of Canada. http://laws-lois.justice.gc.ca/eng/acts/B-9.01/.

Canadian Northern Economic Development Agency (CanNor). 2013. *CanNor Supports Northern Connectivity: Northern Territories Plan Improvements to Connectivity*. Whitehorse: Press Release, 5 March. Accessed 10 December 2013. http://www.cannor.gc.ca/mr/nr/2013/11nr-eng.asp.

Canadian Radio-Television and Telecommunications Commission (CRTC). 1978. *Telecom Decision 78–7. "Bell Canada, General Increase in Rates."* Ottawa: CRTC, 10 August.
– 1985. *Telecom Decision 85–16. "Bell Canada – Interexchange Rates in the Remote North."* Ottawa: CRTC, 7 August.
– 2005. *Report to the Governor in Council: Status of Competition in Canadian Telecommunications Markets. Deployment/Accessibility of Advanced Telecommunications Infrastructure and Services.* Ottawa: CRTC. http://www.crtc.gc.ca/eng/publications/reports/PolicyMonitoring/2005/gic2005.pdf.
– 2012. *Telecom Notice of Consultation CRTC 2012-669-1: "Review of Northwestel Inc.'s Regulatory Framework, Modernization Plan, and related matters".* Ottawa: CRTC, 6 December. http://www.crtc.gc.ca/eng/archive/2012/2012-669.htm.
– 2015. *Telecom Notice of Consultation CRTC 2015-134: "Review of Basic Telecommunication Services".* Ottawa: CRTC, 9 April. http://www.crtc.gc.ca/eng/archive/2015/2015-134.htm.
Carpentier, N., P. Dahlgren, and F. Pasquali. 2013. "Waves of Media Democratization: A Brief History of Contemporary Participatory Practices in the Media Sphere." *Convergence (London)* 19 (3): 287–94. http://dx.doi.org/10.1177/1354856513486529.
Castells, M. 2009. *Communication Power.* Oxford, New York: Oxford University Press.
Crawford, S. 2013. *Captive Audience: The Telecom Industry and Monopoly Power in the New Gilded Age.* New Haven, London: Yale University Press.
David, J. 2012. *Original People. Original Television. The Launching of the Aboriginal Peoples Television Network.* Ottawa: Debwe Communications Inc.
Evans, M.R. 2008. *Isuma: Inuit Video Art.* Montréal: McGill-Queen's University Press.
First Nations Innovation Project. Accessed 14 Dec. 2013. http://fn-innovation-pn.com.
Fiser, A. 2010. "A Map of Broadband Deployment in Canada's Indigenous and Northern Communities: Access, Management Models, and Digital Divides (circa 2009)." *Communication, Politics & Culture* 43:7–47.
Fiser, A., and A. Jeffrey. 2013. *Mapping the Long-Term Options for Canada's North: Telecommunications and Broadband Connectivity.* Ottawa: The Conference Board of Canada.

Freedman, D. 2008. *The Politics of Media Policy.* Cambridge: Polity.

Gibson, K., S. O'Donnell, and V. Rideout. 2007. "The Project-Funding Regime: Complications for Community Organizations and their Staff." *Canadian Public Administration* 50 (3): 411–36. http://dx.doi.org/10.1111/j.1754-7121.2007.tb02135.x.

GwaiiTel. 2006. "GwaiiTel Launches High Speed Internet Services in Haida Gwaii." B.C.: GwaiiTel, 28 November. http://www.gwaiitel.com/newscontd.html.

Heeks, R. 2002. "i-Development not e-Development: Special Issue on ICTs and Development." *Journal of International Development* 14 (1): 1–11. http://dx.doi.org/10.1002/jid.861.

– 2009. *The ICT4D 2.0 Manifesto: Where Next for ICTs and International Development?* Manchester: University of Manchester, Development Informatics Working Paper Series. Accessed 4 December 2013. http://www.sed.manchester.ac.uk/idpm/research/publications/wp/di/di_wp42.htm.

Hudson, H.E. 1974. *Community Communication and Development: A Canadian Case Study.* Unpublished PhD dissertation, Stanford University.

– 1977. "The Role of Radio in the Canadian North." *Journal of Communication* 27 (4): 130–9. http://dx.doi.org/10.1111/j.1460-2466.1977.tb01868.x.

– 1984. *When Telephones Reach the Village: The Role of Telecommunications in Rural Development.* Norwood, NJ: Ablex.

– 1990. *Communications Satellites: Their Development and Impact.* New York: Free Press.

– 2006. *From Rural Village to Global Village: Telecommunications for Development in the Information Age.* New York: Routledge.

– 2011. "Rural Broadband: Strategies and Lessons from North America." *Intermedia* 39:12–8.

– 2013. "Beyond Infrastructure: Broadband for Development in Remote and Indigenous Regions." *Journal of Rural and Community Development* 8 (2): 44–61.

Jacobs, P., D. Berrouard, and P. Mirellie. 2009. *Nunavik: A Homeland in Transition: An Environmental and Social Evaluation of Northern Development: The Kativik Environmental Quality Commission, 1979–2009.* Kuujjuaq: Kativik Environmental Quality Commission. Accessed 6 December 2011. http://site.ebrary.com/lib/sfu/Doc?id=10368047&ppg=1.

Kenney, G.I. 1971. *Man in the North: Parts I and II.* Montreal: Arctic Institute of North America.

Kleine, D. 2013. *Technologies of Choice? ICTs, Development and the Capabilities Approach*. Cambridge, London: The MIT Press.

Löblich, M., and M. Wendelin. 2012. "ICT Policy Activism on a National Level: Ideas, Resources and Strategies of German Civil Society in Governance Processes." *New Media & Society* 14 (6): 899–915. http://dx.doi.org/10.1177/1461444811432427.

McChesney, R.W. 2013. *Digital Disconnect: How Capitalism is turning the Internet Against Democracy*. New York, London: The New Press.

McMahon, R. 2011. "The Institutional Development of Indigenous Broadband Infrastructure in Canada and the U.S.: Two Paths to 'Digital Self Determination'." *Canadian Journal of Communication* 35:115–40.

– 2013. *Digital Self-etermination: Aboriginal Peoples and the Network Society in Canada*. Unpublished PhD dissertation, Burnaby: Simon Fraser University.

McMahon, R., M. Gurstein, B. Beaton, S. O'Donnell, and T. Whiteduck. 2014. "Making Information Technologies Work at the End of the Road." *Journal of Information Policy* 4:250–69. http://dx.doi.org/10.5325/jinfopoli.4.2014.0250.

McMahon, R., H. Hudson, and L. Fabian. 2014. "Indigenous Regulatory Advocacy in Canada's Far North: Mobilizing the First Mile Connectivity Consortium." *Journal of Information Policy* 4:228–49. http://dx.doi.org/10.5325/jinfopoli.4.2014.0228.

McMahon, R., S. O'Donnell, R. Smith, B. Walmark, B. Beaton, and J. Woodman Simmonds. 2011. "Digital Divides and the 'First Mile': Framing First Nations Broadband Development in Canada." *International Indigenous Policy Journal* 2 (2). http://dx.doi.org/10.18584/iipj.2011.2.2.2.

McMahon, R., S. O'Donnell, R. Smith, J. Woodman Simmonds, and B. Walmark. 2010. *Putting the 'Last-Mile' First: Re-framing Broadband Development in First Nations and Inuit Communities*. Vancouver: Centre for Policy Research on Science and Technology (CPROST), Simon Fraser University, December. Accessed 10 September 2013. http://www.firstmile.ca.

Mignone, J., and H. Henley. 2009. "Impact of Information and Communication Technology on Social Capital in Aboriginal Communities in Canada." *Journal of Information, Information Technology, and Organizations* 4:127–45.

Moll, M. 2012. "Appendix B: A Brief History of the Community Access Program: From Community Economic Development to Social Cohesion to Digital Divide." In *Connecting Canadians: Investigations in Community Informatics*, edited by A. Clement, M. Gurstein, M. Moll, and L.R. Shade, 485–90. Edmonton: Athabasca University Press.

Moll, M., and L.R. Shade. 2013. "From Information Highways to Digital Economies: Canadian Policy and the Public Interest". Paper presented at the World Social Science Forum, Montreal, Quebec. October.

Nunavut Broadband Development Corporation. 2010. *Submission to the Digital Economy Consultations on behalf of the Nunavut Broadband Development Corporation*. Iqaluit: Nunavut Broadband Development Corporation, 9 July. Accessed 10 October 2013. http://de-en.gc.ca/wp-content/themes/clf3/upload/1891/Digital%20Economy%20submission%20-%20NBDC.pdf.

O'Donnell, S., M. Milliken, C. Chong, and B. Walmark. 2010. *Information and Communication Technologies (ICT) and Remote and Rural First Nations Communities: An Overview*. Paper presented at the conference of the Canadian Communication Association (CCA), Montreal, Quebec. June.

O'Donnell, S., S. Perley, B. Walmark, K. Burton, B. Beaton, and A. Sark. 2009. "Community-based Broadband Organizations and Video Communications for Remote and Rural First Nations in Canada." In *Communities in Action*, edited by L. Stillman, G. Johanson, and R. French, 107–19. Newcastle upon Tyne, UK: Cambridge Scholars Publishing.

Pacific Community Networks Association. 2006. *New Opportunities for Canada in the Digital Age: Recommendations on the Future of the Community Access Program*, 10 May.

Paisley, L., and D. Richardson. 1998. "Why the First Mile and not the Last?" in *The First Mile of Connectivity: Advancing Telecommunications for Rural Development through a Participatory Communication Approach*, edited by L. Paisley and D. Richardson. Rome: Food and Agriculture Organization of the United Nations (FAO). Accessed 15 August 2013. http://www.fao.org/docrep/x0295e/x0295e03.htm.

Palmater, P. 2011. "Stretched Beyond Human Limits: Death by Poverty in First Nations." *Canadian Review of Social Policy* 65/66:112–27.

Pickard, V. 2013. "Social Democracy or Corporate Libertarianism? Conflicting Media Policy Narratives in the Wake of Market Failure." *Communication Theory* 23 (4): 336–55. http://dx.doi.org/10.1111/comt.12021.

Potter, D. 2010. "Keewaytinook Internet High School Review (2003-2008)." In *Aboriginal Policy Research VI: Learning, Technology and Traditions*, edited by J.P. White, J. Peters, D. Beavon, and P. Dinsdale, 147–55. Toronto: Thompson Educational Publishing.

Raboy, M. 1990. *Missed Opportunities: A Story of Canada's Broadcasting Policy*. Montreal: McGill-Queen's University Press.

Rideout, V. 2003. *Continentalizing Canadian Telecommunications: The Politics of Regulatory Reform*. Montreal: McGill-Queen's University Press.

– 2008. "Public Interest in Communications: Beyond Access to Needs." *Global Media Journal: American Edition* 7: 1–11.

Roth, L. 2005. *Something New in the Air: The Story of First Peoples Television Broadcasting in Canada*. Montreal, Kingston, London, Ithaca: McGill-Queen's University Press.

– 2013. "Canadian First Peoples' Mediascapes: (Re)framing a Snapshot with Three Corners." In *Mediascapes: New Patterns in Canadian Communication*. 4th ed., edited by L.R. Shade, 364–89. Toronto: Thomson.

– 2014. "Digital Self-development and Canadian First Peoples of the North." *Media Development* 2:5–10.

Roth, L., and G. Valaskakis. 1989. "Aboriginal Broadcasting in Canada: Case Study in Democratization." In *Communication for and Against Democracy*, edited by M. Raboy and P. Bruck. Montreal: Black Rose Books.

Sandwell, R.W. 2012. "'Read, Listen, Discuss, Act': Adult Education, Rural Citizenship and the Canadian National Farm Radio Forum." *Historical Studies in Education* 24:170–94.

Savard, J.F. 1998. "A Theoretical Debate on the Social and Political Implications of Internet Implementation for the Inuit of Nunavut." *Wicazo Sa Review* 13 (2): 83–97. http://dx.doi.org/10.2307/1409148.

Shade, L.R. 2008. "Public Interest Activism in Canadian ICT Policy: Blowin' in the Policy Winds." *Global Media Journal: Canadian Edition* 1:107–21.

Shepherd, T., G. Taylor, and C. Middleton. 2014. "A Tale of Two Regulators: Telecom Policy Participation in Canada." *Journal of Information Policy* 4:1–22. http://dx.doi.org/10.5325/jinfopoli.4.2014.0001.

Strover, S. 2000. "The First Mile." *Information Society* 16 (2): 151–4. http://dx.doi.org/10.1080/01972240050032915.

Unwin, T. 2009. ICT4D: *Information and Communication Technologies for Development*. Cambridge: Cambridge University Press.

Valaskakis, G.G. 1990. "The Issue is Control: Northern Native Communications in Canada." In *Proceedings of the Chugach Conference: Communication Issues of the '90s*. Anchorage: University of Alaska Anchorage, 5–6 October: 15–20.

– 1992. "Communication, Culture and Technology: Satellites and Northern Native Broadcasting in Canada." In *Ethnic Minority Media: An International Perspective*, edited by S. Riggins, 63–81. Thousand Oaks, CA: Sage.

Waugh, T., E. Winton, and M.B. Baker. 2010. *Challenge for Change: Activist Documentary at the National Film Board of Canada*. Montreal: McGill-Queen's University Press.

Whiteduck, J. 2010. "Building the First Nation E-community." In *Aboriginal Policy Research VI: Learning, Technology and Traditions*, edited by J.P. White, J. Peters, D. Beavon, and P. Dinsdale, 95–103. Toronto: Thompson Educational Publishing.

Whiteduck, J., K. Burton, T. Whiteduck, and B. Beaton. 2010. *A First Nations Perspective on a Digital Economy Strategy and an Aboriginal Connectivity Strategy*. Consultation Paper, submitted to Industry Canada's Digital Economy Strategy consultation and to Indian and Northern Affairs Canada. Accessed 20 October 2016. https://www.ic.gc.ca/eic/site/028.nsf/eng/00397.html.

Whiteduck, T. 2010. "First Nations SchoolNet and the Migration of Broadband and Community-based ICT Applications." In *Aboriginal Policy Research VI: Learning, Technology and Traditions*, edited by J.P. White, J. Peters, D. Beavon, and P. Dinsdale, 105–17. Toronto: Thompson Educational Publishing.

Whiteduck, T., B. Beaton, K. Burton, and S. O'Donnell. 2012. *Democratic Ideals Meet Reality: Developing Locally Owned and Managed Broadband Networks and ICT Services in Rural and Remote First Nations in Québec and Canada*. Keynote paper presented at the Community Informatics Research Network (CIRN) Conference, Prato, Italy. November.

# 11

# A "Political Activity": The Inherent Politicization of Advocacy

NICK J. MULÉ AND GLORIA C. DESANTIS

Advocacy as a function of democracy has become increasingly complex, especially in the politicized terrain of the Canadian non-profit sector. How advocacy is understood, conceptualized, defined, and practised has shifted, varied, morphed, and in many instances disguised itself, simply so it could survive in an increasingly threatening climate. What this collection of chapters has sought to do is to determine how this has happened and, importantly, why. Undertaking advocacy in the realm of public policy has its built-in challenges: it is in essence a discussion by representatives of the populace with government at all levels. What is revealed is as varied as the experiences of engaging in public policy advocacy themselves.

For some, engaging in advocacy involved interesting, exciting, and innovative experiences, in some cases involving actors and stakeholders that would have been considered unlikely allies in the not so distant past. For others, the increasing restrictions on their ability to advocate for issues that are deeply important to them and others, is seriously felt, at personal, group, and community levels. In some cases, advocates and stakeholders experienced opportunities to rise to the occasion to effect meaningful change. Yet in other cases, citizens' ability to effectively engage in advocacy was seriously challenged due to lack of resources, structural supports, or, most disturbing, political will.

Our concern is that the varying forms of advocacy activities, not to mention the varying ways by which they are being referred, be congruent with social justice. Advocacy itself is an important way of exercising social justice because it involves civil society communicating with state actors that represent and run the government. The communication toward bettering a marginalized societal issue for the benefit of the populace is an act of social justice (Mullaly 1997; Sen 2009). The very issues discussed in the chapters that warranted advocacy activities (Aboriginals, communication systems, disability-based income supports, the environment, poverty) and the ways advocacy was conducted (coalitions, co-constructed relations between community and government, inside/outside advocacy, organizations, social enterprise) are pursued because a segment of the population is experiencing an injustice that negatively affects their well-being. Issues such as these go to the very heart of people's social existence. The ways by which actors advocate to effect positive change elucidates the degree to which citizens exercise democracy in this country. Addressing societal issues via public policy to correct disparities that negatively affect people's lives may be one way of achieving justice, but, with the complexities that come with advocacy in this country, is it effective?

One challenge that contributes to the complexity of undertaking advocacy in the Canadian non-profit sector, is the reduced funding across the board or its elimination altogether. This has not only affected NPOS engaged in public policy advocacy, it has also affected NPOS who are not. As a result, there are serious deleterious effects: those who do try to voice concerns are being silenced in a sector where many others do not raise their voices out of fear or by choice, negatively affecting public policy advocacy in particular and democracy in general.

In this chapter we draw from the experiences, stories, campaigns, and strategies of collective advocacy shared in the chapters gathered for this anthology to further deconstruct public policy advocacy and the shifting terrain it finds itself on. Even in unsupportive times, due to the creativity, innovation, and resiliency of our contributors, some advocates still experienced successes. As editors, we feel it is important for us to dig beneath the surface to find out how some of these experiences were relayed and why (e.g., ties to government funding/relations affecting future work). We also speak to multiple levels of tensions (internal, interrelational, external), which underscore the political nature of advocacy. We raise questions, and in so doing provide a further critique as to whether such public policy advocacy is efficacious, the implications for actors directly involved, the effect on all stakeholders, and ultimately what it says about advocacy and democracy in Canada. Beyond the collection of chapters here, we also explore the current politicized climate of public policy advocacy we find ourselves in. We look at how the meaning of "advocacy" both in term and in meaning has increasingly become sullied in the public sector, resulting in other sectors having to reinvent, reimagine, and reify. We also deconstruct how state actors are positioning themselves and how civil society actors are repositioning themselves in response and underscore this using a critical analysis on power and the tensions that play out between such actors. Finally, and importantly, we examine how the non-profit sector's terrain continues to shift politically and the implications all of this has on Canadian democracy.

## PUBLIC POLICY ADVOCACY IN CANADA: QUESTIONING VARIED EXPERIENCES, VARIED OUTCOMES

The legal and regulatory premise on which Canada operates sets the parameters in which charities can engage in political activities. Registered charities have the advantage of issuing tax receipts for donations received and being eligible for various funding opportunities, assisting them in both fundraising and budgeting. They are also generally restricted in how many resources and the kinds of activities they can devote to what is considered political, based on a sliding-scale budget formula. In addition, charities that receive provincial funding are then answerable to both the province and CRA. Non-profit organizations without charitable status do not have restrictions on their political activities, but they are not able to issue tax receipts for any donations received and have fewer funding opportunities as a result of not being a charity (CRA 2015b), which reduces their budget. What this demonstrates is that all non-profit-sector organizations, regardless of their charitable status, face challenges in doing public advocacy work because of the antiquated Canadian system.

Parachin reveals through a trajectory of the development of the doctrine of political purposes that the Canadian terrain of permissible advocacy on the part of charities has shifted increasingly toward restrictions as a means of distinguishing the work of charities from politics. Based on less than persuasive case law and what Parachin argues is an emphasis on fiscal matters that value goods and services over ideals, the restrictions strike at the core of justice work for many charities. Although it is agreed there are to be some rules against political purposes it is the broad provisions being administered in the Canadian context that are being questioned in light of progressive approaches being taken in Australia (*Aid/Watch Incorporated and Commissioner of Taxation* 2010) and the UK (Charity Commission for England and Wales 2001). An example is restricting charities to addressing the effects of presenting problems, but not the underlying cause of the problem, as the latter would be seen as political. We start at the premise that every marginalized societal issue has a political foundation. The non-profit sector, whether made up of charities or not, is often at the forefront of dealing with shifting and fluid societal issues. Based on their positioning, they must engage with such challenges, which inevitably become political. Restricting such engagement is a form of repression. It places constraints on the non-profit sector, limiting the sector from fully engaging in public discourse on such issues, disempowering it. If such issues are deemed political and that is seen as negative, and thus untouchable, how then can NPOs adequately carry out their missions and mandates to address the societal issues they are charged with? Sadly, this results in bandaid solutions rather than getting to the root of the problems.

## Economic Resources for Advocacy Work

Advocacy, if understood from the perspective of creating dialogue, opening discussion, considering new ideas and working toward positive change, requires the support and cooperation of tax-supported entities, such as all levels of government, governmental departments and bodies (i.e., CRA), and the courts, which encompass the state. This collaborative understanding places advocacy in a different light and would legitimately be funded by varying governmental levels if the state were truly acting in the best interests of society. Both the Freiler and Clutterbuck (7) and Thompson and Morton (5) chapters illustrate the importance of having these kinds of financial resources, especially when dealing with the anti-poverty issues both chapters discuss. Yet both also outline the devastating effects of losing such funding and the negative implications it has for the advocacy process. Economic resources for advocates are a layer of the terrain that is always shifting because of its very precarious nature. Not only are charities restricted in how many resources they can devote to advocacy, based on CRA rules, NPOs without charitable status are highly disadvantaged when it comes to fundraising; hence the need for the state to provide a political opportunity structure for advocacy to thrive in, outlets for dialogue, and advocacy-based engagement to further develop public policy (Meyer 2004). Yet, as Freiler and Clutterbuck argue, the state's embracing of the neoliberal agenda, which includes tax cuts, wage erosion, and minimizing the state's role in the welfare of the citizenry, creates a chilly climate that diminishes political opportunities within which to advocate.

In an era in which there is less and less funding from the state for services, even less so for advocacy initiatives, those projects fortunate enough to get state funding are vulnerable to potential government cuts, as was experienced by DISC in Saskatchewan in chapter 5. Beyond financial support, civil society needs to sustain public and political support, while simultaneously trying to sustain the state's political will. This can be a very challenging yet important piece of the advocacy process, as outlined in chapter 5. Our current neoliberal climate discourages such initiatives, particularly if societal issues do not support the interests of the market economy. Reduced state involvement in societal issues (hence leaving those most affected to fend for themselves), requires those NPOs who do collaborate with the state to abide by the latter's agenda, as Freiler and Clutterbuck illustrated in chapter 7, with watering down anti-poverty action.

Coalitional work done by organizations may have been precipitated by funding cuts to individual organizations as a means of accessing increasingly limited funds, which, as Burrowes and Laforest point out in chapter 3, created connections for solidarity, debates, and strategic planning. That leads to questions about the varied participation of civil society actors. In our own community-based advocacy work, we have experienced many incidents in which members of coalitions have curtailed or restricted their advocacy strategy or messaging, for fear of the repercussions on their charitable status, sometimes to the extent of not continuing as members of such coalitions. In such circumstances, to what extent are the ideals, mission, and mandate of these organizations being compromised by their membership in such coalitions? Freiler and Clutterbuck (chapter 7) aptly demonstrate this in their example of how the state's involvement in an anti-poverty initiative shifted the focus from poverty eradication to poverty reduction. When such coalitions have a mixed membership of charities and non-profits without charitable status, to what extent is the latter being silenced to protect the charitable status of the former and sustain the work of the coalition? Ultimately, to what extent are advocacy coalitions watering down their message, to maintain access to limited funding and sustain the existence of the coalition?

Dudziak and D'Arcy (chapter 9) present a case study in which rural constituencies in New Brunswick organized around shale gas exploration and fracking in their province. As the authors observantly point out, most organized social movements come together and/or take action in large urban centres. The uniqueness of this case study is that a diverse group of constituents, including First Nations communities, gathered, educated themselves about the environmental threat, organized, and opposed their provincial governments (both Conservative and Liberal). Their advocacy methods were also traditional, yet no less effective, as they successfully exposed that the economic agenda of the state was being used to override the health issues of the affected communities.

## SHIFTING DISCOURSE OF ADVOCACY

The state's increased distancing from funding advocacy can be traced over the past twenty-five years. Burrowes and Laforest (in chapter 3) cite both financial and institutional support for voluntary organizations as well as for their advocacy work (Pal 1993; Jenson and Phillips 2001). Yet, Thompson and Morton (in chapter 5) outline federal funding cuts to organizations in their social assistance advocacy initiative. McMahon, Hudson, and Fabian, in chapter 10, similarly point out and cite how communities in northern Canada are forced to compete with each other for scarce time-limited funding (see also Gibson et al. 2007). Over the past quarter century there has thus been a shifting discourse and shifting practice, particularly on the part of the state, which influences the discourses and practices of NPOs. What do these shifts represent philosophically, theoretically, politically, and practically? In many ways these shifts represent a dialling down of advocacy in Canada, to the point that the state has ideologically redefined advocacy through a pejorative lens, forcing NPOs to contort themselves to survive, rather than question how advocacy has diminished and how this contributes to a silencing of voices, a deterioration of democracy, a process of de-democratization. Provided that government continues to discredit advocacy, Burrowes and Laforest argue that it becomes contingent on non-profit organizations to reverse the shifting terrain that has produced this chilly climate.

One way that several NPOs attempted to stabilize the shifting terrain to secure funding was to become members of coalitions, and engage in evidence gathering and public education – all "safe" buzz words in place of the dirty word "advocacy." As the chapters in this book demonstrate, framing advocacy within such discourse does not suggest that the effects of advocacy are any more or less important, but simply what authors are sharing as a trend they are participating in. Yet this raises deeper issues about the effect of such shifting discourses on the very concept of advocacy itself. Does engaging in this shift in discourse contribute to the further sullying of advocacy and any approaches that fall outside the realm of coalition work, evidence gathering, and public education? Do these approaches become acceptable, respectable, and palatable in the eyes of the state (read CRA) and ultimately the public? Do other advocacy actions such as protests, rallies, street theatre, etc. become unacceptable, disrespectful, and unpalatable as a result? Do such shifts in discourse privilege some and marginalize others in our democracy? The experiences relayed in the chapters in this collection answer all of these questions in the affirmative, in effect raising serious questions about the state of advocacy in this country.

## Siloing of Public Policy

Public policies, including information and communication technologies, poverty, the environment, health and wellbeing, etc. and the bureaucratic labyrinth of multiple public policies driven by multiple levels of government and multiple government departments within the same level of government, can pose a challenge to collaborative advocacy work. How advocates and/or advocacy coalitions position themselves can affect the advocacy process from where they are positioned. Freiler and Clutterbuck outline the differences between insider/outsider advocates, but also acknowledge the potential each has to influence the process both in the immediate and the long term. In other words, working from within and working from without can influence public policy. The challenge becomes maintaining consistent goals and objectives between the two groups.

In chapter 10, McMahon, Hudson, and Fabian discuss not only making good use of political opportunity structures such as the state working with Aboriginal populations, but also actually creating an infrastructure to address telecommunications needs in the North through public–private partnerships, including Aboriginal NPOs. Such relations included meetings and consultations about regulatory proceedings, with all key stakeholders providing input at the table. Whether it has been the long fraught history between the state and Aboriginal populations, a requirement for more intense collaboration to build information technology, or other reasons, the regular and ongoing communications between public–private partnerships, with both the state and Aboriginal populations at the table, created, for the most part, a very productive process for public policy advocacy. What underlies the productivity of this process and the meeting of advocacy goals is the binding and enforceable decision-making effect of regulatory proceedings, which can contrast greatly with human service consultations in which government is not bound by public input (see chapters 5 and 7). Chapter 10 distinguishes itself from the others because McMahon, Hudson, and Fabian describe relations between the public, private, and non-profit-sector actors as one of engagement, a contrast with the adversarial experiences of others (see chapters 6, 7, and 9). All the same, this was not a seamless process, as the examples in which communities experienced difficulties participating in public consultations show.

Perhaps the most disturbing example of when this does not work is in Ballard's chapter (6), which describes how the very First Nations Peoples most directly affected by a local flood were siloed out of the resolution process, seriously affecting their advocacy efforts. It is extremely difficult to do collective advocacy when strategic policy analysis is impossible due to a network of interwoven policies that are mired in jurisdictional restrictions, political ideology, and poor consultations. This failed response to an environmental disaster, based on colonial policies, became a particular advocacy challenge to the First Nations peoples while they personally faced the effects of this crisis on their own lives. Government policies may appear to be healthy on paper, but in reality these policies control and silence First Nations – even when they embark on their own community development work and formulate their own answers/solutions to a serious humanitarian problem. Adding insult to injury is the way in which the federal and provincial governments engaged in the "duty to consult" process, a process that fell short of any meaningful discussions that adequately addressed the needs and concerns of these First Nations. Furthermore, the role that area non-profits took in aligning themselves with the government during the crisis raises a serious question as to whether non-profits feel it is safer to side with government in "helping" First Nations Peoples, regardless of its effectiveness, so as to protect their own existence. Is this a deeper and disturbing level of advocacy chill? Interestingly, the duty to consult policies of the federal and provincial governments got this First Nations community nowhere, leaving the community with no capacity to challenge the policy quagmire! Since the time of the flood (2011), until the summer of 2015, when sod was turned for a new settlement, they had been a homeless and landless community.

## Public Policy Co-construction/Collaboration

The term "public policy co-construction" was first coined by Vaillancourt (2009) to describe a process in which civil society actors, including NPOs and state actors, meaning representatives of government, work together to create public policy that addresses the issues at hand – in essence, co-constructing public policy. In chapter 8, Vaillancourt and Aubry describe such a process. In Quebec, approximately 1,500 NPOs created a grassroots anti-poverty movement that forced the provincial government to pay attention and act on proposals originally framed by the community. What is noteworthy about this model and unique in this Québec case is that large masses of people were allowed into the room and got a seat at the table instead of being left out of deliberations. This was no hollow "consultation" process but rather one in which the authors highlight that legislation requires those most affected by such legislation to participate. This process may have been further supported by the fact that Québec uniquely funds such an independent community advocacy structure.

Several chapters focused on experiences engaging with the state using a collaborative advocacy model (see chapters 3, 5, 7, and 10), some with degrees of success, others less so. This has major implications for the collaborative development of public policy and as such needs further attention. For example, civil society actors can try to influence society and political actors through their advocacy work, in effect influencing the public policy-making process. On the other hand, we have seen political actors via the weight of their elected power become ideologues privileged to the point of ignoring civil society actors. Once again, it is critical for civil society actors to be aware of the possibility of such dynamics if they are to maintain their integrity in the advocacy goals and objectives they have set for themselves.

Although correspondence, dialogue, even collaborations between NPOs and the state are important, what is crucial is for NPOs to be aware of the risk of systemic limitations borne of who is or is not invited to the table, co-optation, and silencing. Does the "honour" of being at the table with the state create an environment of acquiescence? Are agenda items kept off the table so as not to offend? Do government limitations (i.e., funding) and/or dialogical processes (i.e., trade-offs, passivity) in turn curtail discussion, compromising the democratic process? Do "successes" on some fronts result in others, and, ultimately, the pursuit of justice, being further marginalized? The chapters in this collection as well as our own personal experiences provide evidence to respond to these questions once again in the affirmative. These are questions all advocates need to keep in mind if and when they engage in "collaborations" with the state.

Evidence-based research in the name of "education" as opposed to "advocacy" can have a depoliticizing effect because it narrows the scope for action, as Burrowes and Laforest point out, particularly when civil society actors are engaged in collaborative work with the state, as demonstrated by Freiler and Clutterbuck in chapter 7. Such evidence-based policy making between organizations/coalitions and government can become increasingly insular, with a real risk of co-optation, far removed from the public citizenry and broader engagement. Just as some have questioned whether coalitions properly represent the interests of the citizenry (Putnam 2000; Skocpol 2003), we also question to what extent the co-optation process impedes coalitions' representation of the best interests of the citizenry, given the survival needs of coalitions and organizations. Also, the state's slant toward attempts at meeting the needs of the majority can inevitably contribute to developing policy that can further marginalize the marginalized. If the questions that need to be asked are not being asked, if the critiques that need to be tabled are not being tabled, and if the difficult discussions required to grapple with the core issues are not taking place, the political process has then been severely compromised, resulting instead in a process of depoliticization.

## Internal Advocacy Strategy Tensions

The northern Canada (10), Ontario (3, 7), Québec (8), and Saskatchewan (5) chapters all discuss and provide examples of the strategy-based tensions that can arise within coalitional groups, particularly those that split between state collaborators and grassroots activists. Constant and ongoing communication between such groups is key. They also need to check in on their political positioning, as this too can shift and vary among group members during the advocacy process. This calls for advocates to engage in a reflexive process with each other on an ongoing basis, a way of checking in to ensure that the state is not inadvertently (or sometimes willfully) redirecting the goals and objectives of the advocacy initiative. Such reflexivity can prevent divisions within advocacy circles and formal coalitions (see chapters 3, 7, and 8 for examples).

Establishing and maintaining a reflexive process is necessary given the systemic challenges imposed on coalitions, which consist of groups and organizations of varying non-profit status and size. Our own experience in community activism has repeatedly demonstrated ongoing tensions in such circumstances. Messaging or demands can be watered down due to charities' fearing the message may be interpreted as too political. In fact, ongoing membership of charities within mixed coalitions can prove tenuous due to the concern that their very involvement may jeopardize their charitable status. Grassroots groups and/or non-profit organizations without charitable status are often put under pressure by charities in the coalition to carry out the more politicized actions. This is often an unfair request, given their lack of resources.

## An Alternative Approach?

Another element of the shifting terrain on public policy advocacy in Canada is the development of new models and approaches, such as the community contribution company (C3) featured in chapter 4. In BC, the C3 is a new hybrid model that commits for-profit corporations with a social enterprise mandate to benefit society at large or a segment of society in need, without any restrictions on the amount of advocacy they can do. Although currently not regulated, the C3 is overseen by its stakeholders. NPOs are welcome to work with them to raise capital to address marginalized societal issues. This is a very new model and one that is currently in development, so the jury is still out. Beyond understanding the structure of this model and how it works, it is also important to consider its larger implications. Questions arise, such as, do C3s have unrestricted advocacy provisions because for-profit corporations are involved? Therefore, if NPOs want unrestricted advocacy along with decent funding should they align themselves with a for-profit corporation? Is the C3 being devised as a model to diminish charities and NPOs? In essence, will the most well-resourced and unrestricted model for public advocacy become the C3 (which is more akin to a for-profit corporation)? Is this a model that will slide down the slippery slope of neoliberalism? What are the implications for public policy and democracy in general?

In the absence of regulation, stakeholders can form C3s through unanimous shareholder approval without community interest testing. Although this creates a model sans regulations, which may appeal to many who are critical of existing regulations on advocacy for charities, it does not clearly spell out the voice and place of the public interest. Does this create a socioeconomic divide between those that can invest in shares and those that cannot? In the end, does this mean that it is shareholders that are determining the "best interests" of the community (i.e., "public interests") on the marginalized societal issue the C3 has been founded to address? This has real implications for democratic decision making. It is further complicated by various levels (i.e., majority vs. super majority and protecting minority stakeholders). It also has the potential of creating an "insider world" of shareholders far removed from individuals without the capacity to be shareholders. In addition, why is the BC government not interested in regulations and what are the potential implications of this? Is the government seeking to offload addressing some marginalized societal issues (i.e., have non-profits seek funding via the private sector) hence decreasing the demand for government funding and the role of the state, and turning over such societal responsibilities to corporations?

## Concluding Summary of Chapters

The chapters in this collection have demonstrated the shifting terrain of public policy advocacy enacted by non-profits in Canada. To say this terrain is diverse is simplistic: just as the Canadian physical landscape is vast in breadth, so are the experiences of NPOs engaged in public policy advocacy, as illustrated in these chapters, drawn from across the country. The authors delve into the depths of the terrain and how it is organized, structured, regulated, policed, and, as such, navigated in terms of public policy. Often, public policy advocacy does not stop once a government agrees to develop a new policy or program. Some chapters show that advocacy continues to sort out details (see chapter 5) or monitor progress (see chapter 8) or lack thereof (see chapter 7).into the developmental and implementation phases.

A fundamental *non-shift* in every chapter is that NPOs rose to advocate for needed public policy and program changes as a result of people getting together to identify, define, develop, and implement needed changes as they saw them. Advocacy can be grassroots-driven, organized informally or formally, in professional employment settings or outside. These chapters show us that the spirit of Canadians to engage in the democratic process through advocacy to better their own lives and the lives of those around them remains palpable, regardless of the limiting effects of the doctrine of political purposes (see chapter 2) or government's disdain for advocacy. The next section takes up this latter point.

## ADVOCACY: A MALNOURISHED TERRAIN

We have chosen *terrain* as a metaphor to look at collective public policy advocacy in Canada because terrain symbolizes the very basis on which nourishment through fertilization allows growth and development. Such a terrain represents grounding, a foundation on which a concept like collective public policy advocacy can grow and flourish and thrive within a democratic environment for the betterment of the country. Yet terrain is not static, and depending on how it is toiled and maintained, and considering the influence of the climate, its ability to produce can be variable. As we point out in the introduction, advocacy as a concept and its association with public policy has a multiplicity of meanings and interpretations, and regardless of the context – whether it be philosophical, ideological, theoretical, political, geographical, or regulatory – its discourse and how it is applied practically is fluid. The experiences, stories, data gathered, and insights featured in the chapters of this book demonstrate the fluidity of collective public policy advocacy and indicate that the terrain is indeed shifting.

Contextually, it is noteworthy to recognize the richness of the voluntary sector in Canada. Canada has over 170,000 non-profit organizations (Hall 2005), 86,288 of them charities (CRA 2015a). Although it is difficult to determine how many of them engage in collective public policy advocacy, the missions and mandates of many of them speak to an involved and committed civil society that wants to contribute to ongoing prosperity for the country. Yet does the structural apparatus (viz. the state) support the initiatives of those in the non-profit sector to contribute to the democratic process?

We argue in our introduction to this anthology that the political environment is creating a climate of reduced political opportunity structures. Although there are pockets of what appear to be structures for political opportunity, such as the funding of non-profits to advocate (see chapter 3 and Laforest 2011), which is generally no longer the case save for Quebec, and an encouraging of collaborative models, such as co-construction between the state and non-profits (see chapters 5, 7, and 8,), which have produced their own uneasy processes, we question whether these were and are distracting tactics. It has been documented that between 1985 and 2005 the Canadian federal government was engaged in a retrenchment of the welfare state, disabling the representation of civil society organizations in the process (Phillips 2012) mostly through funding cuts (Laforest 2012). Furthermore, governance structures that enact tax penalties and reporting requirements impose tighter regulations on charities (Government of Canada 2012) with professionalized bureaucratic procedures, constraining already underresourced non-profits, resulting in compromised autonomy and capacity to advocate in the process (Evans, Richmond, and Shields 2005).

At press time, we are seeing a new and possibly promising shift in the public policy advocacy terrain, due to the election of the majority Liberal federal government in the fall of 2015. What is new is the perspective the Liberal government brings to how it plans to work with the Canada Revenue Agency (CRA). What sounds promising is that part of the Liberals' election platform includes developing a more positive relationship with the non-profit sector and reviewing and updating how this sector is governed, which will involve developing a new legislative framework that more clearly defines "political activity" (Liberal Party 2015). Although such promises bring a level of encouragement, it is important to recognize the climate in which this shift is being offered, due to the legacy of the past federal Conservative government. We devote the remainder of this section to examining how both the non-profit sector and advocacy in particular have been affected by the previous federal Conservative government, to prove the extent to which the relationship between the non-profit sector, the federal government, and the CRA is in need of repair.

What has become of particular concern is the former federal Conservative government's use of the CRA, an arm's length governmental agency that registers and regulates charities, to diminish advocacy on the latter's part. In 2012 the CRA began a "blitz" on charities by reviewing their registered status if they were deemed to be critical of federal government policy and/or deviated from the Conservative Party agenda. The NPOs most targeted were those in the areas of environmental, human rights, progressive policy, and international development organizations, which provided alternative perspectives to the government's (Voices-Voix 2014a). To demonstrate the federal government's targeted agenda, it extended $13.4 million to the CRA, when the latter's budget was already being massively cut, to carry out a blitz on charities from 2012–2017 (Beeby 2014a). A team of fifteen auditors were brought in to carry out this task. They did fifty-two audits, and more were expected to be launched (Beeby 2014b). The Conservative government also invested over $20 million more to monitor activist groups as well as members of their own party, via the media, who were politically opposed to their agenda or deemed a scandal risk (Fekete 2014).

Such activities have contributed greatly to and exacerbated an already existing climate of "advocacy chill," with implications not only for those being audited and warned that they are being watched, but for other charities as well (Beeby 2014c). In the next section, we delve deeper into "advocacy chill," to demonstrate how extensive its reaches are and the amount of work required to redress its implications.

## "ADVOCACY CHILL": IMPLICATIONS FOR PUBLIC POLICY ADVOCACY

The ideological shift in the terrain on public policy advocacy is happening unevenly across the public and non-profit sectors. The increasing disempowerment of advocacy on the part of the former federal Conservative government has had an indelible impact on the non-profit sector (Lawyers' Rights Watch Canada 2014; Raj 2014), with some taking issue and others choosing to acquiesce and reshape themselves in order to survive. This is further underscored by the legal system's limited parameters on advocacy (see chapter 2). The political ideology of the former federal Conservative government was a right-wing perspective that did not appreciate critiques coming from the left (Voices-Voix 2015a).

The blitz targeting NPOs not aligned with the Conservative government's views came on the heels of that federal government's counter-terrorism strategy which identified "environmentalism" as an "extremist" form of internal terrorist threat (Government of Canada 2013, 9). This kind of ideology entered public discourse in the form of the term "eco-extremist" (McCarthy 2012), planting negative imagery of environmental activists in this country. Accusations of charities (whether environmental or not) being "too political" taints the "good works" purposes of these charities within a sector in which the term "political" is not clearly defined, but is instead being used to raise doubts about their actions. The United Nations Platform for Action Committee (UNPAC), an NPO seeking to hold the Manitoba provincial government to the recommendations of the Beijing UN Fourth World Conference on Women and the parallel NGO Conference, sought charitable status with CRA. CRA staff told them to remove the following terms from their objectives: all mention of equality and inequality; to replace educating "Manitobans about gender equality and the impact that inequality has on the lives of girls and women," with "educate and inform the public about women-centred community economic development" (Voices-Voix 2014c, para. 24). Instead of conducting "research and analysis into gender equality," CRA recommended that UNPAC "advance education by conducting research on women-centred community economic development" (Voices-Voix 2014c, para. 24). Most concerning is that terms such as "public policy" and "positive action" were to be removed in favour of an emphasis on education and research to prepare UNPAC's application (Voices-Voix 2014c, para. 19).

Even NPOs or institutions engaged in safe "advocacy" work such as "evidence gathering" and "public education," had been the target of federal government reprisals, especially if their findings were not in keeping with the state's ideology. Often referred to as the scientific knowledge sector, these included scientists, think tanks, statistical programs, and research projects, all of which represented examples of being muzzled, defunded, or silenced. The better-known examples include:

- Access to Information and its governing Act is in need of reform, but rather than doing so, as the Conservative government initially promised, requests to do so were met with high rates of refusal or delay, information withheld due to political reasons, thus hampering Parliament and the media from accessing information needed to conduct their work (Chase 2012a,b).
- The Canadian Council on Learning was forced to permanently shut down in 2012 when the Conservative government decided not to renew its funding (Voices-Voix 2012).
- The Canadian Policy Research Networks closed down in 2009 due to the loss of long-term funding, most significantly the withdrawal of funds by the Conservative government (CMAJ 2009).
- The Department of Justice received the most severe personnel and budget cuts of any federal department, seriously affecting its capacity to fulfill its mandate (Thompson 2014).
- Environment Canada funding was eliminated for both its climate change and environmental programs, and the department's scientists had to receive permission before speaking to the media (Voices-Voix 2014b).
- The Law Commission of Canada had its budget cut in 2006 and closed soon thereafter. Then Treasury Board President John Baird admitted the government was no longer interested in funding bodies that opposed its legislation (*National Post* 2006). Interestingly, in August 2016, the Law Commission of Canada was reinstated (Government of Canada 2016).
- Library and Archives Canada in 2012 saw its staff reduced by 20 per cent due to a $9.6 million budget cut over three years (Government of Canada 2012). In addition, employees were to abide by a code of conduct that muzzled them, implement a snitch line, and require loyalty to the government on and off the job (Munro 2013).
- The National Council of Welfare had its funding terminated by the federal Conservative government in 2012, forcing it to close in 2013 (Monsebraaten 2012).
- Statistics Canada had its mandatory long-form census replaced in 2010 with the voluntary National Household Survey.

All sectors and two senior statisticians at Statistics Canada protested this (Sheikh 2013) and the 2011 NHS was deemed highly problematic (*Globe and Mail* editorial 2013). (The long-form census was restored by the new Liberal government in November 2015.)

Evidence gathering and public education was thus not necessarily a safe route for all NPOs. This decline in the use of evidence-based research to base policy, came with a cost to Canada and Canadians: the silencing of knowledge does not serve democracy well.

In more concrete terms, for charities being audited and investigated, their actual operations are placed in doubt, both in terms of their registered status and the disruption to their work because of the major bureaucratic distraction involved in an audit. In addition, the work of such charities is even further affected during an audit when they have to devote a portion of their limited financial resources to legal advice. For charities not under audit, the "advocacy chill" causes them to lower their profile and reduce their public input to stay out of the line of fire. Some charities were even redirecting their resources (otherwise meant for charitable works) to prepare for a potential audit (Kirkby 2014). The incursion of the former federal Conservative government's ideology via an "arm's-length" regulator, the CRA, has had a chilling effect on those charities engaged in advocacy work in this country, leaving the new federal Liberal government with a very tall order to address.

## FROM DE-DEMOCRATIZATION TO RE-DEMOCRATIZATION

We had close to a decade of a federal Conservative government that increasingly went on the attack against numerous charities in the non-profit sector. Part of the attack included setting up the CRA to accuse some charities of being "too political," when the real question was whether the former federal Conservative government, and by extension the CRA, were being "too political" themselves, targeting charities that were not aligned with that government's objectives. This represented an inverted dynamic that stripped charities of their free speech and free expression on important public policy matters, perverting the democratic process. What appeared to be lost on the former federal Conservative government is the important, and we argue, even necessary, role of dissent and critique, as both serve to hold the state to account and call for mature, constructive reflection on public policy issues that affect Canadians. In effect, this is how civil society and the state communicate and engage with one another. Rather than recognize the necessity of such processes to address important societal issues affecting our country, regardless of political differences, the former federal Conservative government seemed more interested above all else in promoing its ideology. What was at risk was losing the voices of those working on some of the most marginalized societal issues in the country (Canadian Council of Churches 2014). This is important, given that most Canadians believe charities speak to public interest issues, not as an interest group, and that advocacy laws need to be loosened to permit charities to speak more freely to their causes (Muttart Foundation 2013). Sometimes, the voices that rise from the non-profit sector do so to represent the many voices of disenfranchised and/or marginalized Canadians who are either unable to speak for themselves due to the gravity of their circumstances or have knowledge or experiences that fall outside of the understanding of mainstream Canadians. Our concern is that such risks are too high to take.

Structurally, the non-profit sector is already at a disadvantage in its dealings with the state, when compared with the private sector. It does not have the luxury of having lobbyists on staff to advocate for its objectives as the private sector has for its profit-making initiatives, even within the lobbying rules the federal Conservatives instituted. The sectoral terrain was never a level-playing field. The non-profit sector has always been the poor cousin of the public and private sectors. Impoverishing it further through funding cuts and accusations of political impropriety, all designed to contribute to a chilled environment for advocacy, only stilled the waters in the hope of extinguishing dissent. This has exposed the former government's ideological stance at the expense of some of the most marginalized issues in Canada. The price for this can be quite detrimental to the very mandates and missions of NPOs, the people and communities they serve, and the extent to which NPOs can participate in democracy in this country. In essence, it has been a strategy of de-democratization.

What the non-profit sector brings to the democratic process is invaluable, for it is positioned closest to civil society and has the ability to bring forth the very issues, needs, and concerns directly from the frontlines of communities across Canada. The current federal Liberal government presents itself as a responsible, accountable government that welcomes such input to assist in sustaining the health of the governing and democratic process. Will its plan to update governance rules for the non-profit sector usher in an opportunity to re-democratize the country? We believe that if the federal Liberal government is to adequately address the issues plaguing the non-profit sector, such work needs to

- expand the list of charitable purposes beyond the antiquated Elizabethan laws of 1601;
- engage in an in-depth discussion with the sector about advocacy with the intent to amend the CRA guidelines on advocacy; and
- remove the arbitrary and restricting 10–20 per cent resource limits on "political activity."

The Canadian government can look to other jurisdictions, such as Australia and the UK, to study the changes their governments made to assist them in this process (Voices-Voix 2015b). Importantly, underscoring such a review would be the need for the federal Liberal government to enter a dialogue with the non-profit sector and come to a mutual understanding about advocacy, if it expects to make any progress on creating new rules about "political activity."

### Critical Response

Although we commend the creativeness and innovation that NPOs engage in to do advocacy work within the existing constraints, we ultimately take issue with this approach when considering the long-term effects. NPOs should not only find ways to work within the system but also find ways to question and challenge the system. If we do not question and offer alternatives to the current regulatory constraints placed on NPOs in the not-for-profit sector, NPOs will not be able to engage in advocacy work to the capacity needed to truly address their respective missions and mandates. This not only cheats their missions and mandates, but also those they serve and the issues to be addressed, not to mention open and accessible democracy in Canada.

A great challenge of the non-profit sector is its very size and diversity. With over 170,000 NPOs (Hall 2005), it is extremely difficult to organize, let alone come to some form of consensus about the threat to advocacy in Canada. To begin with, many of these NPOs do not see advocacy as part of their mission, others see their work as based on education and/or service provision only, while others skirt advocacy given the current chilly climate. We believe that it is contingent on the non-profit sector to organize and defend its right to advocate, not only to further its respective missions and mandates, the people it serves, and the important issues it undertakes, but for the sake of democracy via freedom of speech and expression. The federal Liberal government's intent to "modernize" the governance rules of the non-profit sector, including creating a new legislative framework, will provide an important opportunity for actors in the non-profit sector to provide their input in shaping such legislation. The long-standing and powerful effect of "advocacy chill" has not given rise to such an opportunity. Given that, to date, none of the major federal parties has made advocacy within the non-profit sector (i.e., take up what the Voluntary Sector Initiative, VSI, process did not) a priority and that even the current federal Liberal government is not specifically naming "advocacy" in their CRA platform, actors in the non-profit sector will need to communicate the inherent role of politics within advocacy when looking at "political activities."

## CONCLUSIONS

What the stories and experiences shared in this book reveal is that despite the numerous challenges the non-profit sector faces, its resolve to take up, attend to, address, and even contest issues in the public policy realm is steadfast. The means and ways of doing so are as diverse as the actors involved. Sometimes they are collaborative and conciliatory, other times confrontational and adversarial. The challenges and conflicts that will inevitably arise in doing public policy advocacy work can play out between NPOs and the state and even within NPOs themselves. Complicating matters even further are the restrictions placed on charities. These include being under-funded or having funds cut, lacking adequate resources to undertake effective advocacy, and the threat of being audited for being "too political," without a clear definition of what the bounds are for permissible political activity. NPOs without charitable status have limited fundraising opportunities, constraining their capacity to do advocacy work. Yet, despite all these barriers, the non-profit sector in this country rises to the challenges in the face of needed public policy that is lacking, or threatened, or public policy that is proving detrimental to our communities and environment. Yet, is it fair that the sector with the least amount of resources and capacity must draw upon such resolve to participate in Canada's democracy?

Canada has been in an era of eroding political opportunity structures with diminishing returns. In the eyes of the former federal Conservative government, silencing dissent served to create an open pathway to surge forward with their ideologies, sidelining the critics and further marginalizing societal issues and the vulnerable in the process. This public policy process worked toward silencing the very voices most affected by the public policy itself, flying in the face of one of the core functions of democracy: public discussion. When a climate is created in which "advocacy chill" permeates, it is no longer a site of democratic process but one of de-democratization. This in turn creates an atmosphere of uncertain public policy advocacy, because the very voices that need to be asserted, self-censor instead to self-protect (Voices-Voix 2015a). A shift to the right in this country empowered the former federal Conservative government to engender a level of distrust toward the non-profit sector, which in turn sidelined and depoliticized public policy advocates.

If we are to reverse this way of "doing" public policy, we urge the current federal Liberal government to act on its CRA platform in a direct and meaningful way with non-profit-sector actors by engaging in a nuanced discussion about advocacy and how it can contribute positively to Canada's re-democratization. Although we do not anticipate that an initiative as large as the VSI will take place, the process of creating a new legislative framework could at least begin to take up advocacy in a far more mutually engaging way than it was during the VSI. We thus urge both state and non-profit-sector actors to enter a dialogue that explicitly includes advocacy when reviewing governing rules. We believe this will contribute to a re-democratization process, and we share the belief stated by the Advocacy Working Group (AWG) of the VSI more than a decade ago: "The AWG is convinced that advocacy must be fully recognized and supported as a legitimate activity of non-profit organizations and charities" (Rektor 2002, 1).

What we propose to nourish and strengthen the public policy advocacy terrain, which in turn will strengthen Canada's democracy, is multilayered and would involve all stakeholders. For one, given that public policy issues affect all Canadians in one form or another, the very issue of advocacy on the part of the non-profit sector in this country needs to be taken up as a national discussion (Broadbent

Institute 2014). It is worth it for Canadians to learn more about this issue and how they are being affected by current circumstances. Informal learning can take place through a national dialogue via broadcast and social media. This volume did not include a detailed analysis of how the media covers public policy advocacy, but that is certainly an area worthy of further examination, including the role the media can play in informing Canadians of its importance. Formal learning can take place in our education system at both the secondary and post-secondary levels, teaching courses on advocacy alongside civics as core curriculum. University faculty, particularly those with tenure (Beeby 2014d), should become public role models who uphold the importance of academic freedom and the right to freedom of speech and freedom of expression (The Progressive Economics Forum 2014) by speaking out on issues that are evidence-based and in the public interest.

The state and the non-profit sector need to return to direct dialogues with each other. The historic VSI dialogues sadly became a lost opportunity for state officials and non-profit-sector representatives to have a meaningful discussion about advocacy, how to understand, value, and define it. The state, regardless of which party is governing, relevant departments, and the courts, have a responsibility to level the playing field if they are to contribute to strengthening our democracy. Members of the non-profit sector also have a responsibility to challenge the inequities in public policy advocacy the sector is experiencing (Elson 2008). We understand that NPOs are experiencing the advocacy chill as threatening, but we also believe that talking with each other and careful strategizing is required to expose and contest such an environment. Not acting will only contribute further to eroding democracy in Canada. We hope this book contributes in one small way to reversing the de-democratization process.

## REFERENCES

*Aid/Watch Incorporated and Commissioner of Taxation* [2010] H.C.A. 42.
Beeby, D. 2014a. "Timeline: Canada Revenue Agency's Political-Activity Audits of Charities." CBC *News, The Canadian Press.* (5 August). Accessed 25 January 2015. http://www.cbc.ca/news/politics/canada-revenue-agency-s-political-activity-audits-of-charities-1.2728023.
– 2014b. "Foreign-aid Charities Join Together to Challenge Canada Revenue Agency Audits." *Toronto Star, The Canadian Press.*

10 August. Accessed 25 January 2015. http://www.thestar.com/news/canada/2014/08/10/foreignaid_charities_join_together_to_challenge_canada_revenue_agency_audits.html.
- 2014c. "Revenue Canada Targets Birdwatchers for Political Activity." CBC News. 16 October. Accessed 25 January 2015. http://www.cbc.ca/news/politics/revenue-canada-targets-birdwatchers-for-political-activity-1.2799546.
- 2014d. "Academics' Open Letter Calls for Moratorium on Political Tax Audits." CBC News, The Canadian Press. September 14. Accessed 25 January 2015. http://www.cbc.ca/news/politics/academics-open-letter-calls-for-moratorium-on-political-tax-audits-1.2765967.

Broadbent Institute. 2014. "Stephen Harper's CRA: Selective Audits, "Political" Activity, and Right-Leaning Charities." Accessed 27 January 2015. https://www.broadbentinstitute.ca/sites/default/files/documents/harpers-cra-final_0.pdf.

Canadian Council of Churches. April 10 2014. Letter to Prime Minister: Re: Definition of Charitable Activities. *Canadian Council of Churches*. Accessed 27 January 2015.http://www.councilofchurches.ca/wp-content/uploads/2014/04/Letter-to-Prime-Minister-on-Definition-of-Charitable-Activity.pdf.

Canadian Medical Association Journal (CMAJ). 2009. "Independent Policy Think Tank Closes Doors." *CMAJ press release*. 29 October. Accessed 19 February 2015. http://www.cprn.org/documents/51894_EN.pdf.

Canada Revenue Agency. 2015a. Charities Listings. Accessed 24 January 2015. http://www.cra-arc.gc.ca/ebci/haip/srch/advancedsearchresult-eng.action?n=&b=&q=&s=registered&d=&e=+&c=&v=+&o=&z=&g=+&t=+&y=+&p=1.
- 2015b. "Registered Charity vs. Non-Profit Organization." Accessed 8 August 2015. http://www.cra-arc.gc.ca/chrts-gvng/chrts/pplyng/rgstrtn/rght-eng.html.

Charity Commission for England and Wales. 2001. *RR7 – The Independence of Charities from the State*.

Chase, S. 2012a. "Can Access to Information Be Fixed?" *The Globe and Mail*. 23 August. Accessed 19 February 2015. http://www.theglobeandmail.com/news/politics/can-access-to-information-be-fixed/article1871549/.
- 2012b. "Five Ways Ottawa Stymies Access to Information Requests." *The Globe and Mail*. 23 August. Accessed 19 February 2015. http://www.theglobeandmail.com/news/politics/five-ways-ottawa-stymies-access-to-information-requests/article562031/.

Elson, P. 2008. "Where Is the Voice of Canada's Voluntary Sector?" *Canadian Review of Social Policy* 60 (61): 1–20.

Evans, B., T. Richmond, and J. Shields. 2005. "Structuring Neoliberal Governance: Emerging New Modes of Control and the Marketization of Service Delivery." *Policy and Society* 24 (1): 73–97. http://dx.doi.org/10.1016/S1449-4035(05)70050-3.

Fekete, J. 2014. "Federal Government Media Monitoring Keeps Tabs on Political Opponents." *Ottawa Citizen* (Ottawa, ON), 23 September. Accessed 25 January 2015. http://ottawacitizen.com/news/politics/federal-government-media-monitoring-keeps-tabs-on-political-opponents.

Gibson, K., S. O'Donnell, and V. Rideout. 2007. "The Project-Funding Regime: Complications for Community Organizations and their Staff." *Canadian Public Administration* 50 (3): 411–36. http://dx.doi.org/10.1111/j.1754-7121.2007.tb02135.x.

Globe editorial. 2013. "Canada Needs a Proper Census, and It's Not Irresponsible to Say So." *The Globe and Mail* (Toronto, ON), 25 June. Accessed 19 February 2015. http://www.theglobeandmail.com/globe-debate/editorials/canada-needs-a-proper-census-and-its-not-irresponsible-to-say-so/article12793625/.

Government of Canada. 2012. "2012 Federal Budget." Ottawa. Accessed 17 January 2014. http://www.budget.gc.ca/2012/home-accueil-eng.html.

– 2013. "Building Resilience Against Terrorism: Canada's Counter-Terrorism Strategy." 2nd ed. Ottawa. Accessed 25 January 2015. https://www.publicsafety.gc.ca/cnt/rsrcs/pblctns/rslnc-gnst-trrrsm/rslnc-gnst-trrrsm-eng.pdf.

– 2016. *Law Commission of Canada Act*. Ottawa: Justice Laws website. Accessed 12 October 2016. http://laws.justice.gc.ca/eng/acts/L-6.7/page-1.html#h-2.

Hall, M.H. 2005. *Cornerstones of Community: Highlights of the National Survey of Nonprofit and Voluntary Organizations*. Statistics Canada.

Jenson, J., and Phillips, S.D. 2001. "Redesigning the Canadian Citizenship Regime: Remaking the Institutions of Representation." In *Citizenship, Markets, and the State*, edited by C. Crouch, K. Eder, and D. Tambini, 69–89. Oxford: Oxford University Press.

Kirkby, G. "An Uncharitable Chill: A Critical Exploration of How Changes in Federal Policy and Political Climate are Affecting Advocacy-Oriented Charities." Master's Thesis: Royal Roads University, 2014. Accessed 26 January 2015. http://garethkirkby.ca/thesis/posting-final-version/.

Laforest, R. 2011. *Voluntary Sector Organizations and the State*. Vancouver, BC: UBC Press.

– 2012. "Rerouting political representation: is Canada's social infrastructure in crisis?" *British Journal of Canadian Studies* 25 (2): 181–97. http://dx.doi.org/10.3828/bjcs.2012.10.

Lawyers' Rights Watch Canada (LRWC). 2014. "UN Human Rights Council Deputation: The Shrinking Space for Dissent in Canada." LRWC. Accessed 27 January 2014. http://iclmg.cfswpnetwork.ca/wp-content/uploads/sites/37/2014/06/UN+HRC+Shrinking+Space+for+Dissent+in+Canada.23.May_.2014.pdf.

Liberal Party. "Real Change – Canada Revenue Agency." (2015). Accessed 3 January 2016. http://www.liberal.ca/realchange/canada-revenue-agency/.

McCarthy, S. 2012. "Ottawa's New Anti-Terrorism Strategy Lists Eco-Extremists as Threats," *The Globe and Mail*, (Toronto, ON), February 10. Accessed 25 January 2015. http://www.theglobeandmail.com/news/politics/ottawas-new-anti-terrorism-strategy-lists-eco-extremists-as-threats/article533522/.

Meyer, D.S. 2004. "Protest and Political Opportunities." *Annual Review of Sociology* 30 (1): 125–45. http://dx.doi.org/10.1146/annurev.soc.30.012703.110545.

Monsebraaten, L. 2012. "Federal Budget 2012: Ottawa Axes National Council on Welfare." *Toronto Star*, March 30. Accessed 19 February 2015. http://www.thestar.com/news/canada/2012/03/30/federal_budget_2012_ottawa_axes_national_council_on_welfare.html.

Mullaly, B. 1997. *Structural Social Work: Ideology, Theory and Practice*. Don Mills, ON: Oxford University Press.

Munro, M. 2013. "Federal Librarians Fear Being 'Muzzled' Under New Code of Conduct that Stresses 'Duty of Loyalty' to the Government." *National Post*, 15 March. Accessed 10 February 2015. http://news.nationalpost.com/2013/03/15/library-and-archives-canada/.

Muttart Foundation. 2013. "Talking About Charities 2013," Edmonton, AB: Muttart Foundation. Accessed 12 October 2016. https://www.muttart.org/publications/surveys-results/.

National Post. 2006. "Tories' Program Cuts See $1B Savings," *National Post*. (Toronto, ON), 26 September. Accessed 12 October 2016. http://www.pressreader.com/canada/national-post-latest-edition/20060926/281522221573536.

Pal, L.A. 1993. "Advocacy Organizations and Legislative Politics: The Effects of the Charter of Rights and Freedoms on Interest Lobbying of Federal legislation, 1989–91." In *Equity and Community: The Charter, Interest Advocacy and Representation*, 119–57.

Phillips, S.D. 2012. "Dual Restructuring: Civil Society and the Welfare State in Canada, 1985–2005." *British Journal of Canadian Studies* 25 (2): 161–80, 319. http://dx.doi.org/10.3828/bjcs.2012.09.

Putnam, R. 2000. *Bowling Alone: The Collapse and Revival of American Community*. New York, NY: Touchstone.

Raj, A. 2014. "CRA Got Few Complaints About Charities' Politics Prior to 2012," *The Huffington Post Canada*, December 5. Accessed 25 January 2015. http://www.huffingtonpost.ca/2014/12/05/canada-revenue-agency-charities_n_6279178.html?utm_hp_ref=tw.

Rektor, L. 2002. *Advocacy – the Sound of Citizens' Voices. A Position Paper from the Advocacy Working Group*. Ottawa, ON: Government of Canada, Voluntary Sector Initiative Secretariat.

Sen, A. 2009. The Idea of Justice. Cambridge, MA: Harvard University Press.

Sheikh, M.A. 2013. "Good Government and Statistics Canada: The Need for True Independence." *Academic Matters* (May):12–16.

Skocpol, T. 2003. *Diminished Democracy: From Membership to Management in American Civic Life*. Norman, OK: University of Oklahoma Press.

The Progressive Economics Forum. 2014. "Update: A Petition of Academics Against the CCPA Audit." Accessed 27 January 2015. http://www.progressive-economics.ca/2014/09/11/a-petition-of-academics-against-the-ccpa-audit/.

Thompson, E. 2014. "DoJ Hunger Games." *Canadian Lawyer*. 4 August. Accessed 19 February 2015. http://www.canadianlawyermag.com/5219/DoJ-hunger-games.html.

Vaillancourt, Y. 2009. "Social Economy in the Co-Construction of Public Policy." *Annals of Public and Cooperative Economics* 80 (2): 275–313. http://dx.doi.org/10.1111/j.1467-8292.2009.00387.x.

Voices-Voix. 2012. "Canadian Council on Learning." *Voices-Voix*. Accessed 19 February 2015. http://voices-voix.ca/en/facts/profile/canadian-council-learning.

– 2014a. "Canadian Charities and the Canada Revenue Agency". *Voices-Voix*. Accessed 25 2015. http://voices-voix.ca/en/facts/profile/canadian-charities-and-canada-revenue-agency.

– "Environment Canada." 2014b. *Voices-Voix*. Accessed 19 February 2015. http://voices-voix.ca/en/facts/profile/environment-canada

– 2014c. "United Nations Platform for Action Committee". *Voices-Voix*. Accessed 26 January 2015. http://voices-voix.ca/en/facts/profile/united-nations-platform-action-committee.

- 2015a. "Dismantling Democracy: Stifling Debate and Dissent in Canada". *Voices-Voix*. Accessed 9 August 2015. http://voices-voix.ca/sites/voices-voix.ca/files/dismantlingdemocracy_voicesvoix.pdf.
- 2015b. "Human Rights: What the New Government of Canada Must Do." *Voices-Voix*. Accessed 15 February 2017. http://voices-voix.ca/en/document/human-rights-what-new-government-must-do.

# Contributors

FRANÇOIS AUBRY is an economist and a member of the research team at the Laboratoire de recherche sur les pratiques et les politiques sociales. He worked for many years in the research department of the Confédération des syndicats nationaux. His main research interest is the social economy.

MYRLE BALLARD, PhD, is Anishinaabe and has a post-doc in environmental health at the University of Manitoba. She is passionate about her research and advocacy on the environment, sustainable livelihoods, and raising awareness about flooding in her community. She has written technical papers, journal articles, and is a documentary videographer.

ANNA BURROWES received her MPA from the School of Policy Studies, Queen's University and currently works for the BC public service. Her recent academic and professional interests include social policy, non-profit advocacy, community-based research and evaluation, and contemporary social movements.

PETER CLUTTERBUCK is the academic coordinator of the Certificate Program on Community Engagement, Leadership and Development at The Chang School on Continuing Education at Ryerson University. He also works on policy, research, and advocacy issues with the Social Planning Network of Ontario and consults in the non-profit and public sectors.

MARK D'ARCY is a community activist who has worked on environmental issues in New Brunswick with Friends of the UNB Woodlot and the Fredericton Chapter – Council of Canadians. He is the 2012 Phoenix Award recipient from the New Brunswick Environmental Network for his leadership on the shale gas issue.

GLORIA C. DESANTIS, PhD, an assistant professor in the Department of Justice Studies (University of Regina) and founder of the Voluntary Sector Studies Network (Luther College), teaches about advocacy, social justice, and the non-profit sector. She works/volunteers/advocates in the sector and has written technical/policy papers, book chapters, and journal articles.

SUZANNE DUDZIAK, PhD, is an associate professor in the School of Social Work at St Thomas University. Her academic interests include political activism, globalization, social movements, and social development. Before teaching, she worked on policy advocacy initiatives with Aboriginal organizations, unions, and the unemployed in Canada and with community groups in Latin America.

PETER R. ELSON is senior research fellow in the Institute for Community Prosperity at Mount Royal University and adjunct assistant professor, School of Public Administration, University of Victoria. Peter has a MSc in Voluntary Sector Organization (London School of Economics and Political Science) and a PhD in Adult Education and Community Development (University of Toronto). His current research focuses primarily on voluntary sector-provincial government relations; mapping the size, scope and impact of social enterprises across Canada; and public policy engagement by grant-making foundations. He is author of *High Ideals and Noble Intentions: Voluntary Sector-Government Relations in Canada* (2011) and editor of *Funding Policies and the Nonprofit Sector in Western Canada* (2016), both published by the University of Toronto Press.

LYLE FABIAN, a member of K'at'lodeeche First Nation, started his own company, KatloTech Communications Ltd., to help First Nations communities that want to achieve ownership in wireless or fibre technology to support long-term economic gain and independence. Lyle has twelve years of experience in the IT sector, and has earned designations as a Cisco Certified Network Associate and

Fiber Optic Certification from the Fiber Optic Association. His projects include fibreoptic networks installed in K'atl'odeeche First Nation and DeBeers Canada's new Gahcho Kue diamond mine.

CHRISTA FREILER has both "inside" and "outside" experience in anti-poverty policy development and advocacy. She directed the Child Poverty Action Group and worked as a policy assistant to an Ontario cabinet minister. Christa is currently on the board of Legal Aid Ontario and researching what makes cities inclusive.

HEATHER E. HUDSON is an affiliate professor of communications policy at the Institute of Social and Economic Research, University of Alaska, Anchorage. Her research focuses on applications and policies of information and communication technologies for rural and community development. Her latest book is *Connecting Alaskans* (University of Alaska Press, 2015).

RACHEL LAFOREST is an associate professor in the School of Policy Studies at Queen's University. She is the author of *Voluntary Sector Organizations and the State* (2011). She also edited *The New Federal Policy Agenda and the Voluntary Sector: On the Cutting Edge* (2009) and *Government-Nonprofit Relations in Times of Recession* (2013).

CAROL LIAO, PhD/SJD, is an assistant professor in the Allard School of Law at the University of British Columbia. She specializes in corporate law, social enterprise law, and social innovation. Previously, she was a lawyer at Shearman & Sterling LLP in New York. Her research has been published in numerous edited collections and journals.

ROB MCMAHON, PhD, is an assistant professor in the Faculty of Extension at the University of Alberta. He is coordinator and a co-founder of the First Mile Connectivity Consortium, which recently won a Best Practices award from the Canadian Race Relations Foundation (see www.firstmile.ca). His research focuses on how Indigenous peoples and other communities are engaging with the emerging network society.

BONNIE MORTON, BHJ, works with the Regina Anti-Poverty Ministry, which is a social justice ministry. She advocates and educates with and for people living in poverty. Bonnie has written and co-authored numerous article and papers on poverty related issues. Bonnie is completing her Masters in Justice Studies, University of Regina.

NICK J. MULÉ, PhD, is an associate professor in the School of Social Work at York University, where he teaches policy, theory, and practice. He has co-edited LGBTQ *People and Social Work: Intersectional Perspectives* (2015); *Queering Social Work Education* (2016); and *Envisioning* LGBT *Global Human Rights* (2017).

ADAM PARACHIN is an associate professor at the Faculty of Law at Western University. He teaches, researches, and writes in the areas of trusts, estates, and charities law. His research relates predominantly to the legal treatment of "charity," focusing mainly on how charity is privileged and defined in law.

KATHLEEN THOMPSON is the principal researcher at TomKat Communications and the Cannabis Regulatory Research Group. She is also the research director of the Human Rights Research Unit with the International Human Rights Association for American Minorities. Her SSHRC-funded PhD is from the University of Calgary, Faculty of Social Work.

YVES VAILLANCOURT is professor emeritus at the School of Social Work at the Université de Québec à Montréal. He is a member of Laboratoire de recherche sur les pratiques et les politiques sociales and of Centre de recherche sur les innovations sociales.

# Index

Aboriginal Affairs and Northern Development Canada (AANDC), 154, 155, 159, 160, 271
Aboriginal Canada Portal, 278
Aboriginal–non-Aboriginal alliances, 231, 240, 253
Aboriginal non-profits in North: development of ICT4D, 261; digital challenges, 283–4; infrastructure of telecoms and Internet, 267–71, 278, 283; initiatives in ICT4D, 280–1; initiatives in radio and TV broadcasting, 265–7; Internet operators, 268–71; mobilization, 259; networks discussed, 269; policy and regulation of broadcast and telecoms, 273–5; policy and regulation of Internet, 276–85; public policy influence, 260, 300; work with federal government, 277
Aboriginal people: community radio stations, 265, 266; language issues in broadcasting, 265–6; management of broadcasting, 266; population and social issues in North, 262; resources extraction and economy in North, 262; role in ICT4D development, 263; treaty rights, 260, 262. *See also* First Nations
Aboriginal Peoples' Television Network (APTN), 274, 275
Aboriginal Policy Research Conference, 278–9
Accelerated Coverage Plan, 265
Accelerating Social Impact CCC, 98
Access to Information, 309
accountability, as governance criteria, 152, 154–5
adaptability, as governance criteria, 152, 155
"Addition to Reserve" lands, 163
adequacy, 177, 190
advocacy: access to government, 70–1; approaches to, 7–8, 13–14, 15–16; case studies, 22–3, 64; as civic engagement, 6; coalitions (*See* coalitions); *vs.* co-construction of public policy, 205–7; collaborative (*See* collaborative advocacy); community (public)

advocacy (*See* community advocacy); concept of, 202–4; context in Canada, 22; dissociation from, 74–5; environments of, 14–15; evolution in Canada, 3–4, 66–7; experiences and outcomes of, 293–8, 304–5; as function of non-profits, 11–12; funding (*See* funding of advocacy and non-profits); funding cuts (*See* funding cuts/reduction); future of, 83–4; innovative practices, 217, 223–4; insider (institutional) advocacy (*See* insider advocacy); learning about, 315; meanings and boundaries, 5–6, 12, 63–4, 74, 204, 293; negative portrayal of, 69; and news media, 20–1; non-shift in, 305; and participatory governance, 8–10; political (*See* political advocacy); processes and strategies in, 6–7, 22–3, 63–4, 232; reform in law and policy, 314–15; role, 63; shifting terrain (*See* shifting terrain); soiling of, 16–19; terms used in, 13; "terrain" as metaphor, 305; theories of, 7–8; value to public, 18–19

advocacy chill: in coalitions, 65, 66; and Conservative government, 307–10, 314; description and definition, 4, 256n3; and funding cuts, 68–9, 70; and Liberal government, 66; and muzzling, 18; in NB, 252, 254; in Ontario coalitions, 65; and political ideology, 308–9; reasons for, 4; reversal of, 78

Advocacy Working Group (AWG) of the VSI, 314

*Aid/Watch Incorporated v. Commissioner of Taxation* (Australia), 35, 36

"All-Candidates Meetings" in NB, 247, 248

Alward, David, and government, 231

*Amateur Youth Soccer Association v. Canada Revenue Agency*, 49

Amnesty International Trust, non-charitable status, 41, 45

Anik and Anik B satellite, 264, 266, 267

Anishinaabe "pimatiziwin" and "pimachiiywin," 143–4, 149

Anishinabek, vulnerability of, 168

anti-poverty. *See* "poverty" headings

Anti-Poverty Act (Quebec). *See* Quebec Act to Combat Poverty and Social Exclusion

anti-poverty advocacy, approaches to, 187–92. *See also* poverty advocacy

anti-poverty initiatives in SK, 120

anti-poverty movement in Quebec, 207–10

anti-shale gas movement in NB: Aboriginal people in, 231, 240, 253; advocacy activities and strategies, 233–8, 242, 247–8, 251–2; approach of, 238–9; coalition creation and advocacy work, 240–1; coalition members, 232–3, 240–1, 253; economic alternatives to fracking, 238–9, 251–2; in election of 2014, 247, 252; events and actions of, 238–41; *Gasland* screenings, 239–40;

and municipal governments, 252–3; public and insider advocacy, 249–50; public consultations, 231, 250–1, 254; rural areas in, 230–1, 253. *See also* fracking
Anti-Tuberculosis League, 12
*À Part Entière* policy, 218
Arons, A.F., 70–1
asset lock, 91–2, 93, 96, 97
Atkinson Foundation, 182, 183, 185
audits of non-profits: funding increase for, 15, 36; impact on non-profits, 68, 310; introduction of, 4, 68, 307; Policy Statement of CRA, 39; in 2014, 68–9
Australia, political advocacy, 35, 36
awareness organizations, reform of law or policy, 41–2

Baird, John, 309
Bakan, Joel, 101
BC Centre for Social Enterprise, 97
BC Social Innovation Council, 94–5
Bell Canada, 275
Berry, J.M., 70–1
Bill 112 (Quebec). *See* Quebec Act to Combat Poverty and Social Exclusion
Bill 152, the *Poverty Reduction Act* (ON), 185
*Blueprint for Poverty Reduction* (25 in 5), 184
Bouchard, Lucien, and government, 200, 208
*Bowman v. Secular Society*, 38
Bowser, D., 242
*Breaking the Cycle: Ontario's Poverty Reduction Strategy*, 180

British Columbia (BC): community service cooperative, 102, 106–7n8; creation of C3s, 94–5, 98–9; features and regulation of C3s, 95–8; funding cuts by government, 84–5; hybrid legal structures, 83; interest in C3s, 99, 102
*Broadband Canada: Connecting Rural Canadians*, 279
broadband policy in North, 260, 271–3, 276, 279, 282
Broadcasting Act (1991), 267, 273, 274–5, 283
broadcasting in North: Aboriginal initiatives, 265–7; language issues, 265–6; policy and regulation, 260, 273–5, 279–80, 282; radio, 264–5, 266; television, 265–7, 273–5
Browne, P.L., 251
budget of 2012 (federal), 47, 57n2, 68–9
*Building the Information Society: Moving Canada into the 21st Century*, 277
Business Corporations Act (BC), 98

Campaign 2000, 179
Canada Assistance Plan, 112
Canada Business Corporations Act (CBCA), 94, 95
Canada Revenue Agency (CRA). *See* CRA
Canadian Council on Learning, 309
Canadian Federal Court of Appeal, on political advocacy, 35–6
Canadian Human Rights Act, employees with disabilities, 117
Canadian Northern Economic Development Agency (CanNor):

radio and TV broadcasting, 264–7; telecoms and Internet infrastructure, 267–71, 283
Canadian Policy Research Networks, 309
Carrefour de pastorale en monde ouvrier de Québec, 208–9
Carters Professional Association, 14
CBC (Canadian Broadcasting Corporation), in North, 264, 265
Charest, Jean, and government, 221
charitable donations, 52–3, 86
charitable status: and doctrine of political purposes, 47–9; eligibility/ineligibility, 17, 37; fiscal aspects, 48–9; and law of charity, 37, 47–9; and political activity, 34, 40, 295; and public benefit, 44–6; and reform of law or policy, 41–2; revoking of, 17; self-censorship by charities, 42; shifting terrain, 37; 10 per cent rule, 40
charities. *See* non-profit sector and organizations
"Charities and their Participation in Political Activities" (video, CRA), 14
Charities Directorate of the CRA, 34, 36
charity: and government programming, 52; *vs.* government/state, 51–6; legal meaning, 37–8
charity law. *See* law of charity
Child, C.D., 76
child poverty, 176–7, 178–9, 180, 192
Child Poverty Action Group (CPAG), 176–7, 178

Child Poverty Report Card, 179
civic engagement, 6
civil society, definition, 203
coalitions (advocacy coalitions): advocacy chill in, 65, 66; description and definition, 8, 64, 65; dissociation from advocacy, 74–5; finances and resources, 67; framework for, 8; in Ontario (*See* Ontario coalitions); as strategy, 65, 66–7, 72, 299; tensions and reflexive process in, 303; ties between, 77–8. *See also* specific coalitions in case studies
co-construction of public policy: *vs.* advocacy, 205–7; Bill 112 and Anti-Poverty Act, 216, 222–4; civil society in public policy, 205–6, 219, 301; democratic aspect of, 206, 207, 222; description, 301; and new government, 221–2; for poverty and social exclusion, 223; stakeholder participation, 218–19, 222–4
*A Code of Good Practice on Policy Dialogue*, 12
co-empowerment, 115
collaboration: definition and success factors, 114; in initiatives in SK, 121–2, 124–5
collaborative advocacy: disability income program in SK, 124–5; DISC and government, 114–16, 118, 122, 124–5, 127–9, 133–5, 136; early initiatives in SK, 118–19; interventions and actions in, 116; limitations in, 302; as model, 114–15, 301–2; process goals and empowerment, 115–

16. *See also* co-construction of public policy
collective advocacy, 7, 8
Collective for a Law on the Elimination of Poverty (Collectif pour un Québec sans pauvreté): in mobilization, 208–11, 219–20; on national action plans, 214–15
*Commissioners for Special Purposes of the Income Tax v. Pemsel*, 38
common law, and charitable status, 37
Communications Technology Satellite (Hermes), 266
community advocacy: adequacy in PRS, 190; and agendas, 193; in anti-shale gas movement, 249–50; definition, 188, 249; disadvantages, 188–9; *vs.* insider advocacy, 187–9, 299; and public policy, 300–1
community contribution company (C3): as alternative model, 303–4; creation in BC, 94–5, 98–9; features and regulation of, 95–8, 303–4; interest in BC, 99, 102
community interest company (CIC): as model for C3s, 95–6; in United Kingdom, 89, 90, 91–4, 97–8
community service cooperative, 102, 106–7n8
*Connecting Canadians*, 277–8, 279
Conservation Council of New Brunswick (CCNB), 239, 240
Conservative government: and advocacy chill, 307–10, 314; audits of non-profits and use of CRA, 4, 15, 307, 310; broadband policies in North, 279, 282; criticism of by non-profits, 69–70, 307, 308; doctrine of political purposes, 36; environmental regulation dismantling, 240; funding cuts in advocacy, 3–4, 15, 68; political advocacy attacks, 36, 308–11, 314; surveillance of non-profits, 15, 307; use of services from non-profits, 69–70
constitutional rights approaches, 15–16
Coon, David, 252
co-production of public policy, 205–6
corporate entities, as form for non-profits, 83
corporatist co-construction of public policy, 206–7, 219
courts: and doctrine of political purposes, 44–9; legal meaning of charity, 37; neutrality of, 45–6; on political advocacy, 39; and reform of law or policy, 41–2
CPS-022 (CRA) circular/policy statement, 14, 39, 40, 84
CRA (Canada Revenue Agency): audits of non-profits (*See* audits of non-profits); docs. no. 2012-0454251E5 and 2012-0468581E5, 84; and factual information, 55–6; funding increase for audits, 15, 36; law interpretation, 39; permissible activities of non-profits, 17, 84; Policy Statement (CPS-022), 14, 39, 40, 84; and political advocacy, 39–41, 308, 314; and public awareness, 34; regulation of non-profits, 14; revenue

generation by non-profits, 84; 10 per cent rule, 40; terms for non-profits, 11; use by Conservative government, 307, 310
Craig, G., 194
Croll, David, 172, 174
*Crossroads for Canada* (Campaign 2000), 179
CRTC (Canadian Radio-Television and Telecommunications Commission) in North: broadcasting, 265, 273; digital ICTs, 276; policy, 283; regulation of ICTs, 271, 272, 274, 275, 284–5
cuts in funding. *See* funding cuts/reduction

de-democratization process, 311, 314, 315
deep poverty in Ontario, 174, 190–1
democracy: de-democratization and re-democratization process, 311, 314, 315; disadvantage of non-profits, 311; and governance, 9–10, 76–7; participatory democracy, 246–8, 249, 250–3, 254; role of non-profits in, 311–12
democratic co-construction of public policy. *See* co-construction of public policy
Department of Communications (later in Industry Canada), 264, 266, 271
Department of Justice, 309
DeSantis, Gloria, 6–7, 204–5, 232, 252, 256n3
digital infrastructure and technologies. *See* Internet in North

diluted advocacy, 71, 72
disabilities, international and federal initiatives, 116–17. *See also* people with disabilities
*The Disability Inclusion Policy Framework: Government's Response to the Saskatchewan Council on Disability Issues' Disability Action Plan,* 120–1
Disability Income Program Task Team, 121, 134
Disability Income Support Coalition (DISC): challenges, 132–3; collaborative advocacy, 114–16, 122, 125, 127–9, 133–5, 136; events timeline, 122; funding cuts, 132, 133, 135; goal, 110, 113, 127, 133; ground rules, 121–2; key principles and vision, 113–14; members, 110, 112–13, 132; new disability income program in SK, 121–2; partner organizations, 122, 123; public education, 127–8; and shifting terrain, 132–3; task team for disability income, 125; working relationship with government, 121; work model and lens adopted, 113. *See also* Saskatchewan Assured Income for Disability (SAID)
Disability Income Task Team, development of SAID, 111
Disaster Financial Assistance Arrangement (DFAA), 153–4
discourse: definition, 12–13; and shifting terrain, 12–14, 16, 298–304, 305
dividend cap, 91, 92, 93, 97
doctrine of political purposes: and charitable status, 47–9;

description and implications, 34–5, 36; and elections and campaigns, 34; excessiveness of, 55; fiscal/tax considerations, 47–50; and freedom of expression, 47; impact on charities, 44; law and regulations, 34–6, 44; legal restrictions' rise, 37–41; liberal trend outside Canada, 35; and political advocacy, 47–8; prejudice towards perspectives, 42–3; rationales by courts, 44–9; reforms proposed, 50–7; regulatory impact on operations, 41–4; and role of non-profits, 34; and self-censorship, 42; shifting terrain, 35, 50, 295–6
donations, 52–3, 86
Downtown Chaplaincy (now the Regina Anti-Poverty Ministry), 120
Draimin, Tim, 86
Drummond Report, 186
Duncan, Dwight, 184
Duncan, John, 160
Du pain et des roses (Bread and Roses March), 207–8
"duty to consult" First Nations, 15–16, 154, 161, 162, 231

Economic and Employment Summit (Quebec), 208
economic efficiency, as governance criteria, 152–3
educational charities, 40, 43
electioneering, 39, 50–1, 55
elections and campaigns, 17, 34
Elections New Brunswick, 252
Employment Equity Act, 116–17
empowerment of members, 115–16

environmental regulation, dismantling of, 239, 240, 242–6
Environment Canada, 309
*Equal Citizenship for Canadians with Disabilities*, 117
equity, as governance criteria, 152, 153–4
ethical approaches, as ideology, 15
Evans, B.M., 10
Evers, A., 203, 205
evidence-based practices/policies: impact on advocacy, 77, 302; and Ontario coalitions, 75–6, 77; and political advocacy, 308, 310

far North. *See* North (Northern Canada)
Federal Court of Appeal, 49
federal government: and Aboriginal non-profits, 277; advocacy support and funding, 67–9; broadband policy in North, 271–3; broadcasting policy in North, 273–4, 279–80, 282; budget of 2012, 47, 57n2, 68–9; compensation for flood victims, 153–4; C3S creation, 95; environmental regulation dismantling, 240; failure of participatory governance, 9–10, 168–9; flood in LSMFN territory, 9–10, 141, 160–1, 168–9; hybrids creation, 94; influence on provincial governments, 68, 69; initiatives on disabilities, 116–17; jurisdiction of First Nations, 160, 167; participation of non-profits, 10; poverty initiatives in 1960s–70s, 174–5; Program Review (1994–97), 69; public

and non-profit criticism of, 47,
  78, 307; public policy and
  legislation for First Nations,
  145–9; in shifting terrain, 14–15
Federal Task Force on Disability
  Issues, 117
*Final Recommendations of the
  Task Team of Income Support
  for People with Disabilities,*
  122–4, 133
First Mile Connectivity Consortium
  (FMCC), 284–5
First Nations: "Addition to
  Reserve," 163; anti-shale gas
  resistance, 231, 253; assimilation
  by policy, 145; compensation for
  disasters, 153–4; digital strategy
  for ICT4D, 279; "duty to consult,"
  15–16, 154, 161, 162, 231;
  IdleNoMore, 240; importance of
  water to, 152; Internet and digital
  operators, 270–1; jurisdiction by
  federal government, 160, 167;
  non-profits (*See* Aboriginal non-
  profits in North); public policies
  and legislation on, 145–9;
  riparian rights, 149–50. *See also*
  Aboriginal people; Lake St
  Martin First Nation (LSMFN)
  community
First Nations Infrastructure Fund
  (FNIF), 271
First Nations Innovation project,
  283–4
*Flooding Hope: The Lake St.
  Martin First Nation Story*
  (video), 159
flood of 2011 in Manitoba. *See*
  Lake St Martin First Nation
  (LSMFN) community

for-profit actors: advantage with
  government, 311; in hybrid legal
  structures, 88–9, 93, 100–2,
  103–4; and social enterprises, 88
fracking: description, 230;
  economic alternatives to, 238–9,
  251–2; environmental regulation
  dismantling, 239; impact and
  safety, 231; moratoriums, 231; in
  NB, 230–1, 239, 249; and
  neoliberal ideology, 232; political
  agreement in NB, 232; public
  input, 231–2; public resistance
  (*See* anti-shale gas movement
  in NB)
freedom of expression, 47
funding cuts/reduction: advocacy
  and non-profits, 3–4, 15, 68–71,
  297–8; and advocacy chill, 68–9,
  70; and criticism of government,
  69–70; in DISC, 132, 133, 135;
  and fear and stigma of advocacy,
  75–6, 77; in ICT4D, 282; impact
  on activities, 71–2, 74–5, 82,
  86–7, 294, 297–8; in Ontario,
  70–5; overall situation, 84–6,
  297; and soiling of advocacy, 17,
  18; for SPNO, 185; strategies
  resulting from, 71–2, 74–5
funding of advocacy and non-
  profits: core *vs.* project-based,
  69, 71; cuts in (*See* funding cuts/
  reduction); and dissociation from
  advocacy, 74–5; by federal
  government, 67–9; funding
  sources dilemma, 84–7; by
  government, 67–9, 85; and
  muzzling, 17–18, 70; as necessity
  for non-profits, 84–6, 296–7; and
  role of non-profits, 86–7; self-

restriction by non-profits, 69;
and shifting terrain, 67–9; social
enterprises and hybrids, 88–9
funding relationships, muzzle
clauses, 17–18

*Gasland* documentary, 239–40
geography, impact on advocacy, 16
Good, T., 241
governance: and democracy, 9–10,
76–7; description, 8; evaluation
criteria, 152–5; and neoliberal
ideology, 9, 20; of water, 152. *See
also* participatory governance
governance theories in collective
advocacy, 8
*Government Action Plan for
Solidarity and Social inclusion
2010–2015: Quebec's
Mobilization against Poverty*, 215
Government of Manitoba and
LSMFN: consultation of LSMFN,
154–5, 161–2, 166–8; "duty to
consult," 162; failure of good
governance, 155, 168–9; flood
management, 140, 143, 161–2;
governance criteria in flood
crisis, 152–5; housing and
relocation, 161, 163, 166;
jurisdiction of LSMFN, 160, 161–
2, 167–8; view of waterways,
150; water management, 162
Government of New Brunswick:
corporate influence on, 241–2;
economic role of fracking, 238–
9; environmental regulation
dismantling, 242–6; public and
insider advocacy, 249–50; public
input on fracking, 231–2, 252,
254; resource extraction, 242;
shale gas development safety and
impact, 231
Government of Nunavut, broadband
policy and regulation, 276
Government of Ontario: Bill 152,
the *Poverty Reduction Act*, 185;
outreach work, 183; poverty
initiatives pre-PRS, 177, 178;
poverty reduction policy in
1990s, 180; poverty reduction
strategy, 173, 180–1, 183
Government of Quebec: action
plans of Anti-Poverty Act, 213–
15; draft and petition from
public for Bill 112, 210; poverty
policy and strategy, 210; public
policy initiatives, 200–1
Government of Saskatchewan:
benefits in SAID, 126–7;
collaborative advocacy, 118,
124–5, 129, 133–5, 136; costs
assistance plan, 119–20; cross-
department work, 120, 121;
disability strategies, 118, 119–21;
new disability income program,
122; task team for disability
income, 121, 122–6; working
relationship with DISC, 121
government/state: access by non-
profits, 70–1; charitable status
eligibility/revoking, 17, 37; *vs.*
charity, 51–6; corruption of, 242;
dialogue with non-profits, 315;
disadvantage of non-profits, 311,
313; funding of non-profits, 85;
programming and charities, 52;
social investment state, 203; and
soiling of advocacy, 16, 17;
subsidy to charities, 48, 53
Graefe, P., 187, 190

Greason, V., 217
"Great Resource Giveaway" teach-ins, 242, 247, 248
Gronbjerg, K.A., 76
Guillemard, A.-M., 203
GwaiiTel, 270
Gwaii Trust, 270

Haida Gwaii, 270
Harding, Matthew, 52
Harper government. *See* Conservative government
Harris, Mike, and government, 70, 180
Healthy Food Supplement (HFS), in PRS, 184–5, 190, 191
high frequency (HF) radios, 268
House of Commons Standing Committee, Industry Canada, 95
House of Commons Standing Committee on Industry, Science, and Technology, 86, 94
Hudson, C.A., 187, 190
Hudson, H.E., 267
*Human Life International in Canada Inc. v. M.N.R.*, 45, 49
hybrid legal structures: Anglo-American spectrum of, 89, 90; in BC, 83; in Canada, 94; CICs, 89, 90, 91–4, 97–8; C3s, 94–9, 102; emergence, 88–91; for-profit actors in, 88–9, 93, 100–2, 103–4; interest in, 100, 102–3, 104, 105; intermingling of profit and advocacy, 88–9, 93, 96, 98, 100; legislation for, 83; and neoliberal ideology, 101; non-profits in, 88–9, 101–2; potential risks and benefits, 102–5; and power, 101–2

hydraulic fracturing. *See* fracking
hydroelectric projects, and floods, 150

ICT4D (information and communication technologies for development) in North: digital challenges, 283–4; diversity in groups involved, 266; funding cuts/reduction, 282; infrastructure development, 278; initiatives, 280–1; origins, 264; as process, 260–1; projects and stakeholders, 263; regulation and policy in, 271–3, 279–80, 282, 283–5; strategy development, 276–83
ICTs (information and communication technologies) in North: development of, 259–60; origins and history, 264–5; participatory communications, 261–3; policy responsibility, 271–2; provincial and territorial aspects, 261–2; public policy development by non-profits, 259–60, 300; regulation and policy, 271–3, 274, 275, 283–5; technical characteristics, 261
idealism, 33
ideological landscape, in shifting terrain, 15–16
IdleNoMore, 240
Imagine Canada, 14, 67
Income Security Advocacy Centre (ISAC), 182
income supports for people with disabilities: and costs of disability, 131; description, 111–12; in disability action plan in SK, 119; and DISC, 113–14, 121–

2; early initiatives, 117; public education in SK, 128; task team for disability income in SK, 121, 122–6

income tax: and charities *vs.* government, 52–3; and doctrine of political purposes, 47–50; as state subsidy, 48, 53

Income Tax Act: amendments in budget of 2012, 57n2; changes in, 14; permissible activities of non-profits, 17; and political activity, 17, 39–40, 57n2, 84; on political advocacy, 39

Independent Living Movement (ILM), 218

Indian Act, 145, 147, 158, 160

Indigenous and Northern Affairs Canada (INAC) (formerly AANDC), 271

Indigenous people. *See* Aboriginal people

Information Highway Advisory Council (IHAC), 277

Innovation, Science and Economic Development (ISED) (formerly Industry Canada), 271–2

insider advocacy: as approach, 13–14; *vs.* community advocacy, 187–9, 299; dangers of, 13–14, 193–4; definition, 188, 249; disadvantages, 187–8, 189; limits of, 173, 250; and political accommodation, 187, 188; and poverty advocacy, 193–4; in PRS, 173, 182–3, 187–9

institutional advocacy. *See* insider advocacy

Interfaith Social Assistance Reform Coalition (ISARC), 182, 186, 189

inter-group cooperation, 115, 129

International Charter of Good Practice in Using Public Private Dialogue for Private Sector Development, 100

International Classification of Nonprofit Organizations, 11

Internet in North: challenges, 283–4; infrastructure and operators, 267–71, 283; policy and regulation, 260, 271–3, 276–85

Inuit, 265–7, 276. *See also* Aboriginal people

Inuit Broadcasting Corporation (IBC), 267, 276

Inuit Tapirisat (now Inuit Tapiriit Kanatami), 267

Inukshuk project, 267

Irving family, 242

Jenkins-Smith, H.C., 8

Johns Hopkins Comparative Nonprofit Sector Project (CNP), 85, 86

justice and marginalization, 19–20

Kairos North East Justice, 159

K'atl'odeeche First Nation, 270

KFN Community Network, 270, 283

KNET (Kuh-ke-nah Network), 268–9, 279

Laboratoire de recherche sur les pratiques et les politiques sociales (LAREPPS), 202–3

Laforest, R., 10

Lake St Martin First Nation (LSMFN) community and 2011 flood: Anishinaabe philosophy, 143–4, 149–50; community development work by, 165–7; compensation for victims, 153–4; consultation by government, 154–5, 161–2, 166–8; deaths during crisis, 156–7; demonstrations, 163, 164; description and location of LSMFN, 141–2, 149; "duty to consult," 15–16, 154, 161, 162; environmental advocacy, 159; evacuees' struggles, 143, 155, 156–9; and federal government, 9–10, 141, 160–1, 168–9; flood description, 150; flood management by government, 140, 143, 161–2; flood problem history, 149–52; food allowances and dietary needs, 155, 156; governance criteria, 152–5; governments role in problems, 140–1, 143, 300–1; homes and property, 158–9; impact of flood and displacement, 140–1, 143–4, 149, 150–1, 155–6; jurisdiction issues, 160, 161–2, 167–8; lack of advocacy during crisis, 141; meaning of advocacy for, 144; non-profits failure, 10, 141, 155–6, 157–8; participatory governance failure, 9–10, 140–1, 155, 160–5, 167–9; radar base and Halaburda site, 161, 166; relocation, 161, 163, 166; site 9 for settlement, 163, 165, 168

Lamarche, L., 209

Landry, Bernard, and government, 210, 220

Lang, S., on insider and public advocacy, 173, 188, 189, 193, 249, 250

languages, in Northern broadcasting, 265–6

Lankin, Frances, 185

LaPierre, Louis, 231

Law Commission of Canada, 309

law of charity: charitable status, 37, 47–9; and doctrine of political purposes, 34–41, 44; fiscal aspects, 48–9; ineligibility of non-profits, 37; meaning and classification of "charity," 37–8; perfection of, 44–5; on political advocacy, 35–6, 38–41, 47, 57; and public benefit, 44–6; reform (*See* reform in law and policy); role of non-profits, 33, 34–5; shifting terrain of restrictions, 37–41

legal approaches, as ideology, 15

legislation: dismantling of environmental law, 239, 240, 242–6; for First Nations, 145–9; hybrid legal structures, 83. *See also* regulations

Leonard, Craig, 252

Liberal Party: and advocacy chill, 66; audits of non-profits, 15, 36, 306; promise of, 306, 311–12, 313, 314

Library and Archives Canada, 309

lobbying, 50–1, 55, 203–4

lobbyist registries, non-profits in, 17

long-form census, 309–10

McFarland, J., 241

*McGovern v. Attorney-General*, 41, 45

McGuinty, Dalton, and government, 173, 180, 181, 184, 186

Macnaghten, Lord, 38
Magnusson, W., 252
*Managing Bandwidth – Nunavut's Road Ahead*, 276
Manitoba (MB): failure of participatory governance with LSMFN, 9–10, 140–1, 155, 160–5, 167–9; flood control, 149; flood problems history, 149–52; superflood of 2011 (*See* Lake St Martin First Nation (LSMFN) community). *See also* Government of Manitoba
Manitoba Association of Native Fire Fighters (MANFF), 154, 155
marginalized societal issues: participation in, 19–20; role of non-profits, 34
Martin, Paul, 105
Mason, M., 99
Matthews, Deb, 180, 183
media: in advocacy, 20–1; ownership in NB, 241–2, 246–7
member empowerment, 115–16
Mennonite Central Committee (MCC), 158
Metcalf Foundation, 182
Ministry of Social Development and Social Innovation (BC), 94
mission drift, 71, 72
Mouterde, P., 200
multilevel governance in Canada, 9
municipal governments, in anti-shale gas movement, 252–3
muzzling and muzzle clauses, 16–18, 70

*National Anti-Vivisection Society v. I.R.C.*, 41
National Broadband Task Force, 277

National Campaign 2000, 179
National Council of Welfare (NCW), 175, 309
*The National Strategy to Combat Poverty and Social Exclusion* (Quebec), 210
National Survey of Nonprofit and Voluntary Organizations (NSNVO), 84–5
Native Communication Society, 276
neoliberal ideology and neoliberalism: definition and goal of, 9, 20; and fracking in NB, 232; and governance, 9, 20; in hybrids, 101; and poverty advocacy, 193; poverty policy in Ontario, 180; public policy in Quebec, 200; *vs.* social justice, 20; use for non-profits, 87
New Brunswick (NB): advocacy chill, 252, 254; anti-shale gas movement (*See* anti-shale gas movement in NB); corporate influence in, 241–2, 246–7; democracy and public engagement, 246–8, 249, 250–3, 254; "duty to consult", 231; economic alternatives to fracking, 238–9, 251–2; election of 2014, 247, 252; environmental regulation dismantling, 239, 242–6; fracking exploration, 230–1, 239, 249; media ownership, 241–2, 246–7; political agreement on fracking, 232; public consultations, 231, 250–1, 254; resource extraction, 230,

242, 248; rural–urban alliance, 253. *See also* Government of New Brunswick
New Brunswick Anti-Shale Gas Alliance (NBASGA), 232
New Brunswick Environmental Network (NBEN), 232, 240
new media (online), 21
news media (traditional), 20–1
*News to You Canada v. Minister of National Revenue*, 36
New Zealand, political advocacy, 35, 36
Nixon, Robert, 178
*Nobody Left Behind!*, 210
Noël, Alain, 221
non-charitable advocacy, 50–1
non-profit–facilitated collective advocacy. *See* advocacy
nonprofit organizational theories, 8
non-profit sector and organizations (non-profits): Aboriginal organizations (*See* Aboriginal non-profits in North); activities undertaken, 11–12; advocacy (*See* advocacy); alternative forms of corporate entities, 83; audits (*See* audits of non-profits); challenges and opportunities, 312–14; definition and description, 11, 24n1; funding (*See* funding of advocacy and non-profits); funding cuts (*See* funding cuts/reduction); labels and categories for, 10–11; non-shift in advocacy, 305; overview, 10–12; and power, 101–2; revenue generation, 84; role and relationships of, 33–4, 82; size and diversity in Canada, 11, 306, 312; value to public, 18–19. *See also* third sector organizations (TSOs); specific topics
non-shift in advocacy, 305
Northern Gateway Pipeline, 68
Northern Indigenous Community Satellite Network (NICSN), 269–70
Northern Native Broadcast Access Program, 273
Northern Native Broadcasting Policy, 267, 273, 274
North (Northern Canada): Aboriginal non-profits in (*See* Aboriginal non-profits in North); Aboriginal population and social issues, 262; definition, 261; development of ICTs, 259–60; digital challenges, 283–4; diversity in groups involved, 266; high frequency radios, 268; ICT and ICT4D regulation and policy, 260, 271–3, 274, 275, 276–85; Internet/digital technologies (*See* Internet in North); language issues in broadcasting, 265–6; management of broadcasting, 266; participatory communication, 261–3; radio and TV broadcasting, 264–7; resources extraction and economy, 262; telephone services, 268; traditional communications, 264. *See also* ICT4D
Northwestel, 284
Nova Scotia, C3s in, 95
Novick, M., 192
numbered treaties, 141–2, 145, 149

Nunavut Broadband Development Corporation (NBDC), 270, 276
Nunavut Implementation Commission, 276

Office of Disability Issues (ODI), 118, 134
omnibus bills C-38 and C-45, 240
*On Equal Terms*, 218
online media, 21
Ontario (ON): coalitions in (*See* Ontario coalitions); deep poverty, 174, 190–1; early community work, 176–7; election of 2007, 181–2; evidence-based practices, 75–6; funding cuts, 70–5; poverty levels, 191, 192; poverty policy and initiatives, 175–80; poverty reduction and elimination, 172–4, 194; poverty reduction strategy (*See* poverty reduction strategy (PRS) in Ontario); shifting terrain, 70–4; strategies in poverty advocacy, 177–9; welfare system review, 177, 190–1. *See also* Government of Ontario
Ontario Campaign 2000, 182
Ontario Child Benefit (OCB), 180
Ontario coalitions: access to government, 71; advocacy chill, 65; areas of struggle, 64; as case study, 64; coalitions in study, 65–6; and evidence-based practices, 75–6, 77; fear and stigma in advocacy, 75–6, 77; funding sources, 66; funding strategies from cuts, 71–2, 74–5; internalization of norms, 64; membership types and involvement, 66, 72–3; mission drift, 72; poverty advocacy pre-PRS, 178–9; for PRS, 172–4; as solution to funding cuts, 72–3. *See also* poverty reduction strategy (PRS) in Ontario
Ostrom, E., 152
"outsider" advocacy. *See* community advocacy

Pallotta, Dan, 86–7
Parizeau, Jacques, and government, 208
Parker, Lord, 38
Parkes, T., 194
participatory communication, in North, 261–3
participatory democracy, in anti-shale gas movement, 246–8, 249, 250–3, 254
participatory governance: and advocacy, 8–10; failure in LSMFN flood, 9–10, 140–1, 155, 160–5, 167–9
people with disabilities: calls for separate program in SK, 118–19, 120; citizen participation, 218; costs of disability, 131; disability action plan in SK, 119–20; early initiatives in SK, 117–19; employment of, 116–17, 119; extra and occasional costs, 112, 119–20; federal initiatives, 116–17; income supports (*See* income supports for people with disabilities); new disability income program in SK, 121–2; public education in SK, 127–8; task team for disability income

in SK, 121, 122–6; and welfare system, 111, 112
Peterson, David, 177
Phillips, S.D., 69–70
Pickard, V., 260
Pinaymootang community, 157
Plan Institute for Caring Citizenship (Tyze), 94
policy-making processes, 9, 75–6, 77, 302
Policy Statement (CPS-022) of CRA, 14, 39, 40, 84
political accommodation, and insider advocacy, 187, 188
political activity, 34, 36, 295–6; in Income Tax Act, 17, 39–40, 57n2, 84
political advocacy: amendments in budget of 2012, 57n2; attacks by Conservative government, 36, 308–11, 314; Canadian and international law, 35–6; as communication, 311; court decisions on, 39; CRA and Income Tax Act, 39–41, 308, 314; and doctrine of political purposes, 47–8; educational charities, 40; legal restrictions, 38–41, 47, 57; non-charitable advocacy, 50–1; and public benefit, 45–6; regulations on, 34; 10 per cent rule, 40
political environment, in shifting terrain, 14–15, 306–7
political purposes doctrine. *See* doctrine of political purposes
poverty: and "adequacy" principle, 177; child poverty, 176–7, 178–9, 180, 192; and co-construction of public policy, 223; deep poverty in Ontario, 174, 190–1; defined in Quebec's Anti-Poverty Act, 212; early community work in Ontario, 176–7; federal initiatives in 1960s–70s, 174–5; minority report of 1971, 175; participation of poor and excluded, 217–19; policy and initiatives in Ontario, 175–80; public policy in since 1960s, 174–9. *See also* anti-poverty
poverty advocacy: approaches to, 174, 187–92; assessment, 192–3; challenges, 193; coalition-building for PRS, 181–4; coalition fragmentation in PRS, 184–7; coalitions pre-PRS, 178–9; coalition themes for PRS, 182–3; community *vs.* insider advocacy, 187–9; importance, 172; and insider advocacy, 187–9, 193–4; members in PRS coalition, 182, 186; national coalition, 178–9; and neoliberalism, 193; in Ontario election of 2007, 181–2; response to PRS, 180–1; shifting strategies in, 177–9; shifting terrain of discourses, 16; social justice *vs.* poverty alleviation approaches, 187–92
poverty alleviation/reduction: as approach, 174; *vs.* eradication, 191–2; in Ontario, 173–4, 180, 194 (*See also* poverty reduction strategy (PRS) in Ontario); *vs.* social justice advocacy, 187–92
poverty elimination/eradication: *vs.* alleviation, 191–2; government action and commitment, 172, 178; initiatives, 176–7, 178; in

Ontario, 194; in Quebec, 208–9; report cards, 179
Poverty Free Ontario (PFO), 173, 174, 185–6, 187, 191–2
*Poverty Reduction Act* (Bill 152) (Ontario), 185
poverty reduction strategy (PRS) in Ontario (2007–13): and adequacy, 190; assessment, 192–3; building of coalition, 181–4; coalition in, 173–4; development, 173–4; divergent approaches to, 174; evaluation and response to by coalition, 180–1; and financial crisis, 184; fragmentation of coalition, 184–7; funding, 186; government outreach work, 183; Healthy Food Supplement (HFS), 184–5, 190, 191; insider *vs.* community advocacy, 173, 187–9; members of coalition, 182, 186; political accommodation in, 188; problems in coalition, 173, 174; release by government, 180–1; strategy of coalition, 173; themes of coalition, 182–3; timeline of coalition, 186
power, in non-profits and hybrids, 101–2
private sector. *See* for-profit actors
proactive social investment state, 203
Program Implementation Advisory Team (PIAT), 125–6, 129, 133, 134
Program Review (1994–97), 69
Project Peacemakers, 159
provinces and territories. *See* specific provinces or territories

provincial governments: Aboriginal population and social issues, 262; disabilities initiatives, 117; federal influence on, 68, 69; funding cuts of non-profits, 4; and ICTs, 261–2; jurisdiction of First Nations, 167; non-profits criticism of, 78; water governance, 152. *See also* specific Governments
Provincial Interagency Network on Disabilities (PIND), 117–19, 128, 134
PRS. *See* poverty reduction strategy (PRS) in Ontario
public advocacy. *See* community advocacy
public awareness, 34, 35, 55–6
public benefit, and charitable status, 44–6
public education, 127–8, 308, 310
public policy: activities and role of non-profits, 11–12, 33; co-construction (*See* co-construction of public policy); and community advocacy, 300–1; community participation, 207–10, 216–17; co-production of, 205–6; definition, 6; evolution in, 9; and First Nations, 145–9; influence of Aboriginal non-profits, 260, 300; initiatives in Quebec, 200–1; legal restrictions in political advocacy, 39; and public education, 128; reform (*See* reform in law and policy)
public policy advocacy. *See* advocacy
public policy environment, in shifting terrain, 16
public policy-making theories, 8

Public Safety Canada, 153–4
Put Food in the Budget (PFIB) campaign, 185, 186, 190–1
Putnam, R., 77

Qiniq network, 176, 270–1
Quebec (QC): citizen and stakeholder participation, 217–19; community participation in policy and reform, 207–10, 216–17; march of June 1995, 207–8; poverty elimination, 208–9; public policy initiatives, 200–1; social welfare and poverty reform, 208–9. *See also* Government of Quebec
Quebec Act to Combat Poverty and Social Exclusion (Anti-Poverty Act): action plans of government, 213–15, 221; coalition in, 207; and co-construction of public policy, 216, 222–4; community and civil society in, 212–13, 214–15, 219–20, 223–4; contents description, 211–13; definition of "poverty," 212; draft and proposal by community, 209–10; emergence of, 207–10; implementation 2003–13, 211–16; innovative advocacy practices, 217, 223–4; institutions created, 215–16; mobilization and interactions, 207–10; national strategy in, 212–13; and new government, 221–2; and original objectives, 211; participation of poor and excluded, 217–19; petition for, 210; political actors in, 210, 216, 220; preamble and purpose, 211–12; resilience of, 221–2; tabling and passing of, 210
Quebec Women's Federation, 207

radios and radio broadcasting, 264–5, 266
rational choice theories, 8
*The Real Poverty Report* (Adams et al.), 175
*Reconcile Freedom and Social Justice: A Challenge for the Future*, 213–14
Red Cross, in 2011 flood, 155, 158
re-democratization process, 314
reduction in funding. *See* funding cuts/reduction
reform in law and policy: for advocacy in Canada, 314–15; legal restrictions in political advocacy, 39; as non-charitable activity, 41–2, 44; prejudice towards perspectives, 43; and public benefit, 44–5, 46; role of non-profits, 33, 34
Regina (SK), services delivery, 130
Regina Welfare Rights Centre, 120
registered charity, 10–11, 17, 295
registered non-profits, 11
*Re Greenpeace* (New Zealand), 35, 36
regulations: activities of non-profits, 14; of CICs, 91–3; of CRA, 14; of C3s, 96–8; and doctrine of political purposes, 35; impact on non-profits, 41–4; on political advocacy, 34; shifting terrain, 14
regulations in case studies: dismantling of environmental regulations, 239, 240, 242–6; ICT

and ICT4D in North, 260, 271–3, 274, 275, 276–85
Reiser, Brakman, 93
*Re Positive Action Against Pornography and M.N.R.*, 45
research, and evidence-based practices, 75–6
*The Revolution Will Not Be Funded*, 10
riparian rights, 149–50
Roeher Institute, 218
rural communities/areas: alliance with urban areas, 253; mobilization, 230–1, 239–40; participatory communications in North, 261–3

Sabatier, P., 8
Sabine, 193
SARC-Public Awareness Campaign (SARC-PAC), 178
Saskatchewan (SK): anti-poverty initiatives, 120; calls for separate disability benefit program, 118–19, 120; collaborative work, 121–2, 124–5; disability income program, 122–6; initiatives on disability, 117–19; Provincial Interagency Network on Disabilities (PIND), 117–19, 128, 134; public education on people with disabilities, 127–8. *See also* Government of Saskatchewan
*Saskatchewan Assistance Plan Regulations*, 120
Saskatchewan Assured Income for Disability (SAID): beginning of program, 126–7; benefits and funds received, 110–11, 126–7; challenges in, 129–30, 131–3; as collaboration, 111; costs of disability, 131; critical analysis of outcomes, 129–32; disability income program, 124, 125; establishment and development of, 110, 132–6; events timeline, 122; impact on beneficiaries, 131–2; PIAT, 125–6, 129; service delivery issues, 130, 131–2; success factors, 134–5; terminology in, 127; and welfare program, 126, 131
Saskatchewan Council on Disability Issues, 118, 119, 120
*Saskatchewan's Disability Action Plan*, 119–20
Saskatoon (SK), services delivery, 30
Satellite Account, 86
Schragge, E., 249, 250
Scott, Katherine, 69
self-censorship, 42
Selinger, Greg, 154
Sen, A., 19
Shale Gas Caucus, 233, 240
shale gas exploration. *See* fracking
Sheikh, Munir, 185
Shields, J., 10, 70
shifting terrain: in approaches to advocacy, 13–14, 298–9; and charitable status, 37; definition, 12; and DISC, 132–3; and discourse, 12–14, 16, 298–304, 305; and doctrine of political purposes, 35, 50, 295–6; in environments of advocacy, 14–16; experiences and outcomes of, 293–8, 304–5; and funding of non-profits, 67–9; general aspects of, 63–4; geographic and spatial variables, 16; ideological

landscape, 15–16; legal restrictions, 37–41; and non-shift in advocacy, 305; in Ontario, 70–4; policing and surveillance of non-profits, 68–9; and political environment, 14–15, 306–7; in regulations, 14; "terrain" as metaphor, 305
silencing, 16–18, 70
*Sivumuqpallianiq: Moving Forward: Strengthening our Self-Reliance in the Information Age*, 276
Skocpol, T., 77
Slade, Justice, 44
social assistance. *See* welfare system
Social Assistance Review Committee (SARC), 177, 190
social determinants of health lens, 113
Social Enterprise Canada, 88
social enterprises, 83, 87–8
social entrepreneur, 105n1
social exclusion: and co-construction of public policy, 223; national strategy in Quebec, 212–13; participation of poor and excluded, 217–19. *See also* Quebec Act to Combat Poverty and Social Exclusion
social investment state, 203
social justice, 19–20, 294
social justice advocacy, 175, 187–92
social justice approach to poverty, 174
social justice theory, 249
social movement theories, 8
Social Planning Council of Metro Toronto (SPCMT), 176
Social Planning Network of Ontario (SPNO): in coalition, 173, 174, 181, 182–3; deep poverty and welfare reforms, 190–1; description, 173; funding cut, 185; HFS policy, 184–5, 191; PFIB campaign, 185, 186, 190–1; policy initiatives for PRS, 184; and Poverty Free Ontario, 185–6, 187; and public advocacy, 188–9; re-conceptualization of, 187
Solomon, Joel, 99
Southwestern Energy (SWN Resources Canada), 249
space, impact on advocacy, 16
Special Senate Committee on Poverty, 174–5
SSi Micro, 270
stakeholders, in CICs, 92
state. *See* government/state
"state capture," 242
state subsidy, and income tax, 48, 53
Statistics Canada, 309–10
*Statute of Charitable Uses* or *Statute of Elizabeth*, 37, 58n4
subsidy, and income tax, 48, 53
*Summoned to Stewardship* (Campaign 2000), 179
Supreme Court of Canada, 49, 253
surveillance by CRA. *See* audits of non-profits

Taqramiut Nipingat Incorporated (TNI), 265
*Task Team of Income Support for People with Disabilities*, 122–4
tax. *See* income tax
Taylor, M., 194
telecommunications: infrastructure, 267–8, 283; policy and regulation, 260, 273–5

telephone services, in North, 268
Television Northern Canada, 274
television/TV broadcasting, 265–7, 273–5
10 per cent rule, 40
terrain, as metaphor, 305
third sector organizations (TSOs): categories of, 205; in co-construction of public policy, 205–7, 222; definition, 202–3. *See also* non-profit sector and organizations
Thomson, George, 177
*Transitions* report, 177
"Translataphone" service, 275
treaty rights of Aboriginal people, 260, 262
Trudeau government. *See* Liberal Party
25 in 5 Network for Poverty Reduction: in coalition, 173, 181–2; coalition problems, 184; coalition themes, 182–3; declaration, 183; evaluation of and response to strategy, 180, 181; formation, 181, 182; HFS policy, 184–5, 190; "inside/outside" strategy, 173, 187, 188–9; poverty reduction, 192; progress of strategy, 185; work with government, 183
Tyze Personal Networks, 94, 95

UK Charity Commission, 54
UK Companies Act, 92

United Kingdom: hybrids and CICs, 89, 90, 91–4, 97–8; insider advocacy, 193–4
United Nations Platform for Action Committee (UNPAC), 308
United States: financing, 86–7; hybrids, 89, 90

Valaskakis, G.G., 265–6
values/value neutrality, 43, 56
"Voice of the North", 265
"Voice of the People" tour, 247–8
Voluntary Sector Initiative (VSI), 10, 12, 14, 15, 314

Wabanaki Confederacy, 253
Waldram, J., 149
Wall, Brad, 133
water, 152
Wawatay Native Communications Society, 175, 265, 266, 276
Weisner, S., 67
welfare system: description and definition, 111, 112; disability benefit program in SK, 118–19; for people with disabilities, 111, 112; public education on people with disabilities, 128; review in Ontario, 177, 190–1; and SAID, 126, 131
*Winnipeg Free Press*, 154
Winnipeg Humane Society (WHS), 158
Wynne, Kathleen, and government, 186–7